Colors of Art

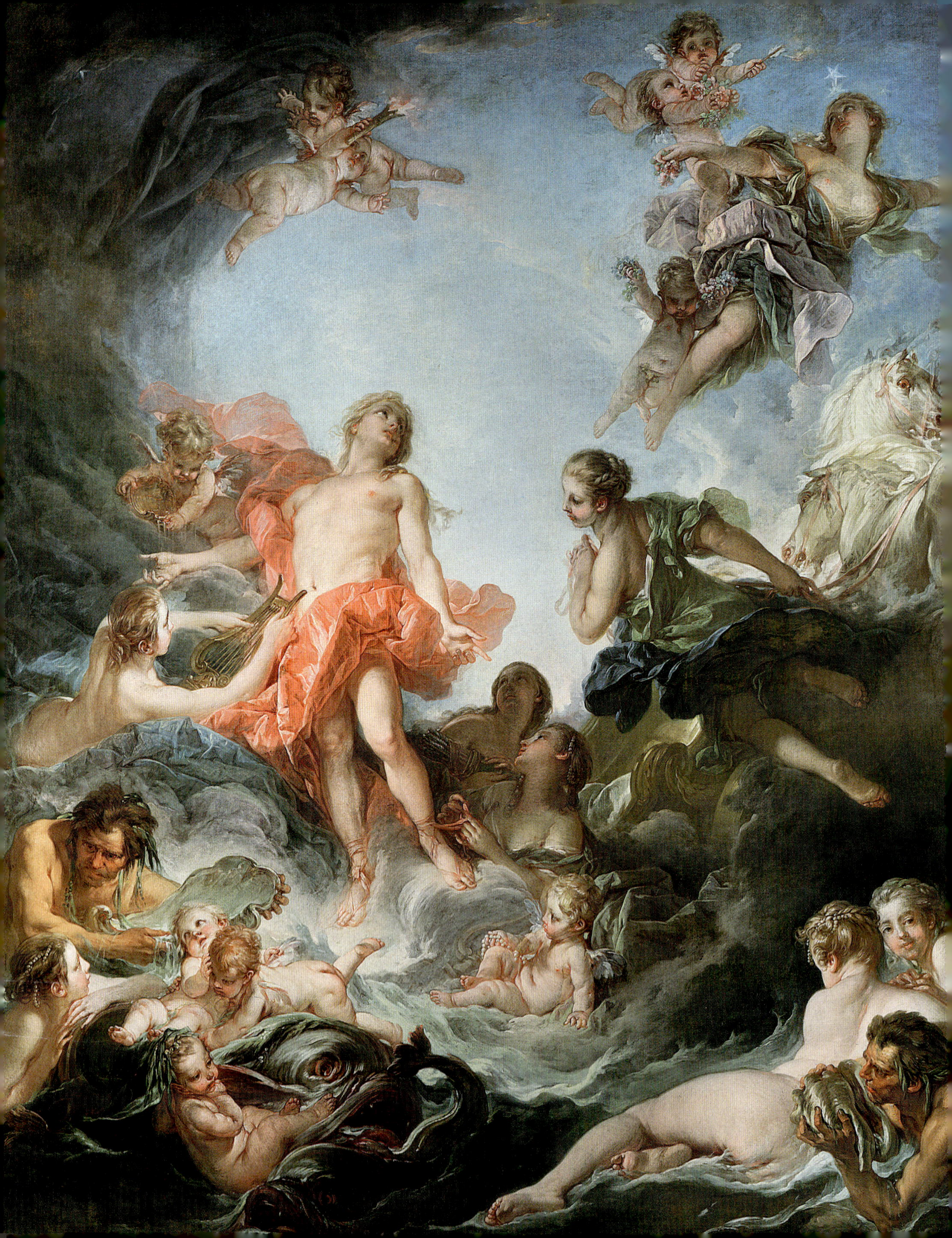

Colors of Art

The Story of Art in 80 Palettes

Chloë Ashby

FRANCES
LINCOLN

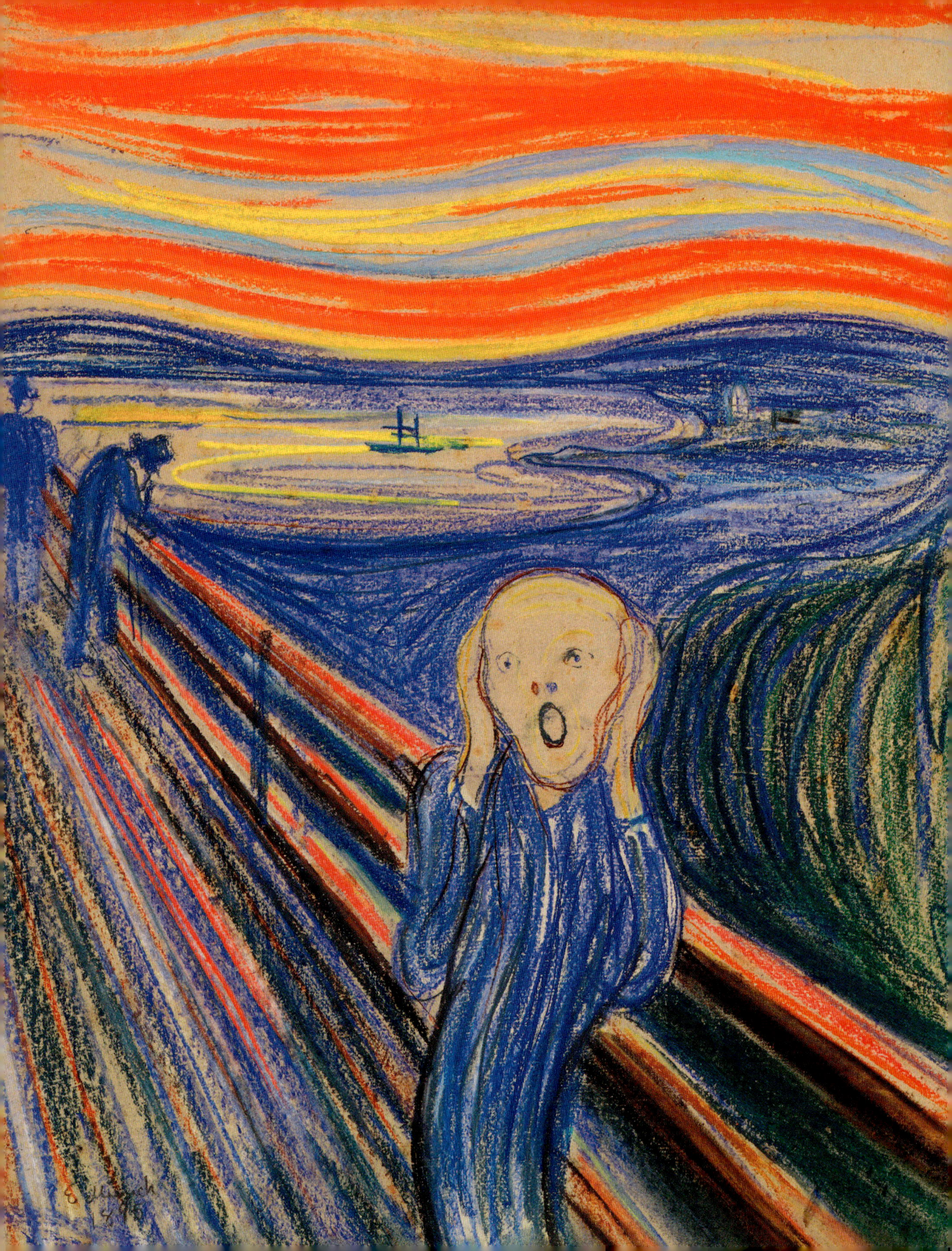

Introduction

Color me in

C6 **M**20 **Y**60 **K**0
R229 **G**201 **B**121

Introduction

Color me in

Opposite: Antoine Vollon, *Mound of Butter*, 1875–85, oil on canvas, 19¾ x 24 in (50.2 x 61 cm).

Can you imagine a world without color? Black-and-white photographs and films give us a rough idea, but our kaleidoscopic surroundings mean that blue, yellow, red, etc. (the list goes on) are constant companions. They're stitched into our clothes, printed in our books, piled on our plates. They hang on our walls and are displayed on our screens. They're at their most vibrant during waking hours, but they're also there, a little fuzzy around the edges, when we close our eyes at the end of the day. As a child, lying in bed in the dark, waiting to fall asleep, I remember marveling at the flashes of blue, yellow, and pink swirling across the underside of my lids. No matter how tight I squeezed my eyes shut, the flashes wouldn't go away.

As with most things readily available to us, we take color for granted. How often do you pause and contemplate a particular shade, why it is the way it is and what it means? When the French conceptual artist Sophie Calle asked a couple of dozen people who had been blind since birth to describe their image of beauty, one replied, "Green is beautiful. Because every time I like something, I'm told it's green. Grass is green; trees, leaves, and nature, too. I like to dress in green." Read this, and then consider the infinite varieties of green you see daily without ever really *seeing* them.

What's your favorite color? It's a question we've all been asked, and one I've been contemplating as I write this introduction. After all, we all have one, don't we? For Claude Monet it was violet (*see page 122*), for Yves Klein it was undoubtedly blue (*see page 200*) and for Flora Yukhnovich it could be pink (*see page 242*). It might strike you as strange that I don't have an easy answer, especially since I've written a book on the colors of art. But even if I did and, let's say, I also found green to be the image of beauty, I could be talking about apple-green, leaf-green, lime-green. Emerald, olive, sage. All things nature-related. Life itself.

It's hard to imagine a world without color, and it's also hard to imagine a world in which color is static, fixed. The history of each hue is unique, and all are subjective and capable of change. The meaning of color fluctuates depending on culture, time, and place. Its appearance shifts, too—according to the medium in which it's rendered, as a consequence of exposure to bright light, damp or heat, and because of varying tastes. After Philip II of Spain remarried, Sofonisba Anguissola retouched the portrait she originally made of the king, replacing his heavy cape with a lighter option in fine black silk, so it would work as a pair with a portrait of his new wife (*see page 48*). When Élisabeth Louise Vigée Le Brun made a copy of her self-portrait in a straw hat, she changed the color of her dress from lilac to pink (*see page 68*).

Art helps us to appreciate and understand color. From prehistoric times to the present day, artists around the world have used their palettes to describe, symbolize, elucidate. They've chosen certain hues to tell stories, and packed their pigments with social, political, and religious references. Color in art can be realistic, as in the standard morning spread in 17th-century Netherlands painted by Clara Peeters (*see page 74*), but it can also be idealized and fanciful—dashed with delicate gilded accents, say (*see page 44*). It can be dulled or saturated to express an atmosphere, an emotion, a mood. It can be pared back to the point of erasure (*see page 193*).

Colors of Art: The Story of Art in 80 Palettes charts the most notable, striking, and madcap uses of color throughout the ages.

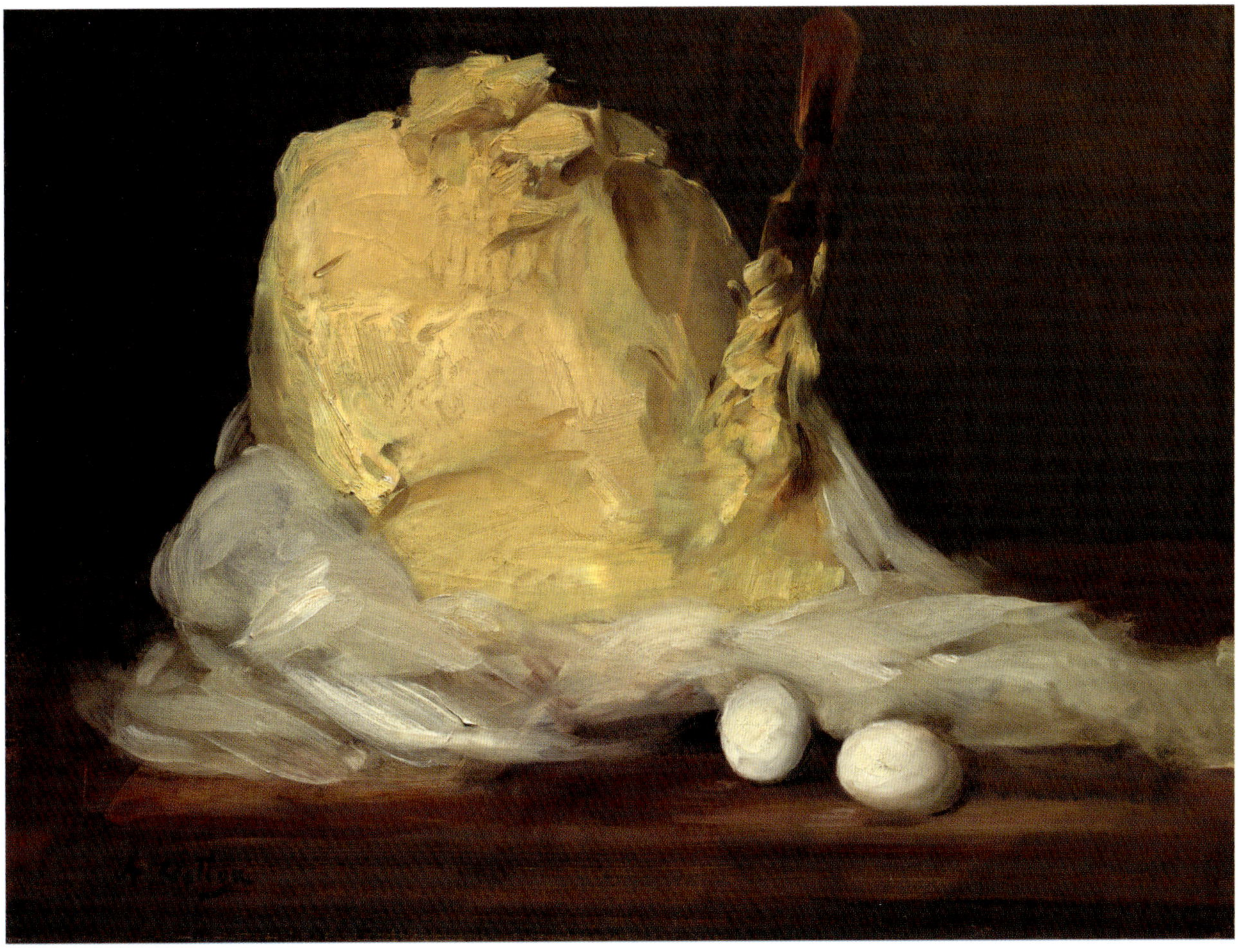

From the earth to semiprecious stones and crushed insects, it explores the unexpected materials used to make pigments and the lengths to which artists have gone to obtain them. It delves into the cost, availability, and desirability of colors, as well as the changing cultural and philosophical attitudes toward practices such as modeling and mixing. It navigates turning points big and small —among them, the Impressionist Revolution (*see page 105*), which was sparked by scientific and technological innovations and a clutch of plucky artists with a radical approach to picture-making. It invites you to look through a bright lens at familiar and lesser-known works.

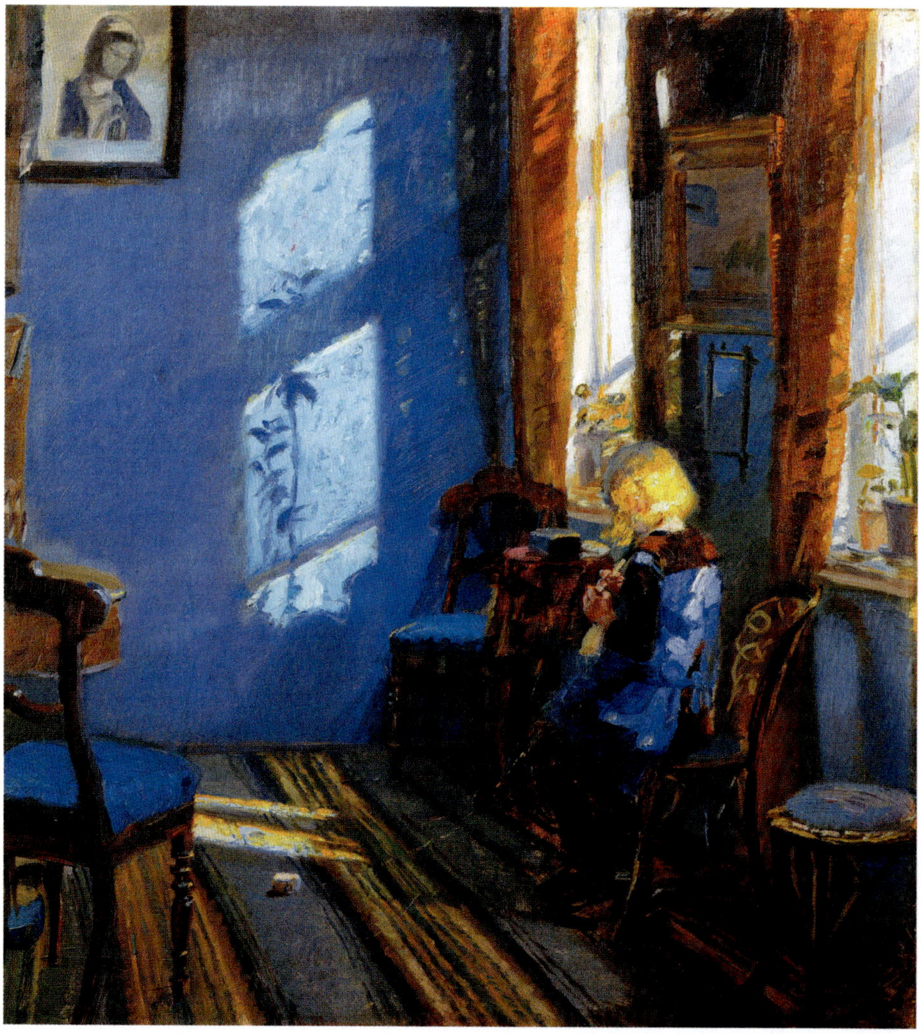

Right: Anna Ancher, *Sunlight in the Blue Room*, 1895, oil on canvas, 25 11/16 x 23 1/16 in (65.2 x 58.8 cm).

Opposite: Édouard Manet, *The Street Singer*, 1862, oil on canvas, 41¼ x 67 5/16 in (106 x 171 cm).

When I was planning my chapters, each of which covers a crucial moment for the colors of art, some works came to me right away. Giotto's heavenly-blue Scrovegni Chapel (*see page 30*), for example, and Édouard Manet's spellbinding portrait of his fellow artist, the beautiful Berthe Morisot, clasping a bunch of violets (*see page 112*). Others, I discovered as I went along. The great Amsterdam artist Rachel Ruysch used a toxic mineral called realgar to obtain the burnt-orange petals of the fiery lilies in her elegant bouquet (*see page 84*). The decorative panel that Henri Matisse painted for the Russian art collector Sergei Shchukin was commissioned as a blue interior, but the artist decided he wasn't happy with the result and painted over it in a raspberry red (*see page 166*). From afar, Agnes Martin's solitary plain field may look like a hazy blank canvas, but up close you'll discover that it's composed of a delicate veil of subtly nuanced color laid over a hand-drawn grid (*see page 202*).

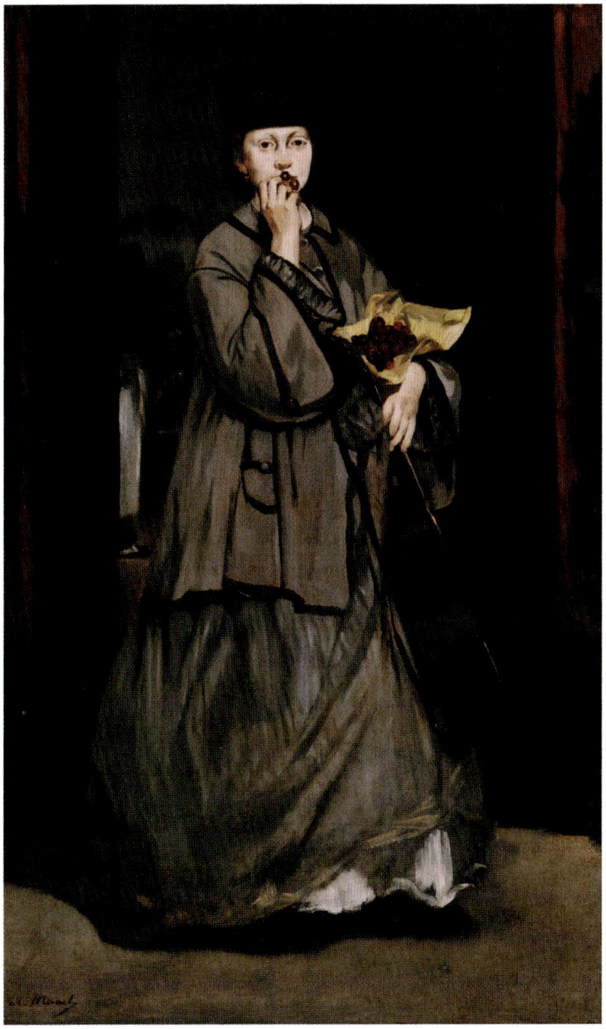

This book isn't definitive—how could it be, considering color's inexhaustible variety? Instead, it's my attempt to capture and celebrate that variety on the page. Each artwork is accompanied by an infographic palette that's intended to help you engage with the colors at play. Rather than representing the amounts of color used on each canvas, the palettes are designed to draw your attention to the hues that I believe have the greatest impact. It's worth saying that they aren't exact replicas of the artists' palettes; pigments can fade over time, and reproductions vary in tone and saturation.

There are many, many more artworks I could have included (some I've snuck into sidebars). My focus is on painting, and color is my jumping-off point, but the art that does appear within these pages can be viewed through countless lenses. Beyond wood panels and canvases, color is wound up with sculpture, video art, and installation: think Louise Bourgeois's mysterious red room, Anish Kapoor's powdery pigment sculptures, and James Turrell's sublime light-filled spaces. Punctuating my mostly chronological case studies are in-depth features on everything from the properties of color and color theory to the Pantone palette, and the complex and unresolved issue of the mostly white Western canon.

The story of art reads differently depending on where and when you're doing the reading—this is just one version, told in 80 palettes. You can read it chronologically from start to finish, or you can dip in and out, flicking through the pages. Wherever you land, you'll find yourself immersed in color—rich, vital, chameleonic.

First impressions

Prehistoric and ancient art

C0 M100 Y100 K25
R158 G11 B12

First impressions

Prehistoric and ancient art

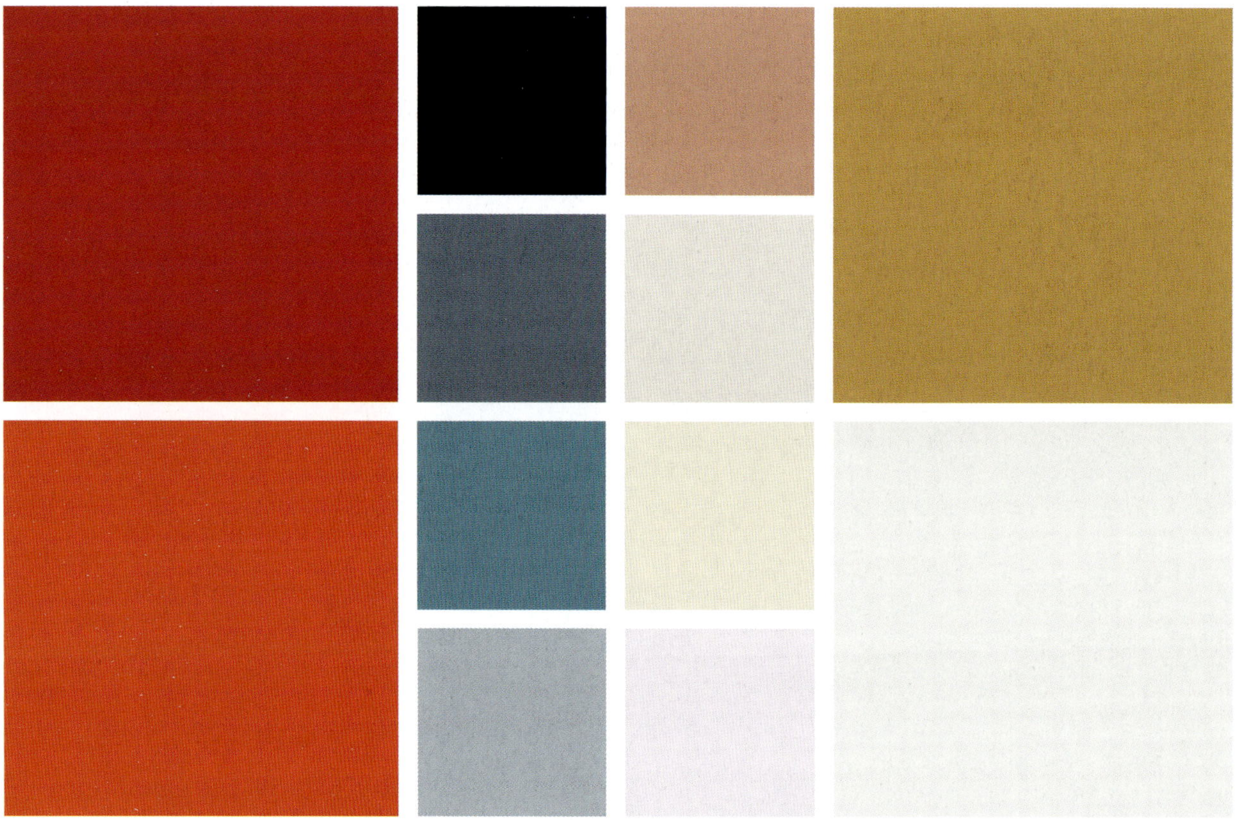

Before there was paint, there was the earth: muddy and rich with promise. For tens of thousands of years, artists have manipulated minerals to make their palettes. They've dug and extracted, ground and bound, and the resulting fiery ochers, dusty coals, dark taupes, and bright whites are the foundational colors of all art.

The creation and use of color pigments is believed to have predated drawing. The discovery of a paint workshop in the Blombos Cave in South Africa—complete with crayon-like lumps of ocher, grinding stones, and shell containers, but zero art on the walls—suggests that pigments were being used as face and body paint 100,000 years ago. In fact, in 2011, among the spear points and other excavated materials, archaeologists found a chunk of rock with a cross-hatched design in red. The initial purpose of color pigments might have been for self-decoration, but they were also used to make decorative objects.

While other prehistoric cave paintings exist in Africa, as well as in the Americas and Australia, it's in Europe that this particular kind of art first became widely known—specifically, in northern Spain and southern France. The first cave paintings would no doubt have been monochrome, made from earth or charcoal combined with a binder as basic as saliva, but the majority have either faded or had something more vibrant superimposed. In 1868 a Spanish hunter stumbled upon the cave of Altamira (*see page 18*) in Cantabria, and in 1940 a group of four teenage boys discovered the Lascaux Cave beneath a tangle of vegetation and tumbled rocks in the Dordogne. Both hunter and boys were searching for missing dogs, and both found painted bison, boar, deer, and horses that appeared to gallop in the flicker of torchlight and were up to 40,000 years old.

From prehistoric cave paintings to the ancient art of Egypt, Greece, and Rome. The ancient Egyptians worked with a palette of six colors: black, white, yellow, green, red, and blue. It was in this part of the world that the first-known artificial pigment was created—more on that later. The classical Greek and Roman sculptures of gods and goddesses, heroes and heroines that we see in museums today might be made of pure white marble, but they were originally painted in bright colors. The loss of pigmentation happened over time, as the organic binding agents that helped the paints to stick, dissolved.

The first writings about color are somewhat piecemeal. In his philosophical poem, *On Nature* (5th century BC), Empedocles developed a theory around four colors (black, white, red, and ochron —the latter a yellowish green) related to the four elements: air, water, earth, and fire. In *On Colors* (4th century BC), formerly attributed to the Greek philosopher Aristotle but more likely written by his follower Theophrastus, color was organized as a scale, with the two principal colors (white and black, or light and dark) at either end and the intermediaries (yellow, red, purple, green, and blue) in between.

Artists have always pilfered from the past, but it was in the late 19th century that modern art began to encounter early humanity in earnest. After visiting the Lascaux Cave, Pablo Picasso (*see page 140*) reportedly turned to his guide and said: "They've invented everything." What he meant by that, only he can know, but we can hazard a guess. He might have been referring to the principles of perspective, naturalism, and animation. He might also have been considering the artists' materials, from their powdered paints and cloths to their lamps and scaffolds. Or, he might have simply been talking about the concept of art—and color—itself.

C37 M23 Y0 K100
R0 G0 B0

C5 M0 Y0 K25
R198 G204 B206

C8 M28 Y75 K10
R203 G169 B80

C8 M8 Y12 K0
R234 G230 B221

Leading the charge

Horses from the Chauvet Cave near the Pont d'Arc

30,000–28,000 BC

Charcoal, hematite, and ocher on limestone,
157½ x 157½ in (400 x 400 cm).

In December 1994, three explorers discovered the world's oldest-known paintings in the Chauvet Cave near the French town of Vallon-Pont-d'Arc. They were observing the limestone cliffs above the Ardèche River when they found the opening. Inside, leaping and running across the walls, was a strange and beautiful medley of more than 300 animals. Rhinoceroses coming head-to-head in battle and buffalos surging across giant panels. Bison and bears. Stags. Lions in search of mates. An owl peering down from its perch. Some species, now extinct, are foreign to us: woolly mammoths and horned wild cows. Others, such as the cavalcade of horses cantering across the rock, are comfortingly familiar. There is also a composite creature, with human legs but the hump and head of a bison—archaeologists call it the Sorcerer.

Deep within the underground warren, where the air was damp and cool, and natural light snuffed, the prehistoric artists got to work. To create their exquisitely detailed drawings, they used a combination of charcoal made from Sylvester pine trees, red hematite, and mineral-rich ocher. Soot-black shading brings the horses into relief, and defines their dark manes and watchful eyes. There's a sense of movement in the fluid lines of their backs and perspective in their staggered positions, with each muzzle diagonally aligned. In places, the cave was coated with a thin layer of brown clay; by partially scraping it away to reveal the white limestone beneath, the artists were able to create a nuanced palette that ranges from pale gray to beige. Every animal has been closely observed, from the rhinos' bulky bodies to their parted lips. There's flesh and fur. The clatter of hooves.

Twenty years after the Chauvet Cave was discovered, a replica built nearby opened to the public (the French government had learned from the damage done to the engravings at Lascaux when it was initially open). Using the same materials, artists copied the original engravings, which remain protected, onto a newly created rock surface. The air of mystery may not be the same, but the animals have once again been brought to life.

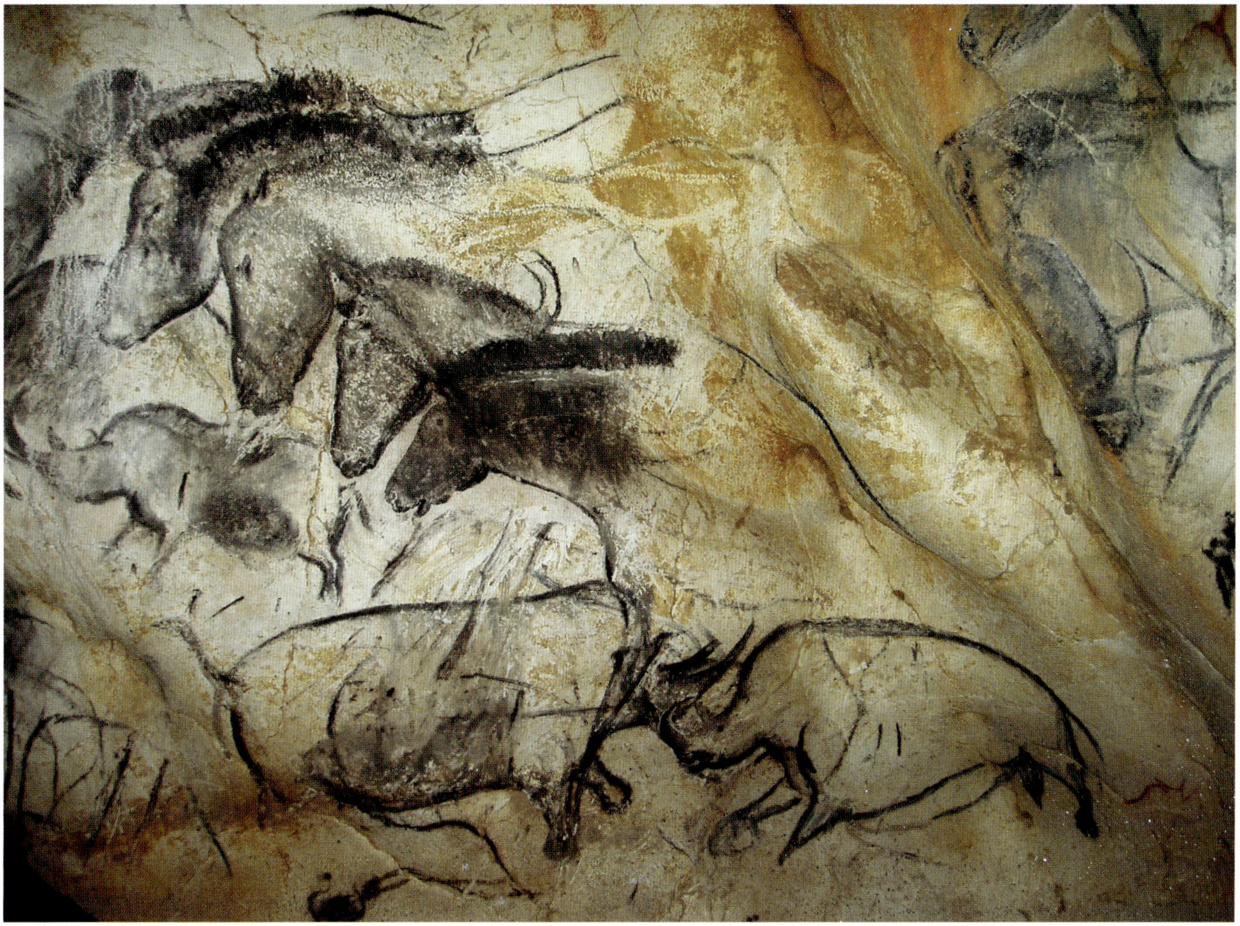

Palette

Charcoal drawings, soot-black shading and ocher-colored clay, with red hematite used in other sections of the cave.

Complementary works

- Charcoal drawing from the Nawarla Gabarnmang Cave in Australia's Northern Territory, 26,000 BC.
- Dappled horses from the Pech Merle Cave in Lot, *c.*25,000 BC.
- Hall of the Bulls from the Lascaux Cave in the Dordogne, 17,000 BC.

C0 M86 Y90 K0
R202 G60 B36

C38 M12 Y0 K100
R0 G0 B0

Prehistoric polychrome

Bison from Altamira

*c.*14,000 BC

Charcoal, manganese oxide, and ocher on limestone, 42$\frac{3}{16}$–66$\frac{7}{8}$ in (125–170 cm) long.

A bison is lightly dozing, eye closed, lips lazily parted. Its hind legs are tucked under its belly, one bent at the hock, letting the others take the weight. There's a pronounced realism in the bulging muscles along the beast's back and the relatively detailed pattern of its pelt, black on varying shades of red. And yet the spaces just above its hooves, together with the simple markings of its shaggy mane, and the mirrored curve of its horns and tail, remind us that this is an artist's impression.

Our drowsy friend is one of hundreds of painted bison, boar, deer, and other wild mammals on the limestone walls of the cave at Altamira in northern Spain, which was excavated by an amateur archaeologist by the name of Marcelino Sanz de Sautuola in 1879. De Sautuola owned the property on which the site was found, and it was his young daughter, Maria, who first craned her neck and noticed the animals leaping across the ceiling. Initially, scientific authorities dismissed the polychrome paintings as fakes, so it wasn't until the early 1900s, when prehistoric art was found in caves elsewhere, that they were pronounced authentic. Today, this UNESCO World Heritage site comprises an entire complex of caves and is known as the "Sistine Chapel of Palaeolithic art."

The paintings at Altamira are unique for several reasons, including the use of up to three colors in each figure. With the bison, the varying shades of ocher are outlined in either black manganese oxide or charcoal, which has been smudged in places to create the impression of three-dimensionality. Adding to its lifelike appearance are the natural contours of the rock, which the artists used to their advantage; they also used a spray-painting technique that involved two hollowed-out bones (*see page 20*). The site has been closed for conservation purposes more than once, most recently in 2002, when a green algae-like mold began to appear on some of the paintings. Twelve years later, it reopened. Debates continue about whether the pigments are strong enough to withstand modern-day visitors. In the meantime, although it may be dozing, the bison remains semivigilant on its feet.

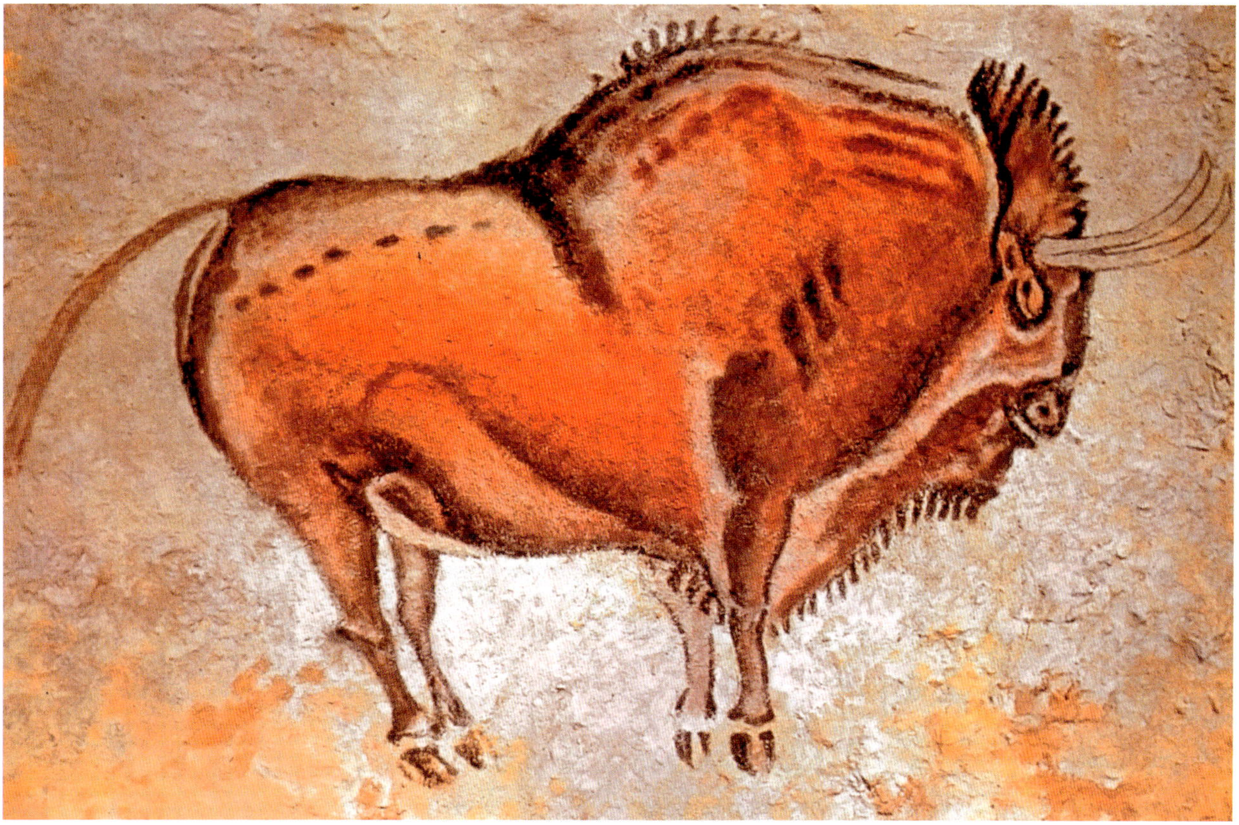

Palette

Varying shades of red ocher outlined in either black manganese oxide or charcoal.

Complementary works

- Hand stencils from El Castillo Cave in Cantabria, *c*.37,300 BC.
- Bison frieze from the Font-de-Gaume Cave in the Dordogne, *c*.14,000 BC.
- Hand stencils from the Cueva de las Manos in Argentina, 7,300 BC.

The nature of color

It makes sense that, in an age before scientific advancements, artists would tap into the natural resources of the Earth to create colors. The first early modern humans to settle in Europe made use of roughly half-a-dozen natural minerals. Though it varied, depending on both culture and climate, the majority used the same basic prehistoric palette: black from manganese dioxide or charcoal; white from chalk; and a range of reds, browns, and yellows from iron-rich ocher, hematite, and goethite.

The process of turning mineral into paint required patience. First, the artist had to locate the mineral, extract or mine the rock, and grind it into a fine powder. This had to be treated, in order to get it to stick to the walls, which had to be prepared by either scraping at the surface or applying layers of plaster. The choice of treatment for the powder depended on the texture, porousness, and moisture of the rock surface: damp surfaces might have been able to handle loose flecks, whereas dry ones required the pigments to be made into pastes or liquids by combining them with binders such as saliva, vegetable juices, and animal fat. At this point, artists were free to explore variations in intensity or hue, by either diluting the pigments with binders or adding other textured materials, such as clay and crushed bones.

It wasn't just the paint that had to be made, but also the tools with which it was applied. As previously mentioned, crayon-like lumps of ocher were found in the Blombos Cave in South Africa, and similar implements were made from charcoal and other malleable rocks. Pastes and liquid paints could be rubbed on with matted animal hair or spongy moss, and there's also evidence of a prehistoric form of spray paint: in the Pech Marle Caves, hollowed-out bones were used to spray pigment directly onto the walls. In Egypt, reeds were chewed at the end to soften the fibers and bound to wooden handles to act as brushes.

It was during the Bronze Age in Egypt that the first-known artificial pigment—Egyptian blue—was created; miners had unearthed the semiprecious stone lapis lazuli and artists were after a less expensive alternative. Unlike the earth colors, which were dug from the ground, blue had to be manufactured by heating calcium carbonate, silica (a copper compound), and nitrate to between 1470°F and 1650°F. Fired together, they formed calcium copper silicate, a glassy substance that was then crushed into a crystalline pigment.

While Egyptian blue retains its intensity thousands of years later, earth colors are susceptible to damage. In the case of prehistoric painted caves in particular, debates have pitted local tourism boards against scientists when it comes to public access: with art this old, anything from body heat to heightened carbon dioxide levels and artificial lighting can be harmful. Controversially, despite fungal damage, the Altamira Cave remains open, whereas the Lascaux Cave has been off limits since 1963. Instead, visitors to the site in southwestern France can explore a replica, where the colors still sing.

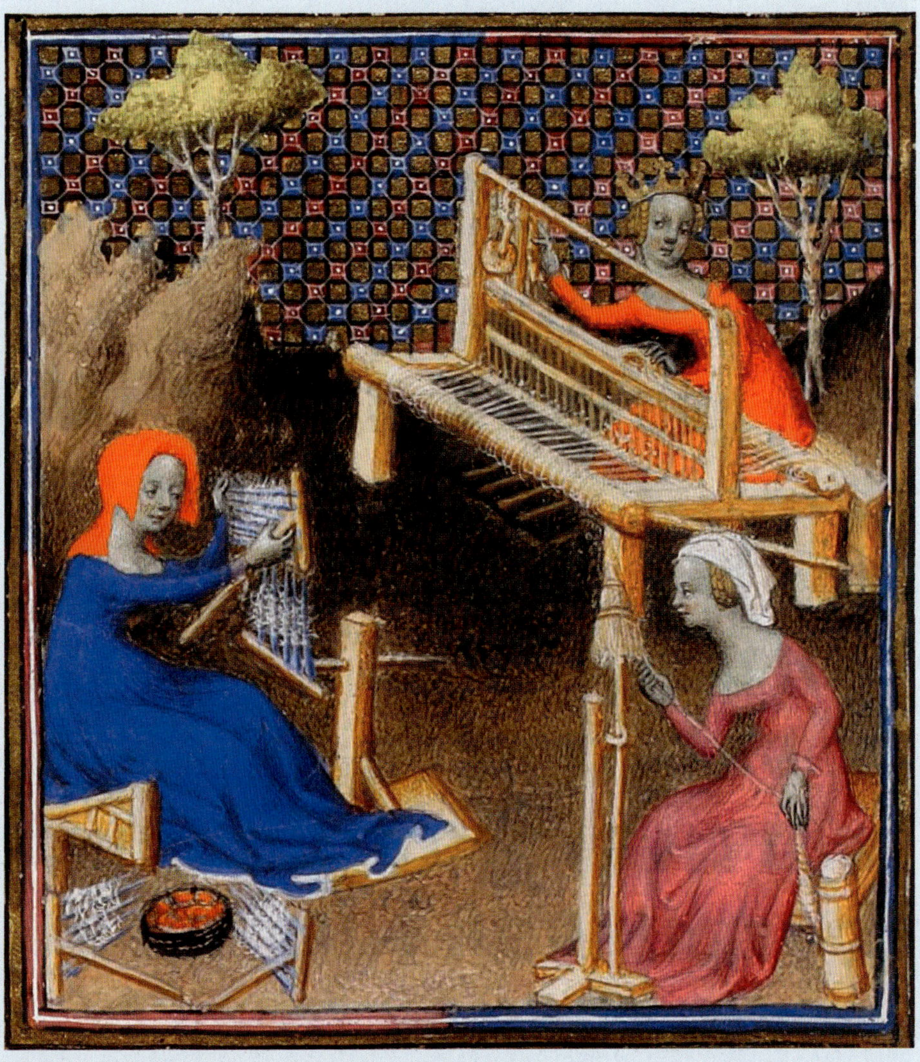

De Claris Mulieribus, *The Story of Thamyris*, 1402, vellum (parchment), 11 x 17 11/16 in (28 x 45 cm).

C75 M15 Y20 K15
R93 G145 B165

C0 M85 Y100 K10
R186 G59 B16

C6 M6 Y16 K0
R239 G235 B216

Into the wild

Nebamun Hunting Birds in the Marshes from the tomb of Nebamun, Thebes

*c.*1,350 BC

Wall painting on plaster,
31⅝ x 38⅝ in (83 x 98 cm).

The tomb-chapel paintings that belonged to the court official Nebamun, a scribe in charge of grain collection for the city of Thebes—as Luxor was then known—are the greatest surviving painted panels from ancient Egypt. The composition is advanced, the details rich, the colors dazzling. Ancient Egyptian tomb paintings were created for two reasons: to commemorate a life and to convey the kind of lifestyle hoped for in the afterlife. As the hieroglyphic caption on this fragment reads, Nebamun is "enjoying himself and seeing beauty."

A hunt through bright reed beds on the Nile River teems with black-and-white wagtails, Egyptian red geese, tiger butterflies, feathery ducks, scaly tilapia, and shiny pufferfish. Nebamun, tall and taut, dominates the scene in a black wig and a beaded collar, the red ocher of his skin standing out against the creamy white background. Together with his wife Hatshepsut and their daughter, he glides through the watery blue marshes on a papyrus skiff. In one hand he holds a throw-stick and in the other a trio of decoy herons; a bunch of lotus flowers hangs over his arm. A tawny cat joins in the hunt: it has delicate whiskers, a gilded eye, and a dark tail that looks like it's been dipped in ink; one bird is caught in its paws and another in its mouth.

The burial house, which was discovered by a Greek grave robber called Giovanni d'Athanasi, was built into the west bank of the Nile. The walls were plastered first with a thick layer of mud and straw mixed with paste, and then with a thin layer of white plaster to create a smooth surface. A team of artists would then have drawn an outline of each scene, before perking it up with the vibrant palette. Like the imagery, chosen for its connotations of fertility and rebirth, the colors have symbolic meanings: the Egyptian blue of the reeds and water is a sign of regeneration and future promise; the red ocher of the skin is a sign of strength and victory. It might appear to be almost impressionistic in its free-flowing depiction of everyday life, but every element of this great hunt scene is here for a reason.

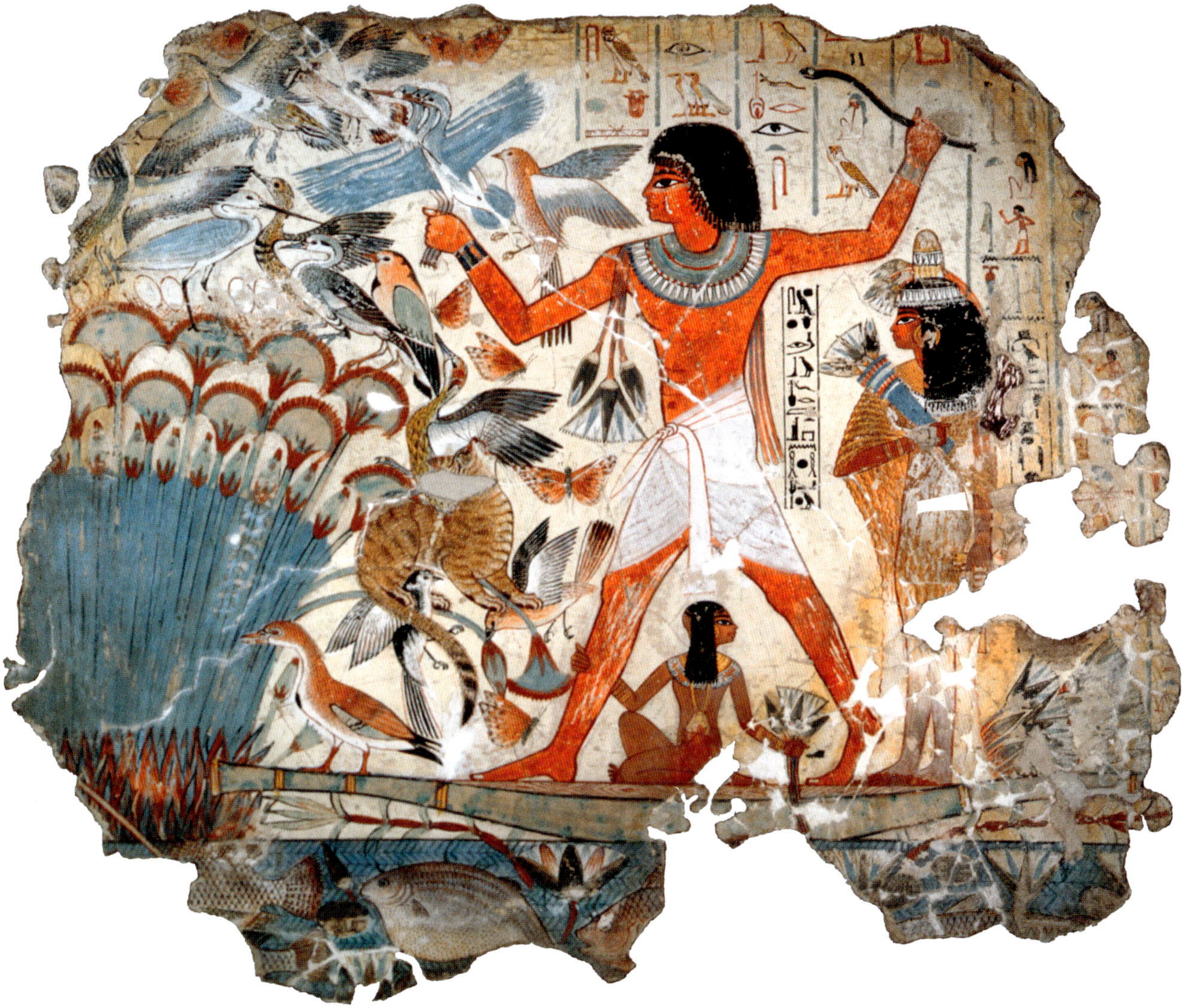

Palette

Egyptian blue and red ocher against a thin layer of white plaster.

Complementary works

- Hippopotamus (William), *c.*1961–1878 BC.
- Coffin of Khnumnakhtca, 1850–1750 BC.
- Book of the Dead for the Chantress of Amun, Nauny, *c.*1050 BC.

Full of flavor

Tomb of the Diver (detail)

*c.*470 BC

Fresco on limestone,
96⅛ × 31½ in (244 × 80 cm).

C8 M35 Y40 K8
R203 G165 B138

C63 M32 Y26 K20
R100 G125 B140

C0 M3 Y0 K5
R243 G240 B242

The paintings that cover the five local limestone slabs of this small sarcophagus in Paestum, an ancient Greek city in southern Italy, place the deceased at the center of a symposium: a social gathering devoted to conversation, poetry, music, politics, and copious drinking. Fit and healthy bare-chested men, with robes slung lazily around their hips and laurel garlands in their hair, recline on sofas lined with blue cushions. In this detail, which shows one wall of the sarcophagus, two men raise their glasses as if calling for a top-up, while a third turns to watch the display of affection between a couple sitting on the end, one of whom is playing a lyre.

Among the thousands of Greek tombs from this period, the fully decorated Tomb of the Diver is the only example painted with figurative scenes to have survived wholly intact. After white plaster had been applied to the slabs, and the design sketched out, the convivial scene was brought to life. The red ocher of the baseboard and the banqueting figures, which was enriched with manganese, was painted directly onto the plaster and, once dry, a black outline was used to add anatomical details. Despite the British statesman William Gladstone's claim that the Greeks didn't see the color blue—based on the word's absence from Homer's epics, which instead described the sea as "wine-dark"—the frescoes in the tomb feature blue pigments. The intense shade of the cushions was likely derived from Egyptian blue, which was the most common of the blue colorants available in antiquity.

The painted scenes on the four walls of the sarcophagus resemble the decoration of ancient Greek cups, jugs, and wine-mixing vessels that would have been used at symposia at the time. On the underside of the lid, though, is a more unique scene that gave the tomb its name: a nude diver plunging past a tower into the depths of a stream. His figure, cast in a dark red ocher, slices through a creamy white sky toward death itself.

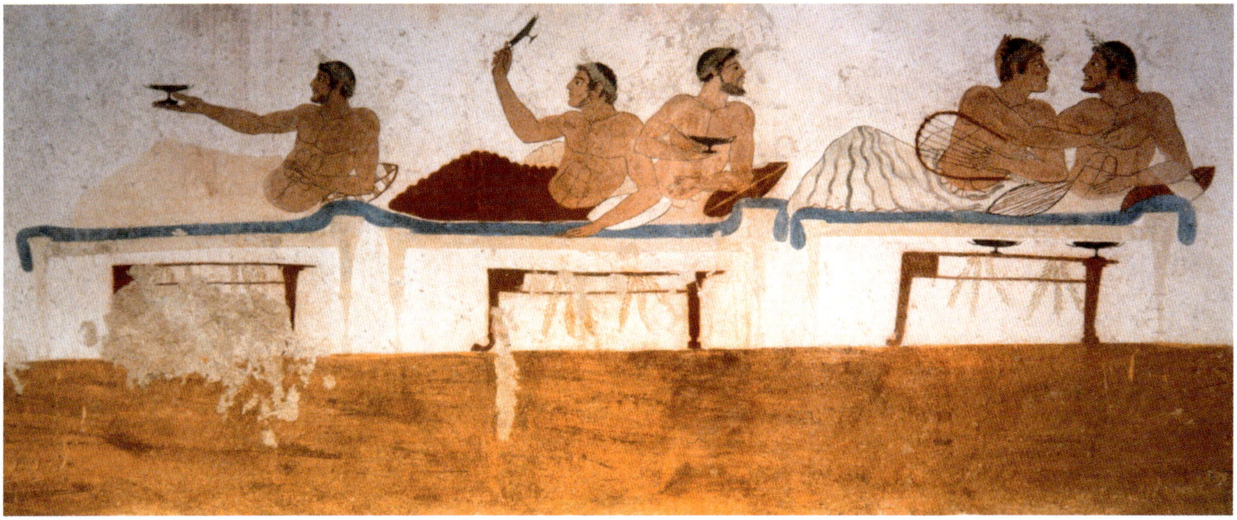

Palette

Red ocher enriched with manganese, white plaster, and a shade likely derived from Egyptian blue.

Complementary works

- Red-figured cup, *c*.490–480 BC, attributed to the Brygos Painter.
- Ram's head rhyton, 480–470 BC.
- Banqueting scene from the Etruscan Tomb of the Leopards, *c*.470–450 BC.

Ordering the world

The Renaissance

C8 M0 Y0 K25
R193 G201 B206

Ordering the world

The Renaissance

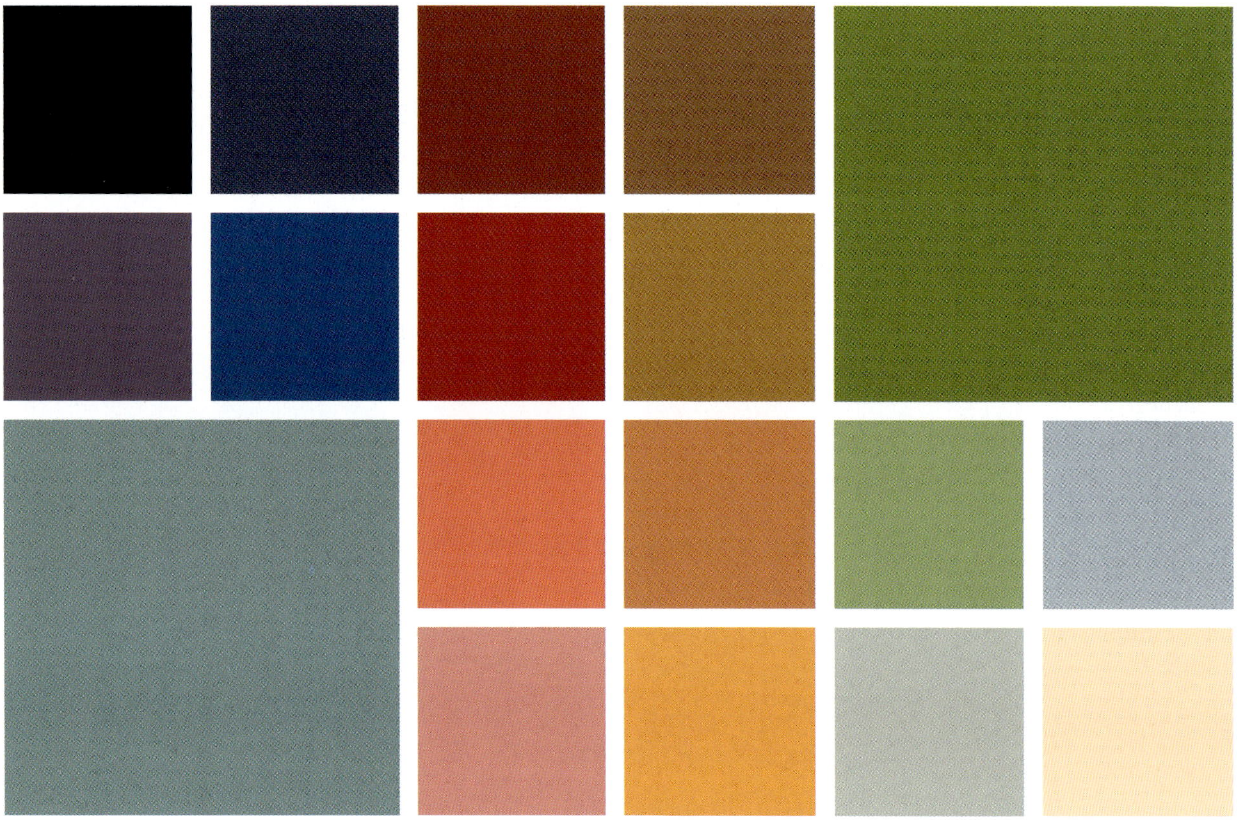

Color is a language like any other. Throughout art history, it has been charged with meaning, even if that meaning has changed according to culture, time, and place. It's both a description and a symbol, packed with social, religious, and metaphorical references. Of course, such connotations depend on the intent of the individual artist, but during certain periods there have been stark commonalities. Take the time often regarded as the pinnacle of artistic achievement: the Renaissance.

After the Black Death swept across Europe in 1348, the continent bloomed like a spring flower after a cold and dank winter. By the 15th century, Italian merchants were making money, and art and architecture flourished. Although there was a revival of interest in subjects, techniques, and materials from Greek and Latin antiquity, artists weren't content to reproduce classical art and culture. Instead, they wanted to create something fresh. They sought to paint people, objects, and landscapes that were real, with a sense of depth.

The colors with which they achieved their purpose were used carefully and meaningfully. What's more, a color's meaning was often connected to its availability and cost. The brilliantly saturated ultramarine blue, made from the semiprecious stone lapis lazuli, was so expensive and hard to come by that it was reserved for especially significant subjects. Gold was regarded as a heavenly material because of its pure and stable properties. Used alone, white might represent peace and calm, green loyalty, and red passion—but together the trio symbolized the three theological virtues of faith, hope, and charity. In portraiture, color was used to convey a sitter's values and status in much the same way as a strategically placed still life, and in this chapter you'll find everything from ornate gold-and-silver costumes to an inky-black cloak. Despite the 15th-century humanist Leon Battista Alberti's demotion of black and white to noncolors in his 1435 treatise *De Pictura* (On Painting), which otherwise mostly maintained and extended Aristotle's color ideas, the two appear fairly frequently.

Helping to make colors rich and scenes realistic was the new medium of oil painting, whose "secret" was discovered by the Flemish artist and alchemist Jan van Eyck (*see page 38*) in the 15th century, or so the story goes. According to the Tuscan art historian Giorgio Vasari and his Dutch counterpart Carel van Mander, van Eyck stumbled upon said secret while dabbling in alchemy, and a visiting Sicilian then carried the formula back to Italy and it spread throughout Europe, supplanting tempera. In fact, there's evidence that artists used oils as early as the 12th century, but van Eyck's masterful manipulation of the medium was unprecedented.

Beyond that, how artists achieved this newly desired realism is up for discussion. It was in 16th-century Italy that debates surrounding *disegno* versus *colore*, and planning versus process, first stirred. In Tuscany artists favored linear clarity, while in Venice color composition was, in writer Paolo Pini's words, "the true alchemy of painting." Michelangelo was drawing's darling; in his hands, forms are clearly defined, color transitions sharp, and surfaces smooth. In Titian's (*see page 46*) works, nothing is distinct—at least not up close. It's through color that the Venetian artist created a sense of perspective, building up the figures in the foreground and affording the distant hills little paint. He stroked and smudged and dabbed and daubed. At times, he even swapped his brush for his fingers—how else do you think he got those bodies looking so fleshy?

Blue-sky thinking

Giotto

The Lamentation

*c.*1305–06

Fresco on plaster,
79 × 73 in (200 x 185 cm).

Six hundred years after Giotto painted the Scrovegni Chapel near Padua in Italy, the French novelist Marcel Proust described it as "so blue that it seems as though the radiant day has crossed the threshold with the human visitor." In fact, the luminous shade of the chapel's interior makes the sky pale in comparison. If anything, this bright and brilliant blue looks like it's spilled out of heaven. It's fitting, then, that decorating the interior is a cycle of frescoes narrating events in the lives of the Virgin and Christ.

Commissioned by the wealthy Scrovegni family, Giotto painted the private chapel in the early 14th century. Uninterrupted by architectural features, he prepared the walls with a layer of mortar (a mix of sand, lime, and water), followed by a moisture-repellent layer of plaster. On top, he sketched out the composition, first in charcoal and then with sinopia (red ocher dissolved in water), before adding a second layer of thin plaster. In parts, Giotto followed the ancient art of *buon fresco* (true fresco) and applied his pigments directly onto the plaster while it was still wet. To avoid the darkening of his heavenly blue, he applied azurite to patches of dry plaster, *a secco*.

Enter the chapel and you find yourself surrounded. The story begins at top right, and spirals down and around the room in three tiers. *The Lamentation*, showing Christ being mourned by his mother and his followers—with their golden haloes, and pink, violet, and green robes—is part of the bottom tier. Paving the way for Renaissance painting, Giotto abandoned the flat and stylized look of Byzantine art in favor of naturalism. The emotions of his figures shine through in their gestures and expressions. Mary tenderly cradles her son, one hand on his shoulder and another on his chest; her brow is bent with grief, and you can almost hear the cry escaping from her open mouth. Mourners raise their arms in disbelief, while angels tear at their hair. The slope of the hill directs our attention toward Christ's body, limp and all too human.

C78 M55 Y0 K0
R80 G105 B171

C6 M44 Y86 K15
R189 G136 B48

C6 M24 Y20 K0
R227 G200 B189

C70 M70 Y35 K0
R96 G85 B118

C26 M9 Y28 K5
R191 G202 B180

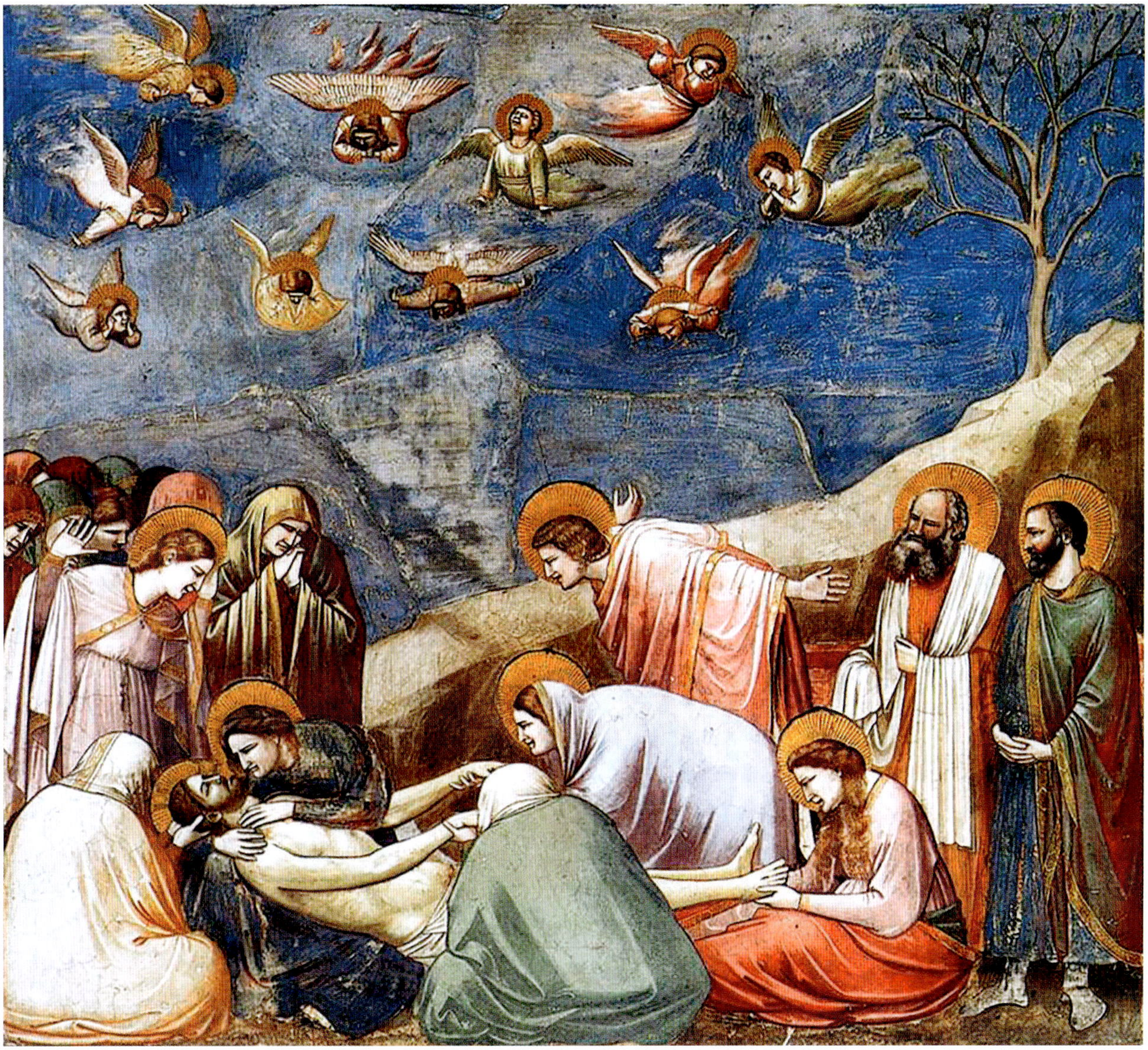

Palette

A heavenly azurite blue sky, golden haloes, and pink, violet, and green robes.

Complementary works

- Duccio, *The Transfiguration*, 1307/08–11.
- Fra Angelico, *The Dormition and Assumption of the Virgin*, 1424–34.
- Andrea del Castagno, *The Holy Trinity, Saint Jerome, and Two Saints*, c.1453.

C0 M38 Y84 K0
R228 G167 B59

Go for gold

Simone Martini and Lippo Memmi

Saint Ansanus Altarpiece *(Annunciation)*

1333

Tempera on wood, gold background, 72⅜ × 66⅛ in (184 x 168 cm).

Gold takes center stage in this elaborate 14th-century altarpiece, which emits a lustrous glow. The entirely gilt backdrop gleams, free from contextual framework, conjuring an otherworldly realm. In this space, shadows don't exist; the scene is awash with a divine light that shines on the figures, intricately rendered in tempera and adorned with golden details.

It was created by Simone Martini and Lippo Memmi for the altar of Saint Ansanus in the Cathedral of Siena. The scene, well documented in art, is the assumption of the Virgin Mary. The Archangel Gabriel is clutching an olive branch and has just touched down, as suggested by his fluttering cloak and parted peacock-feathered wings; he kneels before Mary to inform her of her pregnancy. Startled, Mary leans away from the celestial messenger and draws her dark cloak tight around her. Above the vase of lilies is the Holy Spirit, in the form of a dove encircled with angels. To the left is Ansanus, patron saint of Siena, bearing its black-and-white banner, and to the right is a holy martyr thought to be either Ansanus's mother, Maxima, or Margaret.

The gilt backdrop was achieved by coating the wood panel with a cushiony layer of reddish clay and positioning a fine sheet of gold on top, before burnishing the entire thing to a sheen; artists appreciated reddish gold for its connotations of light's warmth and heat. Using a technique called *sgraffito*, the makers applied paint on top of Gabriel's gilded mantle and then scraped it away to achieve an intricate brocade pattern. The archangel's greeting to Mary is rendered as a raised inscription; each halo is stamped with decorative patterning and incised rays fan out from the dove's beak. Further painted details include the marble floor, Mary's throne, and the half-closed book in her hand. Though the figures are depicted in a nonrealistic space typical of Gothic-style Byzantine art, the artists succeeded in conjuring a convincing sense of animation and emotion. And their use of gold—a precious earthly material—to represent the spiritual realm reinforces the coexistence of human and divine.

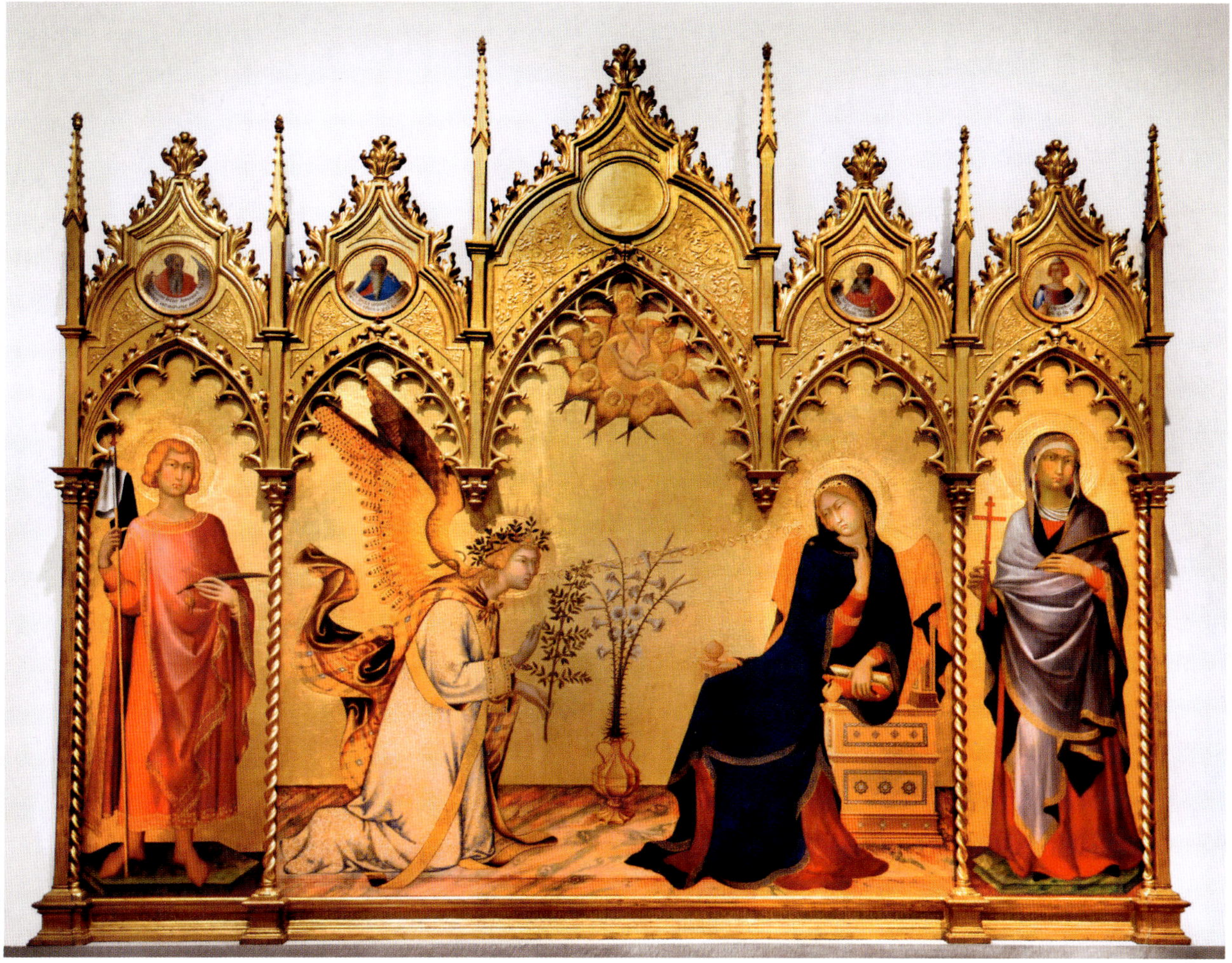

Palette

An entirely gilt backdrop adorned with golden details.

Complementary works

- *The Ladder of Divine Ascent* from Saint Catherine's Monastery in Sinai, 12th century.
- Cimabue, *Santa Trinita Maestà*, 1283–91.
- Bulaki, *Three aspects of the Absolute*, 1823.

C100 M62 Y6 K24
R26 G74 B129

C8 M41 Y83 K10
R195 G146 B58

Reserved for the Virgin's robes

The Wilton Diptych

*c.*1395–99

Tempera on oak,
20⅞ x 14⅝ in (53 x 37 cm).

Among the few English panel paintings to have survived from the Middle Ages is this small portable altarpiece commissioned by Richard II, who ruled over England from 1377 to 1399. The folding diptych comprises two hinged oak panels and was made for the king's private use. The combination of deeply personal religious and secular imagery presents Richard as he wished to be seen: divinely appointed, ruling with the blessing of the Virgin Mary and Christ.

Dressed in an embroidered robe, colored with vermilion, and a gold crown dotted with white-lead pearls, the young Richard kneels in prayer. Presenting him to the Virgin and the Christ Child is John the Baptist, barefoot and cradling the Lamb of God, together with England's patron saints (the former kings Edward the Confessor, holding a ring, and Edmund, with the arrow that killed him). Unlike Richard, who resides in a wooded landscape, the Virgin and her son are surrounded by angels in the garden of paradise. One attendant angel holds a white flag with the red cross; this is England, in the form of a standard, offered by Richard to the Virgin. The moment captured in paint shows Christ raising his hand to bless the banner, and the Virgin presenting the sole of her son's foot for the king to kiss—confirming the holy nature of his rule.

By the 12th century, the Virgin's robes were usually blue, reinforcing her role as both the Queen of Heaven and the sky-like bridge between God (heaven) and humanity (Earth). The bright and intense shade here is ultramarine, the most prized and costly blue around. The infant Christ is bundled in a gold cloth, symbolizing the divine, well-paired with the carefully stamped gilding. Throughout, the intricate details are exquisite—note the tips of the feathered gray-white wings, the angels' red-gold curls, and the white hart badges on their robes. This medieval treasure may have been used for personal religious devotion, but it has the appearance of a high-end luxury object.

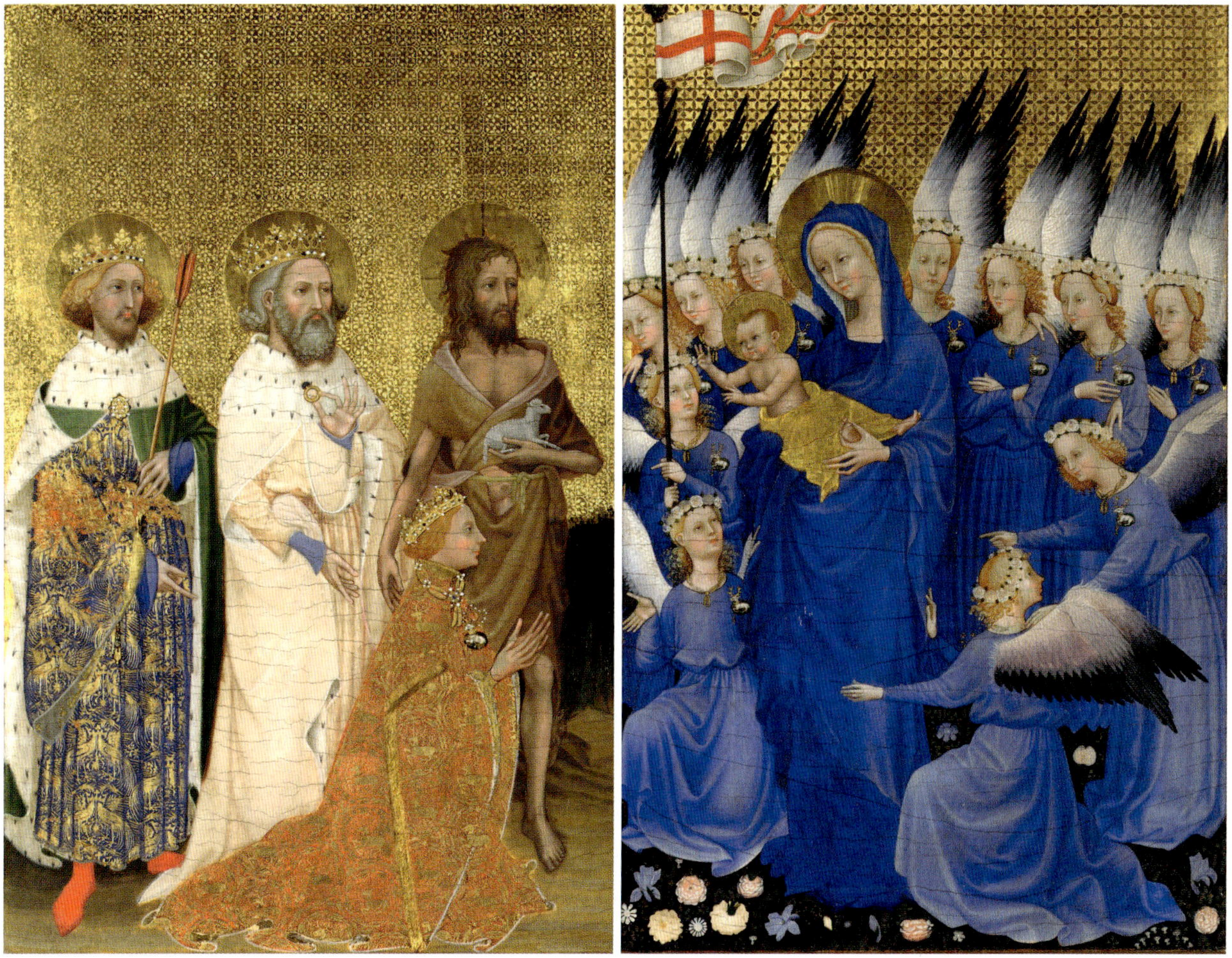

Palette

Ultramarine meets gold.

Complementary works

- *Christ Pantocrator* from Saint Catherine's Monastery at Sinai, 12th century.
- Nardo di Cione, *Three Saints*, *c.*1363–65.
- Filippo Lippi, *Madonna and Child with Two Angels*, *c.*1465.

C12 M90 Y82 K18
R156 G47 B42

C10 M48 Y28 K0
R205 G150 B152

Saints in red

Masaccio
Saints Jerome and John the Baptist
*c.*1428–29

Tempera on poplar,
$49\frac{3}{16}$ x $23\frac{3}{16}$ in (125 x 58.9 cm).

John the Baptist reappears in this portrait painting by the Florentine Renaissance master Masaccio, which originally formed part of an altarpiece in the church of Santa Maria Maggiore in Rome. On top of the camel-hair tunic he wears in *The Wilton Diptych* (*see page 34*), John the Baptist has a pink cloak. Beside him, on a grassy knoll blooming with wildflowers, is Saint Jerome in a red cloak and his cardinal's hat. Jerome was closely linked with the church, having been baptized by its founder. His relics had been moved there in the 13th century, and it may be a model of Santa Maria Maggiore that he's clutching in his right hand.

Jerome was living near Bethlehem when he supposedly pulled a thorn from a lion's paw; ever since, the animal, shown here at his feet, was said to have become his protector. As well as a cardinal, he was a scholar who translated the Bible from Greek to Latin—hence, the holy book in his right hand, open at the first page of the Old Testament, which describes the world's creation. John the Baptist carries a cross, symbolizing the crucifixion, and a scroll bearing the first words he spoke about Christ while preaching in the desert. It was while he was in the wilderness that he wore his signature ragged tunic.

Masaccio's double portrait formed the left-hand panel of the altarpiece, which was double-sided. On the reverse of this painting is another double portrait: Masolino's *A Pope (Saint Gregory?) and Saint Matthias* (*c.*1383–1436). Masaccio's figures are more robust and painted with egg tempera; by mixing his own tempera with oil, Masolino was able to achieve subtle shifts in tone and light. Still, set against a golden background, it's the former pair who stand out in their dazzling red and pink robes—Jerome's painted with brilliant vermilion and John the Baptist's with the more subdued red lake.

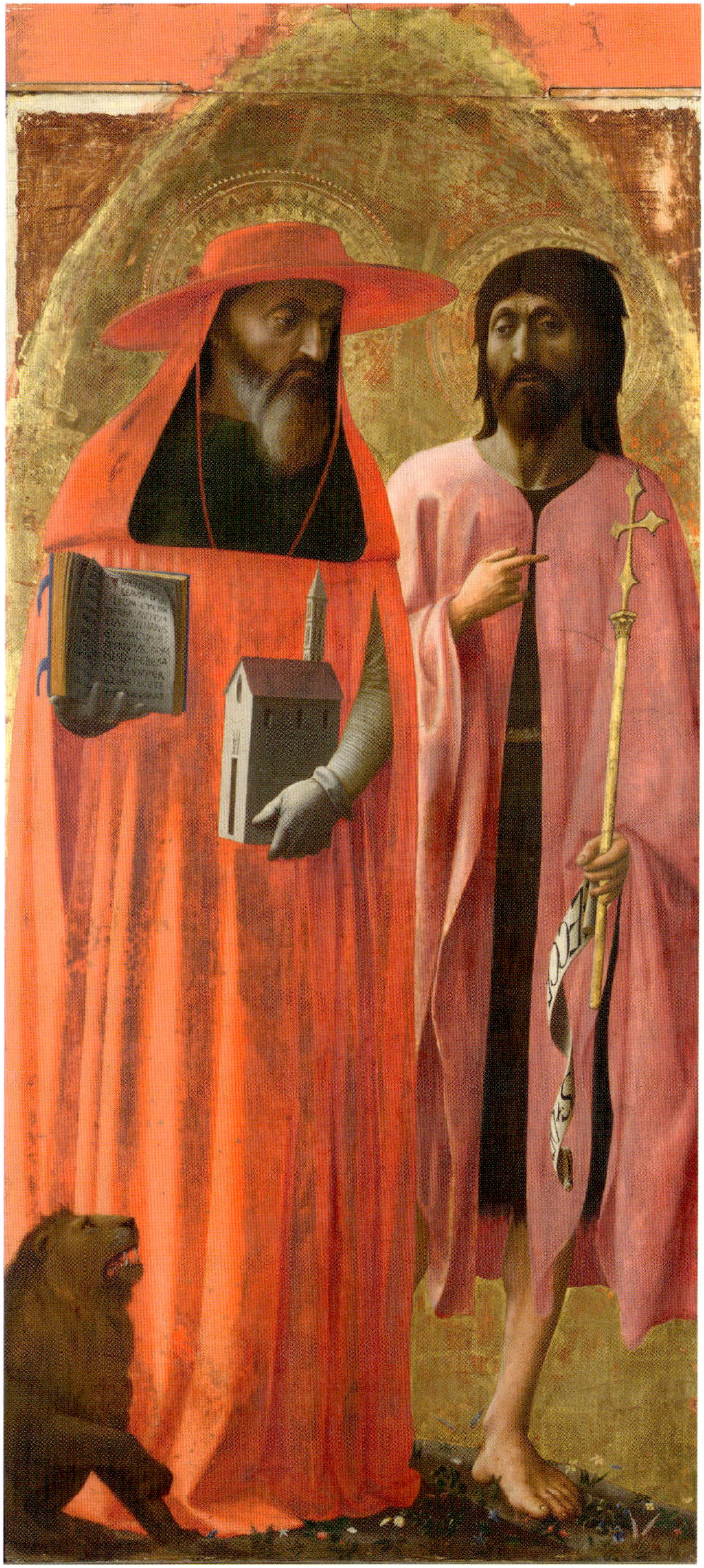

Palette

Vermilion and red lake.

Complementary works

- Frescoes from the Villa of the Mysteries in Pompeii, mid-1st century BC.
- Masolino da Panicale, *A Pope (Saint Gregory?) and Saint Matthias*, *c*.1383–1436.
- Piero della Francesca, *Flagellation of Christ*, *c*.1455–60.

C16 M100 Y100 K24
R141 G24 B21

C38 M12 Y0 K100
R0 G0 B0

C6 M50 Y64 K10
R194 G133 B89

Pioneer of oil paint

Jan van Eyck
Portrait of a Man (Self-Portrait)
1433

Oil on oak,
10¼ x 7½ in (26 x 19 cm).

The Flemish artist and alchemist van Eyck sought an alternative medium to egg tempera after growing frustrated with the way his paintings would crack in the sun while drying. He decided to change the binder and, after trying several liquids, settled on combining his colored powder pigments with a mixture of linseed and nut oils. He might not have been the first to discover the "secret" of oil paint, but his technical ability to conjure a luminous sense of realism and depth by building up thin washes of transparent oil glazes was unprecedented.

Let's start with the flamboyant red *chaperon*, a fashionable 15th-century headdress; in fact, it was more of a hood, usually worn around the neck and shoulders, but here it's been piled up on top of the sitter's head. Van Eyck applied thin layers of red lakes (pigments derived from natural liquid dyestuffs) over other colors —among them vermilion—to create the impression of highlights and shadows dancing across the folds and creases of the lustrous fabric. His mastery of the medium extends to the sitter's face, which the optical effects of oil paint render convincingly lifelike. The whites of the eyes have been mixed with small amounts of blue and red; the irises are painted ultramarine, and the pupils black and white. The cheeks and chin are daubed with stubble in dark brown and blueish white.

The contrast between the brightly lit face and the dark background is striking. But van Eyck's palette wasn't as limited as the portrait before us would suggest. The high-collared *houppelande*—a long-sleeved overgown worn later on in the Middle Ages—was originally a purplish brown, while the background, overpainted in black, was once blue. The sitter, who observes us with an appraising gaze, is almost certainly the artist himself. He leans forward, as if looking in a mirror, and his eyes are variously focused, concentrating on one and then the other. The artist's motto "Als Ich Can" (as I [ich/Eyck] can—but not as I would) is given in Greek capitals on the frame and, as well as riffing on his name, it draws attention to his dazzling colors and painterly skill.

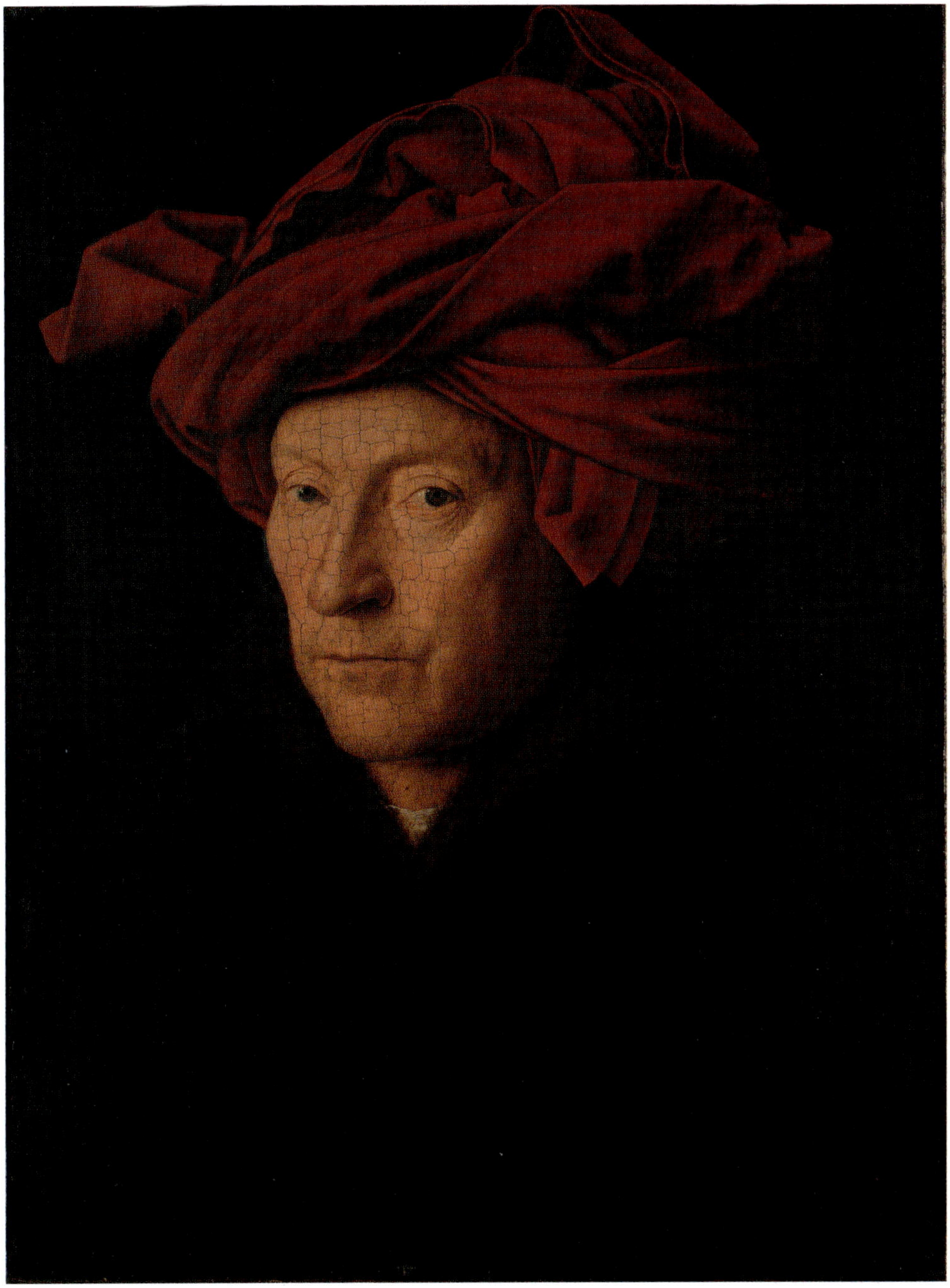

Palette

Red lake and vermilion, black and beige.

Complementary works

- Jan van Eyck, *Portrait of a Man (Léal Souvenir)*, 1432.
- Leonarda da Vinci, *Lady with an Ermin*, 1489.
- Hans Holbein the Younger, *A Lady with a Squirrel and Starling (Anne Lovell?)*, c.1526–28.

A roaring trade

Throughout the ages, an artist's palette has depended on the price and availability of colors; for the majority of history, artists or their apprentices were responsible for preparing their own paints. Once obtained, lumps of raw material had to be cleaned, cooked, ground, and purified into pigments, which were then mixed—with resins, egg, and ultimately oil—and made into paint. It was a laborious process that took time and effort, and had a knock-on effect on the handling of the paint.

Some colors were obtained nearby, from natural sources or local merchants and apothecaries, while others came from abroad. The commercial revolution of the 13th century sparked an increase in maritime trading with new colors more readily imported from overseas. Pigments arrived on ships into Venice—a major international port that maintained a powerful position in the East–West Mediterranean Sea trade—and from there spread across the continent.

In the medieval period, traders brought to the West two new pigments from Asia. First came a new version of red vermilion, known as Chinese red, extracted from the natural ore cinnabar. Introduced during the late 8th or early 9th century, the highly expensive (and toxic) pigment was used mostly in Gospel illuminations, until a cheaper synthetic alternative was produced in the 1300s. In the 12th century, another bright and beautiful color arrived in Venice: ultramarine (meaning "beyond the sea"), a long-lasting blue made from the rare stone lapis lazuli found in a single quarry in what's now Afghanistan. In his 1390 treatise *Il Libro dell'Arte* (The Craftsman's Handbook), the Italian painter Cennino d'Andrea Cennini assessed the rare color's character and shared instructions for its hours-long processing. For some time, it was prohibitively expensive—even more so than gold—and used only by prosperous artists commissioned by wealthy patrons.

In addition to the colors developed in classical antiquity—from yellow-red realgar and lead white to azurite and Egyptian blue—the Renaissance color palette was enhanced with newly discovered pigments. There were red hues derived from insects:

carmine, a natural red dye, was created from the crushed-up cochineal insects that feed on cactus plants in Central and South America; red lake, from India, was also obtained from insects and became the third most costly pigment, after gold and ultramarine. A new bright and transparent yellow pigment, gamboge, was made from the resin of Southeast Asian trees. With the new medium of oil paint, artists also began to mix and layer existing colors to produce more naturalistic effects.

Throughout art history, new materials have been added to artists' palettes, and the Renaissance was a turning point. New pigments brought with them new possibilities, and their use in artworks was directly related to their obtainability. As time went on, cheaper alternatives were created, so all artists could achieve the visual effects of, say, a rich and luminous blue. But for now, such colors were a mark of status.

Giovanni Bellini, *The Feast of the Gods*, 1514–29, oil on canvas, 67 x 74 in (170.2 x 188 cm).

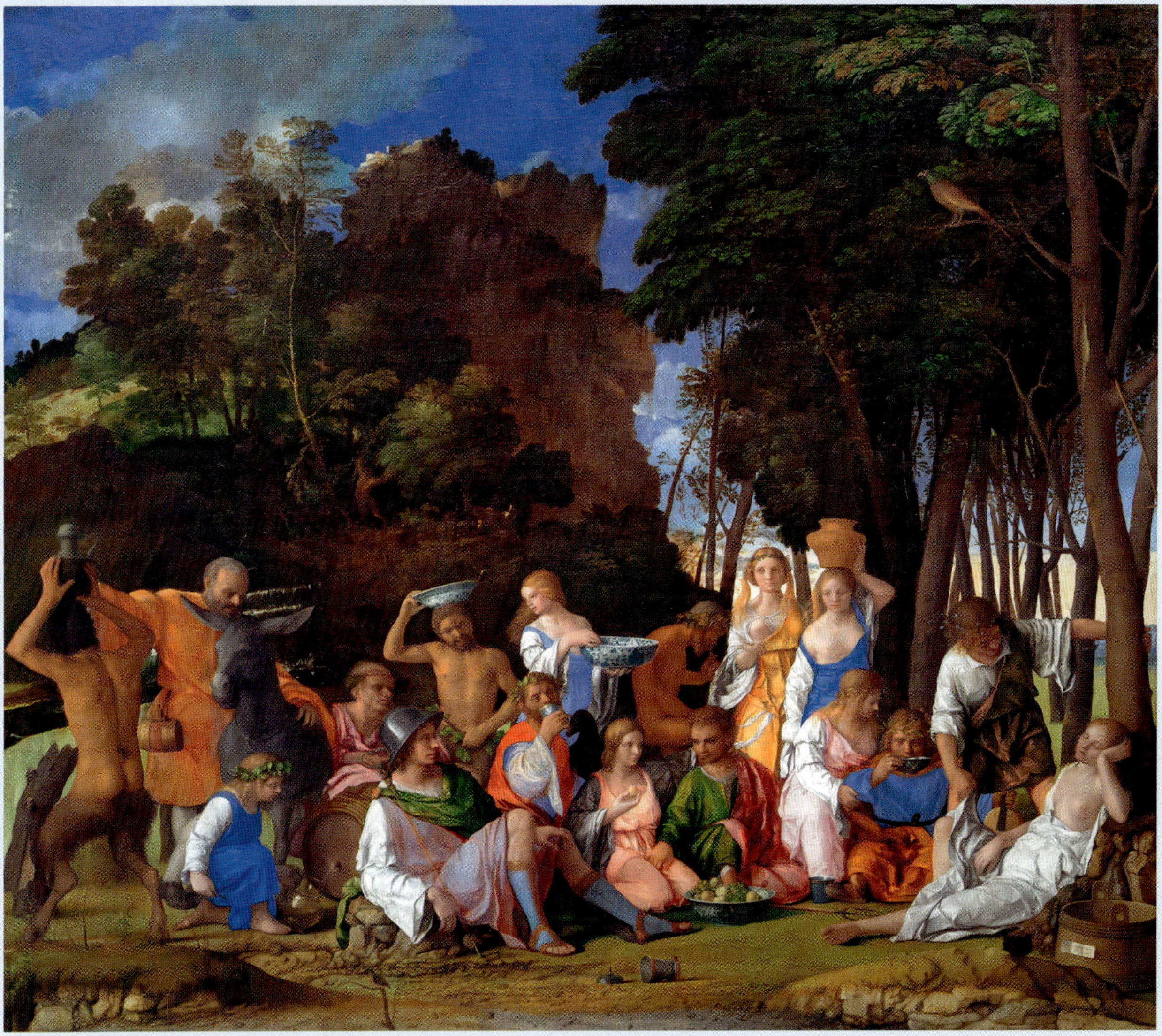

In the balance

Rogier van der Weyden
The Magdalen Reading
Before 1438

Oil on mahogany, transferred from another panel, 24½ x 21⅜ in (62.2 x 54.4 cm).

C40 M15 Y85 K30
R130 G139 B57

C0 M0 Y5 K5
R245 G245 B236

C74 M50 Y16 K30
R72 G91 B124

C28 M90 Y90 K31
R121 G44 B31

C16 M44 Y66 K35
R144 G112 B71

A young woman in a lush green dress sits on the floor, with her back against a carved wooden cabinet. She holds a special edition of the Bible, whose white book jacket picks up on the shade of her veil, tucked behind her ears. Loose locks of red hair escape from beneath the fluted cloth, just as her gold underdress escapes from beneath her hem. Her dress, cinched at the waist with a blue belt, is reminiscent of 15th-century clothing, while the room is the kind you might have seen in a medieval merchant's house. And yet the headdress reminds us that this isn't a contemporary figure: she is Mary Magdalene, a sinner who became a saint.

A surviving fragment of a larger lost painting, this poetic scene originally formed part of an altarpiece of the Virgin and Child with saints. To the left are parts of other figures: Saint John the Evangelist kneels, his toes poking out from his red robe; beside him is Saint Joseph, wearing a blue cloak, and clutching amber beads and a stick. Through the window, a river cuts through a field, with figures strolling along its grassy banks. On the cabinet are golden objects, and beside Mary Magdalene is a small pot of oil with which she is said to have anointed Christ's feet.

Like his fellow Flemish master van Eyck (*see page 38*), van der Weyden had a flair for precision, paying attention to small details, such as the letters in the Bible and Mary Magdalene's lips. The gray fur trim of her robe—itself a verdant mix of verdigris, lead-tin yellow, and lead white—was painted wet on wet with black, white, and gray. Color is beautifully balanced across the panel, with the gilded clasps of the Bible mirroring Mary Magdalene's undergarment, and the red cushion (a combination of vermilion and carmine) echoing the partial figures' robes. And where there's color, there's meaning: the white of the veil and book jacket symbolizes the saint's purity, while the visual link between her robe and the landscape hints at her emotional journey.

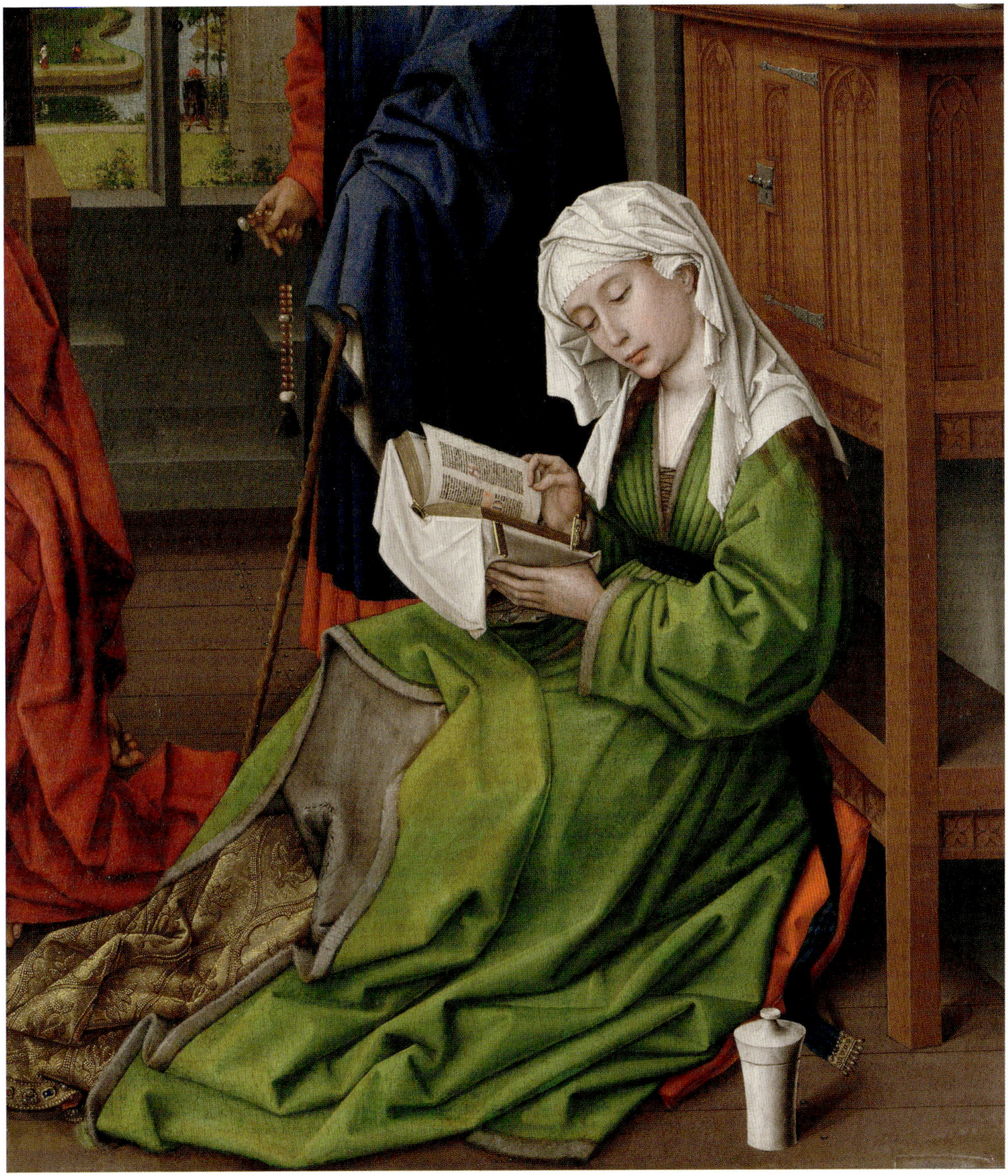

Palette

Green, white, blue, red, and ocher shine brightest.

Complementary works

- Plautilla Nelli, *Saint Catherine with the Lily*, 1465.
- Barbara Longhi, *Madonna and Child*, 1580–85.
- Michelangelo Merisi da Caravaggio, *Penitent Magdalene*, c.1594–95.

C42 M15 Y56 K5
R158 G174 B126

C48 M15 Y26 K15
R136 G162 B161

C0 M12 Y25 K0
R246 G227 B194

C8 M69 Y54 K0
R197 G103 B97

C0 M48 Y82 K5
R213 G142 B58

Watch it glimmer

Sandro Botticelli
The Birth of Venus
Late 1470s or early 1480s

Tempera on panel,
67⅞ x 109⅝ in (172.5 x 278.9 cm).

If you were to glance at the Florentine artist Sandro Botticelli's decorative canvas, you'd be forgiven for thinking that the color scheme had been chosen for its naturalistic qualities. Beneath a pale blue sky is a silky green sea rippling with wavelets of white, while to the right is a grassy bank sprouting tall, leafy, green trees. Look closer, though, and you'll soon see that the artist has infused his scene with flickers of otherworldliness. Like the subject, the palette of *The Birth of Venus* is ethereal.

Although artists in central Italy had turned away from the extensive use of gold by the late 15th century, Botticelli's painting is dashed with delicate gilded accents. Fine highlights streak Venus's long flowing hair, the grooves of the giant shell and Zephyr's steely wings. The rosy flowers wafting through the air are dashed with gold, as are the slender tree trunks and the grass. The technique the artist used is fittingly known as "shell gold," named after the mussel-shell mixing containers in which the powdered precious metal was combined with an egg-white binder. The paste was then applied to the canvas with a brush and, once dry, burnished to a sheen.

It wasn't only the use of gold that elevated Botticelli's masterpiece from the everyday. He also lent the scene a luminous quality by using carefully crushed alabaster in his ground and thinning his tempera paint to create an overall air of hazy transparency. Despite the title, the ancient Greek goddess of love and beauty has already been born from her scallop shell, which, like her flesh, is illuminated a bright and pearly white. Botticelli captures the moment she rides to shore—propelled by the breath of Zephyr, god of the winds, who is tangled up with Aura—and is greeted by one of the Hours, holding out a fluttering floral pink cloak to preserve her modesty. The setting might be recognizable, but the story and the palette—like Venus herself, an idealized classical figure at the center of the composition—are radiant and mythical.

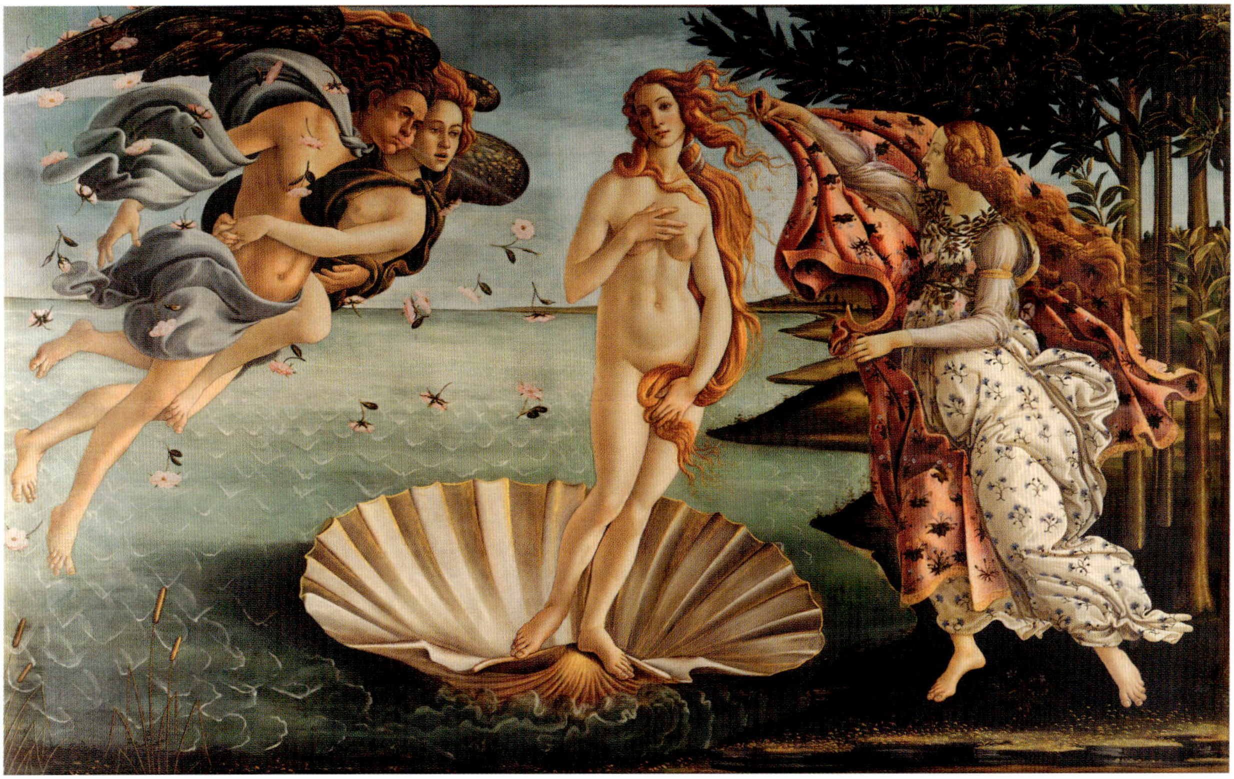

Palette

Pearly whites, pinks, and golds against green and blue.

Complementary works

- Piero del Pollaiuolo, *Apollo and Daphne*, *c.*1470–80.
- Michelangelo, *The Creation of Adam*, *c.*1512.
- Titian, *Danaë Receiving the Golden Rain*, 1560–65.

C84 M52 Y5 K15
R60 G96 B150

C14 M82 Y64 K10
R168 G67 B70

C6 M13 Y10 K6
R224 G213 B210

C0 M0 Y2 K5
R245 G245 B242

Port of opportunities

Titian
The Rape of Europa
1559–62

Oil on canvas,
70 × 81 in (178 × 205 cm).

The last of the seven *poesie* (poetic pictures) that Titian was commissioned to paint for King Philip II of Spain is the most staggering. The scene from Ovid's *Metamorphoses* (AD 8) shows the Princess Europa being dragged across the briny sea by Jupiter, king of the gods, in the guise of a bull. Her ladies-in-waiting stand helplessly on the shore, waving wildly, while a trio of putti—two tumbling through the air, a third clinging to a silvery fish—follow in pursuit. This is a monumental image of climactic emotion, which Titian conveys through sensual textures and subtle variations of lustrous color.

The great Venetian artist sets his lyrical drama against an epic sky that shifts from deep blue to fiery bronze. The sea darkens the further it stretches from the shore; Jupiter has almost lugged Europa to the point of no return. The princess's creamy-white body is bathed in light. Her legs are slightly parted, the soles of her feet red raw. In her left hand she clutches the horn of the bull, which ripples through the water, grizzly and gray; in her right is a crimson sash that casts a shadow over her face. The bull holds our gaze, his alarming brown eyes the most in-focus part of the painting.

Titian made the most of the exotic materials arriving into Venice on ships from the East. For Europa's sash, he used carmine; a shade with connotations of both passion and danger, it appears in stark contrast with the princess's white robe and the ultramarine sky. Titian worked swiftly and spontaneously, experimenting with texture and painting wet on wet. He preferred to work with coarse canvas, and the weave can be seen through the more diluted patches of oil paint.

Titian ignored the ancient rules that prohibited the melding of pigments, as laid out by the Greek writer Plutarch, who in his essay collection *Moralia* (AD *c.*100) said "mixing produces conflict." Well, Plutarch was right—mixing does produce conflict, and that's the exact emotion Titian was trying to evoke. Just as Europa is being swept across the sea, so the artist's brushstrokes sweep across the canvas. He painted with feeling, and he captured feeling in paint.

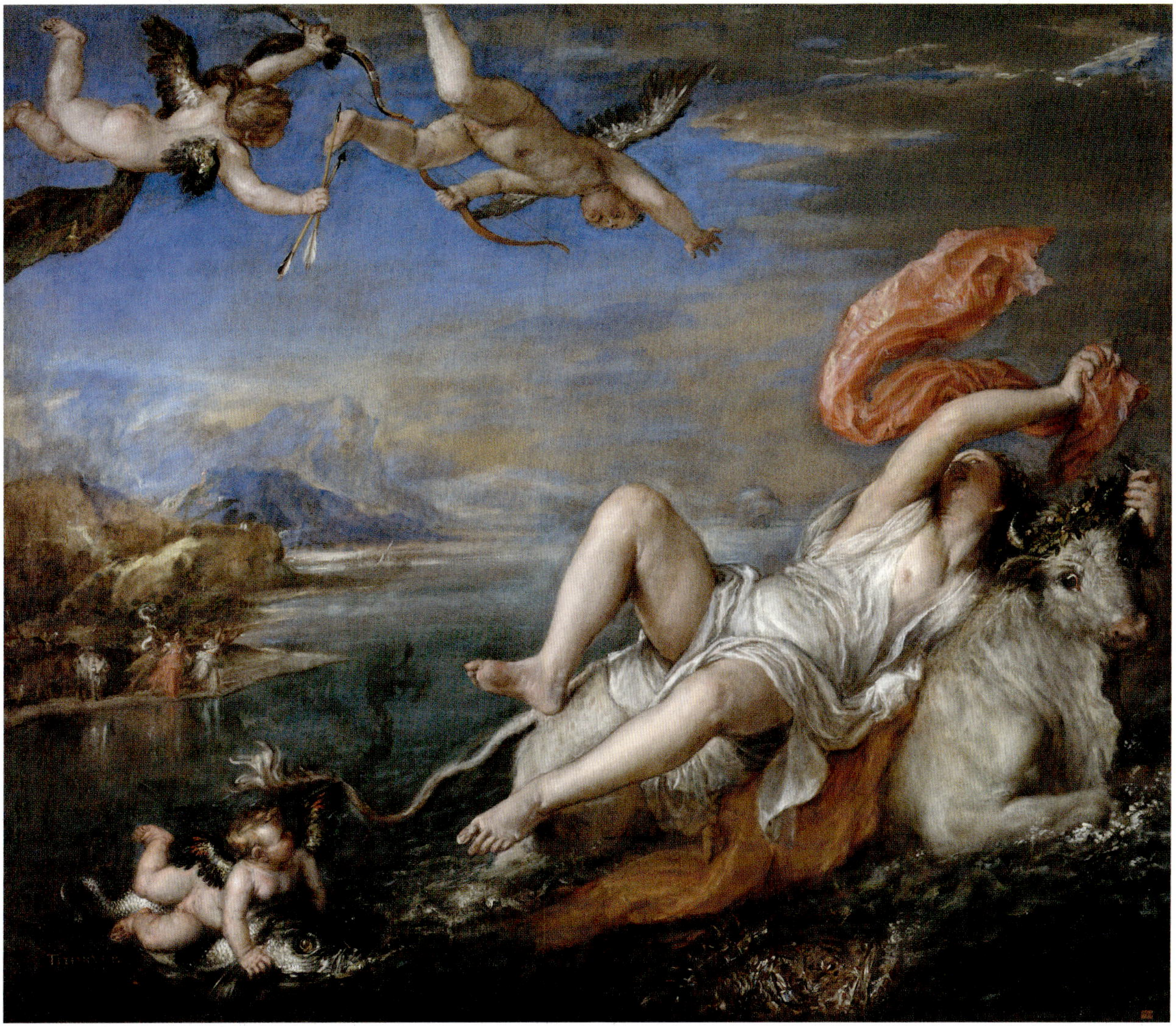

Palette

Every color, from carmine to lead white, beneath an ultramarine sky.

Complementary works

- Paolo Veronese, *The Rape of Europa*, *c.*1570.
- Jacopo Tintoretto, *The Origin of the Milky Way*, *c.*1575.
- Guido Reni, *The Rape of Europa*, 1637–39.

Change of dress

C40 M12 Y6 K100
R0 G0 B0

C2 M0 Y0 K6
R239 G242 B243

Sofonisba Anguissola

Philip II

1565

Oil on canvas,
$34\frac{5}{8}$ x $28\frac{5}{16}$ in (88 x 72 cm).

Color takes on new meaning in commissioned portraits: just as the style of dress communicates a sitter's values and status, as well as wider social and spiritual regulations, so too does its shade. Black drifts in and out of art history, but in the 16th century it was a favorite among kings and nobles, who regarded it as a symbol of power, dignity, and cultural refinement.

After receiving early encouragement from her father, the Italian noblewoman Sofonisba Anguissola enjoyed a long and prosperous artistic career that extended into her 90s. She traveled to Spain in 1559 to serve as a lady-in-waiting for Philip II of Spain's third wife, Elizabeth of Valois, and ended up working unofficially as his court painter for fourteen years. When she painted this portrait, the king was married to Valois; almost a decade later, in 1573, she retouched it so it would work as a pair with a portrait of his fourth wife, Anne of Austria. Philip originally wore a short and bulky cape known as a *bohemia* and pointed to the Order of the Golden Fleece medallion on his chest. Anguissola replaced the heavy cape with a lighter option in fine black silk and moved his right hand to the arm of the chair, evoking a sense of regal authority. With the sword hanging from his waist and the rosary beads he's rolling between forefinger and thumb, the image is one of grace and refinement.

The palette might be spare, but the portrait is rich in details. The pristine white collar and cuffs are brilliant accents against the luscious black cloth, and the king's pale blue eyes are all the more piercing against a plain gray backdrop. Anguissola applied her paint in subtly blurred brushstrokes, creating the impression that the painting is diffused with light. There's a soft modeling to Philip's pinky-white fingers and face. Funnily enough, the king chose not to have any age-related updates to his visage.

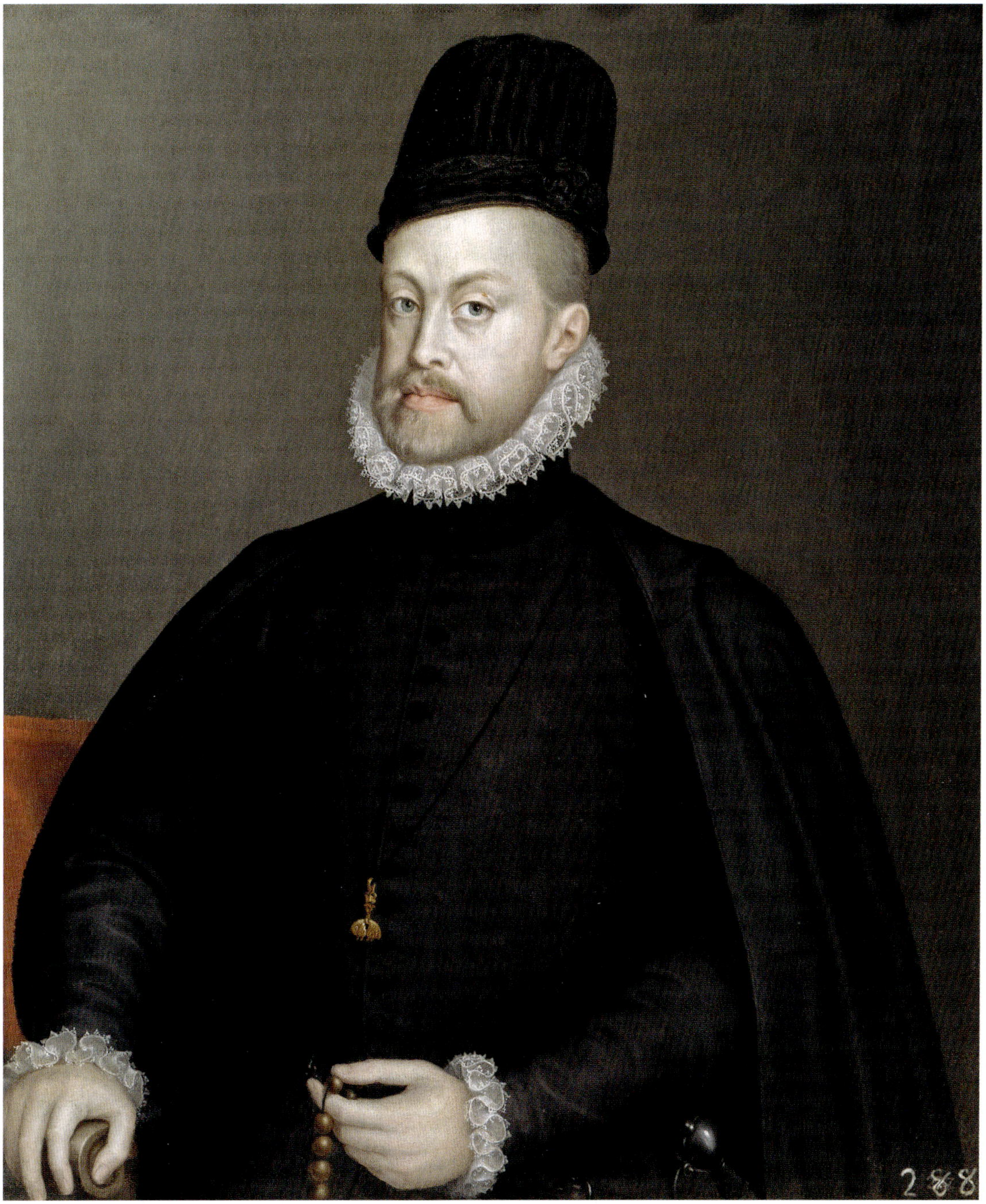

Palette

Things are black and white.

Complementary works

- Giovanni Bellini, *Portrait of the Doge Leonardo Loredan*, 1501–02.
- Catharina van Hemessen, *Portrait of a Man*, c.1552.
- Anthony van Dyck, *Portrait of Sofonisba Anguissola*, 1624.

C8 M0 Y0 K25
R193 G201 B206

C0 M45 Y75 K10
R206 G143 B71

Family portrait

Lavinia Fontana
Portrait of Bianca degli Utili Maselli, Holding a Dog and Surrounded by Six of Her Children
1605

Oil on canvas,
39 x 52½ in (99 x 133.5 cm).

This meticulous family portrait shimmers with silver and gold. The attention to detail of the embroidered clothing and sumptuous jewelry is quite remarkable. And yet beneath the glitzy costumes and formal arrangement is a tender snapshot of motherhood. Lavinia Fontana was the daughter of a prominent Bolognese painter and the first woman to gain a place at the Accademia di San Luca in Rome. Throughout her career she painted dozens of portraits—and this is undoubtedly one of her finest.

Crowned with a rosy floral headband, Bianca degli Utili, the wife of the Italian nobleman Pierino Maselli, stands at the center of the composition, with three children either side. Like their mother, those to her right pay attention to the artist and meet our gaze; those on her left, on the other hand, are a little distracted. Against the plain gray background, the decorative textiles, which provide insight into the fashion at the time, are especially rich. The five boys wear matching outfits, while mother and daughter wear different dresses, as well as gold earrings and pearl necklaces. Fontana used lead white for the delicate lace ruffs and cuffs, each of which varies subtly and has an almost sculptural quality. A combination of lead white and lead-tin yellow was chosen for the opulent golden jewelry and gold thread.

This family portrait isn't just an overt display of wealth. Almost every child—even the well-behaved bunch—clutches a keepsake, such as a colorful bird tied to a chain, a tempting dish of fruit, or a quill and pot of ink. With one hand, the only girl, Verginia, clings onto her mother's forefinger; in the other, she clutches the paw of the small dog—a symbol of fidelity—sitting in Bianca's arm. Verginia is also the only child to have her name inscribed above her head, which might suggest that the portrait was either painted for her or in her honor.

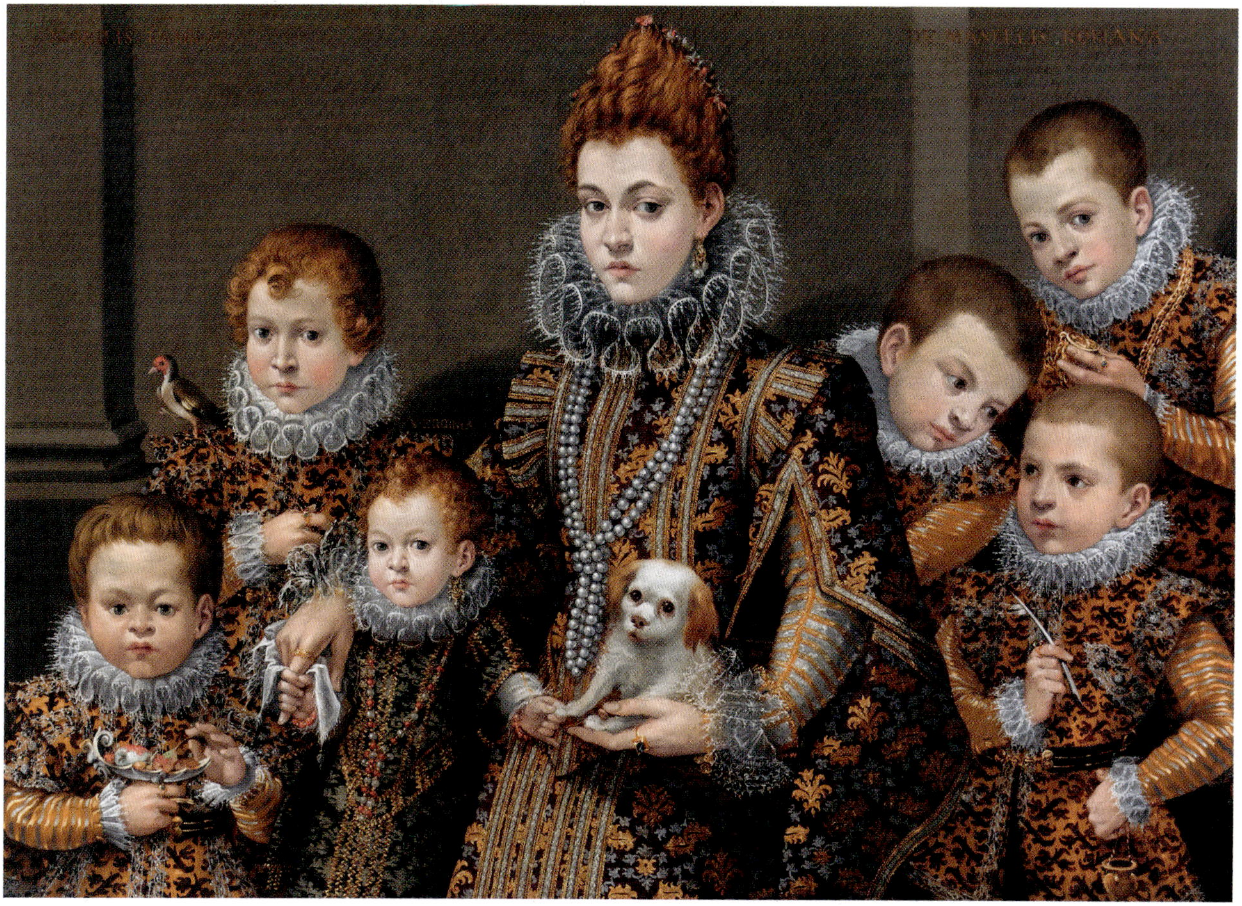

Palette

Shimmering strokes of silver and gold.

Complementary works

- Lucas Cranach the Elder, *Saints Genevieve and Apollonia*, 1506.
- Anthony van Dyck, *Lady Elizabeth Thimbelby and Dorothy, Viscountess Andover*, c.1635.
- Mary Beale, *Self-Portrait of Mary Beale with her Husband and Son*, c.1659–60.

Cutting loose

Baroque and Rococo

C5 M32 Y10 K0
R224 G187 B197

Cutting loose

Baroque and Rococo

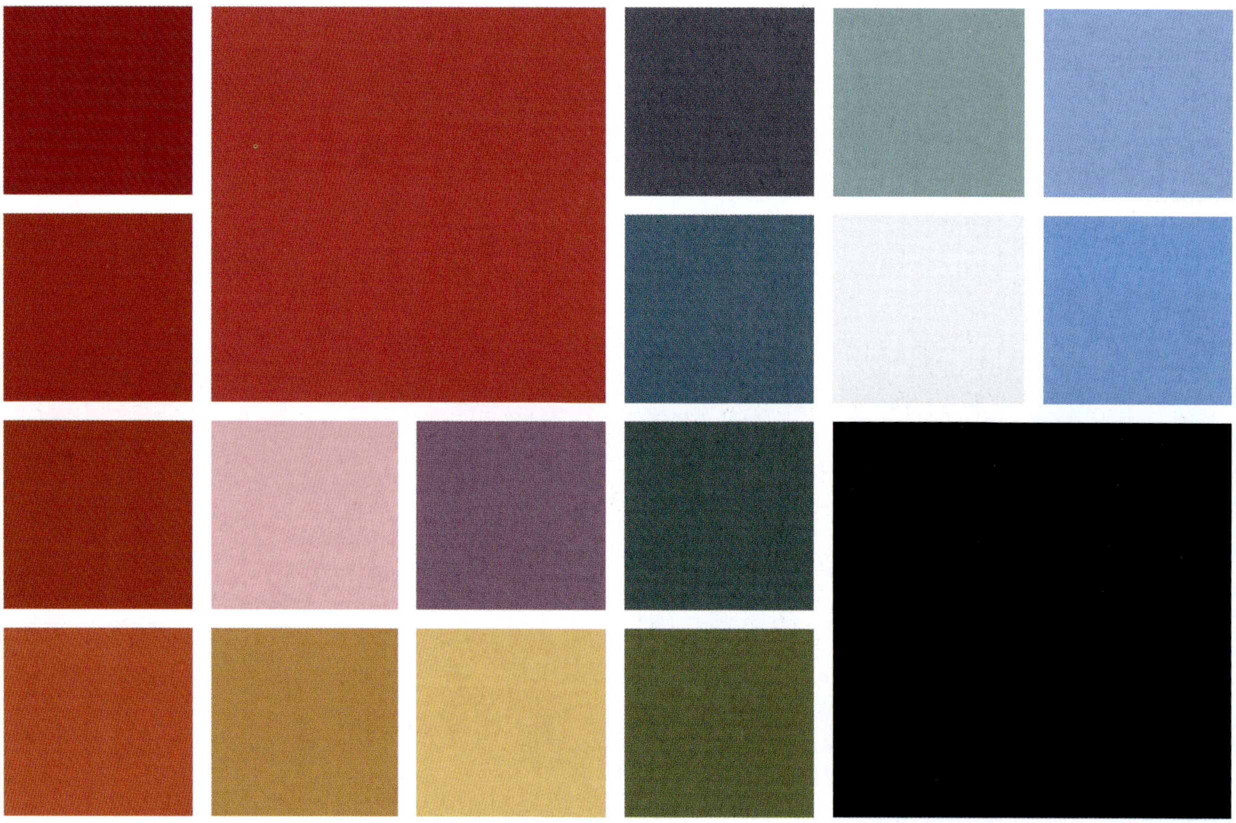

If the Renaissance was about establishing order, the period that followed was about shaking things up. By the end of the 16th century in Italy, artists were becoming disillusioned with the often sickly-sweet color schemes, contrived poses, and deep perspectives of the late-Renaissance European style now known as Mannerism. Instead, they developed a taste for more naturalistic art, with a focus on human emotion and drama. Audiences were hankering for clarity, and what better way to give them that than by cranking up the contrast between light and dark?

Color and light are inextricably entwined, and it was in the Baroque palette that the latter was used to its most dramatic effect. In the 17th century, following the lead of the high priest of the Italian Baroque Michelangelo Merisi da Caravaggio (*see page 56*), artists practiced a technique called *chiaroscuro* (Italian for "light-dark"), darkening their shadows to a velvety black and illuminating their subjects with shafts and blades. Earth and ocher colors dominated, with brighter hues mostly veiled. Edges were crisp, subjects undiluted. These were narratives that prized black above all else.

From brusque black structures and razor-sharp silhouettes to rosy cherubs, smooth silks, and fluffy clouds: fast-forward a few decades and skip over to France, and you'll find an even more naturalistic, if also decadent, sensibility. The Rococo began with the graceful landscapes of Antoine Watteau and evolved over time, via the flamboyant scenes of François Boucher (*see page 64*), to the freely painted genre paintings of Jean-Honoré Fragonard. It saw artworks bathed in harmonious washes of color and light, of which lead white was a key proponent. Fundamental to the 18th-century palette, it was this toxic pigment that enabled artists to create creamy pastels, from coral pinks to baby blues.

"Nature is too green, and badly lit," wrote Boucher. Fortunately for him, a vivid new pigment that was cheap and easy to mix was discovered in 1704. The result of a German chemist and color-maker's experiment gone wrong, Prussian blue was the first of the modern synthetic pigments. The first samples arrived in Paris by 1710 and brought with them a revolution in painting, as they allowed artists to blanket their canvases in timeless skies and seas. Boucher himself also used it as the basis for his foliage; in his art, many elements have a blue tinge. In Venice, Italian artists such as Giovanni Battista Tiepolo and Giovanni Antonio Canal, better known as Canaletto, used it to achieve their cool blue-and-white decorative schemes and atmospheric effects.

Together with Isaac Newton's discovery of the color spectrum (*see page 62*), the discovery of Prussian blue enabled artists to reproduce the full color wheel on their palettes. By mixing a small amount with other paints, they were able to experiment with fresh color harmonies. Although seemingly simple, the Rococo paintings of Boucher and his contemporaries revealed a new mastery of advancing and receding complementary colors by blending and layering hues. And so, black—star of the Baroque—was all but banished by the Rococo.

Throughout the history of art, colors have fallen in and out of favor. What was desirable in one time and place was cast aside in the next. And yet one aspect that these two periods that followed the Renaissance have in common is their fondness for excess. Whether packaged in dramatic contrasts of light and dark or saccharine pastels, neither the artists of the Baroque nor those of the Rococo held back.

Theater of light and dark

Michelangelo Merisi da Caravaggio

Rest on the Flight into Egypt

1597

Oil on canvas,
53$\frac{5}{16}$ × 65$\frac{5}{8}$ in (135.5 × 166.5 cm).

Caravaggio was the master of *chiaroscuro.* A native of Lombardy, he arrived in Rome in the early 1590s and caused a stir with narratives in light and dark. He sought to humanize the supernatural and, in doing so, often flouted convention; his desire to portray sacred events in everyday human terms led to a bold realism that sometimes left little room for spirituality. In *Rest on the Flight into Egypt*, a precursor of his most dramatic paintings, the artist takes a biblical subject and sets it on a spotlit stage.

The viewer is enticed into the image by the coquettish angel, who divides the composition, standing with his back to us while playing a violin. The sleeping Virgin's limp fingers and Joseph's planted feet, along with the couple's wilted golden-brown and blue shrouds, subtly translate the angel's ethereal nature into the vulnerability of humanity. The donkey—a velvety shadow on the left, made out mostly by its glossy eye—blocks in the floodlit scene and nods to the fact that these figures are being watched over from heaven above. From the angel's dark and feathery wings to the sharp-edged rocks at his feet, the figures are projected forward. The artist magnified his textures and dramatized his light with the hope of closing the gap between the spectator and the scene, heightening emotion and making the divine physically real.

Caravaggio uses contrasts of color, and light and dark, to tell the biblical story and guide us around the canvas. Our eyes snag on the swirling bright-white cloth of the angel, before gliding to the matching cuffs of the red-haired Virgin and the glint of a glass vase in the woven basket in the lower left corner. The ocher leaves in the tree pick up on the golden shade of Joseph's cloak, as well as the angel's soft curls. Similarly, the Virgin's deep-blue cloak tumbles seamlessly into the patch of verdant vegetation. Against a dark and earthy backdrop, the 17th-century artist illuminates brighter mineral pigments, from lead white and lead-tin yellow to vermilion.

C40 M8 Y0 K100
R0 G0 B0

C2 M0 Y0 K6
R239 G242 B243

C15 M40 Y80 K20
R170 G134 B60

C14 M86 Y100 K20
R152 G54 B21

C60 M21 Y39 K40
R90 G115 B108

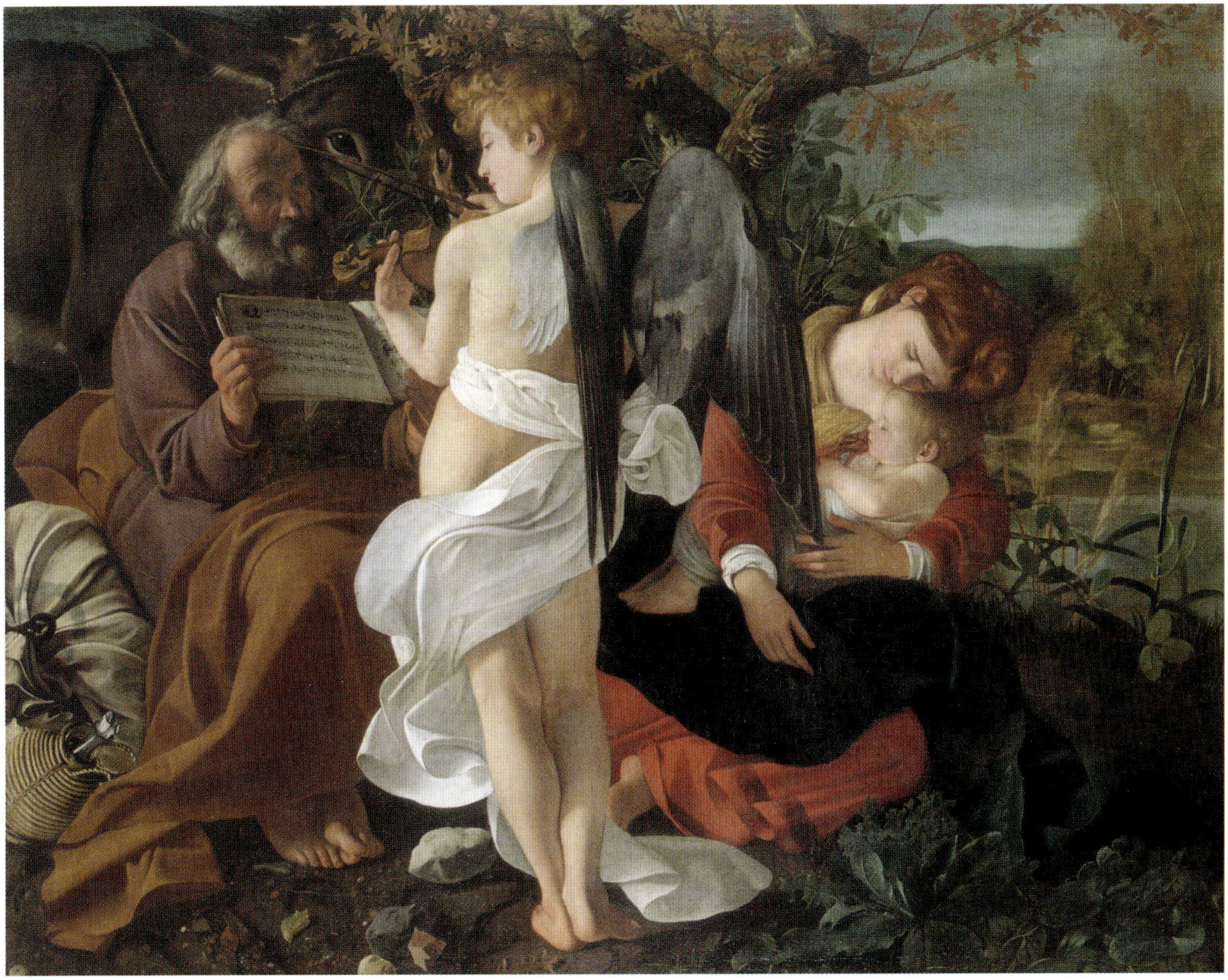

Palette

Carbon black and lead white together with yellow, red, and green.

Complementary works

- Rosso Fiorentino, *Angel Playing the Lute*, 1521.
- Guercino, *Christ and the Woman of Samaria*, 1619–20.
- Rembrandt van Rijn, *The Holy Family with Angels*, 1645.

C40 M5 Y4 K100
R0 G0 B0

C9 M40 Y72 K10
R195 G149 B80

C2 M0 Y0 K6
R239 G242 B243

C16 M100 Y82 K28
R135 G22 B36

C39 M54 Y20 K10
R143 G117 B142

Fan the flames

Artemisia Gentileschi

Judith and her Maidservant with the Head of Holofernes

*c.*1623–25

Oil on canvas,
$7\frac{11}{16} \times 55\frac{7}{8}$ in (187.2 × 142 cm).

The most celebrated female artist of the Italian Baroque was no doubt influenced by Caravaggio (*see page 56*), whose naturalistic altarpieces adorned the churches of her native Rome. She, too, took a realist approach to painting, enlivened by bold colors and dramatic *chiaroscuro*. Like all women artists, Artemisia Gentileschi had to prove herself—and she did so with powerful compositions of life-sized female figures in scenes of intimacy, violence, and ecstasy. Here she captures the aftermath of the often told Old Testament tale of Judith and Holofernes.

The Jewish heroine has just decapitated the Assyrian general leading the assault on her city and is about to escape from his tent in the enemy camp under the cover of darkness. Crouching at her feet is her maidservant, Abra, bundling the bloody head into a sack. The artist painted the same subject a decade earlier, but here she dials up the drama. The two women are engulfed in darkness, with the flickering flame of a single candle illuminating the inside of Holofernes's tent. The deep-red curtain fringed with gold adds to the sense of the spectacle. The scene is made up of sharp diagonals: that curtain, the sweep of golden-yellow folds of Judith's robe, her illuminated raised hand and both her arms, as well as the tightly clutched sword, dripping with blood.

In addition to heightening the drama, the bright color accents and light draw our attention to the narrative. The hilt of the sword gleams, as does its scabbard and the discarded polished-steel gauntlet on the tabletop—items that underscore the women's successful disarming of the general. Although accomplices, they have different social standings, as signified by their robes: Judith's ocher fabric glows gold, as does her embellished diadem, while Abra wears a crumpled white headdress and a blue-and-purple dress that blends more readily with the background. Artemisia used *chiaroscuro* and color to conjure a tense and emotionally fraught atmosphere, but also to describe her characters. Most of all, though, she used them to shine a light on capable female figures.

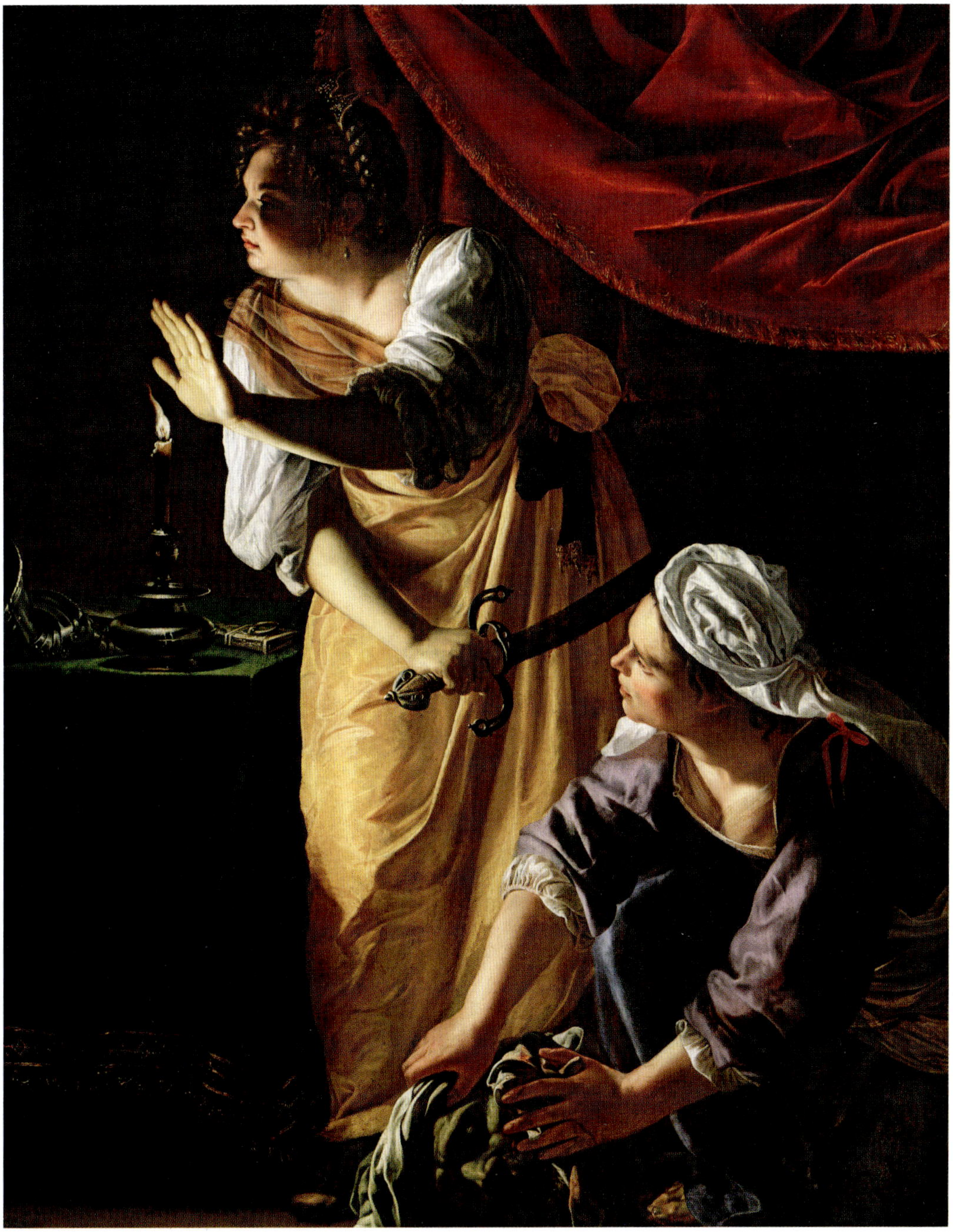

Palette

Golden-yellow, white, red, and purple enveloped in black shadow.

Complementary works

- Orazio Gentileschi, *The Lute Player*, *c.*1612–15.
- Georges de La Tour, *Joseph the Carpenter*, *c.*1642.
- Elisabetta Sirani, *Portia Wounding her Thigh*, 1664.

C9 M20 Y36 K0
R224 G203 B166

C19 M92 Y64 K15
R163 G42 B62

C45 M28 Y19 K45
R103 G111 B120

C0 M2 Y0 K6
R242 G240 B241

Mirror, mirror

Diego Velázquez

The Toilet of Venus (The Rokeby Venus)

c.1647–51

Oil on canvas,
49 x 70¾ in (124.5 x 179.8 cm).

Color is one of several devices used in this prized oil painting to direct our attention toward Venus, the goddess of love. Her smooth, pearly skin is juxtaposed with the satin fabric beneath her, which was originally more purple than gray and has been rendered with lively brushstrokes. Against the sumptuous pink curtain and the dark backdrop, her creamy flesh appears as if it's bathed in light; at the same time, it seems softer than the stark white sheets. Reclining on the bed with her legs bent at the knee and her head propped up in the palm of her hand, she is supported by her son Cupid as she gazes into a mirror, which has pale pink ribbons attached to it, in a nod to his blindfold.

Female nudes were rarely painted in 17th-century Spain, where the Catholic Church frowned upon erotic images, but King Philip IV and wealthy art collectors weren't opposed to hanging mythological paintings of naked figures in their homes. In his only known surviving female nude, the court painter Velázquez combined two traditional representations of Venus—that of her "at her toilet," where she's shown sitting on a bed and looking in a dark-framed mirror, and that of her reclining in a landscape—to create a remarkably original and enigmatic image that captures both an eroticized body and an inner life.

The sensuality of the painting comes in part from the pinks and creams, and Venus's nudity, but also from the artist's clever concealment of her face. She has her back to us and her reflection is blurred. By obscuring her identity, Velázquez adds an air of intrigue that raises the stakes. Also, an air of objectification: the suffragettes famously vandalized paintings of female flesh in their fight for equality and the release of Emmeline Pankhurst, and at the National Gallery in London, Mary Richardson hacked six times at *The Toilet of Venus (The Rokeby Venus)*. In a statement, Richardson said, "I have tried to destroy the most beautiful woman in mythological history."

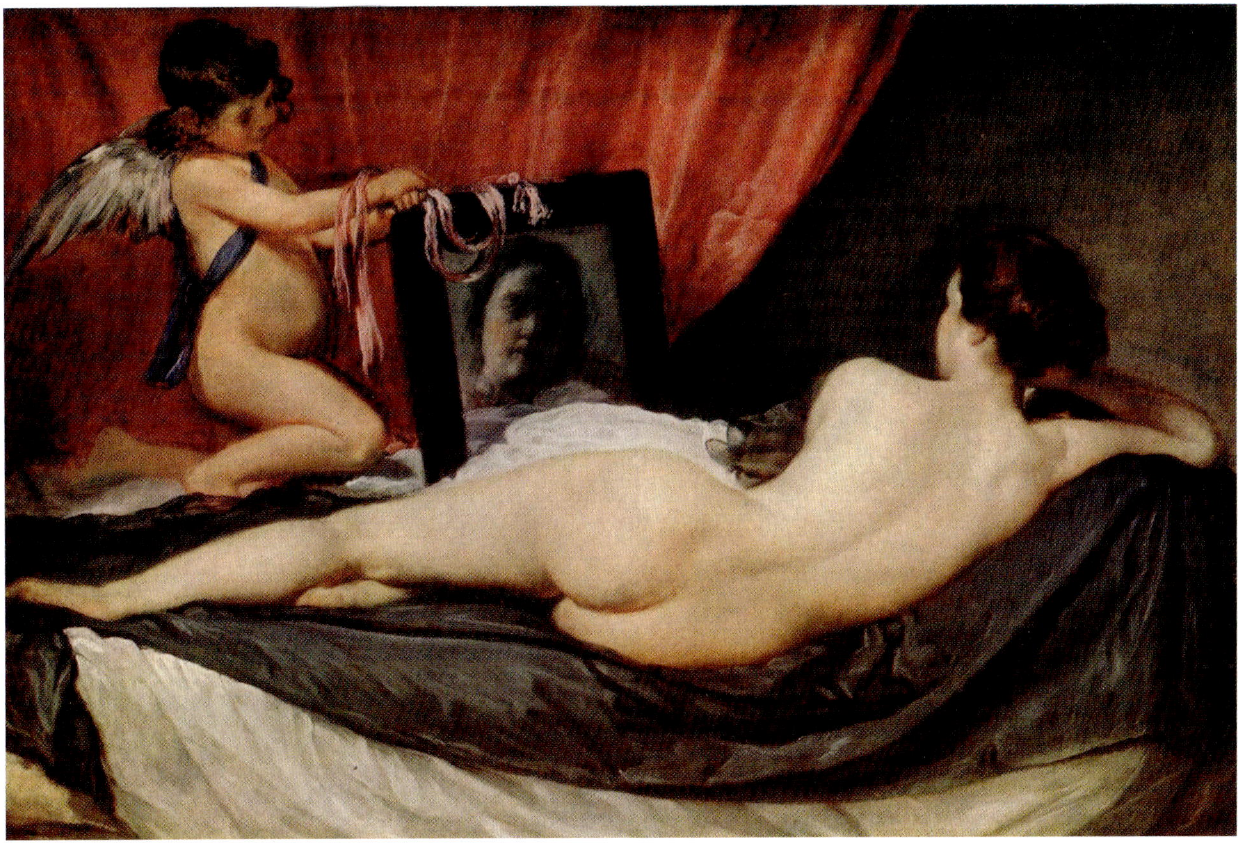

Palette

A sensual mix of cream, pink, gray, and white.

Complementary works

- Francisco Ribalta, *Christ embracing Saint Bernard*, 1625–27.
- Francisco de Zurbarán, *A Cup of Water and a Rose*, *c.*1630.
- François Boucher, *The Toilette of Venus*, 1751.

The color wheel

"Whiteness is the usual color of light," said Isaac Newton, the great 17th-century mathematician and physicist who sparked a revolution in understanding color when he discovered the color spectrum. In 1666 he conducted a series of indoor experiments in which he passed a beam of apparently colorless daylight, or white light, through a glass prism and witnessed it separate into a range of distinct colored rays. He then passed those rays through a second prism, at which point they recombined into white. And so Newton proved that all color is contained within light.

Newton outlined his scientific findings in his treatise *Optiks* (1704) by way of both mathematical formulae and more easily accessible diagrams. The color spectrum might have been continuous, but he identified seven essential hues—red, orange, yellow, green, blue, indigo, and violet—from which he suggested all others were made. Despite its importance in the Aristotelian concept of color, black had no place in Newton's scheme.

Newton mapped his spectral array onto a circle, rather than a linear scale, and in doing so revealed the relationships between different colors and what happens when they appear side by side. In the 18th century, his color circle became something of a prototype, a springboard from which further ideas and approaches were explored. Although revolutionary, Newton's science failed to recognize that artists' materials (such as pigments) blend differently from light, and that color could be a subjective experience as well as a scientific measurement. Subsequent thinkers, including the German polymath Johann Wolfgang von Goethe (*see page 96*), went on to refine his theory, and to study the science of color on a more practical and human level.

Artists were taken with these findings—among them the Czech painter František Kupka (*see page 63*), who alludes to Newton's diagramming in his *Disks of Newton (Study for "Fugue in Two Colors")* (*c.*1912), an abstract painting with theoretical roots. Kupka's work draws on Newton's first color wheel, which sees white take center stage, as well as another of his experiments, which took place a few decades later, in 1717. Known as Newton's rings, it saw the physicist sandwich together two sheets of glass—one flat, one convex—with a layer of air in between. He then directed a beam of light onto the glass and witnessed as the interference of light waves—i.e. light waves reflected from both the top and the bottom simultaneously—created patterns of concentric circles. Kupka's painting shows that when white light, which contains all color, shines onto the glass, the circular bands are colored according to the spectrum.

Newton proved that color isn't simply activated by light, as the ancients proposed, or perceived through light, as was suggested in medieval theory. Instead, he discovered that light is composed of a spectrum of colors, as seen in all their glory in rainbows. He might have made the mistake of trusting maths and science over the experience of the human eye, but regardless, his discovery marked a fundamental change in modern thought and continued to influence color theory for centuries.

Newton's color wheel from Book I, Part II, Proposition VI, Problem 2 of *Opticks*, 1704.

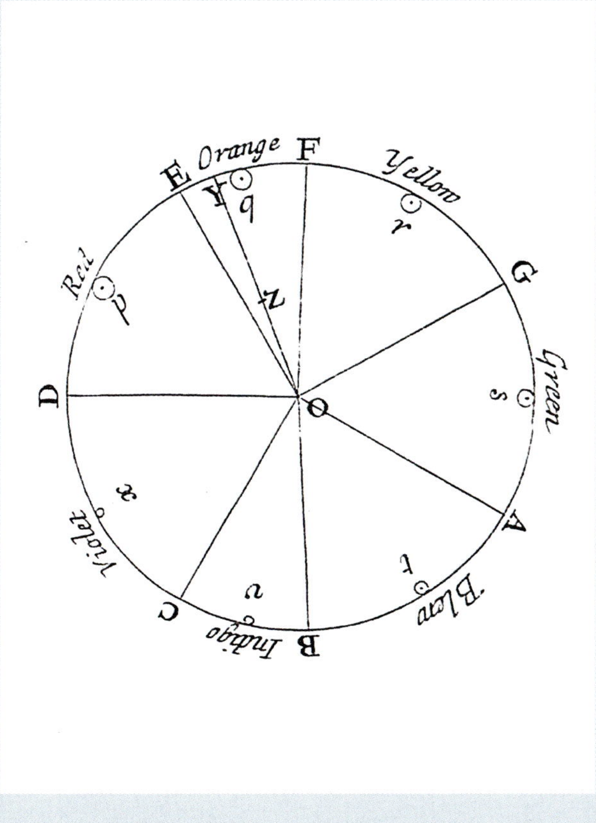

František Kupka, *Disks of Newton (Study for "Fugue in Two Colors")*, 1912, oil on canvas, 39½ × 29 in (100.3 × 73.7 cm).

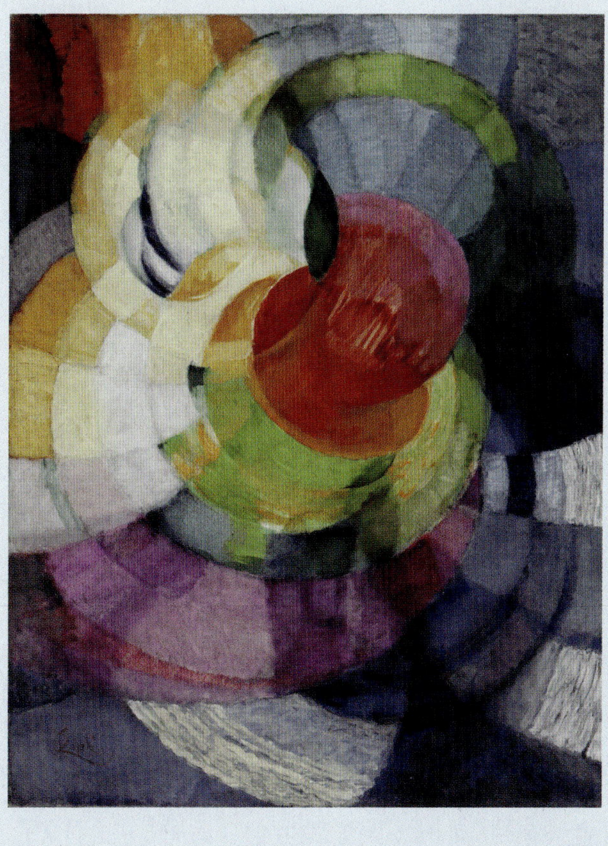

The politics of pink

François Boucher
The Rising of the Sun
1753

Oil on canvas,
149 × 103 in (378 × 261 cm).

C6 M55 Y55 K0
R208 G134 B106

C2 M0 Y0 K6
R239 G242 B243

C6 M19 Y24 K0
R230 G209 B188

C48 M15 Y0 K0
R152 G184 B224

C48 M16 Y24 K0
R152 G179 B183

Few periods in art history are as closely associated with the color pink as the Rococo, a playfully erotic and decorative style that originated in early 18th-century Paris, and Boucher was one of its leading lights. In the 19th century, the Goncourt brothers, who in their writing fashioned an irresistible vision of Rococo France, enthused about his use of pink, "tender and pale like a rain-soaked rose." Others, however, have criticized the painter for over-relying on such a "feminine" color. A peculiar claim, when in this mythological canvas the shade is associated not with gender but with power.

Apollo, god of the sun and symbol of the French kings, is swathed in pink fabric that, together with his pale skin, contrasts with the turquoise and azure blues of the sea and sky. According to Ovid, each day he rode his fiery chariot across the heavens, bringing light to the world, and come evening, he sank back into the waves. The nymph Tethys assists him in his departure, holding the reins of the white horses standing among the clouds, their manes catching the morning light. Above, bare-bottomed cherubs toss and turn, while the sea is populated by bronzed tritons clutching gleaming scallop shells, water nymphs dripping with pearls, and a giant sea creature with a watchful eye.

One of a pair, *The Rising of the Sun* was commissioned by Madame de Pompadour, the powerful mistress of King Louis XV and, in the words of the Goncourt brothers, the "godmother and queen of the Rococo." The large, vertical paintings were to be used as models for tapestries that briefly adorned the king's bedroom in the Château de Bellevue, a country house between Paris and Versailles. By the time she commissioned the works, Pompadour had begun to advise Louis XV, and her role is mirrored in that of Tethys, who bids Apollo goodbye and later welcomes him home. In his art, Boucher combined the political and the mythical with a harmonious, jeweled palette.

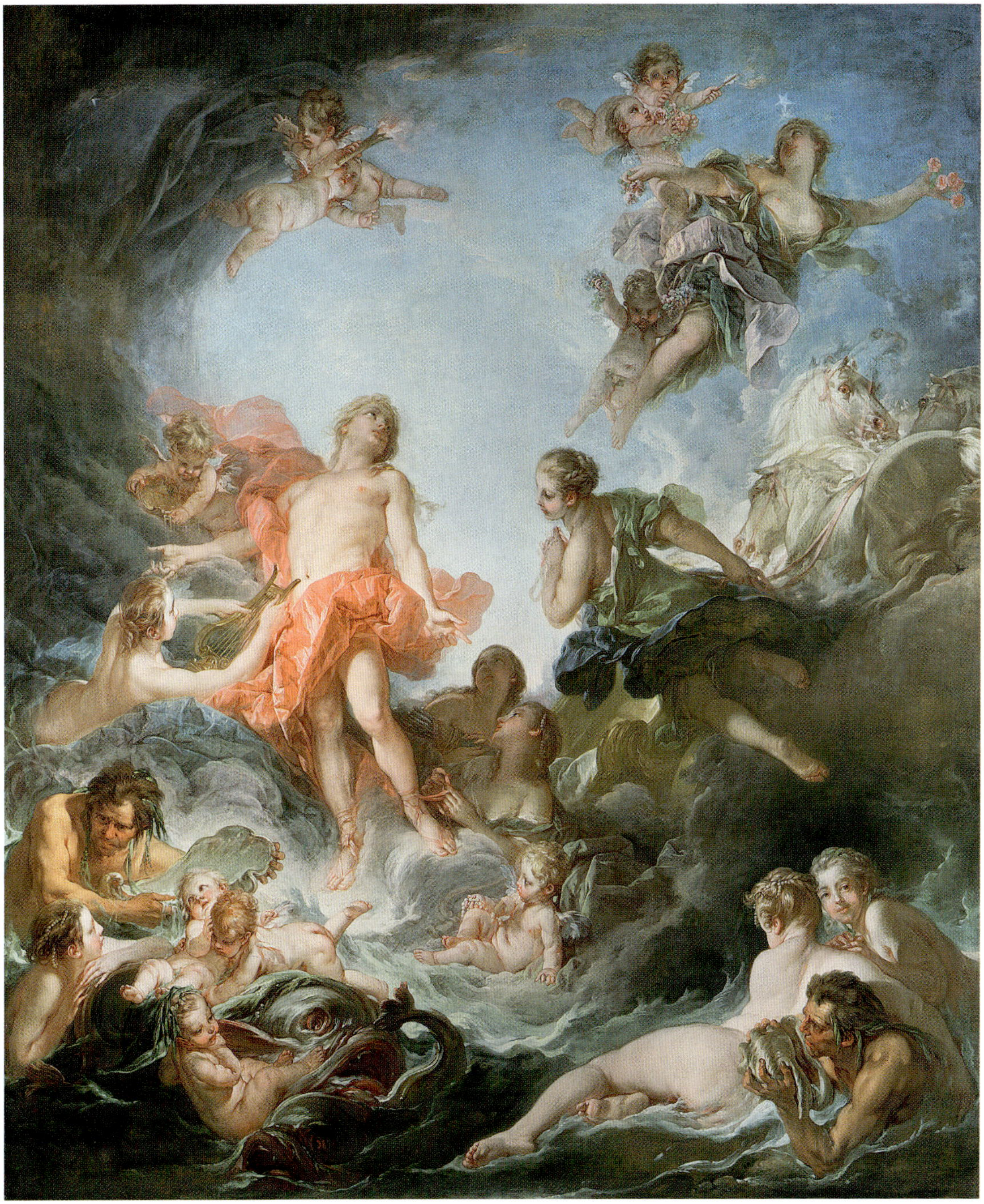

Palette

Pink-skinned putti and nymphs in a turquoise and azure blue morning sky.

Complementary works

- Jean-Antoine Watteau, *Diana at her Bath*, 1715–16.
- Giovanni Battista Tiepolo, *An Allegory with Venus and Time*, c.1754–58.
- Flora Yukhnovich, *Boucher's Flesh*, 2017.

C8 M24 Y60 K0
R223 G192 B119

C0 M0 Y0 K6
R243 G243 B243

C11 M90 Y90 K24
R149 G45 B30

C63 M20 Y20 K29
R95 G129 B144

C34 M15 Y66 K40
R125 G131 B79

Taste the rainbow

Angelica Kauffman

Colour

1778–80

Oil on canvas,
49⅗ x 58½ in (126 x 148.5 cm).

A woman sits on the edge of a wood in a rocky landscape, with mountains rising in the distance beneath a cloudy blue sky. Her auburn hair is loose, much like her golden-yellow and white robes, and her red cloak tumbles toward the ground. In one hand she holds a fistful of brushes and a palette topped with a single daub of white paint; in the other hand she reaches up to collect some more hues from the rainbow. She is a symbolic figure representing Painting or Color, one of the four elements of art. By her feet, shod in delicate gold sandals, a chameleon represents the varied hues found in nature.

Inspired by her fellow artist Joshua Reynolds's *Discourses on Art*, a series of lectures given at the Royal Academy and published in 1788, Kauffman—who was born in Switzerland in 1741—produced four neoclassical paintings that represent the elements of art: *Invention*, *Composition*, *Design*, and *Colour*. The first two allegories are theoretical, the figures reflective, whereas the latter two are more practical, with the figures busily engaged in the act of creation. Commissioned for the ceiling of the Royal Academy's Council Room in its former home in Somerset House, the paintings were part of a scheme with works by the American history painter Benjamin West. They are also the only 18th-century ceiling paintings known to have been created by a woman.

Together with Mary Moser, Kauffman was one of only two women among the original 36 members of London's Royal Academy, founded in 1768; after them, the next woman elected was Dame Laura Knight—more than 150 years later, in 1936. Despite the constraints that women faced during her lifetime, Kauffman became a prominent and progressive artist known not just for her portraits, but also for her history paintings. In all her works—including those personifying the four different aspects of art—she produced, with ambition and creative authority, female-centered compositions of strong and capable women.

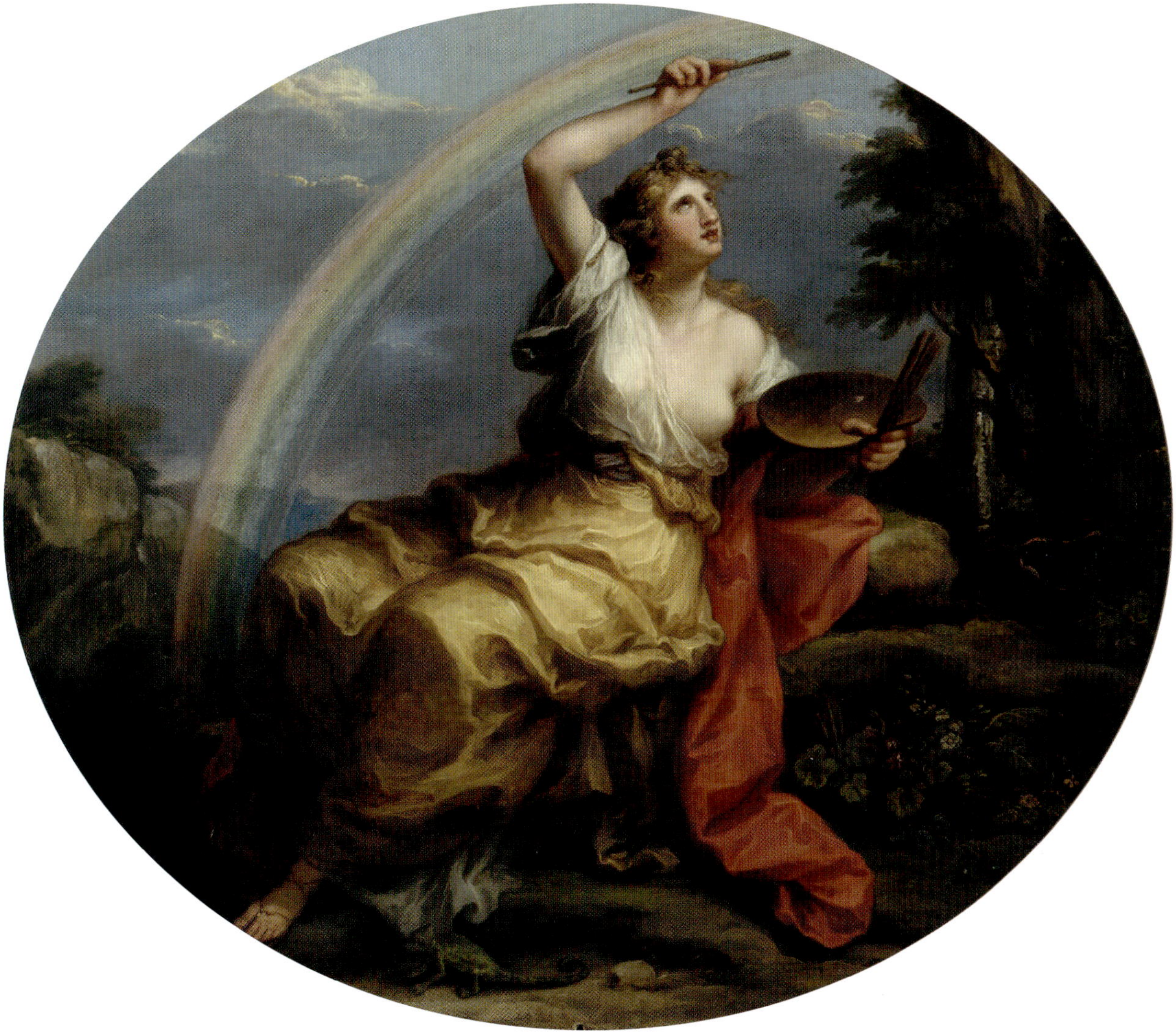

Palette

A rainbow of yellow, white, red, blue, and green.

Complementary works

- Peter Paul Rubens, *The Rainbow Landscape*, *c.*1636.
- Joshua Reynolds, *The Age of Innocence*, *c.*1788.
- Laura Knight, *Spring*, 1916–20.

Color correct

Élisabeth Louise Vigée Le Brun

Self-Portrait in a Straw Hat

1782

Oil on canvas,
38½ x 27¾ in (97.8 x 70.5 cm).

The artist meets our gaze from beneath the brim of a straw hat adorned with fresh wildflowers and a single ostrich feather. Rather than wearing a wig, as women were accustomed to do in formal portraits at the time, her loose golden curls are her own and noticeably unpowdered. Lavish earrings dangle from her lobes and she wears a black wrap over her dusty-pink satin dress, with petallike white frills. Captured in natural light, she clutches a bunch of brushes and a palette daubed with paints, whose startling colors pick up on those daringly combined across the canvas.

Élisabeth Louise Vigée Le Brun was one of only four women to win admission to Paris's Académie Royale de Peinture et de Sculpture in the 18th century. In the years preceding the French Revolution, she was one of the most renowned portrait painters in France, and a friend and favorite artist of Marie Antoinette. Painted at the age of 27, *Self-Portrait in a Straw Hat* was inspired by Peter Paul Rubens's beloved *Portrait of Susanna Lunden* (1622), mistakenly known as *Le Chapeau de Paille* (*The Straw Hat*) despite the fact that the young woman's hat was made of beaver felt. By associating herself with the great artist, and candidly correcting his mistake, Le Brun hoped to enhance her reputation.

This particular self-portrait, housed in the National Gallery in London, is in fact a copy of the original version that Le Brun painted in Brussels in 1782—and there are some significant differences. Perhaps in light of the praise she garnered when the work was displayed at the Salon de la Correspondance in Paris that same year, she made some alterations to the face: here, she looks more self-assured, with fuller eyebrows, almond-shaped eyes and an unabashed smile playing on her rosebud lips. She updated her attire, changing the color of her dress from lilac to a more captivating pink, and in response to quibbles about the limitless blue sky being too basic, she added wisps of clouds. The effect is a frank and joyful self-portrait of an attractive young woman and, more importantly, an accomplished painter.

C60 M50 Y0 K0
R126 G173 B220

C5 M32 Y10 K0
R224 G187 B197

C40 M8 Y0 K100
R0 G0 B0

C0 M0 Y0 K6
R243 G243 B243

C5 M25 Y55 K0
R228 G193 B128

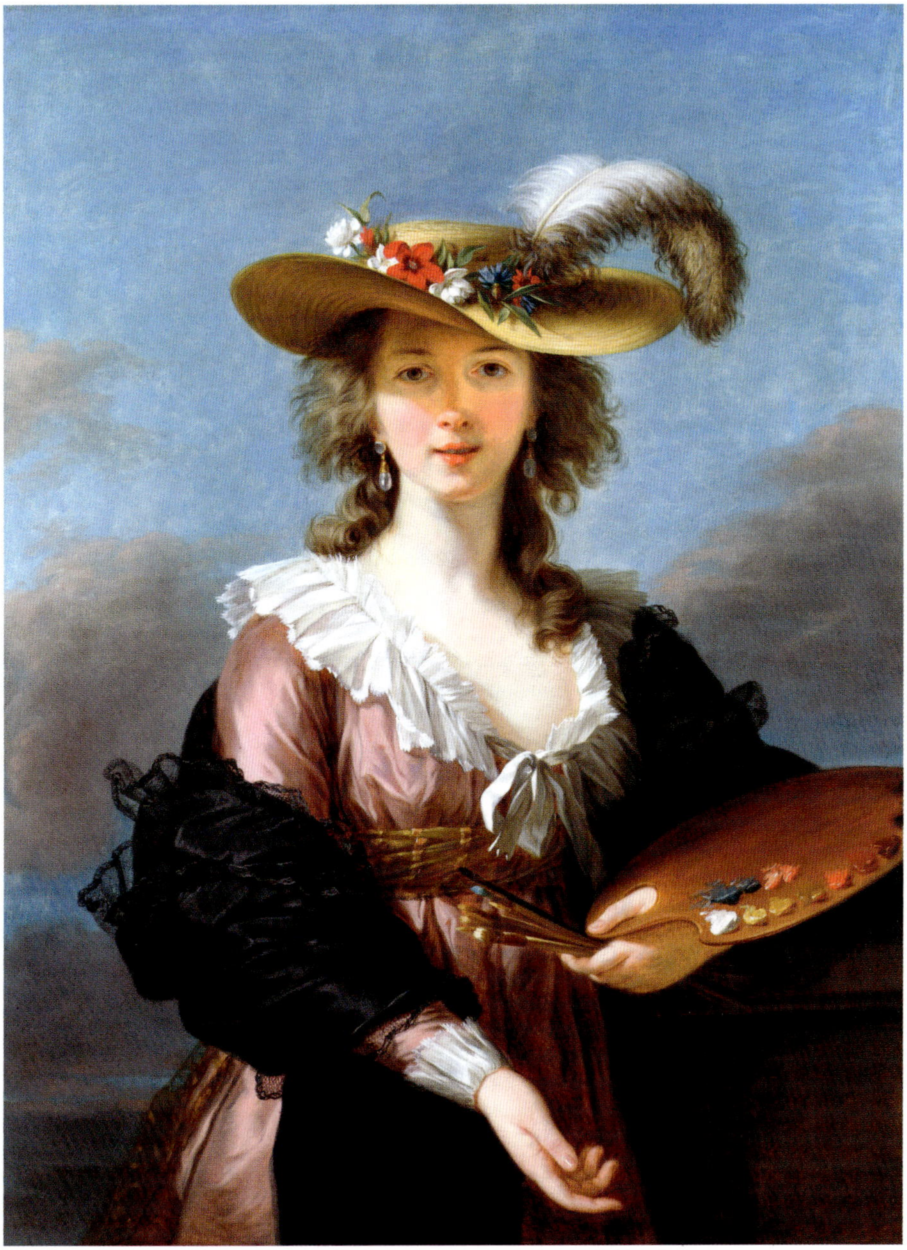

Palette

Dusty pink, black, white, and yellow for the fashion; blue for the sky.

Complementary works

- Peter Paul Rubens, *Portrait of Susanna Lunden (Le Chapeau de Paille)*, c.1622–25.
- Adélaïde Labille-Guiard, *Self-Portrait with Two Pupils, Marie Gabrielle Capet and Marie Marguerite Carreaux de Rosemond*, 1785.
- Jean-Baptiste Pierre Le Brun, *Self-Portrait*, 1795.

Keeping it real

17th-century Dutch painting

C85 M65 Y0 K0
R66 G89 B160

Keeping it real

17th-century Dutch painting

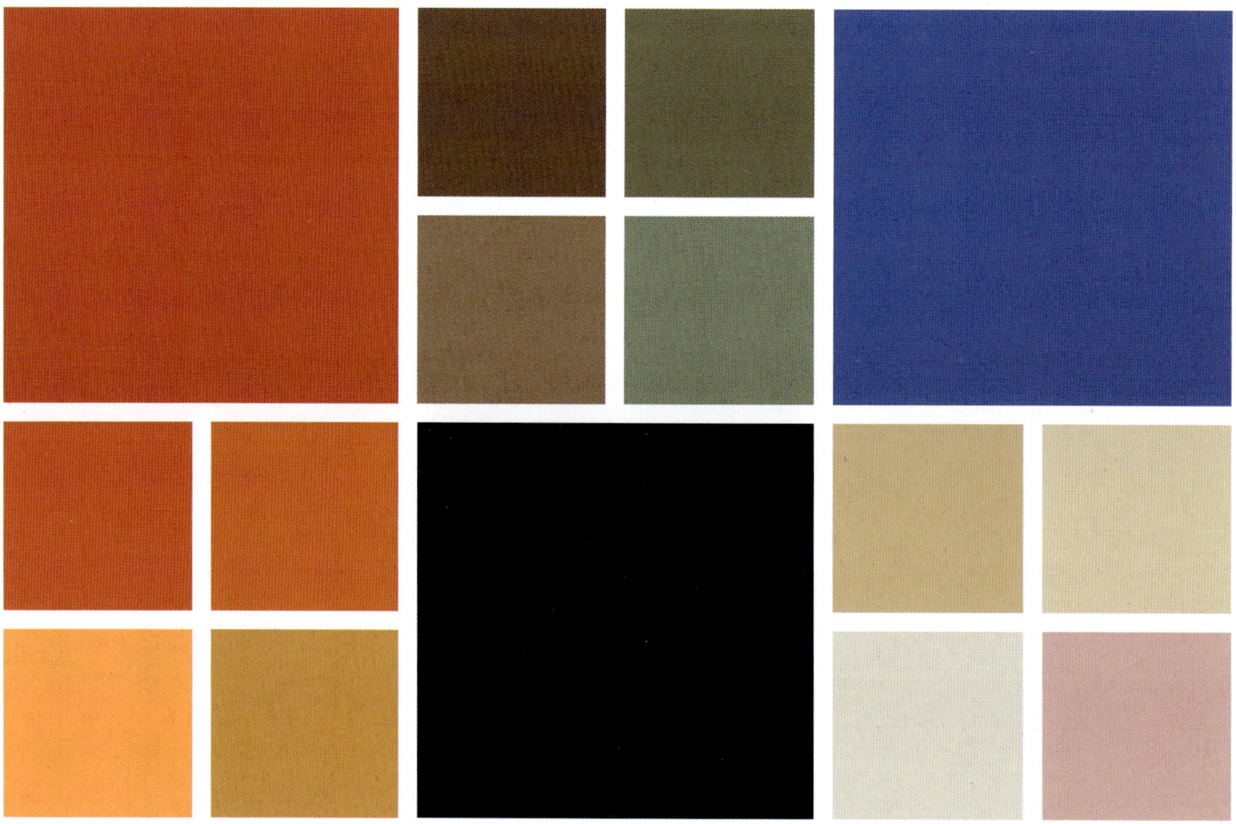

Time to zoom in on one of the world's most beloved art forms: 17th-century Dutch painting. Freed from Spanish Catholic rule in 1648 after 80 years of warfare, the newly independent Dutch Republic experienced an economic and cultural boom. The growing middle and merchant classes were on the rise and in the market for portable lustrous oil paintings that celebrated Dutch life and identity, and reflected their own social status and reputation. The result: a proliferation of decidedly secular and bourgeois paintings that shine a light on the everyday.

This so-called golden age of realism marked a move away from the biblical scenes, as well as the grandiose battles and myths, that provide the loud and proud subject matter of much traditional art. Of course, the Dutch Republic had its fair share of idealists, who sought to emulate the perfection of classical antiquity like their French and Italian peers. But it was the realists, capitalizing on their ability to imitate nature, who produced the art for which the period is best known: still lifes, portraits, landscapes, and domestic scenes somewhat dismissively known as "genre" paintings.

As always, the colors used to conjure these radically real episodes from daily life varied from artist to artist—from Rembrandt van Rijn's (*see page 76*) restricted palette of delicate earth tones to Johannes Vermeer's (*see page 82*) cleverly balanced bright and brilliant shades, which are noticeably purer than those of his rivals. In general, color and tone were used to create a convincing sense of depth and perspective, and compositions are often flooded with white light. After the paint surface was brought to a translucent polish, artists such as Vermeer applied tactile dashes of thick paint on top to add highlights and a sense of texture. These 17th-century painters excelled at creating subtle yet intense light and color contrasts.

The seemingly unassuming still life—from tabletop spreads to flower arrangements—provided artists not only with the opportunity to reflect the abundance and wealth pouring into the nation's ports from overseas, but also to showcase their technical painterly ability. Alongside the Dutch artists on show in this chapter is one of the few known Flemish women artists from the 17th century, Clara Peeters (*see page 74*). She is often credited with helping to introduce the humble *ontbijtje* (breakfast piece) into the Dutch painting tradition.

Remember: ordinary doesn't mean dull; life is rich and diverse, and its depictions no less so. In order to conjure convincing natural appearances, artists decked their works with painstakingly precise details. Surreptitiously, they also tell stories. There's a hidden drama to Carel Fabritius's (*see page 78*) chained goldfinch and Rachel Ruysch's (*see page 84*) tumbling arrangement of blooms. In his luminous scenes of the domestic lives of men and women inside merchant houses by the canals, Vermeer gives the impression that he's pulling back a curtain and inviting us to observe the stage set of a private theater. Each of his episodes of daily life is dashed with intrigue. What's the content of the letter that the mistress of the house is reading? Is that maidservant pouring the milk quietly happy or is she miserably overworked?

The following pages contain detailed recordings of day-to-day life, each one implying a sense of drama, whether through subject matter or style. Upon first glance, you might mistake them for photographs, but look closely and you'll start to pick out painterly strokes that remind you that the scenes are in fact carefully composed depictions—representations of reality, rather than reality itself.

C18 M45 Y80 K20
R163 G125 B59

C15 M24 Y50 K0
R210 G189 B137

C10 M14 Y35 K0
R226 G213 B173

C44 M35 Y64 K25
R125 G123 B86

C5 M78 Y90 K10
R182 G75 B36

Good enough to eat

Clara Peeters
Still Life with Cheeses, Artichoke, and Cherries
*c.*1625

Oil on wood,
13⅛ × 18⅜ in (33.3 × 46.7 cm).

Stand in front of this artwork and your fingers will soon start to itch. The knife ruptures the picture plane and gives a sturdy point of contact—go on, take it. You might want to cut yourself a slice of cheese from the stack on the large silver plate or tear off a chunk of the baked bread and spread it with one of the serrated curls of butter piled up like discarded coats on the blue dish. On the small silver plate is a split artichoke, its green outer leaves giving way to a deep red. The cherries glisten like marbles, each one a perfect crimson sphere dotted with a white reflection.

Peeters is one of the few known Flemish women artists of the 17th century. She started out painting valuable objects, such as goblets and gold coins, and then turned her attention to humble foodstuffs. This piece is an example of an *ontbijtje* and it presents a standard morning spread in 17th-century Netherlands. Peeters's painterly skill shines through in her exquisite rendering of details, from the glint of the knife to the prickly artichoke leaves. The canvas, and the stack of three subtly differentiated cheeses in particular, is alive with color and texture. The pale half-round of young Gouda stands out against the dark backdrop; in front is an older dark wedge, perhaps an Edam, colored with parsley; and on top is a hexagon of sheep's cheese. This may be staple fare, but its arrangement on the stone ledge has been carefully considered. Some see it as a nod to the Netherlands' bounty of dairy; others read it as a religious reminder to refrain from sin.

Either way, Peeters's still life is illuminated. Her cherries are jewellike and her butter velvety smooth. The plates function as mirrors and even the crumbly planes of cheese glow. Is your stomach rumbling? Someone has already pinched a cherry: a single stone is sucked clean of its flesh. The cheese, by the looks of its cuts and fissures, has been tasted, too. Let's dig in.

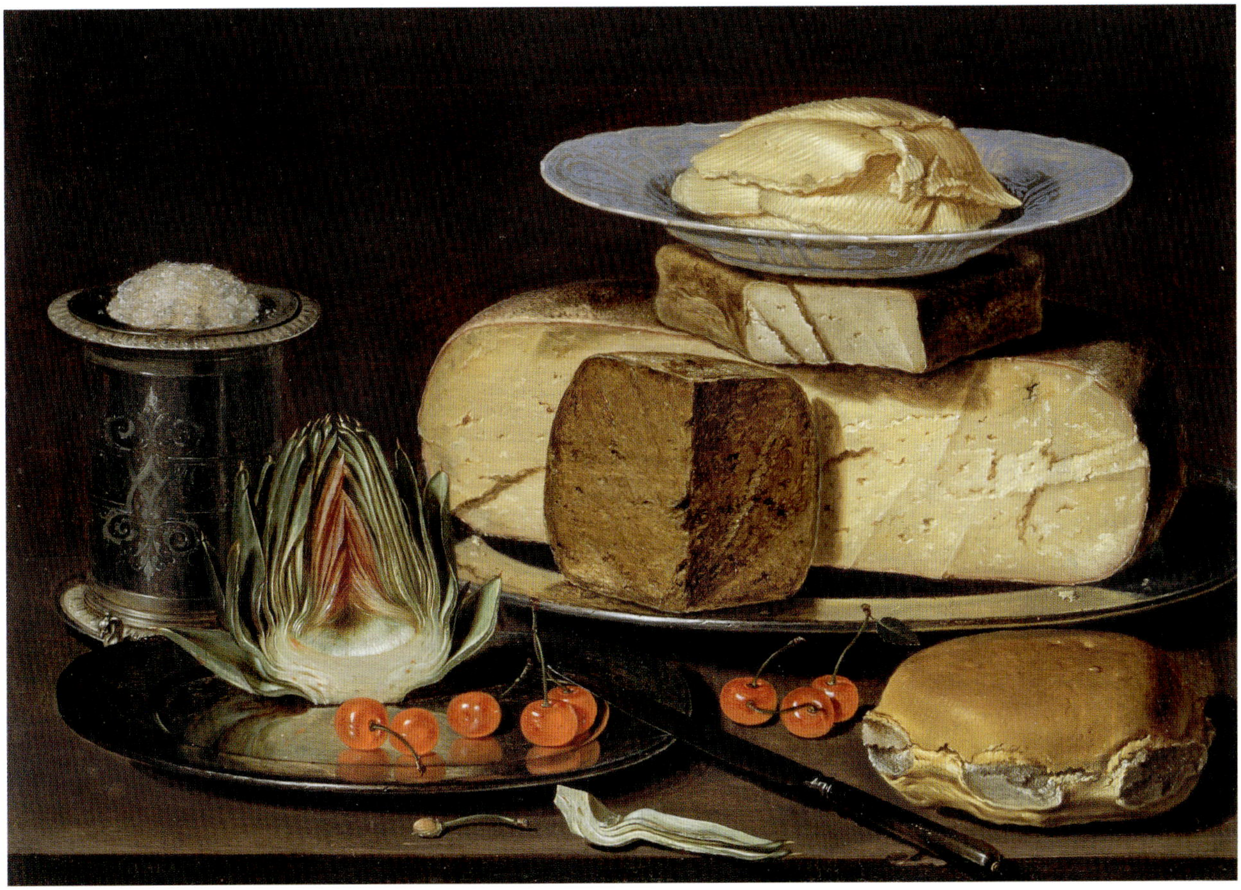

Palette

Shades of yellow punctuated with red and green.

Complementary works

- Louise Moillon, *Still Life with Fruit*, *c.*1637.
- Anna Maria Punz, *Still Life with Kitchenware, Onion, and Kohlrabi*, 1754.
- Antoine Vollon, *Mound of Butter*, 1875–85 (*see page 9*).

Stream of consciousness

Rembrandt van Rijn
A Woman Bathing in a Stream
1654

Oil on oak,
24$\frac{5}{16}$ x 18½ in (61.8 x 47 cm).

A young woman feels her way through a stream, smiling at the way the water ripples against her shins. She's lifting her plain white shift to prevent it from getting damp; her sleeves are bunched around the elbows and her neckline is deep. Her forehead and chest are bathed in a mellow light. Her auburn hair is pulled back from her face, though a stray ringlet suggests it could quite easily come loose. The setting is unclear, but the backdrop is typical Rembrandt, all dark and shadows. To the woman's left, you can vaguely make out overhanging trees, and behind her is a pile of rich robes in red and gold—a prop, perhaps. Or perhaps this young woman is better known than her baggy shift would have us think.

Rembrandt's reductive palette conjures a sense of intimacy. Free from distraction, our focus is on the bather, a beacon in the dark. Eschewing the bright and exotic pigments available in the Netherlands in the 17th century, the artist used readily available earth tones: lead white for flesh; lead-tin yellow for highlights; red and yellow lakes, and yellow ocher, for the robe and its reflection; brown ocher, and both charcoal and bone black, for shadows. Rembrandt's portrait is a masterclass in what can be done with few resources. By combining his limited pigments, and varying textures and translucencies, he found variety. He blended and layered his paints, and brushed them onto the oak panel in thin and thick strokes. The coarse shift is juxtaposed with the bather's smooth, milky skin. In places he applied wet on wet; elsewhere he left the warm ground uncovered.

The identity of the young woman remains a mystery: the model is probably Rembrandt's lover Hendrickje Stoffels, but it's unclear whether she's been caught off guard in a Dutch stream or is posing as a mythological or biblical heroine (most likely Bathsheba, whom the artist painted the same year). There's more than a hint of the erotic in the way she tugs at her shift, and a tenderness to her features. Whoever she is, the scene is naturalistic and real.

C10 M9 Y20 K0
R229 G225 B205

C5 M39 Y80 K10
R201 G151 B64

C25 M44 Y70 K52
R109 G89 B53

C40 M0 Y8 K90
R0 G0 B0

C10 M86 Y94 K10
R172 G57 B31

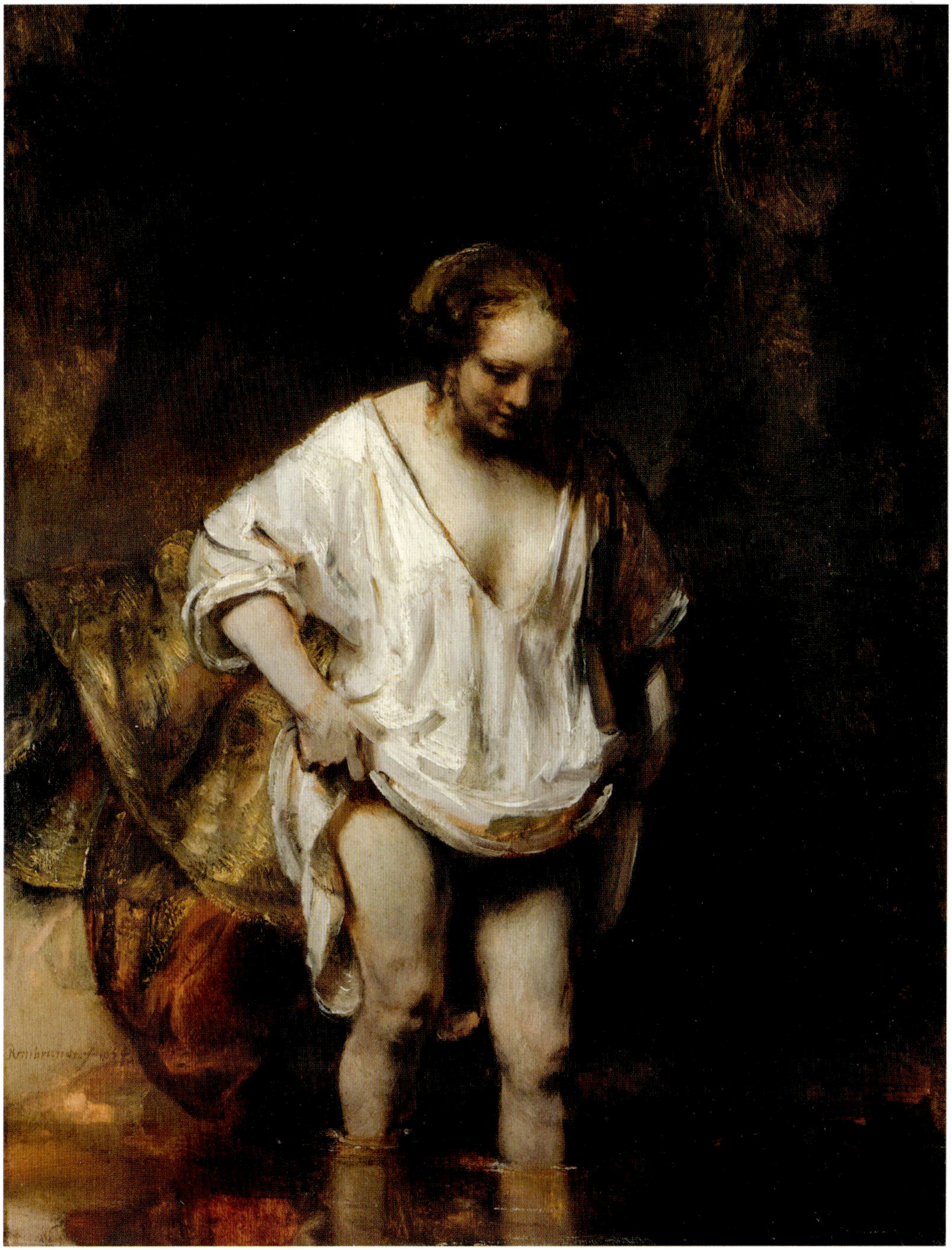

Palette

Lead white for flesh; lead-tin yellow for highlights; red and yellow lakes and yellow ocher for the robe and its reflection; brown ocher, charcoal, and bone black for shadows.

Complementary works

- Jan Brueghel the Elder, *Diana and Actaeon*, 1600.
- Artemisia Gentileschi, *Susanna and the Elders*, 1652.
- Edgar Degas, *Woman Bathing in a Shallow Tub*, 1885.

C5 M5 Y5 K0
R242 G240 B239

C0 M45 Y80 K0
R224 G154 B66

C40 M2 Y0 K100
R0 G0 B0

C24 M40 Y58 K25
R151 G127 B92

Special effects

Carel Fabritius
The Goldfinch
1654

Oil on panel,
9 x $13\frac{3}{16}$ in (22.8 x 33.5 cm).

This charming little painting of a pet bird found fame first in the writing of the 19th-century French journalist and art collector Théophile Thoré-Bürger and later in the best-selling novel of the same name by American author Donna Tartt. The Dutch artist Fabritius was a pupil of Rembrandt (*see page 76*) and a contemporary of Vermeer (*see page 82*). He died young in a gunpowder explosion in Delft and left behind few works; this one was created in the final year of his life.

The creature sits on its perch, which casts a strong tan shadow against the creamy wall, rendered with a lead-white base. The intimate scene is bathed in a chalky light, which catches on the gilded rails and the delicate gold chain, as well as the bird's feet. Fabritius was a pioneer of optical effects, or trompe l'oeil, which he used in his pursuit of the everyday. Glance at the life-sized goldfinch chained to its feeder and you'd be forgiven for thinking it was real. And yet, at the same time, the artist hints at the illusion. His brushstrokes are clearly visible, especially the thick flurry of buttery yellow against black on the bird's wing, and the sandy brown around its characteristic red face. Fabritius daubed and dashed bright streaks over duller shades of brown to accentuate the visual effect of the goldfinch's feathered body, and then contrasted them with the smooth gray box and plastered backdrop. Also bursting the bubble is the prominent date and signature in gray paint.

The Goldfinch has an air of melancholy about it—the artist gives us a popular domestic pet, chained by its foot, with nowhere to go. The panel painting was previously on display in the staircase gallery of the Mauritshuis Royal Picture Gallery in the Hague, but since finding fame, it has been moved to a gallery upstairs, where it takes pride of place. Even in its new location, hanging on a wall beside other works of art, it's easy to be fooled into thinking that this little bird might twitch its feathers as you pass.

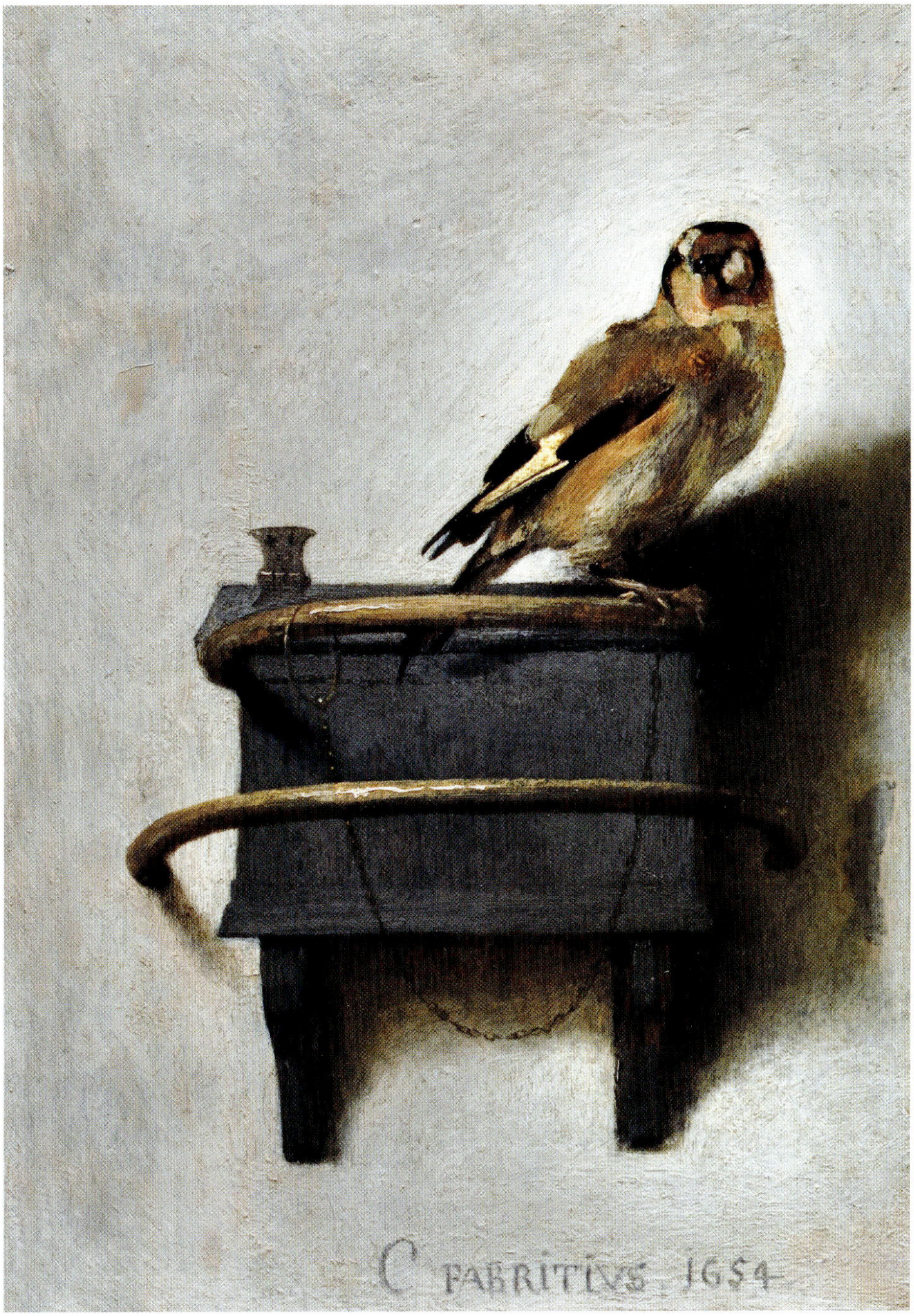

Palette

White, buttery yellow, sandy brown, and black.

Complementary works

- Albrecht Dürer, *Wing of a European Roller*, 1512.
- Jan Baptist Weenix, *A Dead Partridge*, 1650–52.
- Jean-Baptiste Oudry, *White Duck*, 1753.

Risky business

Painting has come at a price for many—and not just in terms of time and energy. Throughout history, artists (and their apprentices) have risked their lives for their work. Before the advent of modern medical science, the common threats of certain art supplies—and in particular pigments—were unknown. Even after such pigments were identified as poisonous, it often took years for them to be banned.

One of the earliest and perhaps most missed of art history's poisonous colors is lead white, used to conjure the impression of milky light. The recipe for making it features in the Roman author Pliny the Elder's encyclopedic *Natural History* (AD *c.*77–79), which recommends mixing metallic lead with strong vinegar. In 17th-century Netherlands, the pigment was made by layering cow and horse manure over lead and vinegar in a sealed room; three months later, the materials would have combined to create flakes of pure white. It was in the late 19th century that scientists discovered that lead was poisonous, but it wasn't until 1978 that the U.S. banned the production of lead-white paint.

We often associate green with healing nature, but it was another poisonous color. In 1775, the Swedish chemist Carl Wilhelm Scheele invented Scheele's green, a bright synthetic pigment laced with arsenic. Affordable and easy to produce, it quickly replaced older green pigments and gained popularity in the Victorian era. By the end of the 19th century, it was largely replaced by Paris green, which was more durable but no less toxic. A favorite of Claude Monet (*see page 122*) and Paul Cézanne, who used it to create zesty emerald landscapes, Paris green wasn't banned until the 1960s. Other poisonous pigments include chrome yellow, a lead-based favorite of Vincent van Gogh (*see page 154*); cadmium red, used extensively by Paul Gauguin (*see page 136*) and Henri Matisse (*see page 166*); and realgar, a natural yet highly toxic orange pigment used by Rachel Ruysch (*see page 84*).

There are several stories of artists who have fallen victim to poisonous pigments—among them Cézanne, who developed diabetes, and Monet, who went blind. François Boucher's (*see page 64*) affection for lead white, which he used to produce his dreamy pastels, might have been responsible for his failure to see color in later life: he told a fellow artist that "he saw only earth colors where others saw vermilion [bright red]," and a pair of glasses and a magnifying glass were found beside his pigments after his death. Most tragically, lead white was used in ointments and cosmetics worn by ancient Egyptians, Greeks, and Romans. And patrons paid the price, too: some believe that the death of the revolutionary French emperor Napoleon Bonaparte might have been caused by the Scheele's green used in the ornate floral patterns on his bedroom wallpaper. In the words of Oscar Wilde, another potential victim, "This wallpaper and I are fighting a duel to the death. Either it goes or I do."

Paul Cézanne, *Hillside in Provence*, 1890–92, oil on canvas, 25 x 31¼ in (63.5 x 79.4 cm).

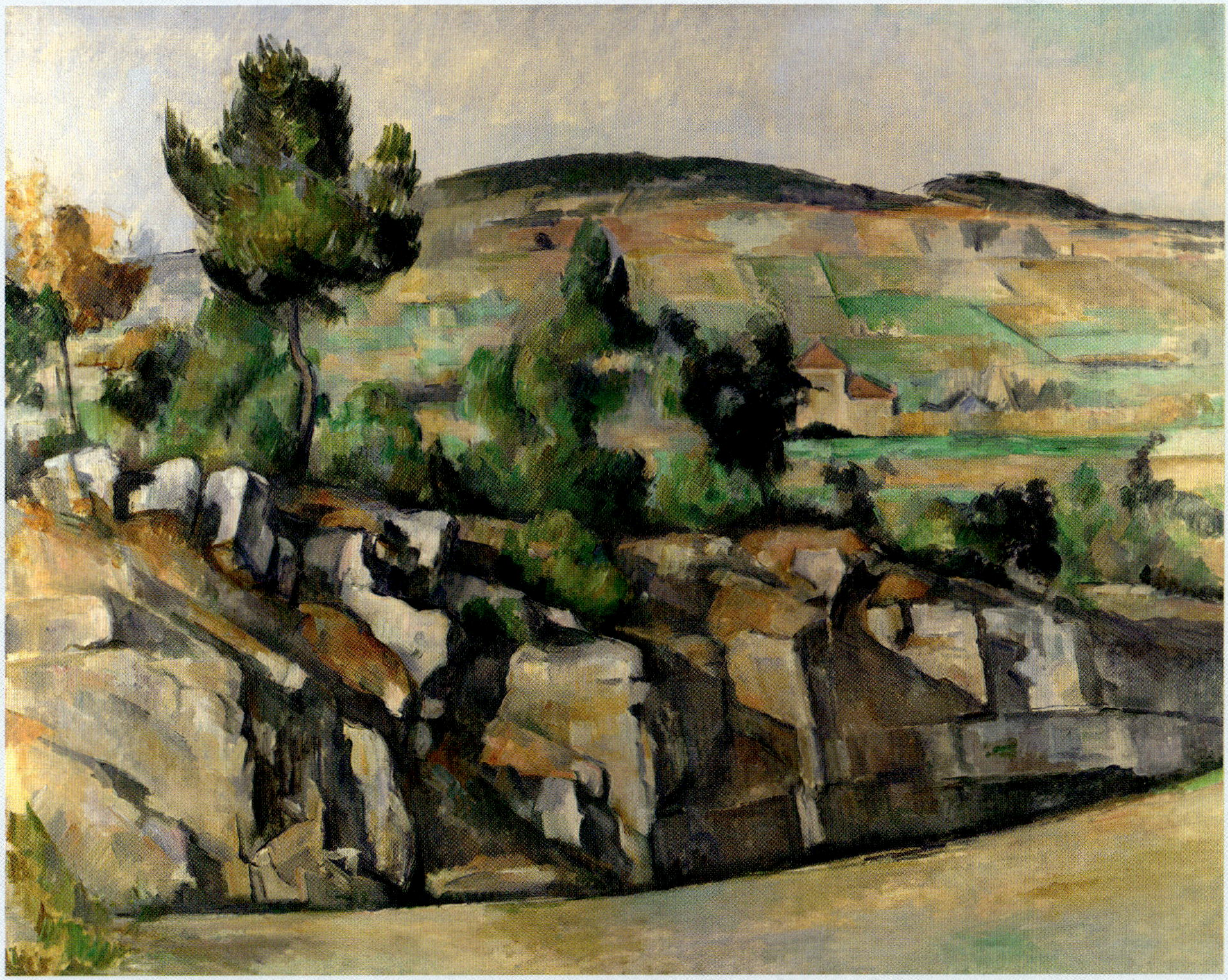

C84 M65 Y0 K0
R68 G89 B160

C5 M14 Y50 K0
R235 G215 B145

C0 M3 Y7 K3
R247 G242 B233

Color in the contract

Johannes Vermeer
The Milkmaid

1657–58

Oil on canvas,
17⅞ x 16⅛ in (45.5 × 41 cm).

When you think about 17th-century Dutch painters, it's easy to forget everybody else and simply focus on the master of everyday beauty: Vermeer. Although relatively unknown during his lifetime, when he was regarded as just another genre painter, he found fame among the early modernists in 19th-century Paris, who appreciated his dazzling domestic scenes. He gave us girls reading and writing letters, a woman with a water jug, a lacemaker, a music lesson, and—one of his most precious and illusionistic paintings—a milkmaid.

A solitary figure stands by a small, cluttered table and a window, and patiently pours milk from an earthenware jug into a two-handled bowl. To her right, a woven basket and polished copper pot hang from hooks on the whitewashed wall; to her left is the plain backdrop of a sparse and scrappy kitchen. Vermeer has centered his composition around two colors, blue and yellow, which meet in the milkmaid's middle. Her corn-colored bodice, rendered with lead-tin yellow, is in harmony with her creamy collar and linen cap, as well as the pearly gray wall—a marvel in light and shadow. Her rich blue apron meets its match in the draped tablecloth and the stoneware jug with the pewter lid. The brilliant blue pigment, ultramarine, was so rare and costly that the amount used by the artist was specified in advance by the patron for the painting.

Like the sunlight filtering through the tiny crack in the window, Vermeer's colors delicately suffuse the canvas, and make convincing its textures and tones. The brightest light shines on the still life of crusty breads, which is brought to life with dots of paint, but it's the milkmaid herself whom Vermeer appreciates above all else. She stands tall, with downcast eyes and parted lips, entirely absorbed in the task at hand. The gentle tilt of her head and the way in which she cradles the jug suggest that she's taking great care. Vermeer not only captured a simple household chore, but also his sitter's sensibility.

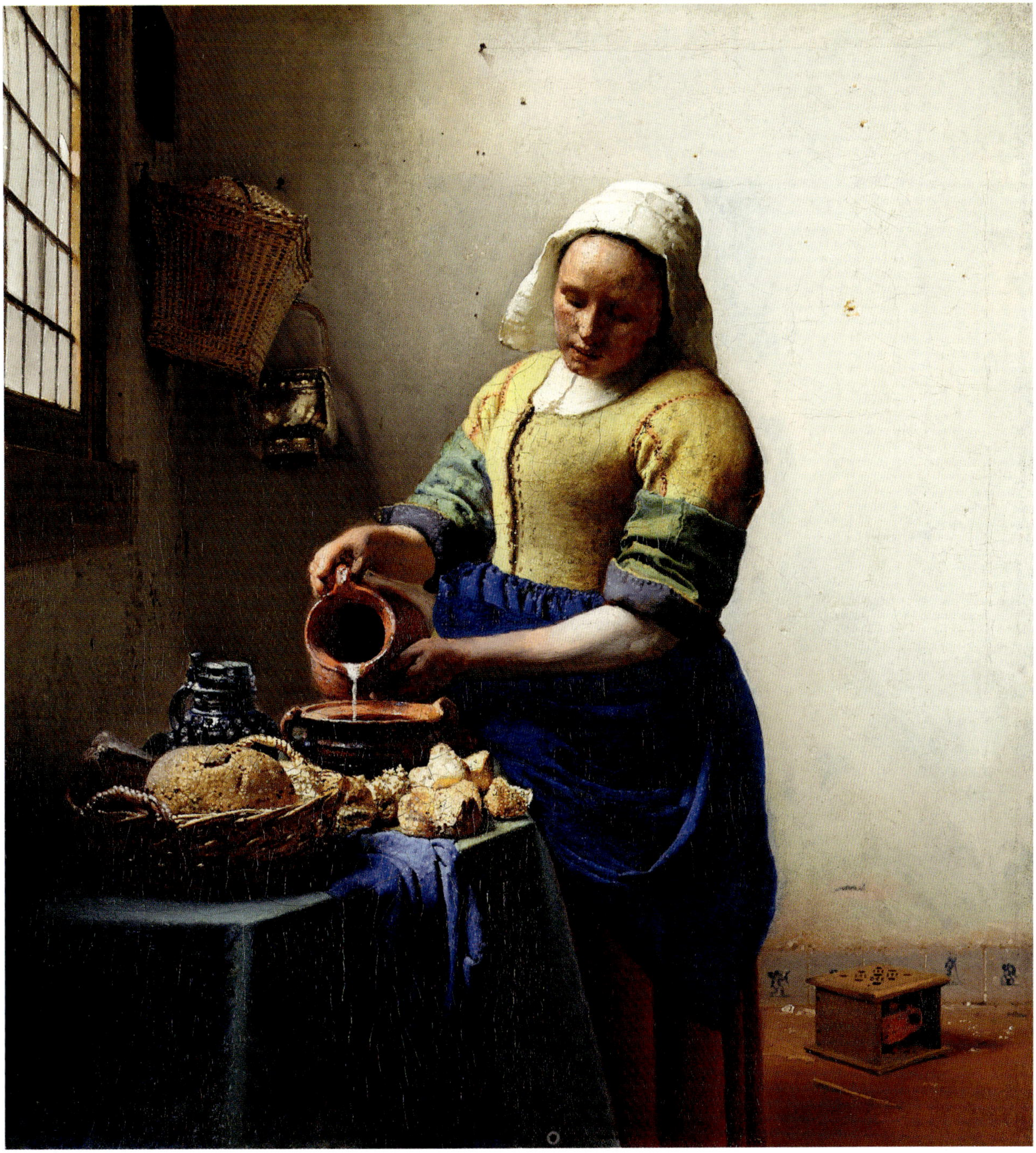

Palette

A corn-colored bodice, a creamy cap, and a rich blue apron.

Complementary works

- Judith Leyster, *The Proposition*, 1631.
- Nicolaes Maes, *Girl at a Window*, 1653–55.
- Pieter de Hooch, *Woman Weighing Gold and Silver Coins*, c.1664.

C0 M70 Y88 K15
R184 G90 B37

C5 M28 Y20 K5
R218 G186 B179

C40 M20 Y48 K20
R142 G152 B122

C70 M60 Y59 K91
R24 G23 B6

Brush with death

Rachel Ruysch

Flowers in a Vase

c.1685

Oil on canvas,
22$\frac{3}{8}$ x 17$\frac{1}{8}$ in (57 x 43.5 cm).

An elegant bouquet shines bright against a dark, undefined backdrop. Look closely and you can glimpse the crowd of stalks lapping up water in the curved glass vase on the stone ledge. Dark-green leaves and a crimson bud become one with the black wall, while snow-white pear blossom and pastel-blue columbine cast a striking shape against it. Pinky-white peonies look soft to touch, as does a sprig of lemon-yellow honeysuckle, which partially conceals a grasshopper. A couple of flame-like lilies have opened up; others are stubbornly closed, as if demanding more daylight. An elegant bouquet, but also one with a life of its own: a wheat stem twists like a ribbon as it stretches toward the right side of the canvas, while a single seed pod skulks over the edge of the shelf.

This great Amsterdam artist was one of the most prosperous flower painters working in the late 17th and early 18th centuries. Against the odds, she won international acclaim and enjoyed a lengthy career that extended into her 80s. Those odds are related to her color palette, but also included the simple facts that Ruysch was a woman working in a man's world and that she bore ten children. In order to obtain the burnt-orange petals of her fiery lilies, the artist used a toxic mineral called realgar, which contains arsenic.

The daughter of a renowned botanist, Ruysch had first-hand knowledge of the flora and fauna she painted—and yet, like most other painters of floral still lifes at the time, she jumbled the seasons in her composition. The pear blossom, peonies, and honeysuckle make you think of spring, while the lilies and wheat have a more autumnal feel. In the foreground, finely veined leaves have grown crinkled and crisp. The presence of the grasshopper and the caterpillar adds both a sense of movement and an air of fragility. But even as she introduced hints of decay into her canvas, with her dramatic lighting and meticulous attention to detail, Ruysch made the ordinary extraordinary.

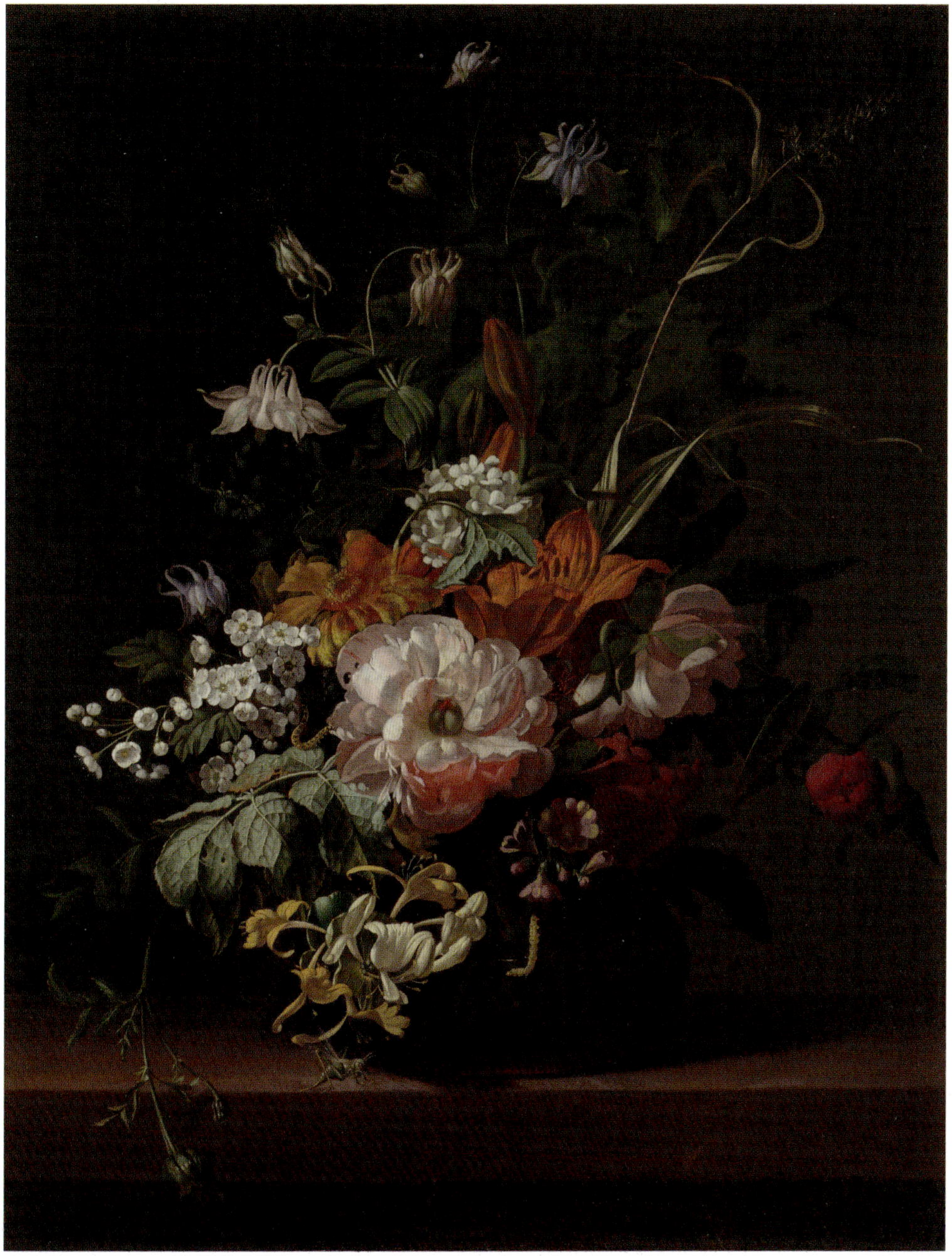

Palette

A dark backdrop enlivened with flame-like lilies, pinky-white peonies, and sprigs of green.

Complementary works

- Ambrosius Bosschaert the Elder, *A Still Life of Flowers in a Wan-Li Vase on a Ledge with further Flowers, Shells, and a Butterfly*, 1609–10.
- Judith Leyster, *Flowers in a Vase*, 1654.
- Mary Moser, *Flowers in a Vase, Which Stands on a Ledge*, undated.

Two sides of a coin

Neoclassicism and Romanticism

C0 M20 Y90 K5
R231 G193 B46

Two sides of a coin

Neoclassicism and Romanticism

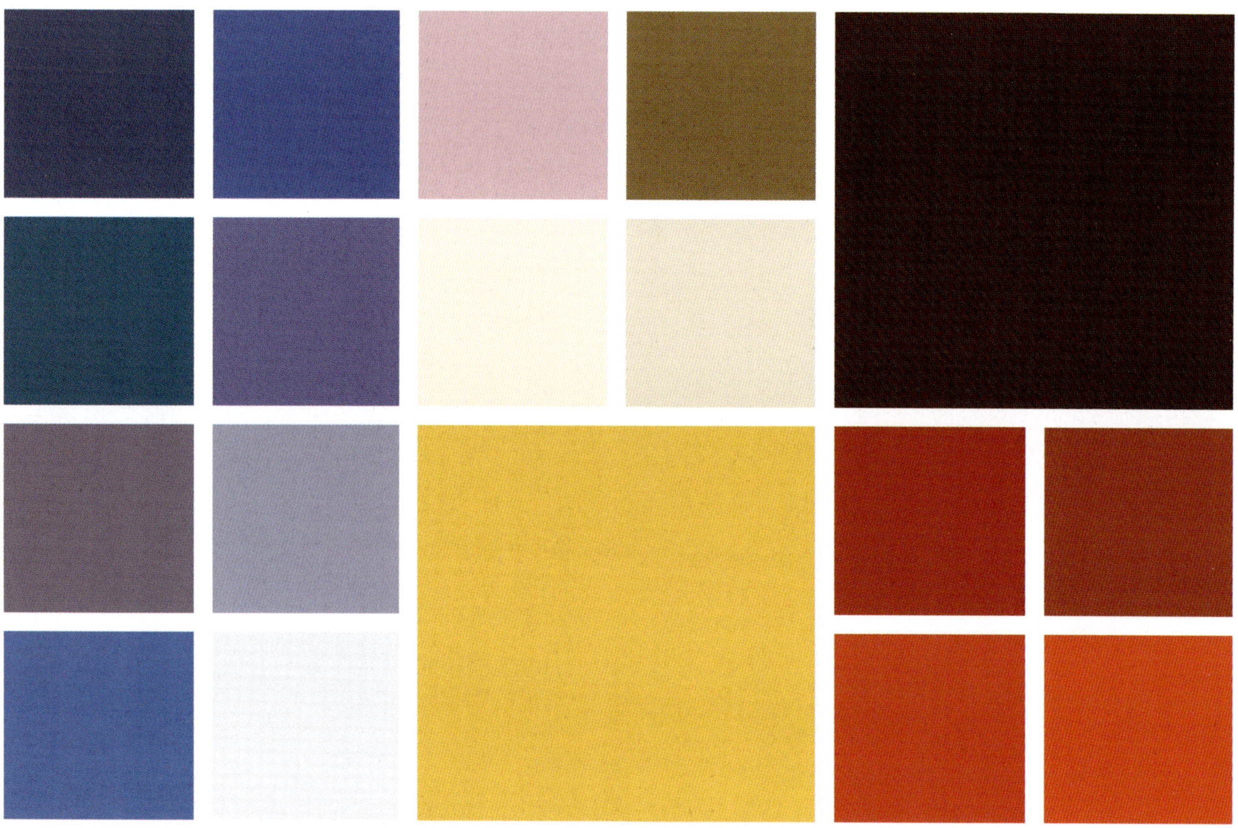

Arguments about *disegno* versus *colore* first flared up during the Italian Renaissance, and in the 16th century, artists, writers, and theorists sparred on the subject with regularity. The art historian Giorgio Vasari was an outspoken advocate for design, which flourished in Tuscany, and is epitomized in the distinct hues and defined edges of artists such as Michelangelo. Over in Venice, Titian (*see page 46*) advocated for color, blending and blurring his paints. The debates were about more than the role of drawing versus color; they were about a preference between intentionality and spontaneity. And they persisted for centuries.

All the way to the 19th century, to be precise. In France, the Academy was such a staunch advocate of drawing that it didn't even include color in its syllabus. Conservative academic training prized diligence and clarity above all else. If students wanted to practice painting, they had to do so in their own time in a private atelier. The neoclassical French painter Jean-Auguste-Dominique Ingres (*see page 100*) was the Academy's shining example, with his naturalistic palette, refined compositions, and smooth and precise forms. He adhered to what he viewed as classical values and techniques, and believed that drawing made up seven-eighths of painting.

The Academy argued that a painting had three layers: the first, a monochrome study of the composition's light and dark tonality, usually in reddish brown; the second, a layer of "dead coloring," which saw the artist begin to add basic patches of color, using cheap and opaque pigments; and, finally, a "second painting" layer, which involved working up meticulous details and glazing. This was the credo of neoclassicism.

At the other end of the spectrum was Romanticism: a movement that emerged in the aftermath of the French Revolution of 1789, in response to the prevailing values of order and restraint. In art, its exponents turned their attention away from the ordered world of the Enlightenment to the powerful and unpredictable natural world, and humankind's place within it. Romantic artists rejected the neoclassical belief in perspectival logic and instead regarded color as a mode of composition. In lieu of crisp forms, they allowed colors and shapes to interact. The polished paint handling favored by the Academy was replaced with freewheeling brushwork. Color was used to express feeling. While neoclassical artists favored smooth creams offset by striking accents with a high finish, the Romantics relied on a palette of intermingling earthy and neutral tones that reflected the wild and uncontrollable power of nature. Artists drew on almost every other pigment available to them, including the newly invented Scheele's green, which was quick and easy to produce but laced with arsenic (*see page 80*).

In France, the leader of the Romantic School was Eugène Delacroix (*see page 94*), who debuted in the Salon, aged 24, in 1822. His ideas about painting's physicality came from studying artists such as Peter Paul Rubens in the Louvre. He was also an admirer of English art and he visited London in 1825, where British artists such as John Constable and Joseph Mallord William Turner (*see page 98*) were painting with a Romantic sensibility. To this crowd, color was dynamic: something to be manipulated and exploited. In Delacroix's words, "Give me the mud of the streets and I will turn it into the luscious flesh of a woman, if you allow me to surround it as I please."

C20 M84 Y90 K19
R147 G59 B35

C85 M59 Y0 K10
R61 G91 B155

C5 M6 Y26 K0
R241 G234 B197

C10 M31 Y11 K0
R215 G183 B195

The color spectrum

William Blake
Albion Rose
1794–96

Color engraving and etching, printed planographically, 10 11/16 x 7 7/8 in (27.2 x 20 cm).

A rainbow of colors explodes from the open arms of this naked youth. There he stands: on the edge of a speckled cliff, legs parted and palms outstretched, head tilted, eyeing something up ahead—liberation, perhaps. His golden curls act as a halo of sorts and a golden-yellow cloud pulses around his head. He is a full-frontal visionary starburst, casting bands of light upon the dark and gloomy earth.

Also known as *The Dance of Albion* or *Glad Day*, and existing in multiple guises (drawing, engraving, etching, and watercolor), this utopian image marked a radiant new dawn for British art. Albion is an ancient, poetic name for Britain, as well as one of the characters in the painter, printmaker, and poet William Blake's personal mythology. Blake was antiestablishment; he rallied against reason and science. The image before us is generally thought to symbolize the country shedding the shackles of physical, political, and spiritual oppression, and—in a moment of clarity and divine perception—transcending the material world and enjoying a revolutionary awakening.

Yet, the meaning of Blake's work is infinitely strange and complex. The ideal human form on display, vaguely reminiscent of Leonardo da Vinci's *The Vitruvian Man* (*c.*1490), might represent universal humanity, but remove it and this radiant explosion of color becomes a remarkable feat of abstraction. Reds, blues, yellows, and pinks fan out from the artwork's center and pick up on the dashes of color heaped up in the lower left-hand corner. To the right, streaks of reddish yellow bring to mind the drip paintings of Jackson Pollock. In this supreme artwork, Blake employed a kaleidoscope of color as a rallying cry for freedom and imagination—in art and in life.

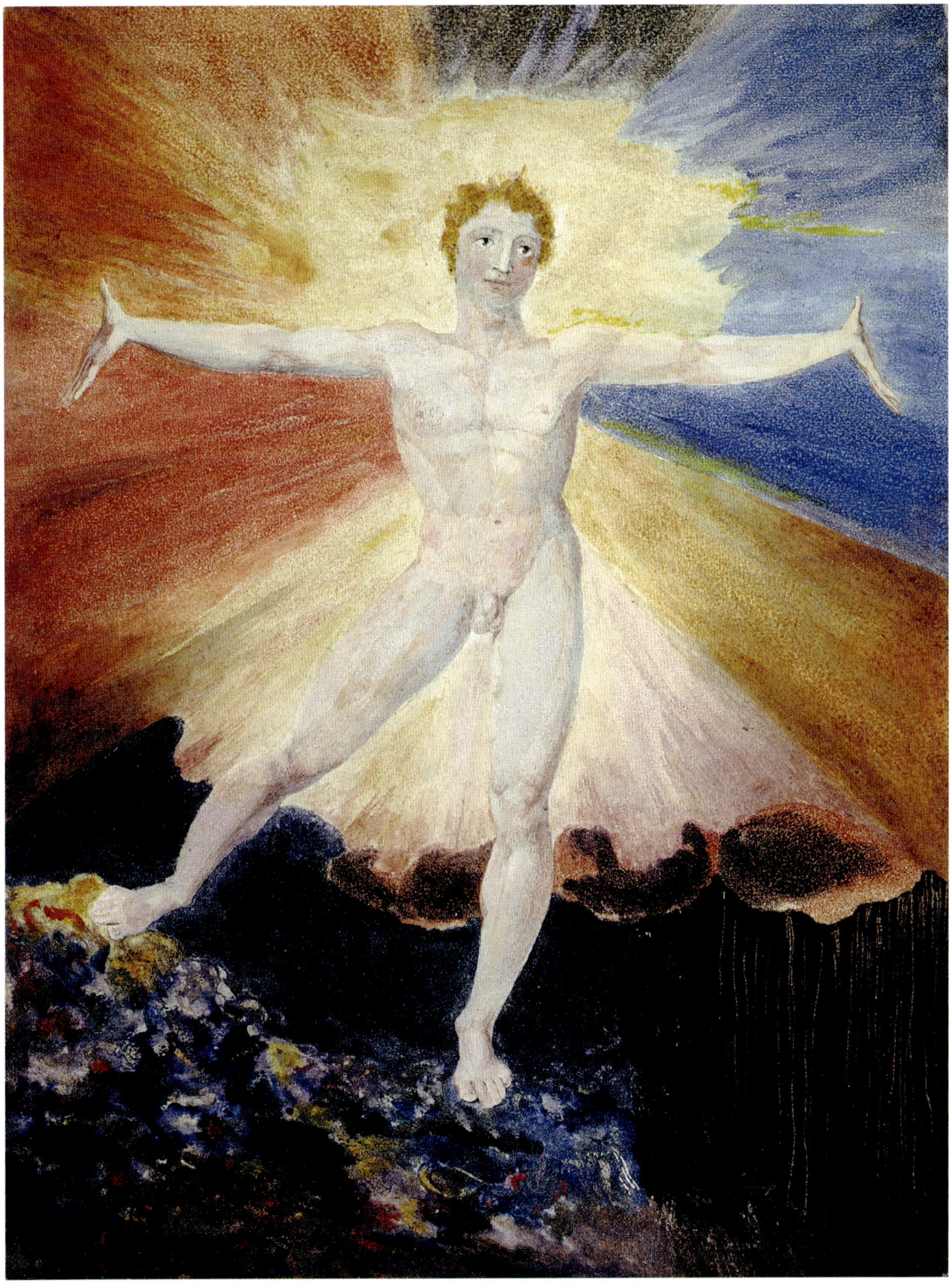

Palette

A starburst of reds, blues, yellows, and pinks.

Complementary works

- Henry Fuseli, *The Shepherd's Dream, from Paradise Lost*, 1793.
- Francisco Goya, *The Nude Maja*, 1797–1800.
- Caspar David Friedrich, *Wanderer above the Sea of Fog*, *c.*1818.

C24 M60 Y79 K75
R69 G47 B16

C5 M6 Y20 K0
R241 G235 B209

C88 M35 Y21 K35
R43 G94 B122

C0 M88 Y100 K30
R153 G46 B7

Political palette

Marie-Guillemine Benoist
Portrait of a Black Woman
1800

Oil on canvas,
31⅞ x 25⅝ in (81 x 65 cm).

Marie-Guillemine Benoist was one of the best-known women painters in late-18th- and early-19th-century France. Trained under the portrait painter Élisabeth Louise Vigée Le Brun (*see page 68*) and the neoclassical master Jacques-Louis David, she presented her work regularly at public exhibitions, including the annual Paris Salon. In 1791 she made her debut with two ambitious history paintings—generally considered a man's subject—and in 1800 she exhibited this striking portrait, which may well have been intended as a political statement.

A young Black woman sits in an armchair draped with a vibrant blue shawl; the sheen on the chair's golden trim is in dialogue with that of the single hoop earring dangling from her lobe. Against her warm dark skin and what we can see of her black hair, her classical robe and intricately wrapped headdress are a bright white. Tied around her waist is a single crimson ribbon; despite its presence, her robe has slipped off her shoulder to reveal her right breast (a symbol of liberty, perhaps). Against the plain beige backdrop, the colors sing. Even the sitter's skin has a glossy shine to it, as do her lips. She turns her head to meet our gaze with a composed and engaging look on her face.

Created in the period between the French revolutionaries' abolition of slavery in 1794 and Napoleon's restoration of it in 1802, the portrait should be viewed in light of emancipation. Although unnamed by the artist, we now know that the sitter was Madeleine, a freed slave from Haiti hired as a servant by Benoist's in-laws. The artist's choice of subject may have simply offered her an opportunity to showcase her painterly skill, but it may also have been more than that. Whether or not she intentionally used red, white, and blue to make a political statement, Benoist's palette recalls the tricolor and possibly marks her support for the integration of Black people into the French nation.

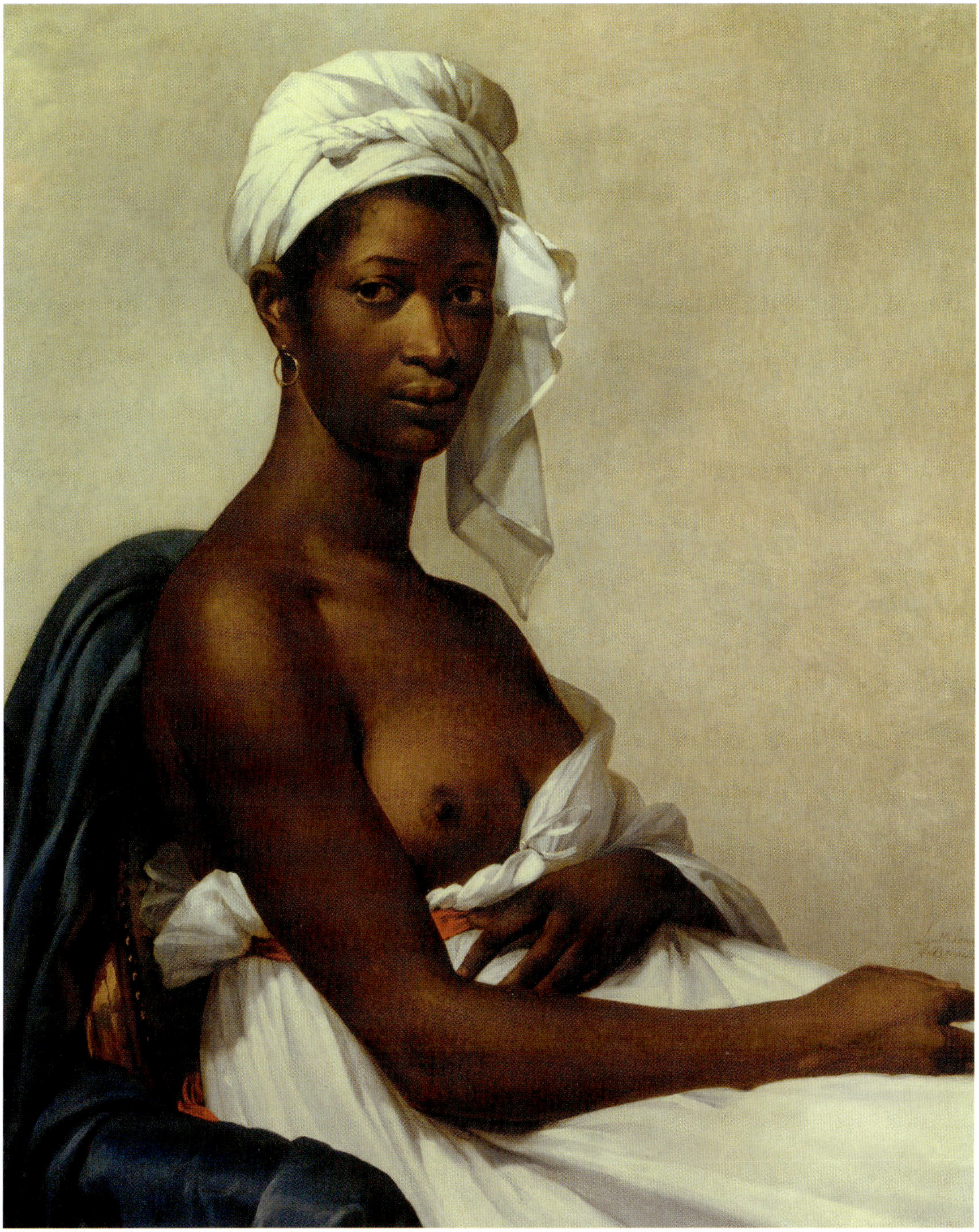

Palette

Bright white robes on warm dark skin, plus a vibrant blue shawl and a crimson ribbon.

Complementary works

- Anne-Louis Girodet-Trioson, *Jean-Baptiste Belley*, 1797.
- Eugène Delacroix, *Liberty Leading the People*, 1830.
- Édouard Manet, *Olympia*, 1863.

C5 M12 Y20 K0
R237 G242 B202

C2 M0 Y0 K6
R239 G242 B243

C25 M42 Y75 K30
R141 G116 B63

C10 M84 Y91 K15
R165 G60 B33

Oh, what a feeling

Eugène Delacroix
Orphan Girl at the Cemetery
*c.*1823–24

Oil on canvas,
26 × 21 in (66 × 54 cm).

For this precocious French painter, colors were mutable and dynamic. It didn't matter to Delacroix that drawing was prized above all else in the Academy; in his art, color would reign supreme. Take this melancholic portrait painted in the 1820s, believed by some to be a preparatory piece for *The Massacre at Chios* (1824). From afar, the palette might seem subdued, even spare. But look closer and you'll discover the artist's expressive use of color.

The young girl is caught in a moment of despair: her head flung to the side, and her teary eyes wide and directed up at the blustery sky. Her lips are parted, perhaps letting out a cry. The sight of two loose curls at the nape of her neck suggests that, despite her rosy cheeks and bare shoulder, there's a breeze. Delacroix used color to evoke emotion, and here the desolation of the orphan girl—a desolation the artist knew himself, having been orphaned at the age of sixteen—is matched by that of the scenery. The cemetery, empty and neglected, is a muddle of murky browns and greens, and even the pale-blue sky has been shrouded with slowly moving clouds in a dreary shade of vanilla. Like the dimly lit patch of greenery to her left, the girl's face is partly painted in shadow. The bright white of her blouse picks up on the glistening white of her eye. The skin tone of her right hand, resting in her lap, is tinged green, lifeless.

In spite of conservative academic artistic training in France, Delacroix blended his colors freely to produce a harmonious painting. And yet, at the same time, almost every element on this canvas has been rendered with a different technique. The blurred backdrop ensures our attention is on the closely cropped girl, desolate and alone. Together with her rosy lips and cheeks, her smooth skin hints at her youth. In contrast, her ragged clothes are roughly painted with harsh strokes. The overall effect is a somber portrait of a lonely, impoverished orphan in a graveyard at dusk.

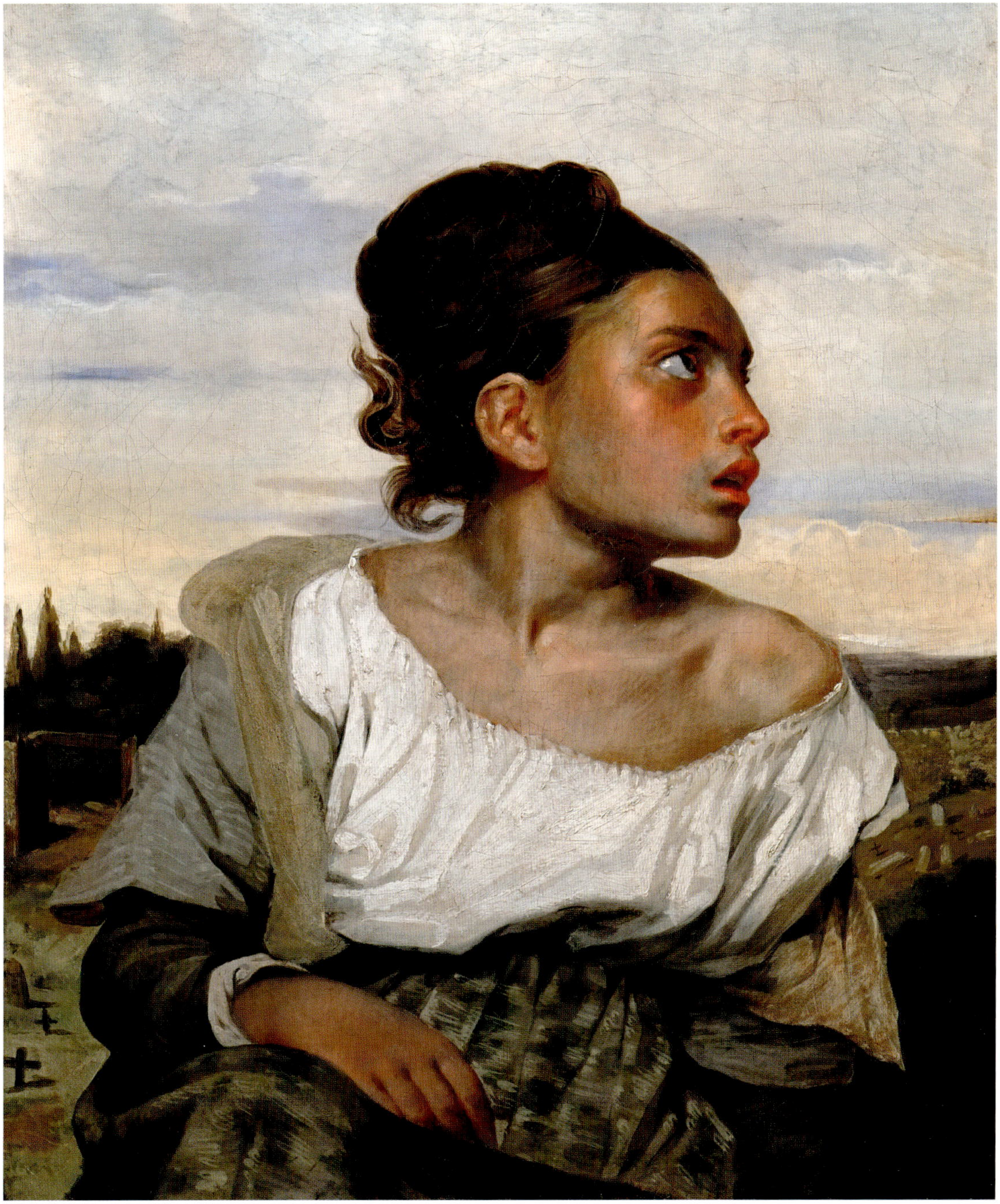

Palette

Vanilla clouds, a bright white blouse, rosy cheeks, and dimly lit greenery.

Complementary works

- Théodore Géricault, *Portrait Study of a Youth*, *c.*1818–20.
- Gustave Courbet, *The Desperate Man*, 1843–45.
- Jean-François Millet, *The Gleaners*, 1857.

How we see color

The German poet and scientist Johann Wolfgang von Goethe was one of several 19th-century theorists to expand on Isaac Newton's color circle (*see page 62*). In 1810 he published a German text called *Zur Farbenlehre* (*Theory of Colors*), which described a more subjective and human experience of color perception. Unlike Newton, Goethe trusted the human eye over math and science; he explored the perception of color in shadows and through mediums from air to dust, and based his conclusions exclusively on personal observations. In his opinion, a Newton-like understanding of physics was a hindrance; he argued that his predecessor's theory of light and color wasn't an elemental principle, but an incidental result.

Goethe also disagreed with Newton's suggestion that colors are contained within white light. Instead, like Aristotle, he believed that all colors arise from the dynamic interplay of the polar opposites of light and dark. On his new symmetrical circle, he placed six colors appositionally, and assigned plus and minus values to each. He wrote: "The colors diametrically opposed to each other in this diagram are those which reciprocally evoke each other in the eye. Thus, yellow demands violet; orange [demands] blue; purple [demands] green; and vice versa."

Goethe's theory was as much about poetry as optics. As well as assigning plus and minus values to each color, he allocated them positive and negative psychological and moral associations. His was a kind of color psychology, proposing that certain shades represented particular ethical values. In his mind, red was associated with beauty, orange with nobility, yellow with good, green with usefulness, blue with commonality, and violet with all things unnecessary. In his own home in Weimar, different rooms were decorated accordingly, with blues and greens (the most welcoming color) in abundance.

Color theory was explored by several artists in the 19th century—among them Turner (*see page 98*), who owned and annotated a copy of the English translation of Goethe's seminal text. Turner's *Light and Colour (Goethe's Theory) – the Morning after the Deluge – Moses Writing the Book of Genesis* (exhibited 1843) is a partial visualization of Goethe's wheel, with color

Goethe's color wheel from *Theory of Colors*, 1810.

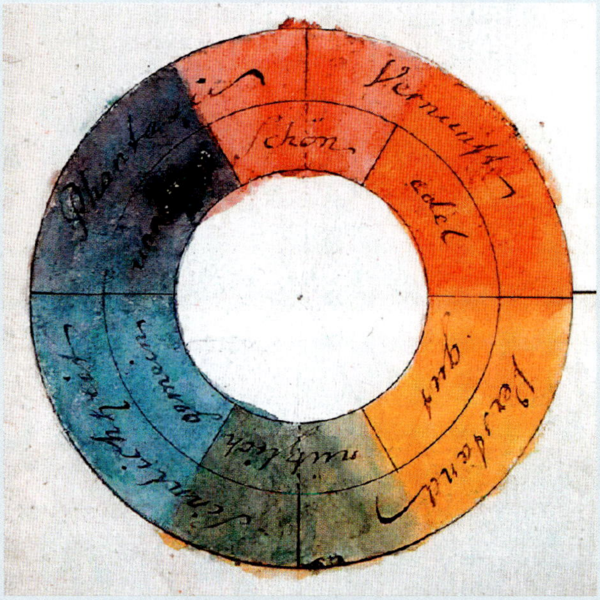

arising from the interaction between light and dark. The light-filled morning in the aftermath of the biblical flood features a triumphant yellow whirl and other colors from the warm side of the spectrum. And yet, the poem that Turner wrote and presented alongside the painting undermines its optimism by emphasizing the ephemerality of the rising sun.

Of course, the search for the laws of color behavior continued, and Goethe's conclusions have since been overthrown, but he was supremely confident. In his own words: "From the philosopher, we believe we merit thanks for having traced the phenomena of colors to their first sources, to the circumstances under which they appear and are, and beyond which no further explanation respecting them is possible."

Joseph Mallord William Turner, *Light and Colour (Goethe's Theory) – the Morning after the Deluge – Moses Writing the Book of Genesis*, 1843, oil on canvas, 31 x 31 in (78.7 × 78.7 cm).

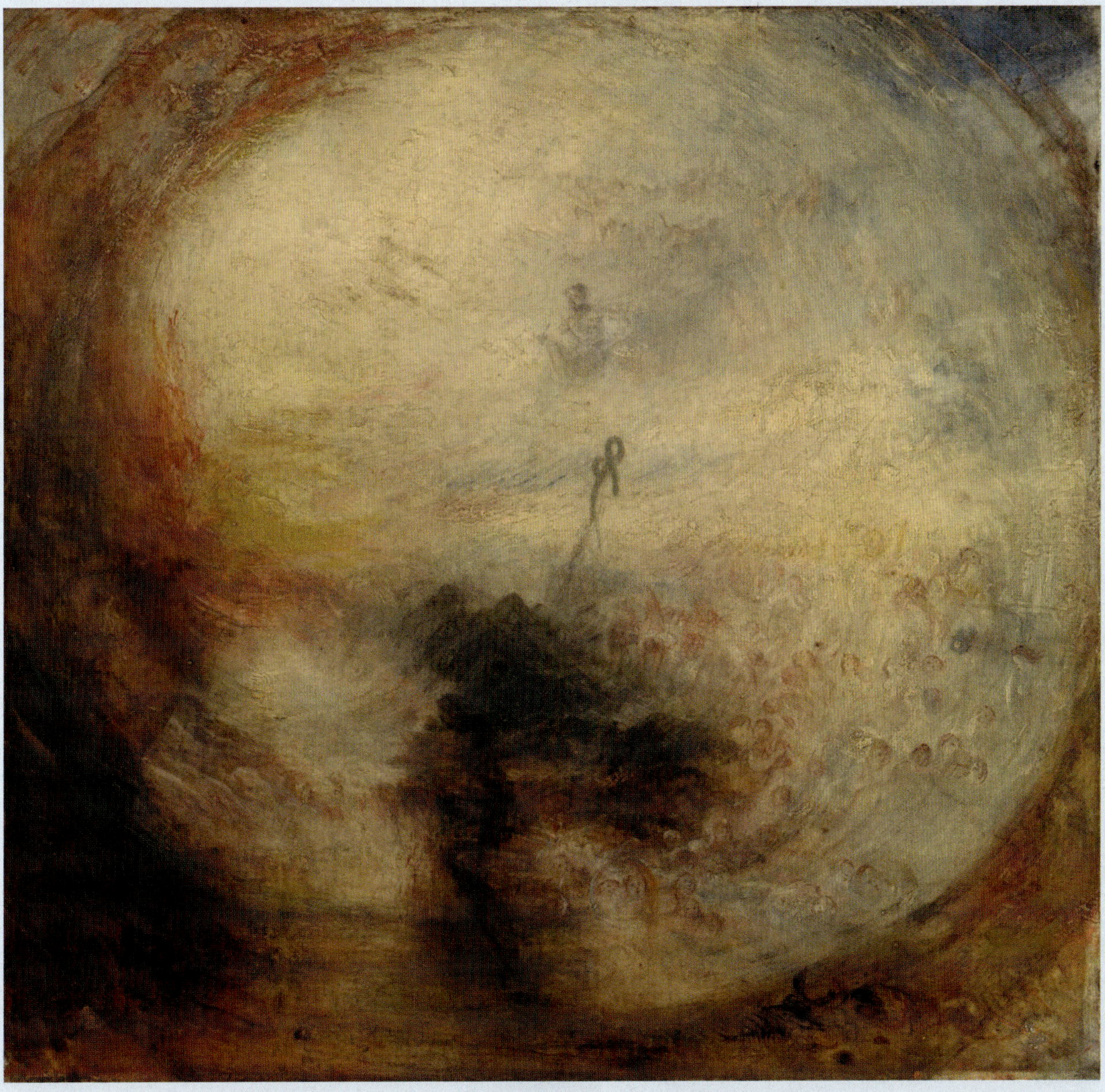

C2 M0 Y0 K6
R239 G242 B243

C0 M21 Y90 K5
R230 G191 B46

C0 M84 Y100 K10
R187 G61 B16

C84 M45 Y0 K5
R64 G112 B175

C66 M52 Y0 K15
R95 G104 B158

On fire

Joseph Mallord William Turner

The Burning of the Houses of Parliament

1835

Watercolor and gouache on paper, 11⅞ x 17½ in (30.2 × 44.4 cm).

It was early evening on October 16, 1834, when London's Houses of Parliament caught fire. As the blaze swept through the Lords and the Commons, thousands of spectators gathered to witness the destruction of the historic buildings. Among them was Turner, who hired a boat to get a better look at the searing blazes of light. The conflagration might have been a national disaster, but for the artist it was a spectacle, and an opportunity to create raw and explosive art.

The sky is ablaze in this oil painting, which the artist made back in his studio after producing rapid pencil and watercolor sketches at the scene. A great swirl of molten red, orange, and yellow stretches up into the sky—where it takes on a golden-bronze shade—and down into the glassy Thames, where it's reflected in the water. The dazzle of flames divides the canvas in two and seeps across the painterly surface, which has been rendered with violent swathes of contrasting colors and assumes a hazy glow. On either side of the blaze are rough glimpses of Westminster Bridge and the two towers of Westminster Abbey, as well as crowded boats of onlookers. Dashes of pale blue and violet, in the river and sky, provide relief from the plumes of smoke and crackling heat.

An artist of the Romantic age, Turner often loaded his art with historical and mythological references. And yet his late works have more in common with the art of the Impressionists and Abstract Expressionists. Rather than building up his layers of oil paint from light to dark, as tradition dictated, he painted on a light ground to achieve translucence. He animated and intensified his scene with saturated colors that verge on the supernatural. At the time, his paintings were ridiculed for their lack of representation and finish. Today, they are among his greatest achievements, energetic and inventive. They are optical explorations of light, tone, color, and atmosphere, as well as studies of the sublime.

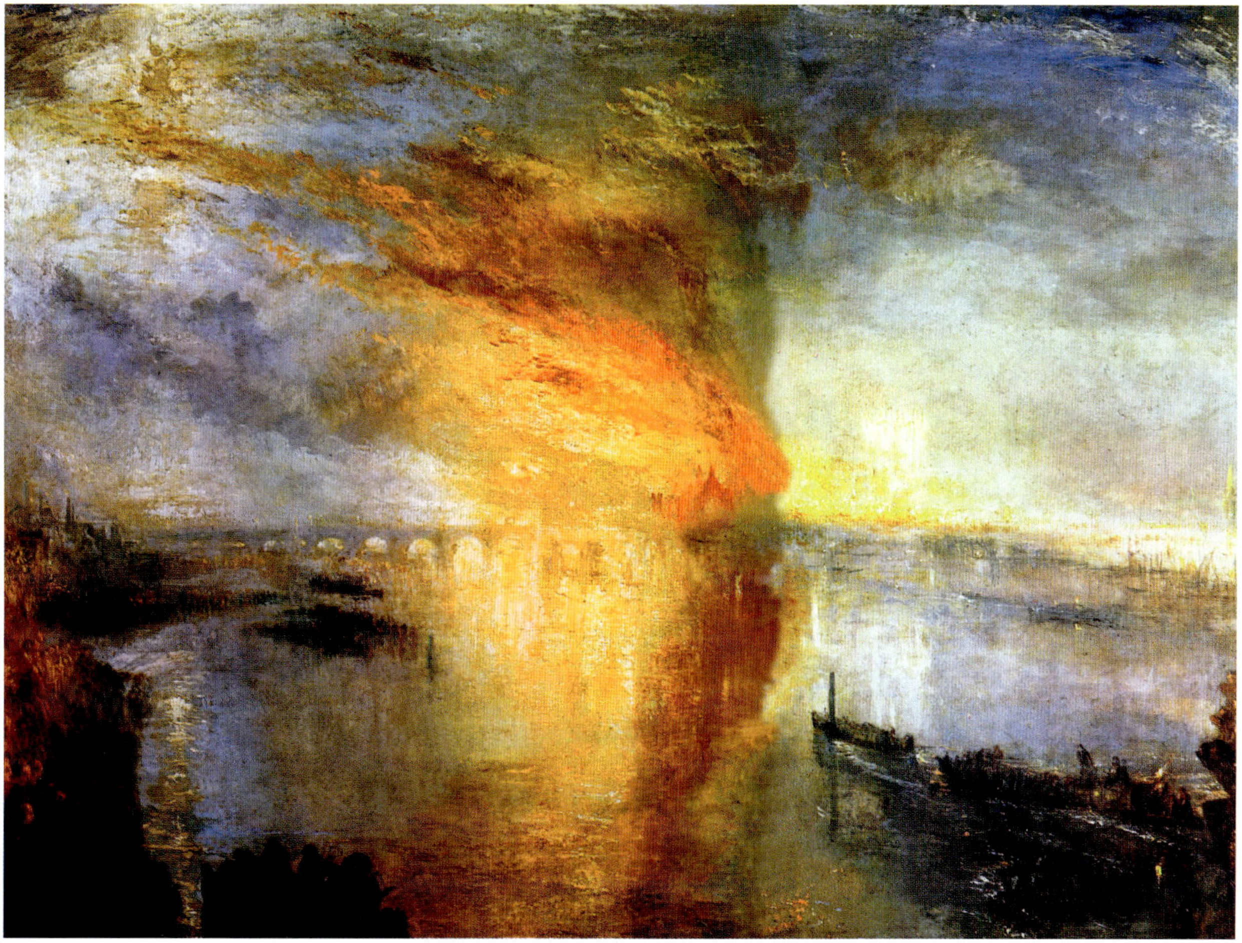

Palette

A great swirl of molten red, orange, and yellow, with dashes of white, pale blue, and violet.

Complementary works

- Claude Lorrain, *Seaport at Sunset*, 1639.
- John Constable, *Rainstorm over the Sea*, c.1824–28.
- Claude Monet, *Houses of Parliament, Sunset*, 1904.

Academic approach

Jean-Auguste-Dominique Ingres

Comtesse d'Haussonville

1845

Oil on canvas,
$51\frac{7}{8} \times 36\frac{1}{4}$ in (131.8 × 92.1 cm).

C85 M65 Y20 K30
R53 G71 B109

C44 M30 Y9 K0
R154 G163 B193

C59 M55 Y24 K10
R111 G106 B134

C5 M89 Y100 K10
R178 G50 B20

C0 M6 Y12 K0
R251 G241 B225

A distinguished member of the Academy, Ingres prized drawing over color. Unlike Delacroix (*see page 94*), his compositions are controlled and precise, and his smooth colors stay firmly inside the lines. Take his softly lit portrait of the Comtesse d'Haussonville, an image so carefully detailed and highly finished that it appears almost photorealistic.

The young Louise de Broglie is captured in her boudoir, leaning back against an upholstered fireplace, with one hand draped across her waist and the other raised. The canvas is painted with a palette of blues and purples—from the deep indigo velvet mantel-cover to the dusty walls and the Comtesse's lavender satin gown, which falls in intricate light and dark folds. The gemstones in her jewelry are blue, as are her doe eyes. Against those harmonized shades, contrasting colors pop. The mirror appears in a gold frame, and various gilded objects sit on the mantelpiece. Pink and red wildflowers stand in an ornate vase, and a brilliant vermilion red ribbon adorns the young woman's hair. To the right of the fireplace is the Comtesse's discarded mustard-yellow shawl, and at the center of it all is her flawless skin, a milky white. In the mirror, we get a glimpse of the bare nape of her neck.

Despite her elevated social class (her husband was a diplomat and, like Ingres, a member of the Academy), the Comtesse was known for being outspoken and independent. She once said of herself, "I was destined to beguile, to attract, to seduce, and in the final reckoning to cause suffering in all those who sought their happiness in me." Ingres produced several preparatory drawings of this portrait and eventually settled on a coquettish pose—the young woman stroking her jaw as she meets our gaze—and an intimate interior scene. The canvas might be controlled and precise, in an intricately orchestrated symphony of blues, but the flashes of red in the Comtesse's ribbon and her rosy cheeks hint at seduction and intrigue.

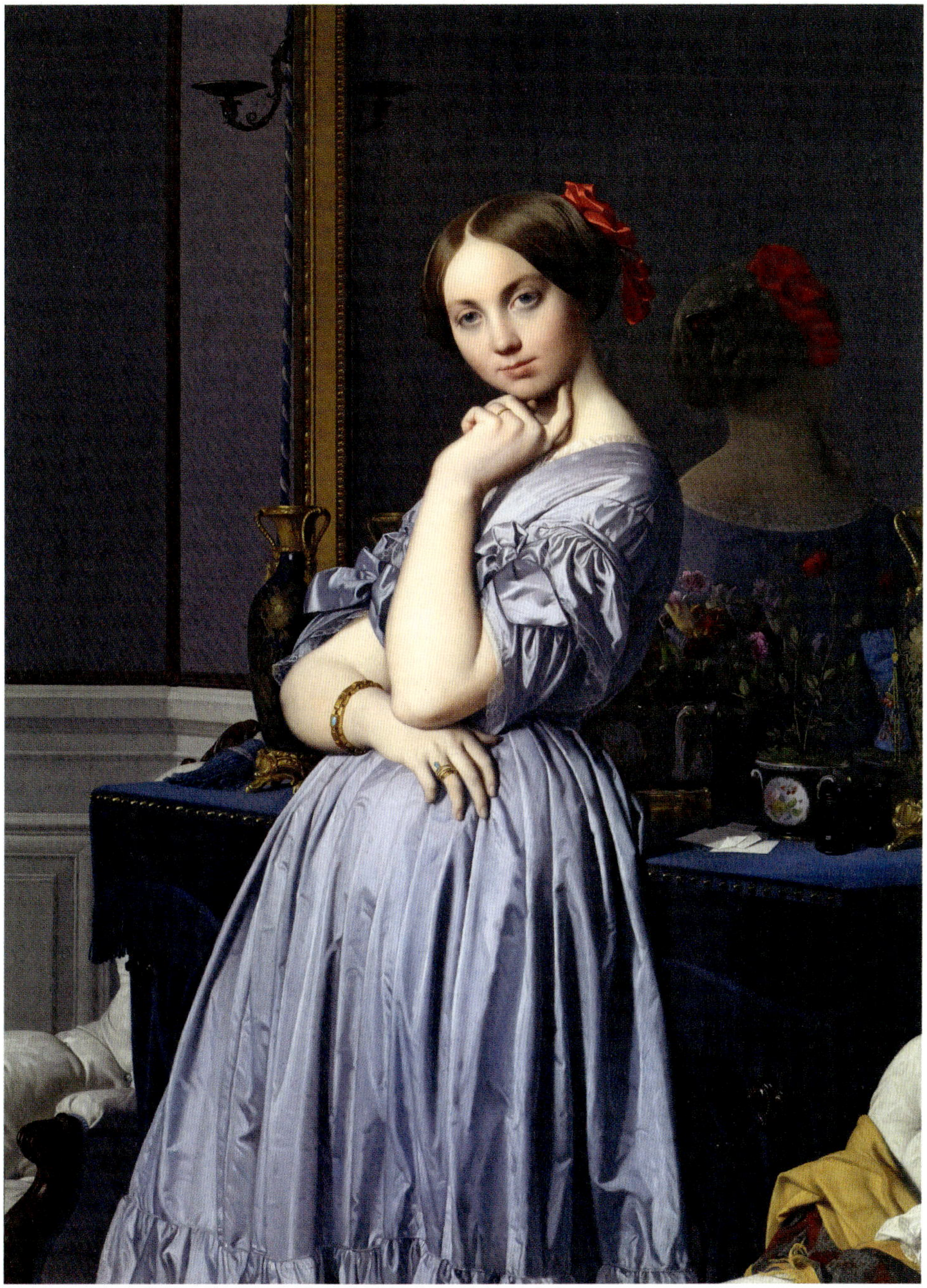

Palette

Blues and purples, from deep indigo to lavender, with flashes of brilliant vermilion and milky white.

Complementary works

- Thomas Gainsborough, *The Blue Boy*, c.1770.
- Marie-Denise Villers, *Portrait of Charlotte du Val d'Ognes*, 1801.
- Anne-Louis Girodet-Trioson, *Portrait of Hortense de Beauharnais, Queen of Holland*, c.1805–09.

Let there be light

Impressionism

C40 M45 Y20 K15
R139 G126 B145

Let there be light

Impressionism

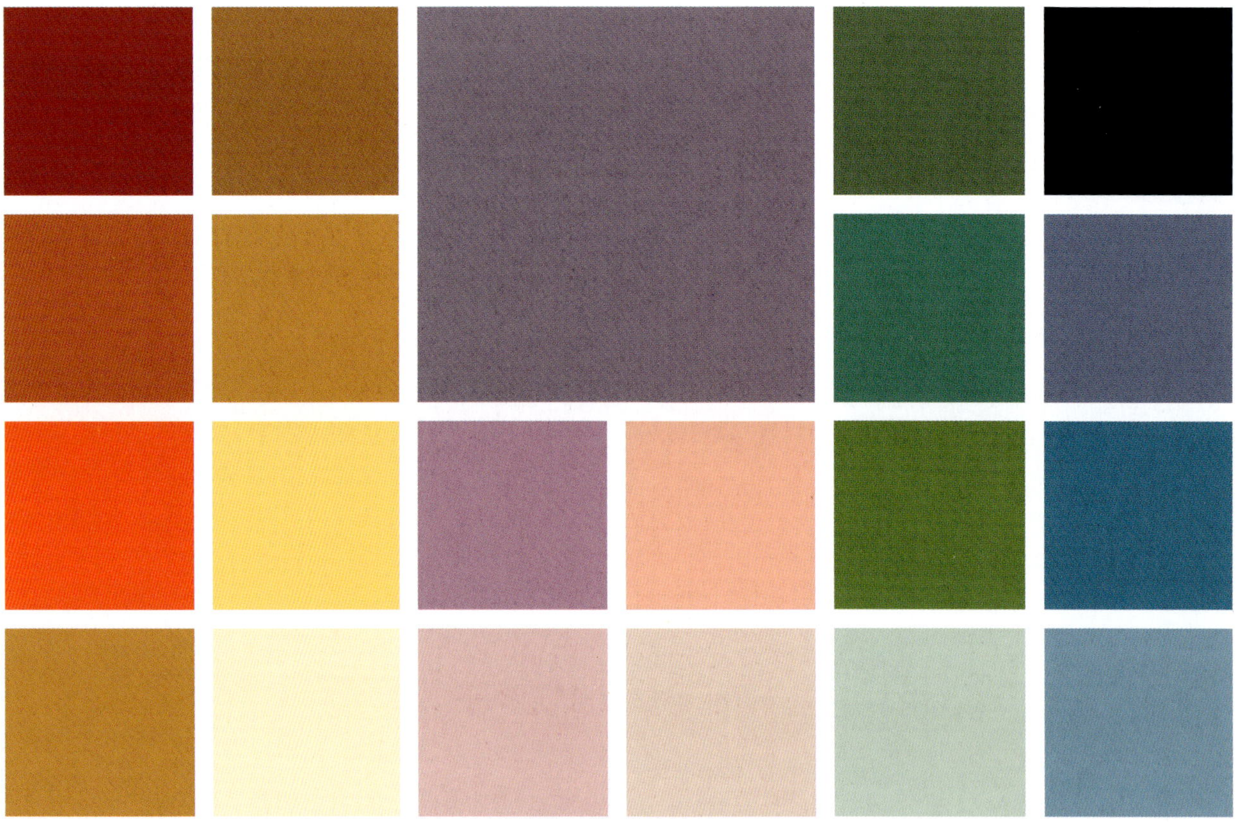

There was more than one French Revolution. Almost a century after the political convulsions of 1789, a clutch of plucky artists with a radical approach to picture-making sparked a painterly revolution, with color in the vanguard. They turned away from traditional subjects—historical, mythological, religious—and instead took up modern life itself: beautiful and mysterious, thrilling and strange. They were preoccupied with visual experience and the act of looking. They wanted to capture a mood, the play of light, a fleeting moment in time—and they did so with a vibrant palette that defied artistic convention.

Impressionism emerged in France toward the end of the 1860s, by which time modern chemistry was in full swing. Since the Renaissance, artists had made do with the same twenty or so natural pigments—many of which were unstable or toxic, at least to some degree. Scientific advances meant that, by the mid-19th century, 40 new chemical elements had been discovered and, between 1800 and 1870, around twenty synthetic pigments were readily available (*see page 114*).

In the hands of the Impressionists, colors began to leap and dance. Snow white was whirled with pink and blue, while human flesh was dashed with violet and green. They sought to record the world as it was, living and breathing, rather than how they had been told it was supposed be. The kind of observation they strove for was immediate and could only be achieved by working directly from life—they had to get out of their studios and into the cafés, streets, and fields.

Scientific advances came hand in hand with technological innovations in paint storage: in 1841 the little-known American painter John Rand provided artists with a tidier alternative to keeping paint in pigs' bladders sealed with string. He invented the collapsible tin paint tube, so not only were premixed colors cheaper than ever, but they also came in a convenient portable form. When painting *en plein air*, the Impressionists paid attention to the weather, their brushstrokes becoming broken and bumpy as they hurried to commit to canvas a passing cloud or a fleeting rain shower.

The great advantage of being outdoors was the ever-changing light. Claude Monet (*see page 122*) once said that "light is the principal person in the picture" and the Impressionists paid attention, above all else, to the atmosphere that it conjured. They sought to capture the way woozy evening light tiptoes over the surface of water and the effect that morning rays have when they filter through trees. They returned to the same scenes again and again to chart the atmospheric changes, depending on the time of day, the weather or the season.

The 19th century brought with it a radical new vision and vibrancy of color that went against established academic traditions. Rather than attributing color to objects and scenes, the Impressionists let it be the lead. They were inspired in part by the everyday subjects, a sense of clarity, and the luminous colors of Japanese woodcut prints; in 1853, Japan's ports reopened and foreign imports—among them ukiyo-e (pictures of the floating world)—flooded European shores. The Impressionists, too, sought to create a sense of balance in their art, using contrasting or complementary hues. They worked quickly and spontaneously, and the result is shimmering and bright. This is the Impressionist Revolution.

C24 M30 Y35 K10
R177 G162 B146

C25 M5 Y25 K0
R203 G218 B196

C5 M40 Y70 K10
R201 G151 B84

C0 M6 Y25 K0
R251 G239 B200

C0 M0 Y6 K0
R255 G254 B243

C58 M15 Y15 K5
R126 G167 B189

Tropical light

Camille Pissarro
Two Women Chatting by the Sea, Saint Thomas
1856

Oil on canvas,
10⅞ x 16⅛ in (27.7 x 41 cm).

Few paintings are more beautifully drenched in light than this calm coastal landscape. Two Afro-Caribbean women pause on a dusty path: one is dressed in creamy white and has a big basket of freshly laundered sheets balancing on her head, while the other, in rich blue, carries a smaller basket in the crook of her arm. The warm rays of the West Indian sun illuminate the folds of fabric, and the stationary women cast shadows on the ground as they engage in conversation. The beach beyond is empty, except for a group of figures by the smooth and glassy water. In the distance, purples hills extend across the horizon.

Born in 1830 on the island of Saint Thomas, in what's now the U.S. Virgin Islands, Pissarro never held French nationality. At the age of twelve he was sent to school in France, where he became interested in painting, and when he permanently relocated there in 1855, his focus was on tropical beach scenes like this. In such early works, he combined the color and light of the Caribbean with the gentle palette of the Barbizon painters, who first expressed the importance of painting landscapes outdoors. It was during classes at the Académie Suisse in Paris that he met Monet (*see page 122*) and Paul Cézanne, and settled on a new pictorial language.

Later, Pissarro would become infatuated with grays and blacks, but there's something striking about the way he used colors when he started out. There's a serenity to this landscape, achieved by his use of pale pigments, from the pearly blue water to the soft brown vegetation and the milky yellow light. In the foreground, the women stand tall, with a dignity imparted by their stature and classical folds. Pissarro's family owned a dry-goods business on Saint Thomas, and he depicted humble workmen and women throughout his career. His may not be the first name that springs to mind when you think of the artistic revolution of the 19th century, but it should be. "We learned everything we do from Pissarro," said Cézanne in the 1890s. "It's he who was really the first Impressionist."

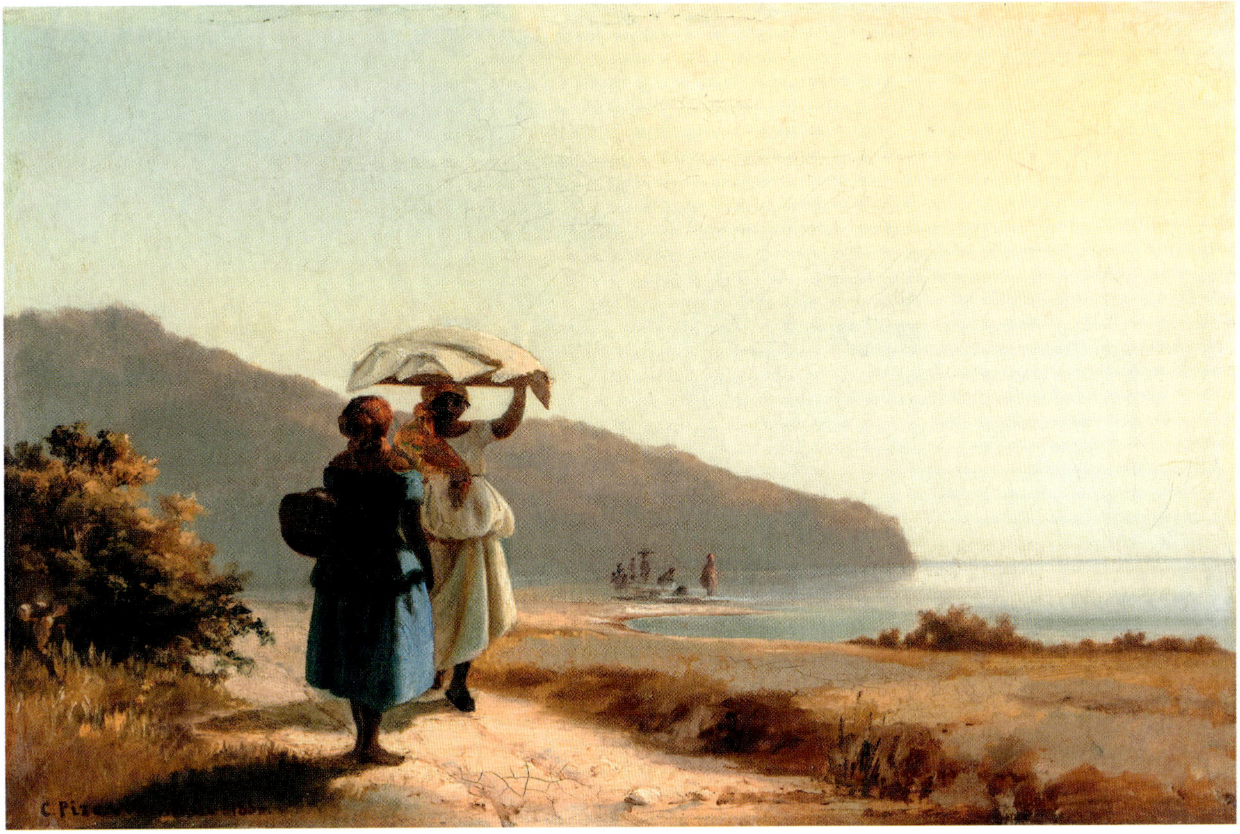

Palette

A wash of pale pigments, from pearly blue water to soft brown vegetation and yellow light.

Complementary works

- Édouard Manet, *Beach at Boulogne*, 1869.
- Claude Monet, *The Thames below Westminster, c.*1871.
- Paul Cézanne, *Hillside in Provence*, *c.*1890–92.

Garden variety

Frédéric Bazille
Young Woman with Peonies
1870

Oil on canvas,
23⅝ x 29½ in (60 x 75 cm).

The profusion of flowers in this intimate portrait offered Bazille an opportunity to paint with a bold and brilliant palette. The pale pink peonies in his sitter's hand stand out against the beautifully highlighted greenery, while among the seasonal blooms in the wicker basket are red and yellow tulips, bright-white anemones, pale-blue forget-me-nots and more tumbling green leaves. Bazille and his contemporaries looked to the Dutch tradition of floral still lifes but stripped away any symbolic or moralizing element. Instead, their focus was simply on the pleasure of painting from nature, and the texture and color combinations that such lush arrangements afforded.

Bazille was born and raised in Montpellier, southern France, and it was in the town's botanical gardens that he studied different flower species. He produced two versions of *Young Woman with Peonies* in the spring of 1870, before returning home for the last time—he died at the age of 28 in the Franco-Prussian war. Both works combine figurative painting with the still-life genre and exhibit a technical mastery of the medium of oil paint. In the second work, his sitter is busy arranging flowers in a glossy earthenware vase, seemingly unaware of our presence. Here, she's posed as a vendor and meets our gaze as she extends the clutch of peonies toward us.

The trope of a Black female model with a bunch of flowers crops up in several mid-19th-century paintings, among them Édouard Manet's (*see page 112*) *Olympia* (1863). Bazille's portrait may be a tribute to Manet's more radical work—and to the artist himself, whose favorite flowers were peonies. Unlike in *Olympia*, though, where the model, Laure, is portrayed against a dark background, Bazille's model is center stage and bathed in light. She's dressed in modern attire: a cream shirt with a scalloped collar, a plaid headscarf, and a pair of coral earrings. Her skin is a warm brown and, together with the slate-gray backdrop, it intensifies the splashes of color in the flowers.

C45 M26 Y30 K25
R126 G137 B135

C5 M50 Y85 K25
R170 G116 B44

C49 M10 Y88 K30
R118 G139 B55

C0 M90 Y100 K0
R201 G50 B20

C0 M36 Y30 K0
R230 G179 B162

C0 M15 Y71 K0
R244 G213 B99

C0 M0 Y0 K6
R243 G243 B243

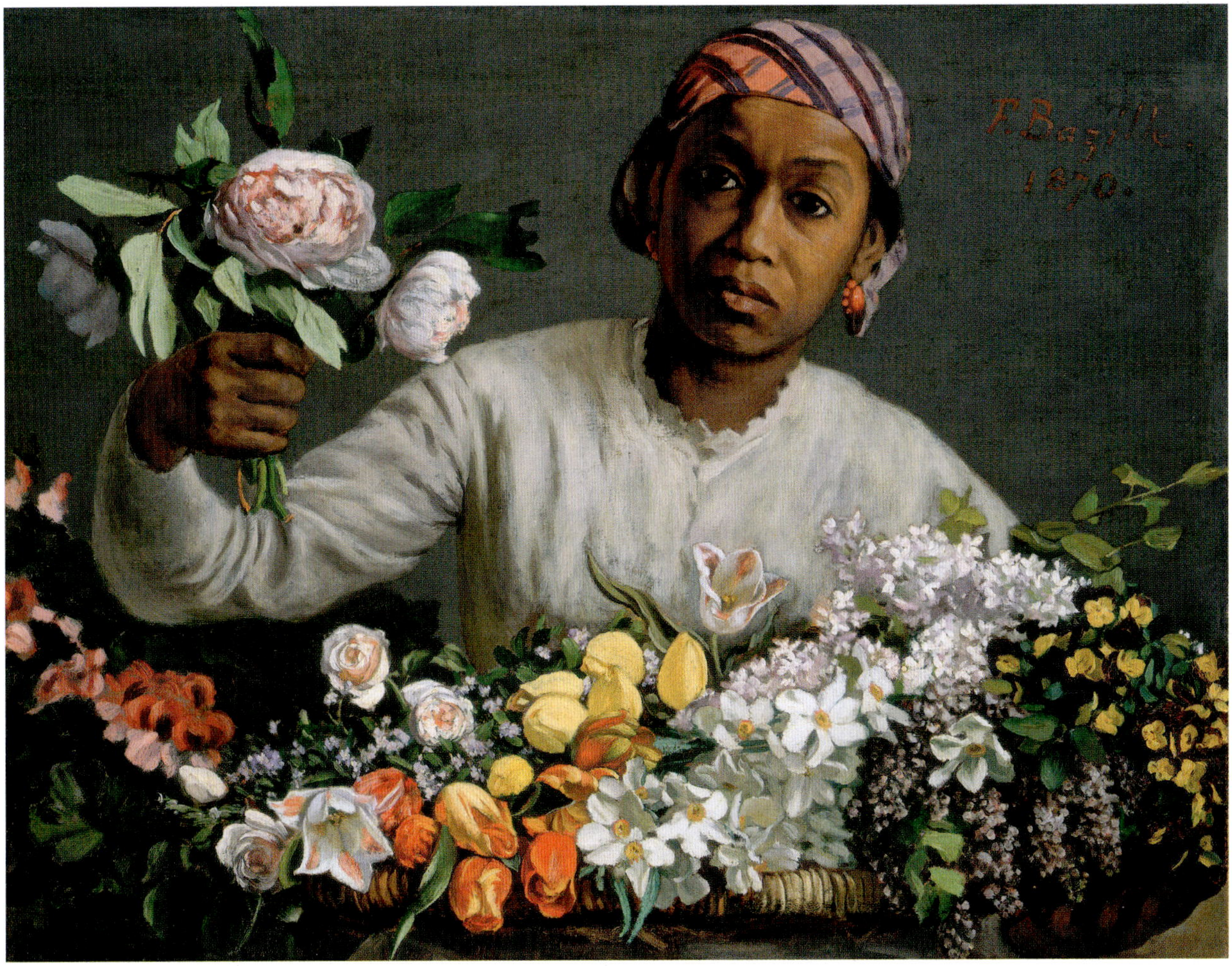

Palette

Pale-pink peonies, red and yellow tulips, bright-white anemones, pale-blue forget-me-nots, tumbling green leaves, and warm brown skin.

Complementary works

- Henri Fantin-Latour, *Flowers and Fruit*, 1866.
- Édouard Manet, *In the Conservatory*, 1878–79.
- Max Liebermann, *Flower Shrubs in Wannsee Garden*, 1919.

C5 M21 Y20 K0
R231 G206 B193

C5 M14 Y20 K0
R236 G220 B200

C0 M3 Y6 K0
R253 G248 B240

In harmony

James Abbott McNeill Whistler
Symphony in Flesh Colour and Pink: Portrait of Mrs Frances Leyland
1871–74

Oil on canvas,
77⅛ × 40¼ in (195.9 × 102.2 cm).

"I cannot see that it is at all a likeness," wrote Dante Gabriel Rossetti of Whistler's portrait: an elegant arrangement of color, form, and line. Defying convention, Whistler resisted narrative and instead focused on art's abstract elements. Some criticized his works for failing to fulfill the traditional function of portraiture; he responded by asking what the public cared about the identity of portraits. Of course, in this instance, his sitter is named, and although Mrs Frances Leyland is almost subsumed in color and tone, her beauty and wistful demeanor are immortalized in paint.

Commissioned by Frederick R. Leyland, one of Whistler's greatest patrons in the 1870s, *Symphony in Flesh Colour and Pink* shows the wealthy collector's wife with her back to the viewer, her head in profile and her hands clasped. She wears a loose-fitting sheer pink chiffon gown over a white underdress and stands in front of a dusty pink wall, on a chequered rug that's been laid across a parquet floor. The flowering snow-white almond blossom—a nod to Whistler's love of Japanese prints—is echoed in the appliqué flowers on Frances's dress. The artist designed both costume and interior to harmonize with one another, and chose the pink-and-cream color scheme to offset his model's creamy complexion and auburn hair. With oil paint diluted to a thin sauce-like consistency, the paint surface is soft and sensual—especially that of the luminescent floral gown.

This hazy portrait, which Whistler never considered finished, is one of several that home in on one or two colors and satisfy the artist's aesthetic ideals. A leading light of Aestheticism, Whistler placed equal weight on fine art and design, and promoted art for art's sake. Ignoring the rules of perspective, he made no attempt to show the rug or the floor receding into space; instead, he deliberately painted the details flat against the picture plane. Conceived as a single beautiful object, the portrait brings together in perfect harmony subject, setting, costume, and mount, which he also designed.

Palette

What it says on the tin.

Complementary works

- Gustave Caillebotte, *Woman at a Dressing Table*, 1873.
- Thomas Eakins, *Portrait of Maud Cook*, 1895.
- Cecilia Beaux, *Ernesta*, 1914.

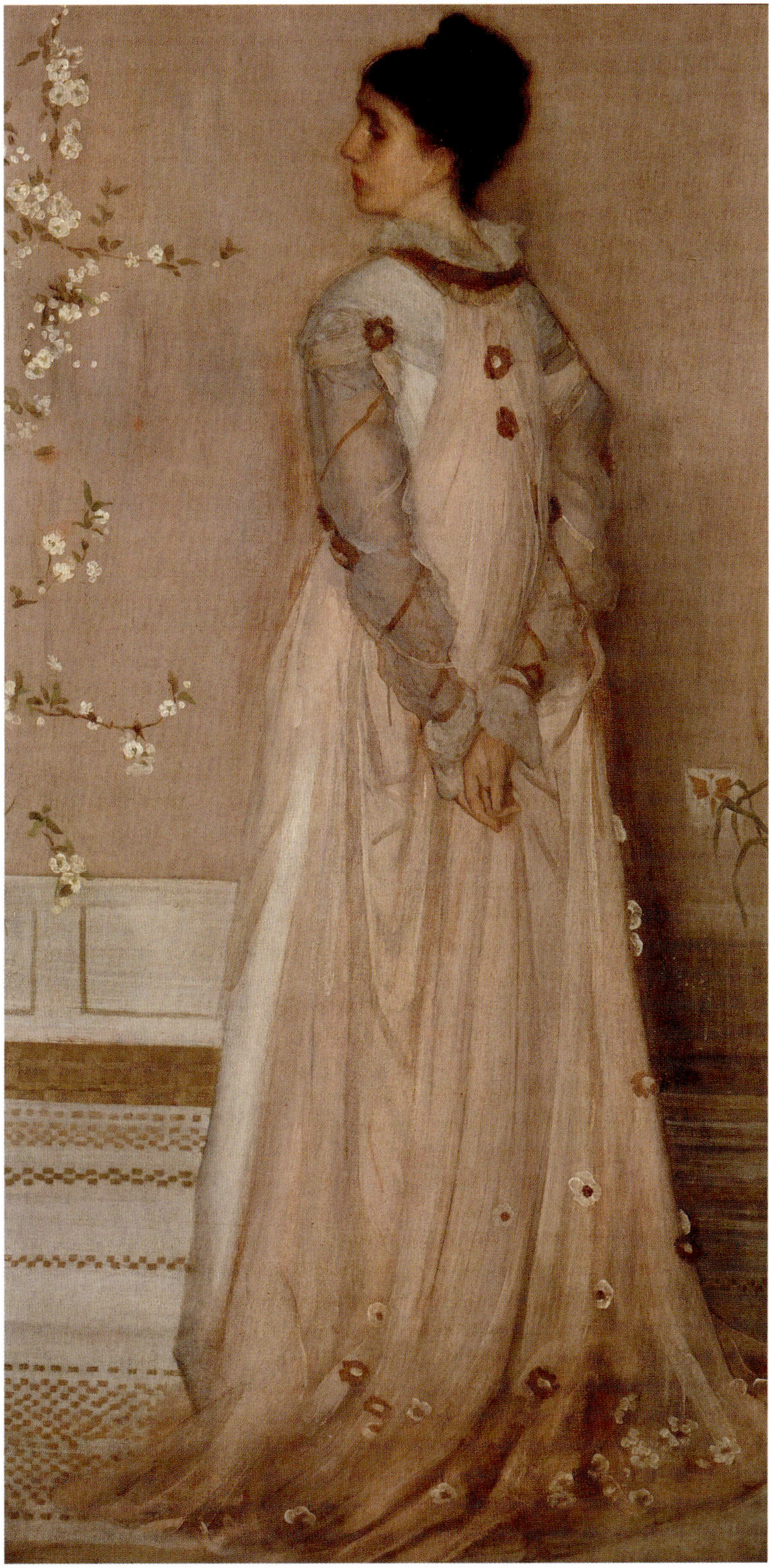

C40 M12 Y0 K100
R0 G0 B0

C30 M20 Y20 K20
R158 G162 B162

C10 M15 Y25 K0
R225 G213 B190

C28 M30 Y45 K25
R149 G140 B115

C64 M34 Y15 K15
R102 G128 B157

Paint it black

Édouard Manet

Berthe Morisot with a Bouquet of Violets

1872

Oil on canvas,
$21\frac{11}{16}$ x 15 in (55 x 38 cm).

Manet's spellbinding portrait of his fellow artist, the beautiful Berthe Morisot (*see page 116*), who would later become his sister-in-law, is as much a study in tone as it is a study in character. The color black was considered best avoided by the Impressionists, with whom Manet was loosely associated, but here it takes center stage, covering more than half the canvas. Against the pearly gray backdrop, Morisot is statuesque, and yet there's movement in her intense cloak and elaborate hat, which themselves contain expressive strokes of light and dark. Another fellow artist, Camille Pissarro (*see page 106*), observed that Manet "made light with black."

Morisot is portrayed in mourning at her father's funeral, with one half of her face in shadow. She wears a black cloak and matching hat, with wide black ribbons falling loose alongside her brown hair. Against her creamy skin, her lips are a dull pink, her hollow eyes dark (in fact they were green) and lined with kohl, and her eyebrows sharp like wings. It's easy to miss the earrings dangling from her lobes and the titular bouquet of violets in her hands—a dash of bright blue, inches below her white shirt. On the right-hand side of the canvas is a dark strip of shadow, which almost threatens to take over the pale and empty backdrop, glowing a silvery yellow.

During his career, Manet studied the works of Titian (*see page 46*) and Peter Paul Rubens, as well as the Black Paintings of Francisco de Goya and the frank creations of Diego Velázquez (*see page 60*). He revisited the past in his paintings of modern life, and the result is art that's at once old and new, clear and complicated. Manet presents us with images that are startlingly direct, and yet so often the subject is hidden in plain sight. His portrait of Morisot is about the formal attributes of color, but also about capturing in color what's going on inside her head.

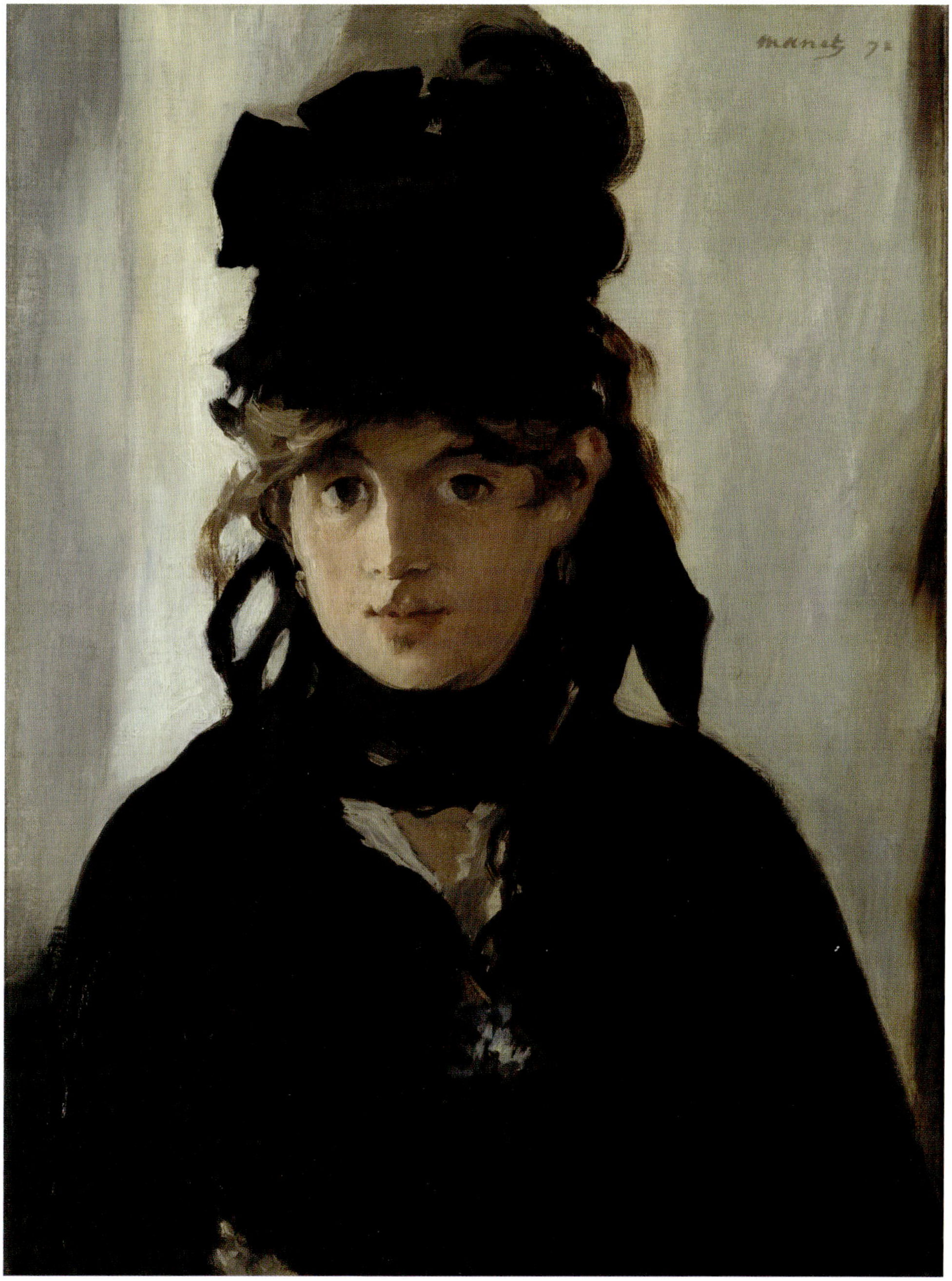

Palette

Black clothing, creamy skin, a dash of bright blue, and a backdrop of gray and silver.

Complementary works

- Diego Velázquez, *The Lady with a Fan*, *c*.1638–39.
- Thomas Gainsborough, *Portrait of Margaret Gainsborough*, *c*.1778.
- John Singer Sargent, *Portrait of Madame X*, 1883–84.

Color chemistry

It was the invention of Prussian blue in the 18th century that sparked the modern age of chemical paint synthesis. Until that point, artists had mostly been relying on the same assortment of fewer than twenty naturally colored pigments. Although the first known artificial pigment—another shade of blue—was in fact created thousands of years earlier in ancient Egypt (*see page 20*), its recipe had been lost to history in the Middle Ages, and our understanding of its origination is unclear. The story of Prussian blue, however, is well told.

It was 1704 and the German alchemist (and potential model for Doctor Frankenstein) Johann Konrad Dippel was sharing a lab in Berlin with the Swiss dyer and color maker Johann Jacob Diesbach. One day, Diesbach was working on a batch of cochineal red when he accidentally created an intense blue instead. It turned out that it was the result of a chemical reaction caused by some potash provided by Dippel, which had been diluted with animal oil and contained elements of blood. And so the world's first documented synthetic pigment was born.

Dippel swiftly monetized his colleague's mistake and marketed the new pigment, whose formula was then published in 1724 by an English chemist. By the late 1720s, Prussian blue was available throughout Europe, where it was used not only by artists, but also in dyes and wallpapers. It launched an industry that flourished in the decades that followed and had a significant impact on artistic practice, particularly that of the Impressionists. Once one chemist had worked out how to make blue synthetically, others followed, seeking both new shades and substitutes for existing pigments that were either prohibitively expensive or poisonous.

The advent of modern chemistry meant that the Impressionists had at their fingertips an array of affordable and stable colors. As scientists discovered new elements and began to understand how they combined, they realized that several produced brightly colored compounds that could be used as pigments. Among the new synthetic ones that became available between 1800 and 1870 were bright and opaque cobalt, chromium, and cadmium. There were cobalt blues, chrome yellows, and emerald and viridian greens, as well as a cheap synthetic ultramarine (the French Society for the Encouragement of National Industries, established in 1801, offered a financial reward for whomever could devise a method for manufacturing the pigment industrially). The arrival of mangolese violet meant that artists no longer had to mix red and blue to make purple, while the availability of cadmium orange removed the need to mix red and yellow. Although still toxic, Paris green was more durable than Scheele's green.

With synthetic pigments came specialist paint manufacturers: businesses that catered to what was becoming a popular pursuit. Paints were made using grinding equipment powered, first by horses, and later by steam; for fine art they were bound with oils, whereas for amateurs they were suspended in a water-soluble gum and turned into easy-to-handle watercolors. The industry bloomed, as did artists' palettes. Of all the turning points in the history of color, this was the finest.

Pierre-Auguste Renoir, *Dance at the Moulin de la Galette*, 1876, oil on canvas, 52 × 69 in (131 × 175 cm).

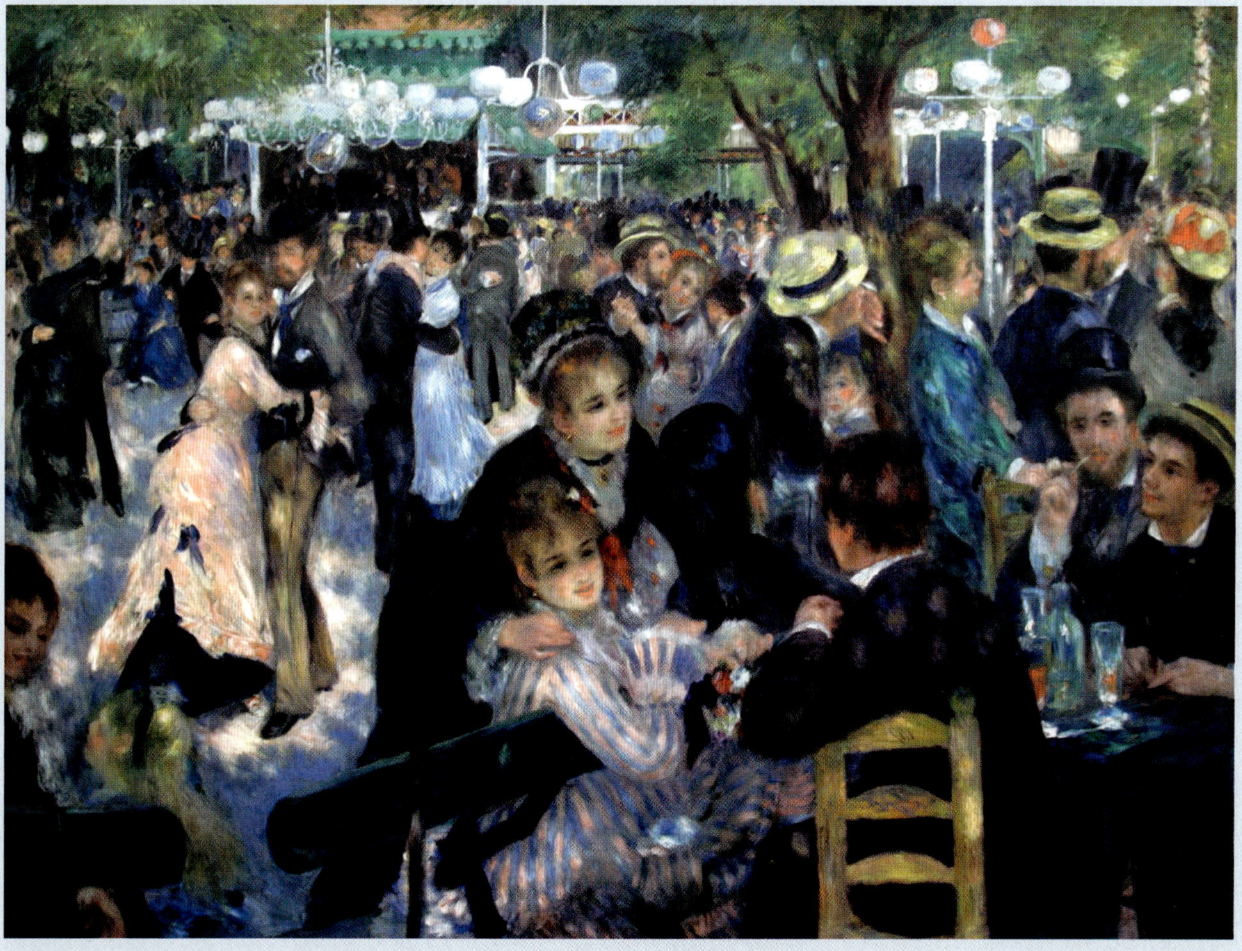

In praise of paint

Berthe Morisot
In the Country (After Luncheon)
1881

Oil on canvas,
39⅜ x 31⅞ in (100 × 81 cm).

C40 M43 Y20 K15
R140 G129 B147

C82 M15 Y15 K25
R58 G126 B156

C38 M10 Y52 K10
R161 G179 B132

C78 M10 Y53 K25
R71 G130 B112

C12 M94 Y98 K8
R169 G40 B27

C0 M0 Y4 K6
R243 G243 B236

A woman sits by a window that overlooks a garden. A muddle of dark and light foliage has both depth and movement, drawing our eye toward the backdrop, while echoing the bunch of grapes on the table. The red and white flowers inch forward onto the hat that frames her face, together with the white lace collar of her fashionable high-necked gown. She sits upright, with one hand creeping toward the glass jug and the plate of lemons, and the other resting on the back of her chair, clutching a blue fan. Her dress, which is a similar shade of violet to the wooden beams between the glass panels, teeters on transparent. Critics accused Morisot of leaving her canvases unfinished, but there's meaning in her deliberately feathered strokes and restless whirl of color.

Despite showing at seven out of the eight Impressionist exhibitions and leaving behind a body of work to rival Manet's (*see page 112*), after her untimely death in 1895, Morisot—like the woman in her painting—all but disappeared. Audiences dismissed her art as "domestic," since her central characters are women and children, and her settings living rooms and gardens. In recent years, thanks to the work of feminist scholars and exhibitions such as that which began at the Musée national des beaux-arts du Québec in 2018, this key figure of the Impressionist movement is being appreciated for her fresh and radically free brushwork.

Like her fellow Impressionists, Morisot paid attention to life's surfaces—a tangle of greenery, a froth of lace, the way light strikes glass. There's something decorative about this close-up of a solitary woman staring, but that's not to say it lacks meaning. On the contrary, almost fading into the background, the woman is remote, her dark eyes downcast, her lips locked. Her expression could pass for composed, but it could also be more than that—bored, perhaps, of having to pose? As well as a visual appreciation of paint itself, Morisot's work is a psychological portrait of an inner life—and life's impermanence.

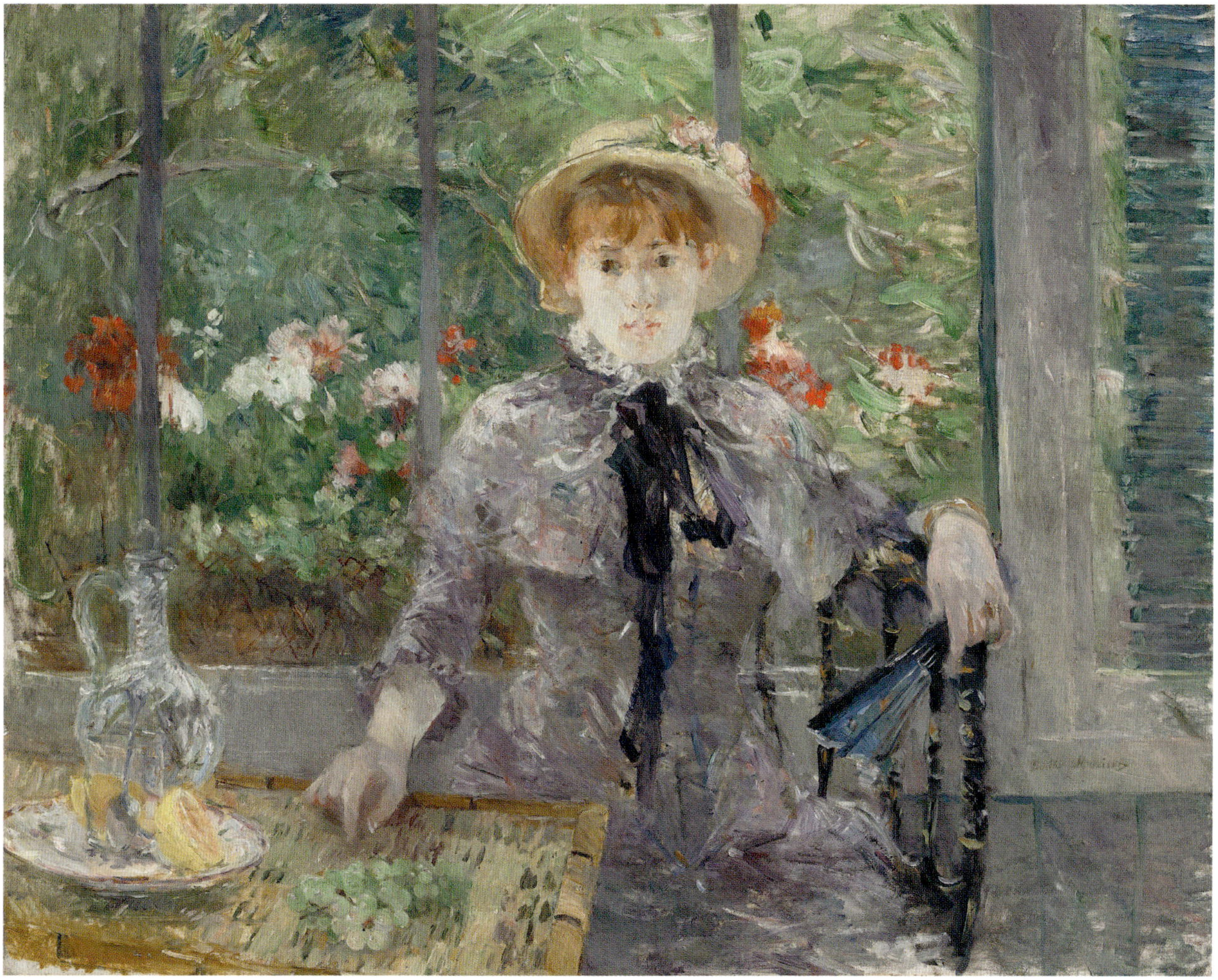

Palette

A restless whirl of violet, blue, and green, with red and white flowers.

Complementary works

- Eva Gonzalès, *Awakening Woman*, 1877–78.
- Marie Bracquemond, *Afternoon Tea (The Snack)*, *c.*1880.
- Childe Hassam, *Celia Thaxter's Garden, Isles of Shoals, Maine*, 1890.

Internationally inspired

Mary Cassatt
The Child's Bath
1893

Oil on canvas,
39½ × 26 in (100.3 × 66.1 cm).

C58 M20 Y68 K30
R102 G125 B83

C5 M83 Y100 K25
R157 G58 B13

C20 M52 Y10 K5
R180 G134 B164

C4 M0 Y0 K6
R236 G240 B243

C80 M40 Y20 K15
R69 G111 B144

After visiting an exhibition of Japanese prints at the École des Beaux-Arts in Paris in 1890, Pittsburgh-born Cassatt—who made waves both in the U.S. and in France—was energized by the flattened picture planes, asymmetrical compositions, and broad swatches of contrasting colors and decorative patterning. In response, she produced a series of her own prints, using aquatint and drypoint, that culminated in this tender oil painting. Like Morisot, she was drawn to intimate scenes of daily life—in particular the intimate bond between women and children.

A mother—or maybe she's a nanny or a nurse—wears a stripy robe in white, lilac, and green, and sits with a small girl propped up on her knee. One arm is wrapped protectively around the child's waist, while the other washes her feet in a bowl of water. Both gaze toward the water, engaged in the task at hand and apparently unaware of our presence. The vivid colors of the robe are echoed around the canvas—the white in the girl's towel and the ornate jug in the foreground; the lilac in the floral wallpaper; and the green in the golden-handled chest of drawers. The setting is most likely a bedroom; on the floor is a Persian-style carpet in shades of red and brown.

Cassatt masterfully directs our eyes around the canvas with colors and lines. The bold stripes of the woman's dress lead our gaze—like hers—toward the child's feet, while the curve of the jug's handle mirrors the arch of the little girl's arm. Their heads touch, and the palpable sense of connection is completed in the holding of hand and foot; thanks to the lack of formality, we, too, feel within touching distance. Even the loose lock of hair that falls forward on the woman's forehead finds its match in the blue apostrophe-like swirl on the wall. Throughout are dashes of blue—outlining the towel and the girl's legs, as well as in the woman's hair. The effect is a bold and rhythmic image of the everyday.

Palette

A stripy robe in white, lilac, and green, a red carpet, and dashes of blue.

Complementary works

- Henriette Browne, *A Greek Captive*, 1863.
- Marie Bashkirtseff, *In the Studio*, 1881.
- Marie Bracquemond, *Under the Lamp*, 1887.

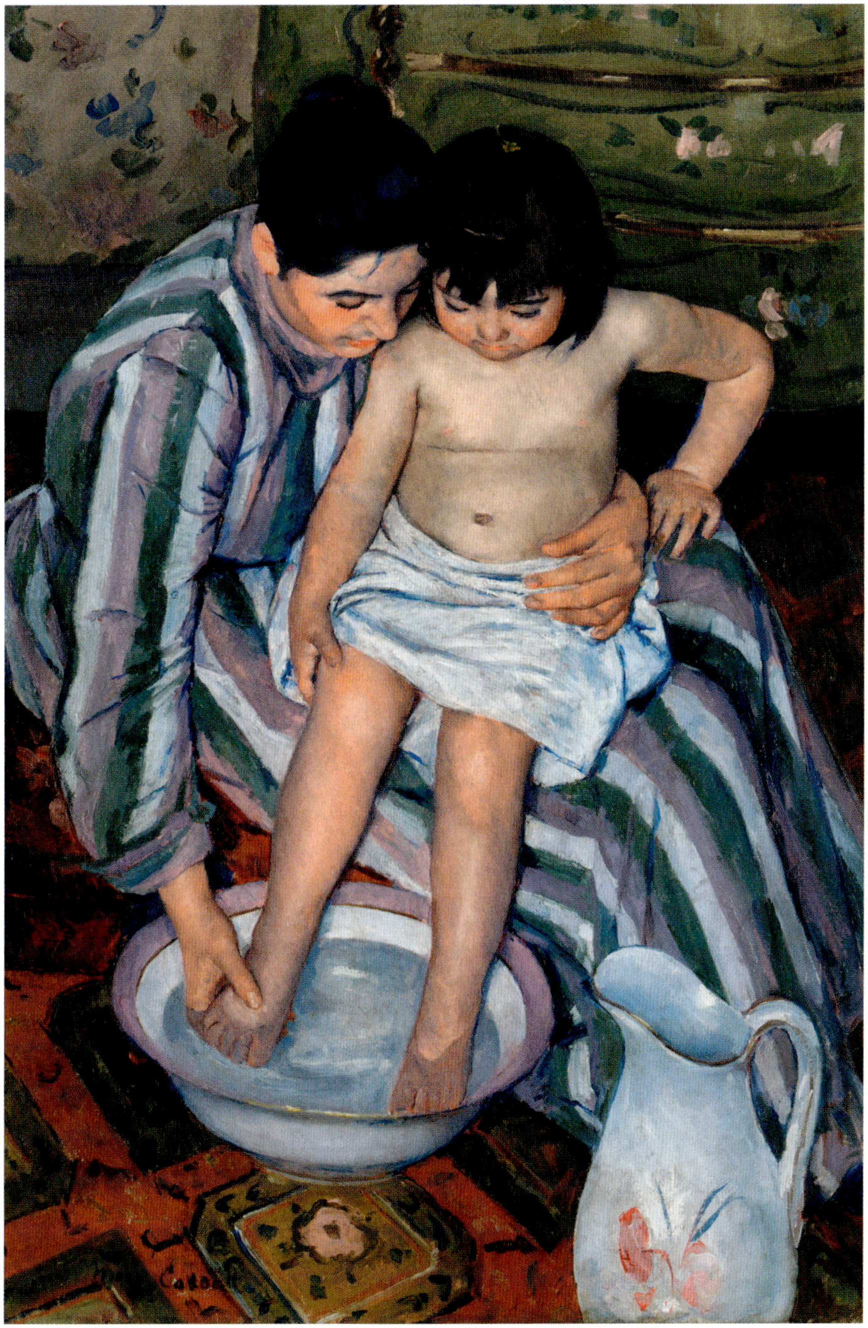

C12 M100 Y100 K30
R137 G21 B17

C0 M73 Y100 K20
R175 G80 B0

C6 M31 Y15 K0
R223 G187 B190

C5 M44 Y88 K10
R198 G141 B46

C5 M11 Y20 K0
R238 G226 B203

Hot head

Edgar Degas
Combing the Hair
1896

Oil on canvas,
5⅝ x 57¾ in (14.3 x 146.7 cm).

Hair brushing might not sound like a loaded subject, but in 1896 it was scandalous for a woman to untangle her tresses in public. The presence of a peeled-back curtain on the left of Degas's vast canvas hints at the fact that we're seeing something we shouldn't. The composition toggles between intimacy, eroticism, and violence —and that's before we even get to the fiery orange-red palette. In losing himself in variations of one color, the artist cranks up the claustrophobic nature of the scene. This is a shade associated with a range of emotions: love, lust, violence, and shame. Just looking makes the heat rise to one's cheeks.

The advent of new synthetic pigments in the 19th century didn't entirely wipe out old materials. Masaccio (*see page 36*) made use of vermilion-based red paints during the Renaissance and Degas did, too—in his case, red lead, Indian red, vermilion, and red lake, depending on the desired level of intensity. He painted over a white ground, which emerges from beneath the thinly coated tablecloth and at the curtain's tail end. He applied his paint in rough, rapid strokes, as though rushing to capture this stolen glimpse of a private scene. The force of his twitchy brush marks echoes that of the act he depicted: the way the seated young woman leans back and clings onto the crown of her head suggests that her maid is pulling hard and she's in pain.

Relief from the heat comes briefly in the form of the yellow comb and brush, as well as the maid's pink blouse. But the harsh black outline swiftly refocuses our attention on the underlying menace of this otherwise ordinary domestic scene. The back of the chair is groggy with shadow, the line ragged and vague. Elsewhere, it's crisp—the mistress's face is punctuated with sharply dashed eyebrows and dots for nostrils. The titular hair itself is uncontained, its color spilling out. In this late work, Degas moved away from the Impressionists' spontaneous use of color and used his reds as a metaphor for something altogether more unsettling.

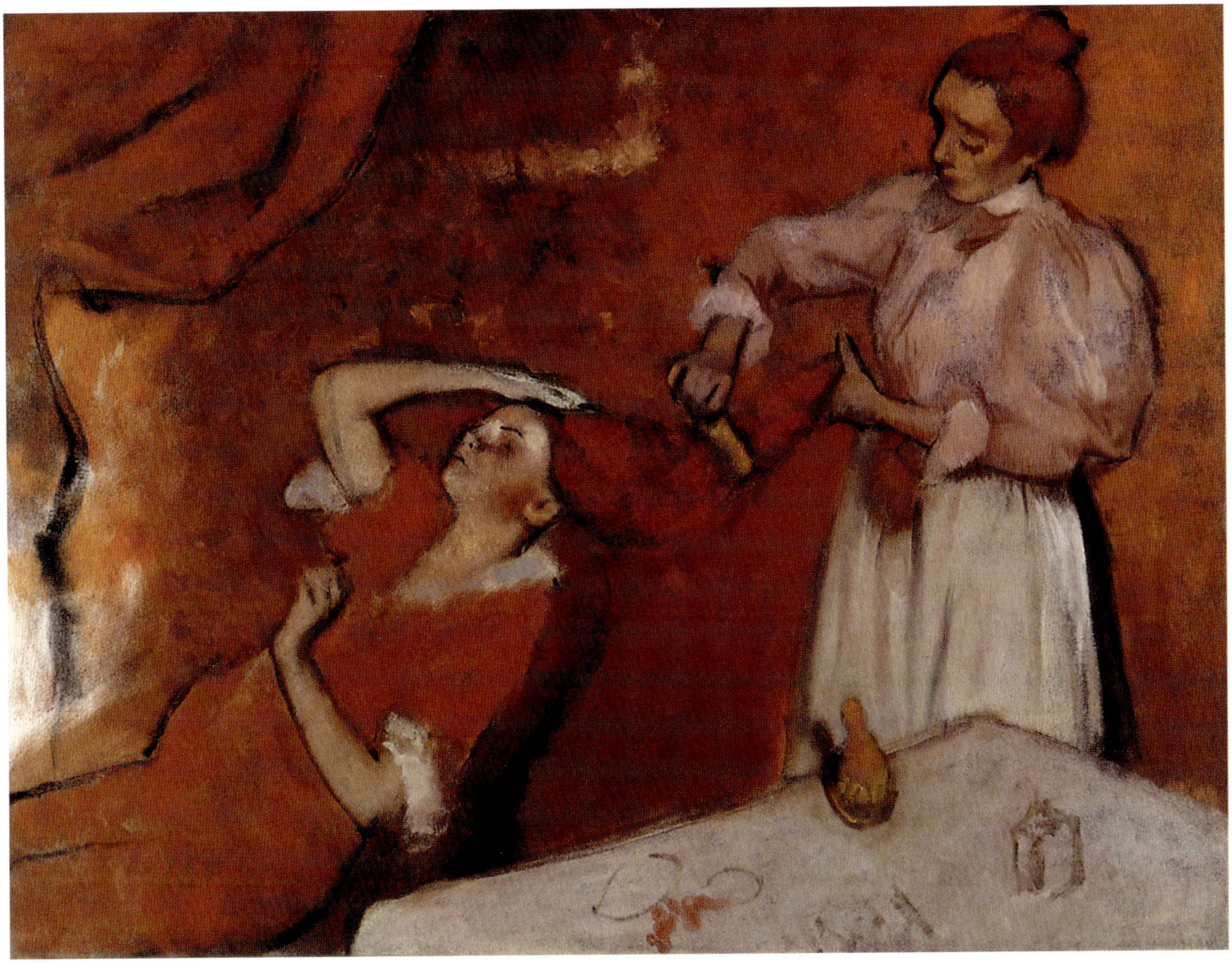

Palette

Fiery orange-red, with relief in the form of the yellow comb and brush and the maid's pink blouse.

Complementary works

- Richard Redgrave, *The Sempstress*, 1846.
- Jean-Louis Forain, *The Tub*, c.1886–67.
- Cecily Brown, *Combing the Hair (Côte d'Azur)*, 2013.

C68 M45 Y0 K10
R96 G117 B171

C34 M36 Y10 K0
R170 G160 B187

Get some air

Claude Monet
Waterloo Bridge, Blurred Sun
1903

Oil on canvas,
25⅞ × 39¾ in (65.7 × 101 cm).

There have been several theories—some more outlandish than others—as to why violet is so prevalent in Impressionist paintings. At the time, some critics suggested it was a symptom of "violettomania," a condition associated with hysteria. Others believed that Monet and his colleagues had the rare ability to see ultraviolet light, which is invisible to most eyes. Either way, the Impressionists' depiction of the world with such vibrant colors was unprecedented.

Monet's preference for this particular hue sprung from his belief that shadows were colored. Violet made sense as the complementary color to yellow (the sun), because it appeared opposite it on the spectrum. And so he used varying shades of violet, rather than black or gray, to create the impression of shadows and graduations of light. In this canvas from his sublime London series, the undulating arches beneath Waterloo Bridge and the distant chimneys billowing smoke on the factory-lined South Bank are a deep blue-purple, while the highlights on the rippling Thames are flecked with a pale pinkish violet. The only break from the violet is offered by the red and yellow daubs of paint dotting the bridge, designating the headlights of passing vehicles. In response to critics, Monet replied: "I have finally discovered the true color of the atmosphere. It is violet. Fresh air is violet. Three years from now everyone will work in violet."

Monet visited London three times between 1899 and 1901, and painted some of the city's most recognizable landmarks. From his window on the fifth floor at the Savoy hotel, he rose each morning and studied Waterloo Bridge in various weather conditions, before painting 41 variations of the stone structure upon his return to his studio in Giverny, northwest of Paris. His favorite: when the city was cloaked with fog and mist, its edges filed down and softened. With his carefully coordinated palette, he creates the impression that the architecture is dissolving into its surroundings: a harmonious and near-abstract impression of color, atmosphere, and ever-changing light that seems to shimmer.

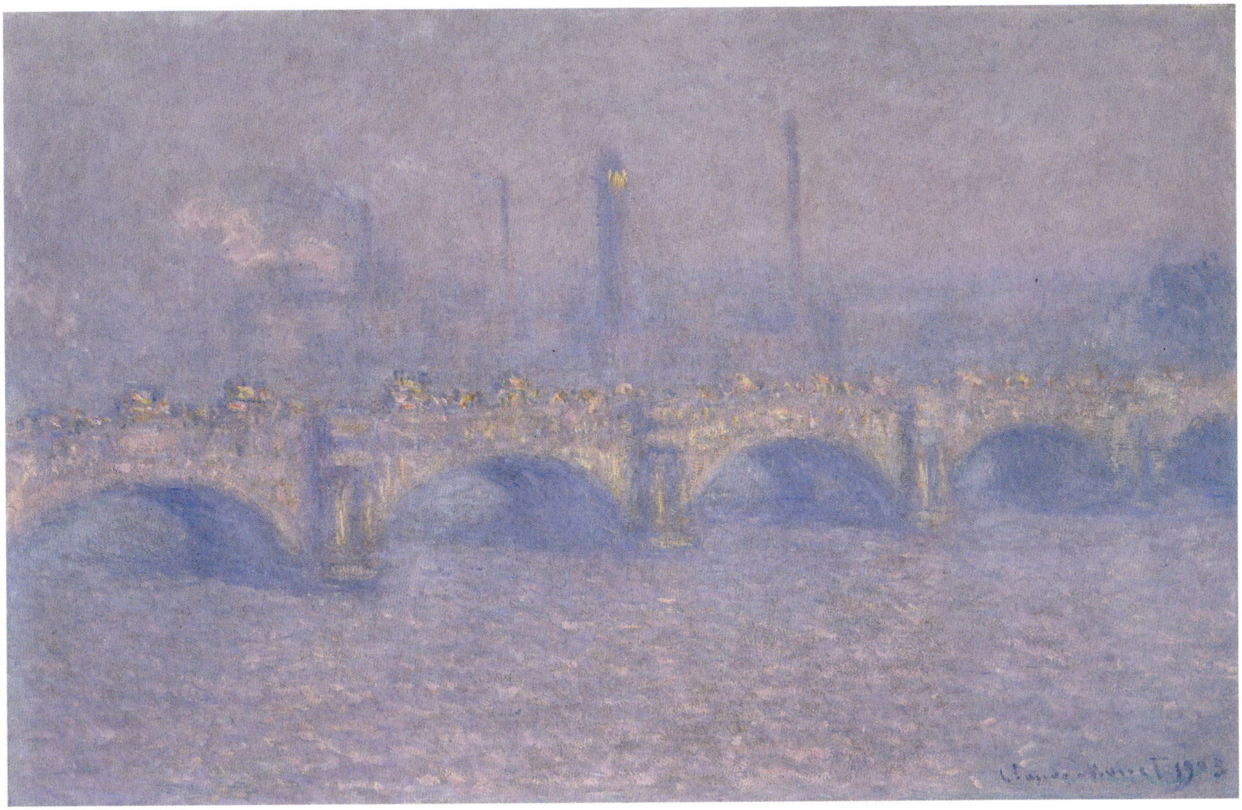

Palette

Varying shades of violet.

Complementary works

- Auguste Renoir, *Nini in the Garden (Nini Lopez)*, 1876.
- Armand Guillaumin, *Landscape with Ruins*, 1897.
- Francis Bacon, *Portrait of Michel Leiris*, 1976.

On the edge of the spectrum

From Pre-Raphaelites to Postimpressionists

C80 M40 Y20 K50
R49 G79 B101

On the edge of the spectrum

From Pre-Raphaelites to Postimpressionists

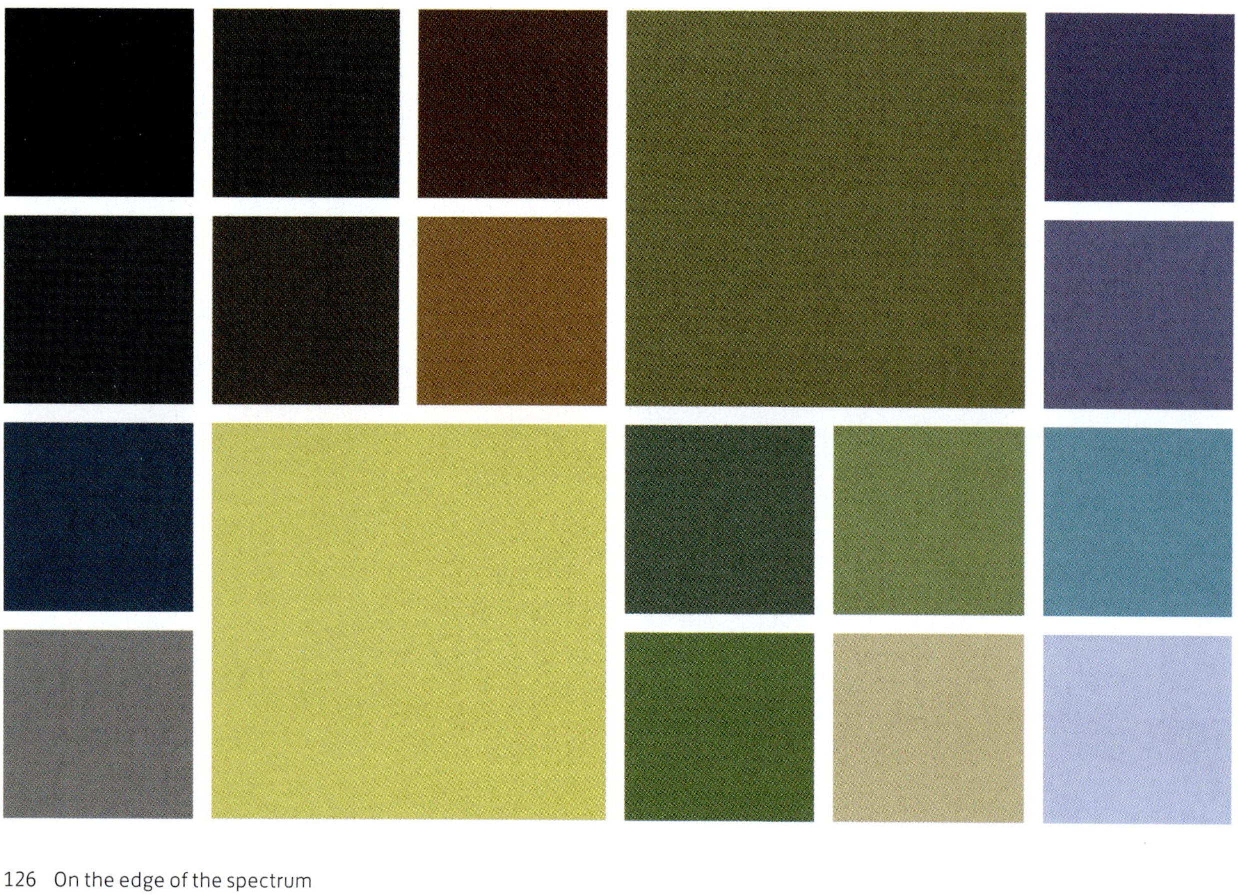

No matter how hard you try, the history of color—like the history of art—can't be packed into neat and tidy boxes. What one school sees as rules, another sees as rough guidelines; others disregard those completely and push the boundaries with their palettes, reconsidering what color is and could be. It's time to meet the outliers—groups and individuals who have flourished at the fringes.

In Paris in 1886, the Impressionists held their eighth and final exhibition. The show reunited several artists who had pitched up in previous years and also marked the debut of the Postimpressionist era. While their forebears were unified by a single approach—capturing mood, the play of light, a fleeting moment in time—these artists, who worked both alone and collectively, incorporated an assortment of techniques, subjects, and styles. Like the Impressionists, they let color lead—but on their palettes, color became artificial.

Across the varied works produced in and around Paris at the turn of the 20th century are common threads: emotional symbolism, saturated hues, and painterly brushstrokes. Led by Paul Cézanne and Paul Gauguin (*see page 136*), the Postimpressionists—so-called by the painter, critic and curator Roger Fry—placed emphasis on subjectivity and imagination. Rather than creating a realistic representation of the subjects they encountered in the studio or out on the street, they sought to evoke the sense of an inner world. As Fry writes in *An Essay in Aesthetics* (1909): "Art appreciates emotion in and for itself."

Out of this unwieldly group came smaller groups—among them, the self-proclaimed Nabis (Hebrew for "prophet"). Inspired by the liberating possibilities of Gauguin's experiments in abstraction, Paul Sérusier, Pierre Bonnard (*see page 142*), Édouard Vuillard (*see page 130*), and Maurice Denis embraced the decorative function of painting. Their works comprise flat patches of pure color and simplified forms with bold contours; like the Impressionists, they were inspired by the broad planes and repetitive patterns of Japanese prints. The Nabis freed color and form from their traditional representative functions and used them instead to express emotional and spiritual properties.

From Paris to London: a decade or so before the Impressionists rebelled against artistic convention across the pond, a secret society of young and plucky artists was founded in the U.K. capital. Inspired by the theories of the art critic John Ruskin, the Pre-Raphaelites came together in 1848 to create art that was true to nature. Revolting against the Royal Academy of Art's promotion of the ideal (epitomized by Raphael) and what they regarded as trivial genre painting, they sought to explore in paint the themes and subjects of religion, literature, and poetry, and recreate the vivid style of the Renaissance.

"As brown as my grandmother's painted tea tray" is how William Holman Hunt, who established the Pre-Raphaelite movement together with Dante Gabriel Rossetti and John Everett Millais, once described academic art. In comparison, he and the Pre-Raphaelites used the mid-19th century's newly synthesized pigments to create images with intense, bright colors. Among the vivid new pigments available was an emerald green, as seen in Millais's meticulously painted *Ophelia* (1851–52). The brotherhood—as the movement was known, despite the daring and talented women associated with it (*see page 128*) —used zinc white as a stark base coat to achieve maximum luminosity.

The possibilities are endless with a chapter on artists who wrote their own brief, but it would be wrong not to include a footnote on the Surrealists. Officially founded by the French writer and poet André Breton in 1924, when he wrote *The Surrealist Manifesto*, the movement explored the inner workings of the mind, championing imagination and the irrational over logic and reason. Artists employed dreamlike imagery rendered in either a highly saturated or monochrome palette. The aim: to unravel the unconscious.

C0 M55 Y20 K0
R218 G140 B155

C5 M74 Y89 K30
R152 G72 B30

C34 M70 Y76 K55
R90 G57 B36

Think pink

Evelyn de Morgan

Night and Sleep

1878

Oil on canvas,
$42\frac{13}{16}$ x $62\frac{1}{8}$ in (108.8 x 157.8 cm).

Night drifts through an evening sky of lightly spun clouds in a dusky-pink robe, her brown cloak billowing out like a bedsheet and casting a shadow over the rural landscape. Floating alongside her is her son, Sleep, in a bright-red hat and a single-shouldered russet robe that falls to just above the knee. He's clutching an armful of pink poppies—a nod to the opium poppies from which the Victorian sleeping drug laudanum was made—and casually scattering them across the earth. Night's eyes are closed, Sleep's lids heavy. The allegorical scene is soft and mesmerizing, and at the same time sculptural—the folds of fabric reminiscent of classical stone-carved drapery.

De Morgan, who was born in 1855, painted this richly colored canvas when she was just 23. Despite her wealthy upper-class background, and the social conventions that discouraged her from working, she became one of the first women to enrol at the Slade School of Art, where she developed a rigorous creative practice. Throughout her career, she looked to both classical and Renaissance art: the composition of this early oil painting was inspired by Botticelli's *The Birth of Venus* (*see page 45*), with Night and Sleep replacing Zephyr and Aura, and poppies replacing roses. Her rich and jewellike palette is characteristic of the Pre-Raphaelites, with whom she was associated; her style was often compared to that of Edward Burne-Jones. She was one of the few women mixed up with the brotherhood to receive formal training and become a professional artist.

A spiritualist with a keen interest in mythology, de Morgan uses color here to conjure atmosphere and create a sense of movement. Caught between her brown cloak and the russet robe of her son, Night drifts forward, pink and featherlight. Depicted in a matching shade, the strewn poppies plot the pair's path, and the cloak stretches out to the sides of the canvas, shrouding us in darkness, along with the sky. There's beauty and innocence in the luscious shades, and yet the brown adds a hint of melancholy.

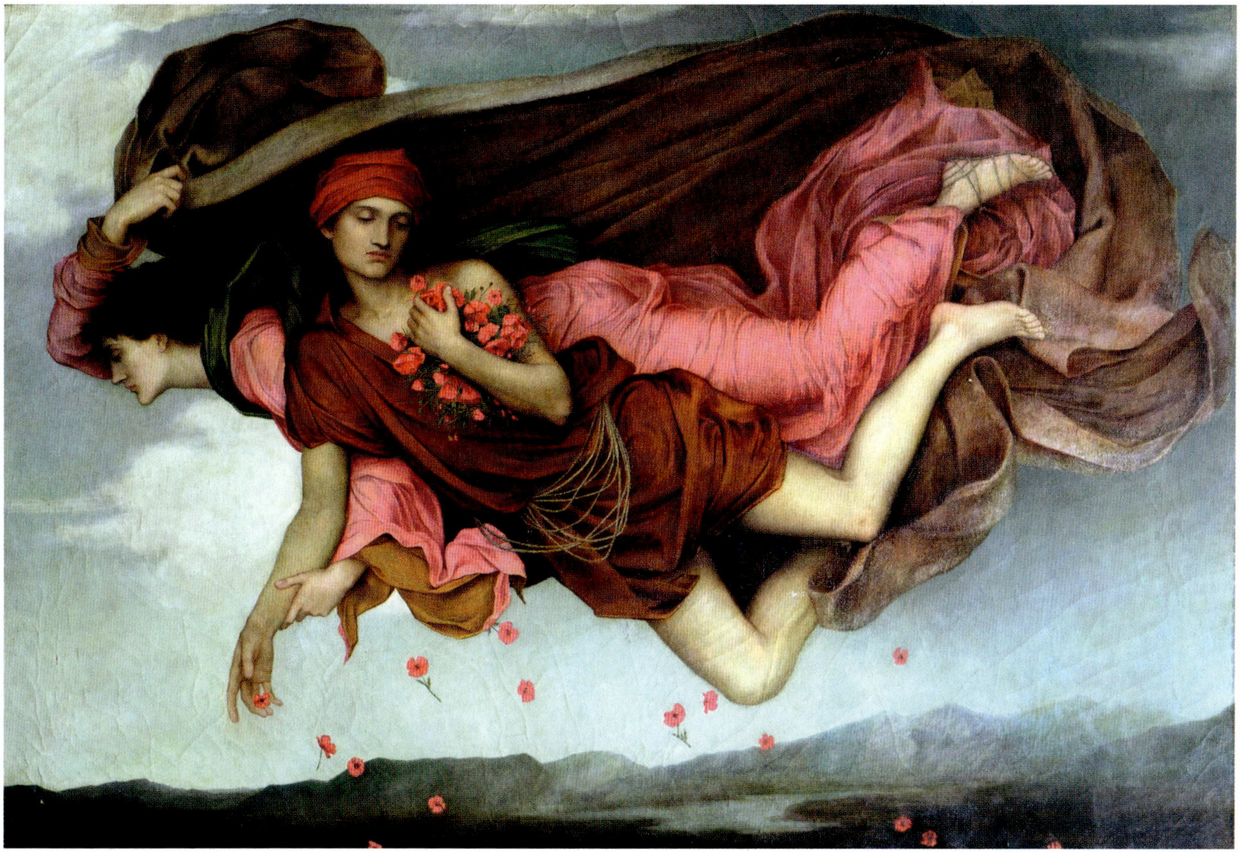

Palette

Dusky-pink, russet, and brown robes and cloaks.

Complementary works

- John Everett Millais, *A Huguenot on Saint Bartholomew's Day*, 1851–52.
- Ford Madox Brown, *The Last of England,* 1855.
- William Holman Hunt, *Isabella and the Pot of Basil*, 1868.

C24 M50 Y89 K45
R118 G89 B31

C5 M60 Y88 K5
R198 G116 B45

C0 M14 Y60 K0
R245 G217 B125

C40 M24 Y10 K5
R159 G169 B192

C80 M53 Y25 K58
R44 G60 B80

Letting color loose

Édouard Vuillard
The Suitor
1893

Oil on millboard panel,
$12\frac{1}{2}$ x $14\frac{5}{16}$ in (31.8 x 36.4 cm).

Color threatens to take over in this ornamental panel: a mass of mustard, lemon, and saffron yellow. You can just make out the curve of a table in the foreground and, alongside it, a wicker stool with stubby legs. To the left, a large table is topped with a lilac sheet, and beyond is the arched back of a chair and what looks like a wardrobe, tall and straight. To the right, a glass door into another room. Amid it all, three figures: the artist's mother and sister—absorbed in their task, each clutching at fabric—and his fellow bearded Nabi in navy blue, peering around a door whose outline has dissolved into the mottled wallpaper.

Inspired by medieval tapestries, Vuillard the theater designer began painting decorative interiors in the 1890s. His mother had a sewing business, which she ran from their various Paris apartments. Far from providing a refuge, the artist's domestic scenes distill episodes of bourgeois life and family drama. One of his first major paintings, *The Suitor* nods to the opening act of his sister Marie's unhappy marriage to the painter Kerr-Xavier Roussel, who had an affair. Like the furniture, the figures almost disintegrate into the background—a reflection perhaps of 19th-century social constraints. This might be a bright and lavish work, but beneath the surface is a knotty subtext: the painted patterns are rich with secrets.

More than anything, though, Vuillard's work is about color. The swatch of material in electric blue. The luminous yellow in Marie's hair and the speckled design of her dress. The navy shadow of her mother, who reaches forward as she works. Scraps of bright white provide a quick reprieve. The painting teeters on abstract—and yet, like Bonnard (*see page 142*), Vuillard is able to create a sense of texture and depth within his flat and decorative designs. Stare at the painting for long enough and the colors begin to blur, until you're left with one great chromatic field of pleasure.

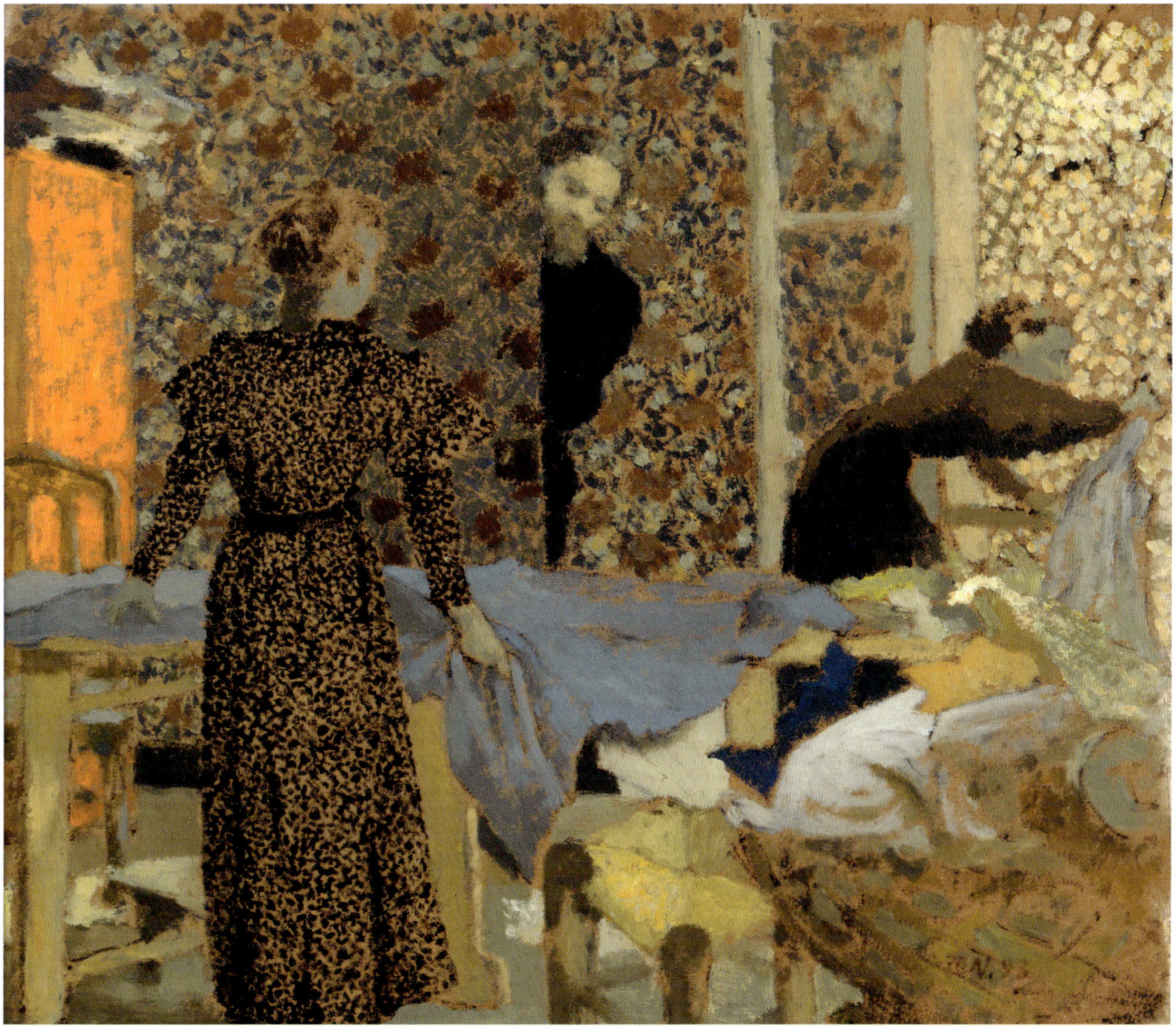

Palette

A mass of mustard, lemon, and saffron yellow, a lilac sheet, and a bearded Nabi in navy blue.

Complementary works

- Paul Sérusier, *The Talisman*, 1888.
- Maurice Denis, *September Evening*, 1891.
- Njideka Akunyili Crosby, *Mother and Child,* 2016.

Artist's block

Félix Vallotton

The Visit

1899

Gouache on cardboard,
21⅞ × 34¼ in (55.5 × 87 cm).

C63 M55 Y10 K13
R101 G103 B147

C75 M73 Y15 K24
R72 G67 B113

C63 M25 Y56 K35
R89 G113 B92

C0 M68 Y85 K5
R202 G101 B47

C60 M60 Y60 K60
R64 G58 B49

Born in the Swiss city of Lausanne, Vallotton peeled away from his strict Protestant family to study art in Paris at the age of sixteen. In the 1890s he became associated with the Nabis; Vuillard (*see page 130*) was a lifelong friend and, like his contemporaries, Vallotton was influenced by the Postimpressionist style of Gauguin (*see page 136*), as well as Japanese ukiyo-e. Inspired by these woodblock prints, he created bold images with flat blocks of offbeat color and stylized forms. But his vision is also unique—uniquely strange, some say. Almost all his work exudes an air of mystery.

In *The Visit*, a man and a woman linger at the edge of a highly decorative room. She's dressed in a purple coat trimmed with pink and green, and wears a feather hat dashed with blue; he wears a brown suit. He grips her hand in his and curls the other around her back, gently arched. The cut-out composition is divided in two, with the couple on one side and the promise (or is it a threat?) of an open door to a bedroom on the other. The interior itself—complete with a sickly green wall, orange floor, a blocky purple-blue sofa, and that floral rug—adds to the mounting sense of pressure. Who is the visitor, here? Is the man paying by the hour, or have we chanced upon the culmination of a long and loving courtship?

The extreme color contrasts and linear composition ramp up the puzzling nature of Vallotton's narrative, painted in gouache on cardboard. Though surely gloved, the white tips of the woman's fingers poking out from the man's hand suggest he's squeezing tight. The sharp stripes and zigzags on the floor act as barriers, slowing the pair's progression. And then there's the green carpet, or perhaps it's a shadow, seeping out from beneath the obscure red armchair in the foreground—if that doesn't conjure a sense of unease, what does? Vallotton offers up a narrative and at the same time withholds it.

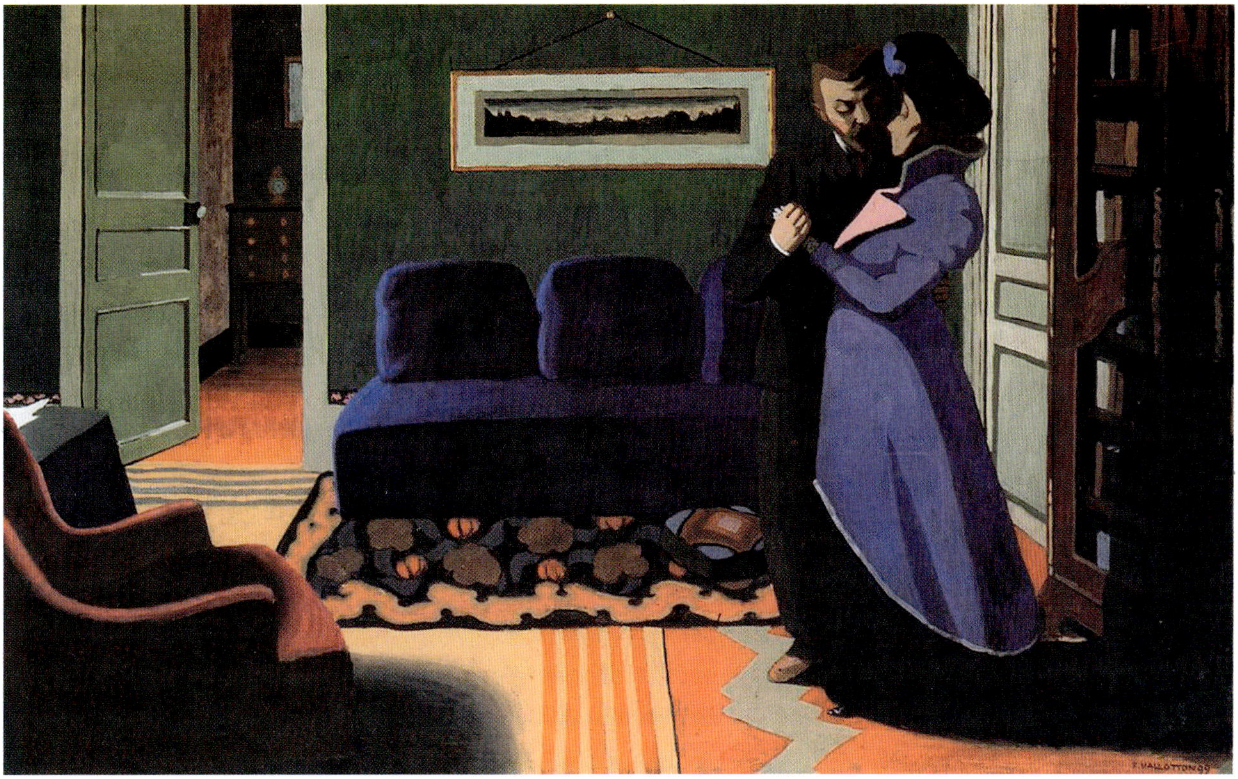

Palette

A woman in a purple coat and a man in a brown suit. Plus, a sickly green wall, orange floor, and a blocky purple-blue sofa.

Complementary works

- Arthur Hughes, *April Love*, 1855–56.
- Ferdinand Hodler, *The Night*, 1889–90.
- Edward Hopper, *Cape Cod Morning*, 1950.

Shades of gray

Vilhelm Hammershøi

Interior. Strandgade 30

1901

Oil on canvas,
$18\frac{5}{16} \times 20\frac{1}{2}$ in (46.5 x 52 cm).

While his contemporaries were creating bright and colorful canvases in Paris, Hammershøi was producing small and precise paintings of gray interiors in his native Copenhagen. Unlike the homes of the bourgeoisie, fussily filled with belongings, he preferred his interiors spare and pure. When he and his wife, Ida Ilsted, moved into their flat at Strandgade 30, he had the decorators paint it plainly and it was furnished minimally. In this geometric canvas, the only pieces of furniture on show are the plain wooden chair, a pair of framed pictures, and what looks like a writing desk. The space is homely but bare, and Hammershøi's rendering of it poetic but melancholy.

There's a great stillness to the Danish artist's canvas. A stillness that's accentuated by the restrained palette and simple patches of color: dark brown floorboards that in places have a steely-gray sheen, pale dove-gray walls with sandy cut outs, eggshell-white doors. He painted with four hues—black, brown, gray, and white —and though he captured all the tones of each, critics struggled to understand his color scheme's subtle nuances. Asked, in an interview in 1907, why he used an austere palette, Hammershøi said, "It feels natural to me. I most certainly think that a picture works best, in purely coloristic terms, the fewer colors it has." He painted slowly and deliberately, applying layer upon layer; sometimes he finished a picture with a thin wash of gray, bathing it in a fine silvery mist.

Hammershøi and his wife lived at Strandgade 30 from 1898 until 1909. Throughout his career, he depicted their flat, often with Ida seen from the back. Here, our eye is drawn to the cold, natural light filtering through the window. Glimpsed through an open door, Ida lurks in the shadows, the hem of her almost black dress just beyond reach of the pool of light on the floor. She holds up her hands, as if she's reading, and her hair is pinned up on her head, revealing the milky nape of her neck. Without her, the canvas would be utterly quiet, still; with her, it's mysterious, dreamlike. In paint, Hammershøi attempts to conjure up her inner world.

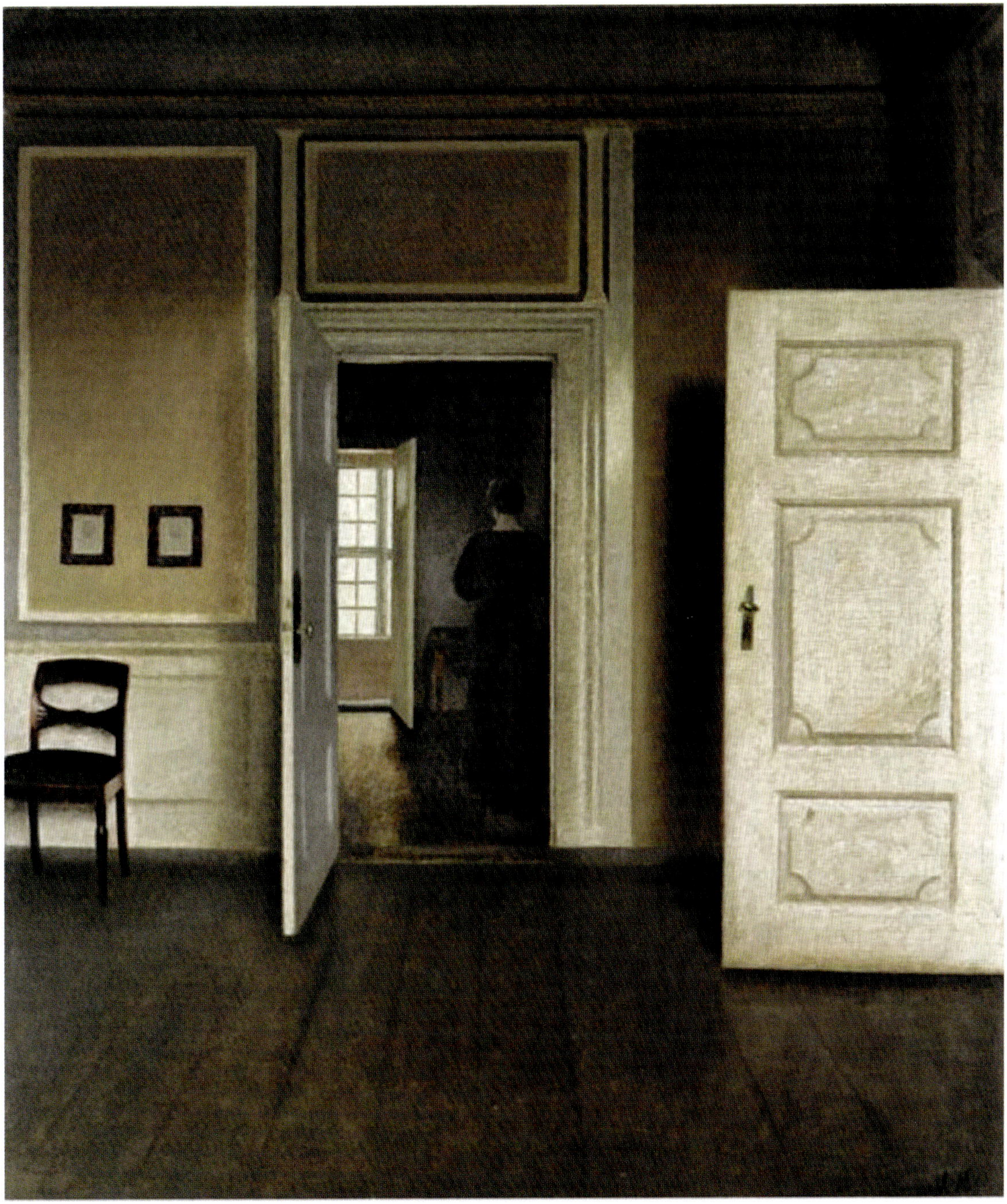

Palette

Dark brown floorboards that in places have a steely-gray sheen, pale dove-gray walls with sandy cut outs, eggshell-white doors.

Complementary works

- Georges Seurat, *Gray Weather, Grande Jatte*, c.1886–88.
- Peter Ilsted, *Interior with Girl Reading*, 1908.
- Carl Holsøe, *Waiting by the Window*, 1935.

C20 M48 Y80 K29
R146 G111 B53

C5 M74 Y85 K0
R199 G90 B48

C53 M50 Y14 K15
R118 G113 B146

C39 M15 Y64 K20
R145 G156 B100

Troubled dreams

Paul Gauguin
Barbarian Tales
1902

Oil on canvas,
$51\frac{3}{16}$ x 35 in (130 x 89 cm).

Gauguin believed that color had the power to spark the imagination. He railed against scientific and literary explanations of its effects, and instead encouraged artists to "join the battle for painting through color" and use it enigmatically. His polychrome palette was more subjective than objective, more otherworldly than real. Together with his subject matter and boldly outlined forms, it contained meaning and, most importantly, mystery.

In this provocative canvas, painted a year before his death in the Marquesas Islands, the Postimpressionist artist uses color to acknowledge his fascination with "exotic" female flesh. Two Polynesian women, beautiful and serene, are depicted among tropical flora and fauna, their warm brown skin glowing in the light. One sits upright with her legs crossed, in the traditional pose of the Buddha, a coral earring shining bright against her black hair. The other leans forward on her knees, with white and green flowers in her fiery locks. A patch of blue sky crowns the jumble of greenery, swirled with smoke, and pale pink and white plants provide relief from the saturated scene. Behind the women is a devilish European interloper, thought to be Gauguin's friend and fellow artist, Meyer de Haan, in a purple-blue robe. His eyes are a lurid green, his red toenails clawlike and his skin a sickly shade of pink.

With funding from the French government, Gauguin had set sail for Tahiti in the 1890s, and he lived and painted in the South Pacific for the rest of his life. He wanted to escape the conventions of European society and unleash his creativity free from so-called civilization. He found pleasure in this new world—and, in particular, in its native women, whom he sensuously painted, often naked. In *Barbarian Tales*, Gauguin appears to acknowledge that his portraits, though striking, are part of a colonial and misogynist fantasy. Crouching behind the stoical bold nudes, who are at peace in the lush setting, the Western voyeur tugs at his beard, uncomfortable and out of place.

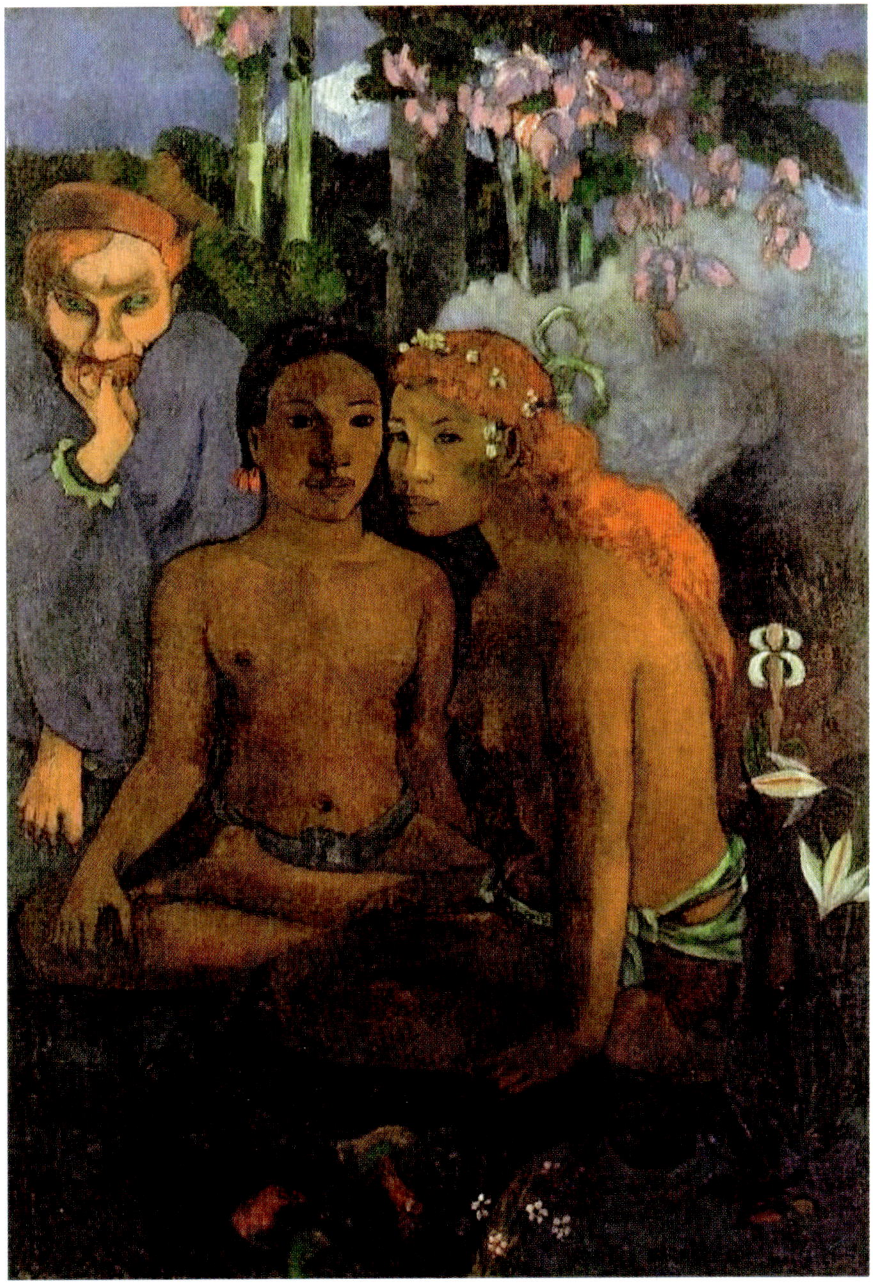

Palette

Warm brown, lurid green, purple-blue, and red.

Complementary works

- Vincent van Gogh, *La Berceuse (Woman Rocking a Cradle; Augustine-Alix Pellicot Roulin, 1851–1930)*, 1889.
- Paul Cézanne, *Bibemus. The Red Rock*, 1897.
- Henri Rousseau, *The Dream*, 1910.

Color communication

One of the reasons why you can't pack the history of color into neat and tidy boxes is because its use and reception vary according to context. Culture, geography, religion, politics: each of these has an impact on how artists, patrons, and viewers interpret an artwork's palette. It depends on its purpose—whether a work is functional or purely decorative—and societal expectations, even regulations. It also depends, quite simply, on what language you speak.

Humans categorize colors differently. In English there are eleven basic color terms: black, white, red, green, yellow, blue, pink, gray, brown, orange, and purple. Several languages don't have words for yellow, pink, and brown, while some use the same term for blue and green. The Russians have two words for blue—*goluboy* (light blue) and *siniy* (dark blue)—and regard them as distinct hues. Some communities have no color terms at all: Bassa, for example, spoken in Liberia and Sierra Leone, has only two words for grouping cool and warm colors: *hui* (blue, green, violet, and black) and *ziza* (white, yellow, orange, and red).

A community's vocabulary is largely determined by context—colors that are considered important or meaningful require a name—but there are some consistencies within different languages. A recent study by MIT cognitive scientists found that in general there are more words for hues in the warm part of the spectrum than those in the cool part. A reflection, perhaps, of the fact that oranges, yellows, and reds regularly appear in the foreground, whereas cooler colors, such as green and blue, are often relegated to the backdrop.

Of course, nothing is fixed—as individuals cross borders, so too do ideas and influences. Context can be personal as well as cultural and an artist's use of color subject to change. The first painting that Amrita Sher-Gil created when she returned from Paris to India in the mid-1930s saw her moving away from the academic style she'd picked up in Europe and revisiting Indian miniature painting traditions. *Three Girls* (1935) is an intimate portrait of three desolate young women on the cusp of adulthood and, most likely, marriage. Their solemn expressions are juxtaposed with the vibrant reds, oranges, and minty greens of their clothes, which in turn contrast with the murky background. "I am personally trying to be, through the medium of line, color, and design, an interpreter of the life of the people, particularly the life of the poor and sad," said Sher-Gil.

So, what does color communicate? It depends on the standpoint of both the artist and the audience, as well as the circumstances in which a work is made and viewed. With her fresh perspective, Sher-Gil interpreted the lives of her three girls as rich with color; with her palette, she drew attention to their plight. After a while, there's only so much that vocabulary can convey—as Louise Bourgeois once said, "Color is stronger than language. It's a subliminal communication."

Amrita Sher-Gil, *Three Girls*, 1935, oil on canvas, 36⅜ × 26³⁄₁₆ in (92.5 × 66.6 cm).

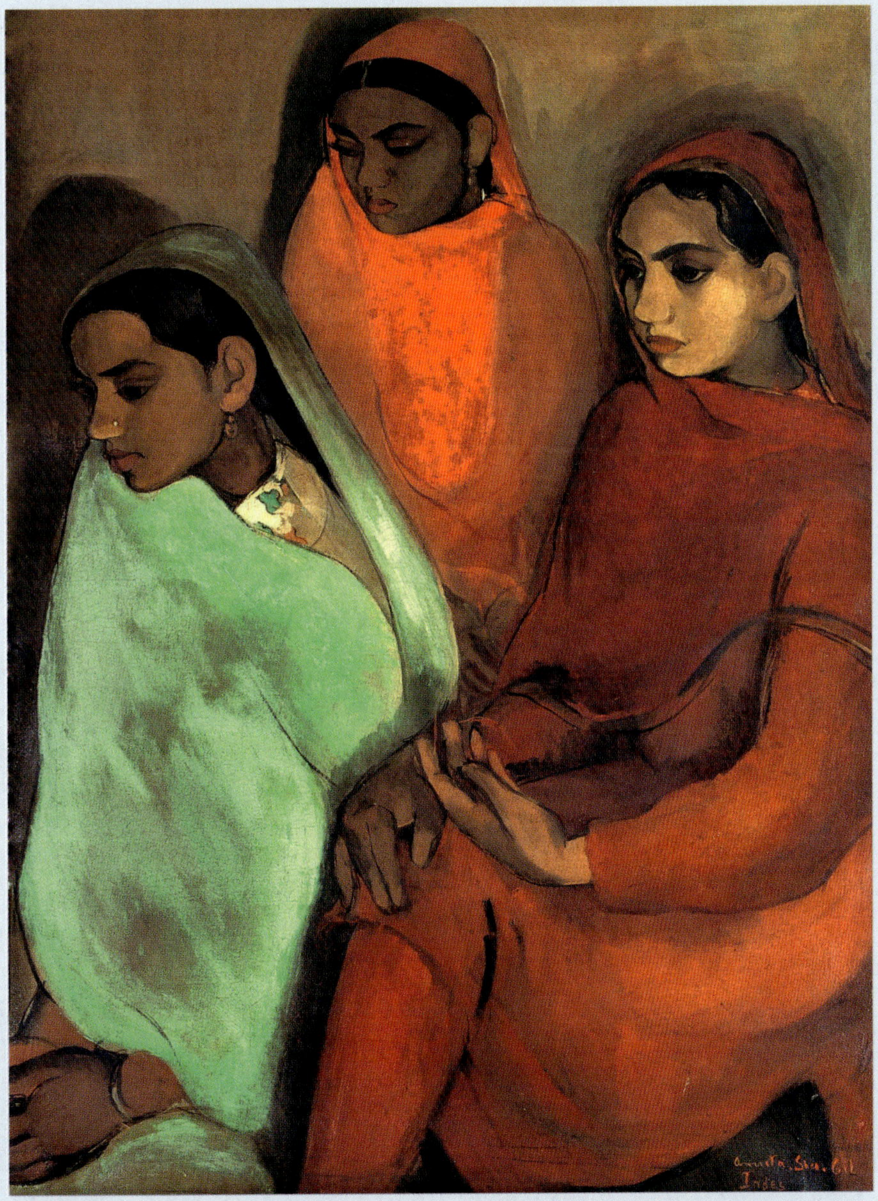

C79 M40 Y19 K50
R51 G79 B102

C69 M10 Y16 K10
R99 G158 B182

C9 M5 Y19 K0
R234 G234 B211

C3 M0 Y0 K6
R237 G241 B243

Feeling blue

Pablo Picasso
The Life
1903

Oil on canvas,
77$\frac{3}{8}$ x 50$\frac{7}{8}$ in (196.5 x 129.2 cm).

It was in 1901 that Picasso plunged into his so-called Blue Period. He was 21 years old, not yet successful, and low on funds. He was also mourning the loss of his close friend and fellow Spanish art student, Carles Casagemas, who had committed suicide at the start of the year after being rejected by the woman he loved. "It was thinking about Casagemas that got me started painting in blue," Picasso later told his friend and biographer Pierre Daix. This vast canvas, created in Barcelona, comprises cold and gloomy shades that reflect the despondent artist's preoccupation with sorrow, isolation, and death.

La Vie, as it's known in French, has been variously interpreted as an allegory of sacred love and a symbol of the circle of life. According to one reading, the naked couple—their outlined skin bruised an unnatural bluish cream—are Casagemas and the object of his affection, the model Germaine Pichot, all of a sudden devoted. Opposite is a woman in a dusky blue robe cradling a baby in a blue-tinted white cloth; Casagemas raises a finger toward the child, as if to acknowledge the future family he could have had. Beyond the group are two paintings: one showing a bare couple huddling together for warmth, the other a solitary woman folded forward over her knees. According to another reading, the painting is autobiographical: Picasso with a lover, reflecting on his infancy and contemplating old age.

Throughout his career, Picasso experimented with color. He painted in twilight blues from 1901 until 1904, and afterward his palette thawed into a blushed rose. At times, he restricted his canvases to monochromatic shades of gray or earth tones. "Colors, like features, follow the changes of the emotions," he said in the 1930s. Here, melancholy seeps toward us, threatening to engulf us as it has done the artist. *The Life* is the culmination of Picasso's obsession with the themes of loneliness and longing—and yet misery is muddled with beauty and elegance.

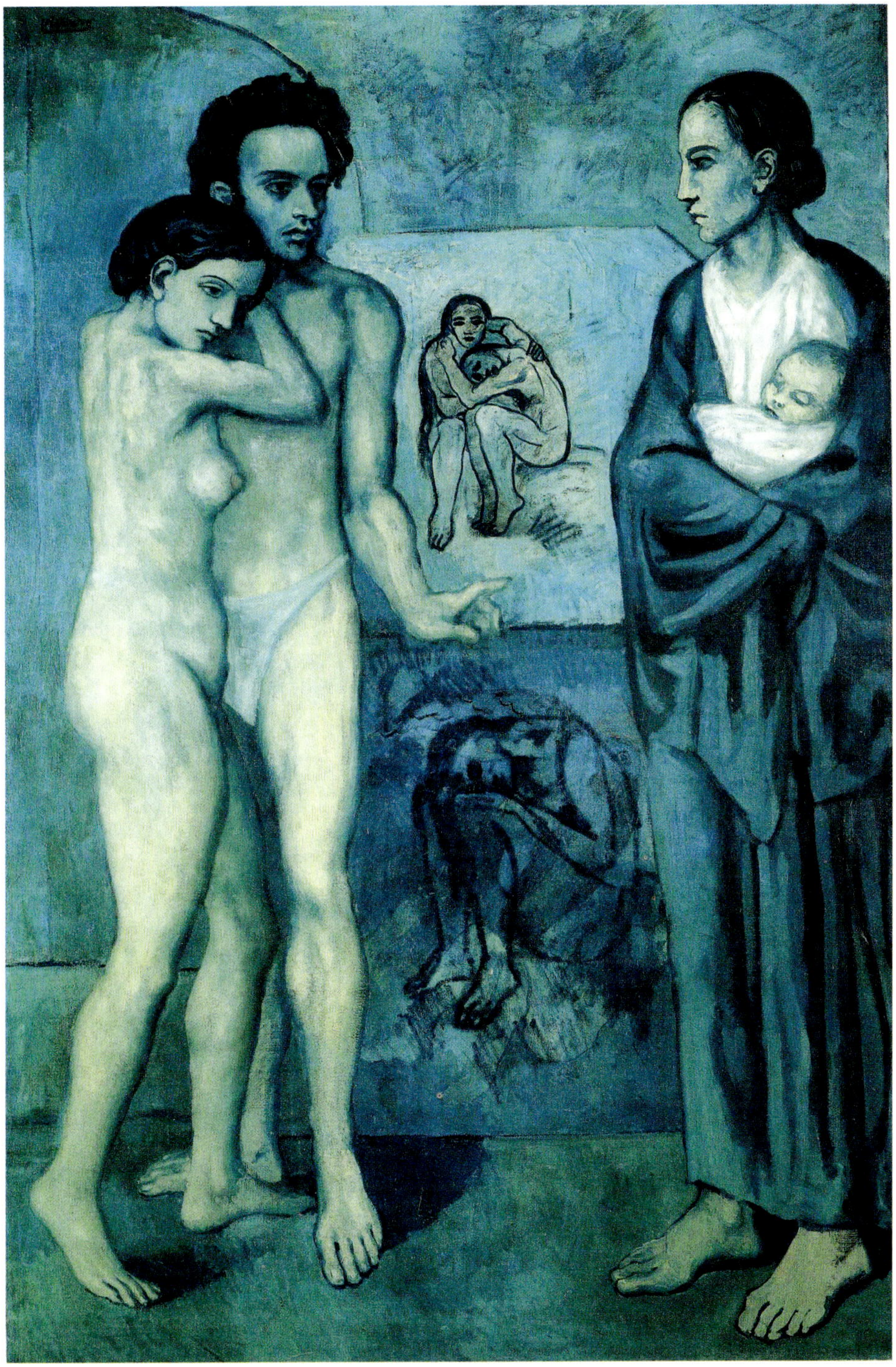

Palette

Twilight blues, white, and cream.

Complementary works

- Chaim Soutine, *Woman in Blue, c.*1919.
- Amedeo Modigliani, *Alice*, 1919.
- Alice Neel, *Benjamin*, 1976.

C58 M20 Y75 K25
R107 G130 B77

C0 M55 Y88 K5
R209 G127 B44

C0 M25 Y97 K0
R237 G190 B19

C25 M47 Y20 K0
R181 G145 B162

C31 M15 Y0 K0
R186 G199 B229

Splendor of color

Pierre Bonnard
The Green Blouse
1919

Oil on canvas,
40⅛ × 26⅞ in (101.9 × 68.3 cm).

The color palette of this oil on canvas by Bonnard slips between reality and a dreamlike state. The bowl of fruit in the foreground is true to life, with red-and-green apples, pale grapes, and clementines that catch the light. A South of France landscape glimpsed through the window is also realistic: painted at dusk, perhaps, the palm trees are swaying against the sea, and the sky is glowing blue, yellow, and green. The natural light illuminates the tabletop, a silvery lilac. When it comes to the two figures, though, reality begins to unravel: the face of the figure on the left is a saturated orange, while the yellow dye of the striped curtain appears to have leaked from the fabric into the hair and flesh of the woman sitting in front of it.

Bonnard's handling of color is at times inventive, at others bizarre, and also controversial: Henri Matisse (*see page 166*) called him "a rare and courageous painter," while Picasso (*see page 140*) described his paintings as a "potpourri of indecision." Bonnard preferred to paint from memory, imagining a scene rather than recreating it. From 1912, his palette became more fervent, almost Fauvist; he intensified his hues and used them to pull out the narrative elements that mattered most. With him through it all was Marthe de Méligny; the pair met in Paris in 1893 and lived together for more than 30 years before they married. She crops up in countless canvases—resting, bathing, gardening.

The French artist captured these everyday moments through color and composition. The hazy vertical and horizontal lines of the yellow curtain and the windowsill provide structure, while the shift in hues from warm to cool distinguishes between indoors and out. Marthe's hair and flesh may be on the brink of blending with the backdrop, but her green blouse stands out. In her husband's art, she never aged, and here she looks younger than her 50 years, blue eyes shining bright. Bonnard used color in a subjective and unconventional way to piece together his past, just as he liked it.

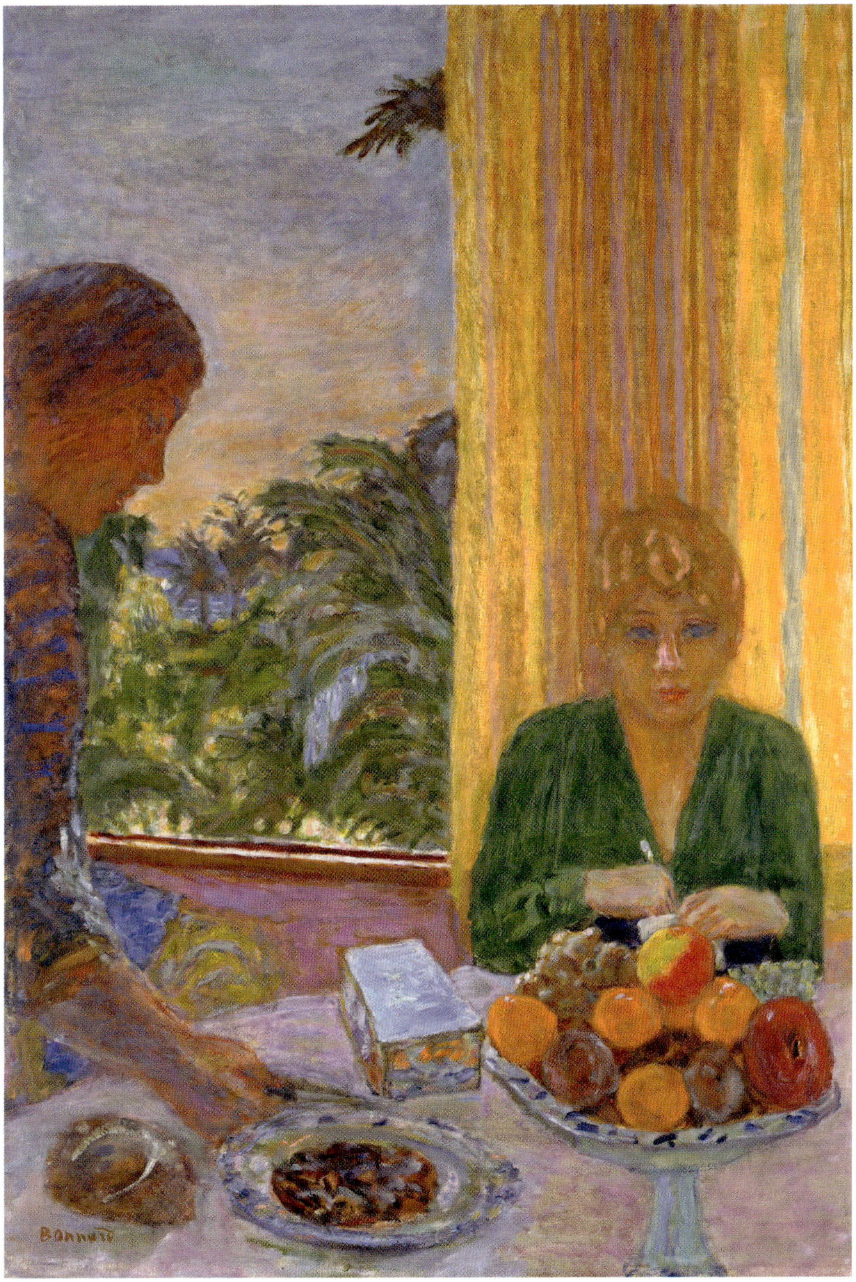

Palette

The titular green blouse, saturated orange skin, a silvery lilac tabletop, and a sky that glows blue, yellow, and green.

Complementary works

- Georges Braque, *Landscape at L'Estaque*, 1907.
- Natalia Goncharova, *Self-Portraits with Yellow Lilies*, 1907–08.
- Frances Hodgkins, *Loveday and Ann: Two Women with a Basket of Flowers*, 1915.

C10 M48 Y30 K0
R205 G150 B149

C10 M88 Y90 K19
R158 G50 B32

C78 M59 Y30 K74
R35 G41 B53

C10 M18 Y55 K00
R223 G202 B132

C24 M30 Y80 K34
R141 G126 B57

C56 M33 Y79 K65
R65 G72 B37

At first blush

Suzanne Valadon

The Abandoned Doll

1921

Oil on canvas,
20⅛ x 13 in (51 x 32 cm).

Two figures perch on the edge of a bed that's topped with a heavy crimson quilt. Both turn to the left, their feet resting one in front of the other on a yellow rug printed with a geometric pattern. The girl, who's naked apart from a flouncy pink hair ribbon, gazes intently at her reflection in a small handheld mirror, while her fully clothed companion towels her dry. Discarded on the floor is a doll, whose rosy ribbon matches her owner's. As the girl turns away, it appears that, just as she no longer needs the comfort of her doll's presence, she also does not wish for the help of her companion.

Valadon began drawing when she was nine and, after a string of unsuccessful jobs, became an artist's model at fifteen. It was partly by observing the techniques of Pierre-Auguste Renoir, Edgar Degas (*see page 118*) and Henri de Toulouse-Lautrec that she taught herself to paint, but the style she developed—with a bold outline and a vivid palette—was very much her own. Throughout her life, she produced frank self-portraits and images of women that raised important questions about aging, beauty, and female desire. Here she explores the complicated stage in a girl's life when she's suddenly more of a woman than a child.

Color contributes to the psychological mood of this intimate coming-of-age portrait. Together with the close crop of the composition, the mossy green tinge of the floor and walls lends the work a claustrophobic and slightly unsettling feel. The pink of the girl's ribbon evokes a youthful innocence, while that of her flushed cheeks hints at her budding self-awareness and sexual curiosity. Her flesh is a muddle of peach, yellow, and green, with a warmth that's missing from the pasty legs of the older woman, clad in smooth, pale stockings. The exposure of the girl's changing body may suggest vulnerability, but the bold border around it also hints at her inner strength and capability.

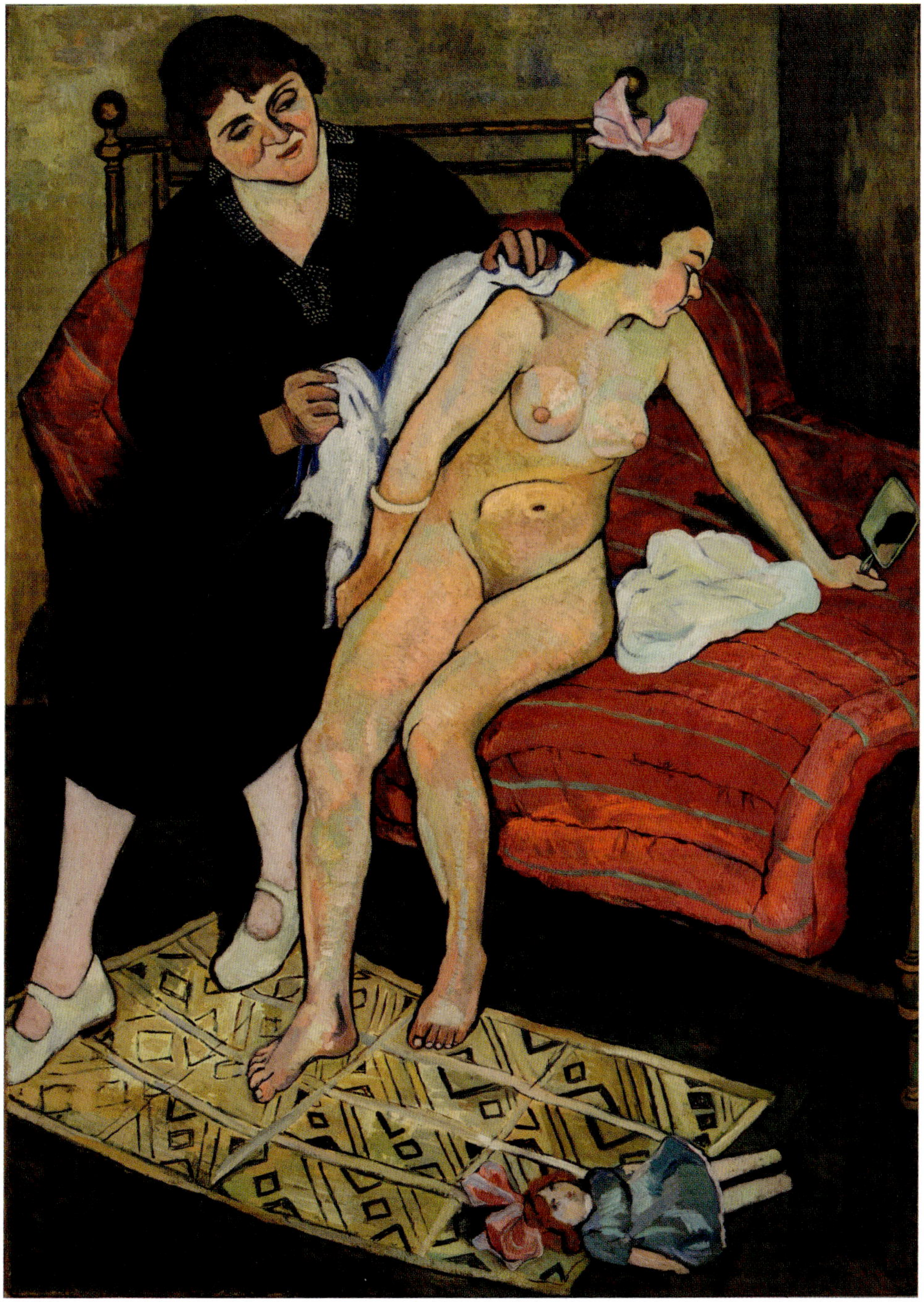

Palette

A flouncy pink hair ribbon, a heavy crimson quilt, a navy-blue dress, a yellow rug, and a green floor.

Complementary works

- Gwen John, *Girl with Bare Shoulders*, *c.*1909–10.
- Florine Stettheimer, *A Model (Nude Self-Portrait)*, 1915–16.
- Madeleine Thien, *Pan Yuliang, Narcissism*, *c.*1929.

In life, as in art

Frida Kahlo

The Two Fridas

1939

Oil on canvas,
$68\frac{5}{16}$ × 68 in (173.5 × 173 cm).

C70 M58 Y0 K20
R84 G91 B145

C58 M45 Y0 K0
R123 G131 B186

C0 M40 Y78 K0
R227 G164 B72

C25 M35 Y69 K25
R151 G132 B79

C0 M3 Y0 K6
R241 G238 B240

C5 M86 Y94 K20
R163 G54 B26

Shortly after her divorce from fellow artist Diego Rivera, Kahlo painted this double self-portrait showing two sides to her personality. On the right is the Kahlo he loved, wearing traditional Mexican dress—an electric-blue top with orange stripes and a moss-green skirt with a pleated hem—and clutching a locket with a childhood image of her unfaithful husband. On the left is the unloved Kahlo, in a colonial-style wedding dress with frilly sleeves and a claustrophobically high lace neck, her face pale and powdered with rouge. Her two sides are connected, not just through the touch of their hands, but through their hearts, brutally exposed. While the heart of her loved self is whole, that of her unloved self is torn open, its main artery severed by a pair of scissors and spilling crimson blood onto her white skirt.

Kahlo took her troubles and translated them into art. In her paintings, she laid bare the near-fatal traffic accident she experienced as a teenager, the dozens of operations that followed, her chronic pain and her dangerous miscarriages. She depicted her physical and inner anguish, which in this portrait one can imagine roiling in the mass of dark blue-and-white storm clouds. Her incendiary marriage to Rivera has quite literally broken her in two. Yet, look at the expression of each Kahlo: fixed, resolute.

Kahlo's use of color heightens the emotion. Sitting on a bench in front of a tempestuous sky, she and her double shine bright. The contrast between the bloodstains and the white wedding dress, as well as the complementary shades of orange and blue on the top, catch the eye. The highlights and shadows in the folds of the clothing give both figures a monumentality reminiscent of classical sculptures, while the flesh glows almost gold. Kahlo may have been exploring her anguish, but something else shines through here—determination. She was bold, revolutionary and an inspiration, especially for the women artists who followed in her footsteps.

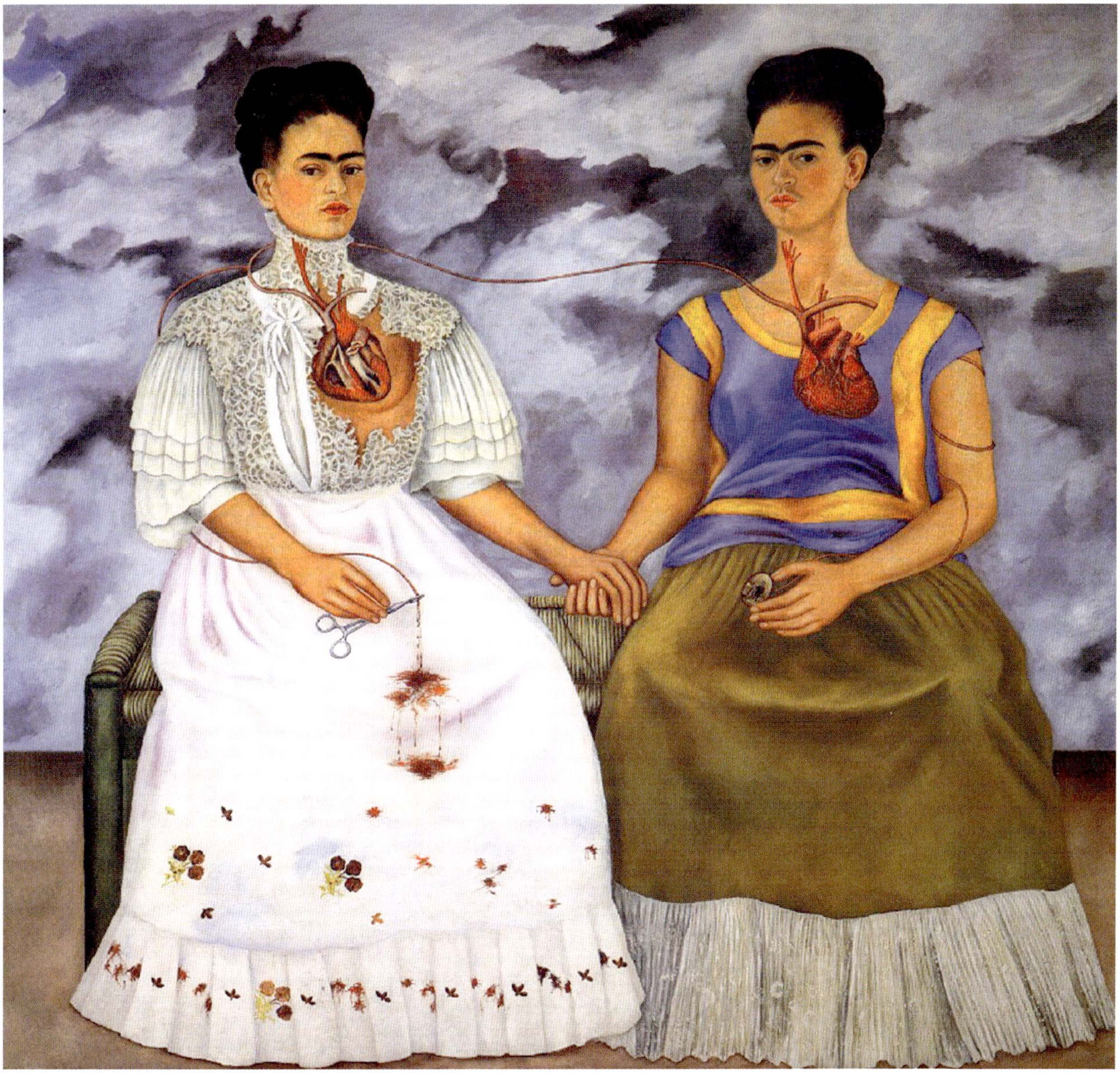

Palette

Dark blue-and-white storm clouds; an electric-blue top with orange stripes and a moss-green skirt; crimson blood on a white skirt.

Complementary works

- Diego Rivera, *Dream of a Sunday Afternoon in Alameda Park,* 1946–47.
- Lubaina Himid, *Between the Two My Heart is Balanced*, 1991.
- Cassi Namoda, *Conjoined twins in soft blue dressing*, 2020.

C30 M19 Y71 K40
R129 G129 B71

C5 M6 Y70 K11
R220 G207 B98

C0 M0 Y3 K6
R243 G243 B238

C6 M18 Y7 K6
R220 G204 B209

C51 M22 Y0 K10
R133 G159 B199

Surrealist tea party

Leonora Carrington

The Old Maids

1947

Oil on board,
22⅞ x 29⅛ in (58.2 x 73.8 cm).

A tea party is taking place, but not one as we know it. Carrington's guests include a colossal woman dressed in blue and white, with coiffed hair that brushes against the ceiling. Hooded folk in pink and green sip tiny cups of tea, while a figure in lemon yellow holds a fork in midair, waiting while a peckish magpie takes a bite of cake. Like her fellow female Surrealists, Carrington drew on witches, fairies, and other mythic figures. The space—sparsely furnished with a single gold chair bearing the image of a lush green landscape, and a sizeable fireplace in which a puny pile of sticks flame orange and yellow—can barely contain these socializing giantesses.

The Old Maids flits between realism and fantasy in both subject matter and color palette. The cawing magpies are realistically rendered in black and white, as is the curly-tailed monkey in brown; through the door is a black cat. The pie has a golden pastry crust, and the cut cake on the table, covered with an off-white cloth, is spread with icing. When it comes to the figures, though, something isn't right—each looks on with a pale moonlike face. The entire painting has a surreal green tinge—even the dark robe of the central figure with petite hands and feet—and the guests are outlined in a hazy yellow. The violet teapot seems normal enough, until you notice that it's transparent.

A writer as well as a painter, Carrington fell in with the Surrealists while studying art in London. In 1937 she met her mentor and lover Max Ernst, with whom she moved to Paris. In Spain during the Second World War, she suffered from anxiety and depression, and it wasn't until she moved to Mexico that she found peace and prominence. Carrington was fascinated with animals and bodies, both human and otherworldly. In her art, she sought to explore themes of identity and transformation; color was a tool with which to liberate our thinking, and to highlight the blurred boundaries between ordinary and strange bodies and beings.

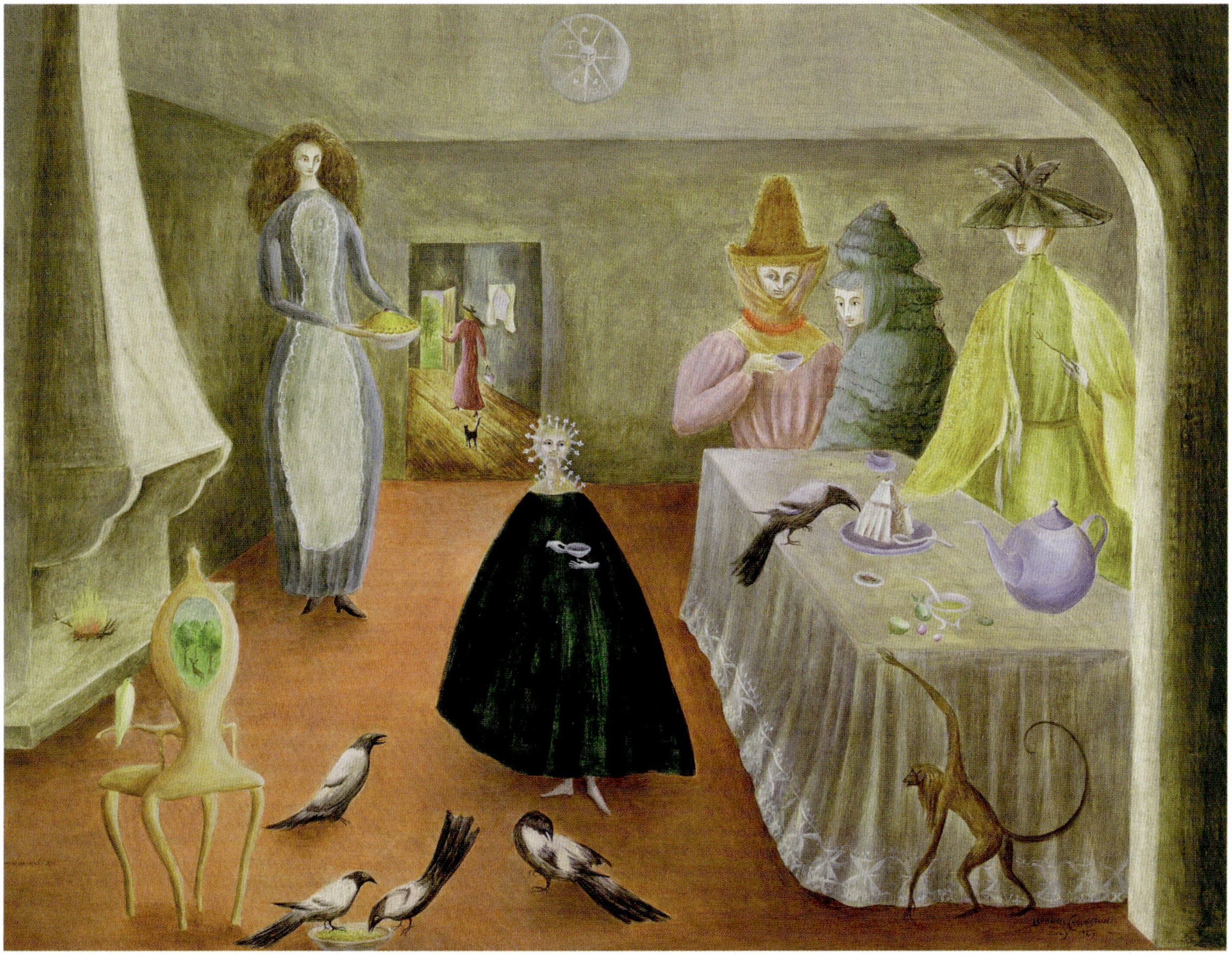

Palette

Socializing giantesses dressed in blue and white, pink and green, and lemon yellow.

Complementary works

- Marion Elizabeth Adnams, *Alter Ego*, *c.*1940.
- Dorothea Tanning, *Eine Kleine Nachtmusik*, 1943.
- Eileen Agar, *Figures in a Garden*, 1979–81.

Express yourself

Expressionism

C0 M55 Y90 K0
R217 G132 B42

Express yourself

Expressionism

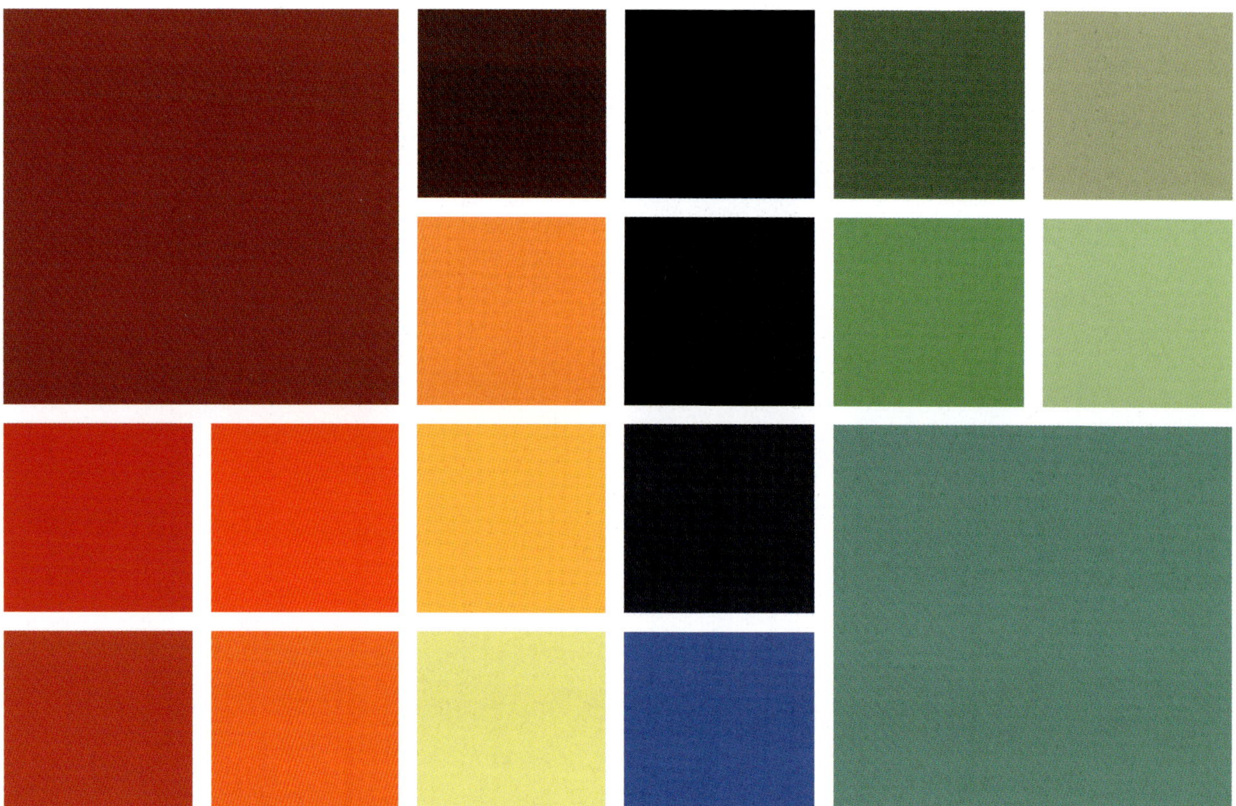

Although the term "Expressionist" is largely applied to works of the 20th century, this new kind of art was arguably invented in the late 1880s by Vincent van Gogh (*see page 154*). Inspired by the Impressionists (*see page 105*) and the symbolic paintings of Paul Gauguin (*see page 136*), van Gogh prepared his palette with luminous pigments, which he applied to his canvases using jagged and feverish brushstrokes. Toward the end of his troubled life, he experienced an unbridled burst of creativity and would work ceaselessly for days and nights, losing himself in his colorful creations. He painted sunflowers in a utopian sea of yellow, plum trees in bloom, and cafés by night. He'd always had a habit of getting overexcited, and he channeled that feeling into art.

Though they both lived for a while in the Paris neighborhood of Montmartre, and moved in similar artistic circles, it's unlikely that van Gogh ever met the Norwegian painter Edvard Munch (*see page 156*). And yet both saw the world through color and produced bold, personal works of art during the same period. They also had psychological breakdowns in common: van Gogh famously cut off his ear before committing suicide, and Munch was hospitalized in 1908 after struggling with depression and anxiety for years. "To paint strong feelings solely by working directly from nature—glowing with passion—infernal fire of the soul—is incredibly taxing for the nervous system," wrote Munch in 1908. "Vincent is an example of that (myself partially so)."

These so-called fathers of 20th-century Expressionism weren't the only artists associated with the movement who suffered for their art. The leading lights of German Expressionism—Max Beckmann and Ernst Ludwig Kirchner (*see page 168*)—also experienced some form of emotional self-abandonment. Expressionist art hasn't always been popular—some see it as overly theatrical, others as messy and crude—and the fact that several of its practitioners believed that artists were incapable of leading normal lives while producing art doesn't help. Today, the trope of the "tortured" artist who must surrender wholly to their practice doesn't fly.

Expressionism took root in the early 20th century in Germany and Austria, where avant-garde artists bared their souls through intense and undiluted palettes. During the First World War, it became entangled with the social tumult; those who enlisted or were drafted made art that recorded their battered sense of optimism and the frightening conditions on the frontlines. After Hitler seized power in 1933, art itself was under attack, and by 1937 German museums were purged of anything deemed ugly and unacceptable. Expressionist works were among those labeled "degenerate"; Nazi officials took against the clashing colors and the loose brushstrokes, not to mention the unapologetically explicit subject matter. Thousands of pieces were confiscated—among them the shocking and sensual portraits of the Austrian artist Egon Schiele (*see page 170*); some were burned, others displayed in one of the most infamous exhibitions of the century. Anything that dared to be subjective was stamped out.

Or at least, that was Hitler's plan. Since then, Expressionism has experienced several revivals. Despite coming in and out of fashion, it reappeared in abstract form in the U.S. in the 1940s and 1950s (*see page 177*), in Germany in the 1960s and 1970s, and again in New York in the 1980s. Its seemingly arbitrary colors are too bright to be dulled, and its brushstrokes too full of movement and life. The Expressionists took up the baton of the Impressionists and continued their quest to overturn centuries-old conventions. Theirs is an art form that beats like a drum.

In sickness, in health

Vincent van Gogh

Two Crabs

1889

Oil on canvas,
418½ x 24 in (7 x 61 cm).

"There are colors that make each other shine, that make a couple complete each other like man and wife." So said van Gogh in a letter he wrote to his sister Willemien from Arles, in the South of France, in 1888. In December that year, he had a row with Gauguin (*see page 136*) and sliced through his own ear with a razor. He was admitted to hospital and released in January 1889, the month he painted this still life. The close-up of two crabs—one upright on its front, the other scrabbling around on its back—perfectly captures his fragile mental state. Four months later, he was confined to an asylum on the outskirts of Saint-Rémy-de-Provence, and the following year he killed himself.

Painted in red and green, the compact canvas is intense and expressive. When van Gogh moved to Paris in 1886, his painting style became loose and bright, like that of the Impressionists. His vivid palette sprung from his observation of their works, nature, and books on color theory. In 1884 he read the French art critic Charles Blanc's *Grammar of Painting and Engraving* (1867), which advocated for the use of complementary colors. Such color contrasts were advocated by Eugène Delacroix (*see page 94*), who used them to heighten drama, and are applied here by van Gogh. As a pair, red and green reinforce each other by their opposition.

Within that pairing are light and dark variations. Growing up in the Hague, the mostly self-taught Dutch artist was surrounded by tonal paintings, from which he learned to accentuate highlights and shadows within one hue. Despite his inner turbulence, van Gogh was very productive. Rendered with thick, fiery strokes of red, orange, and yellow, the crustaceans sit on a luminous bed of pale and zingy greens, so loosely painted it resembles a rippling sea. The crabs are probably dead—possibly cooked, judging from the blush of their shells—and yet, with their crooked legs and shiny black claws, they look alive. Like the crabs, van Gogh's was an existence was one of ups and downs.

C0 M100 Y100 K11
R180 G0 B18

C0 M75 Y100 K0
R207 G87 B16

C0 M28 Y100 K0
R235 G184 B0

C30 M0 Y30 K0
R195 G220 B190

C90 M0 Y98 K0
R59 G153 B68

C65 M0 Y38 K0
R119 G183 B169

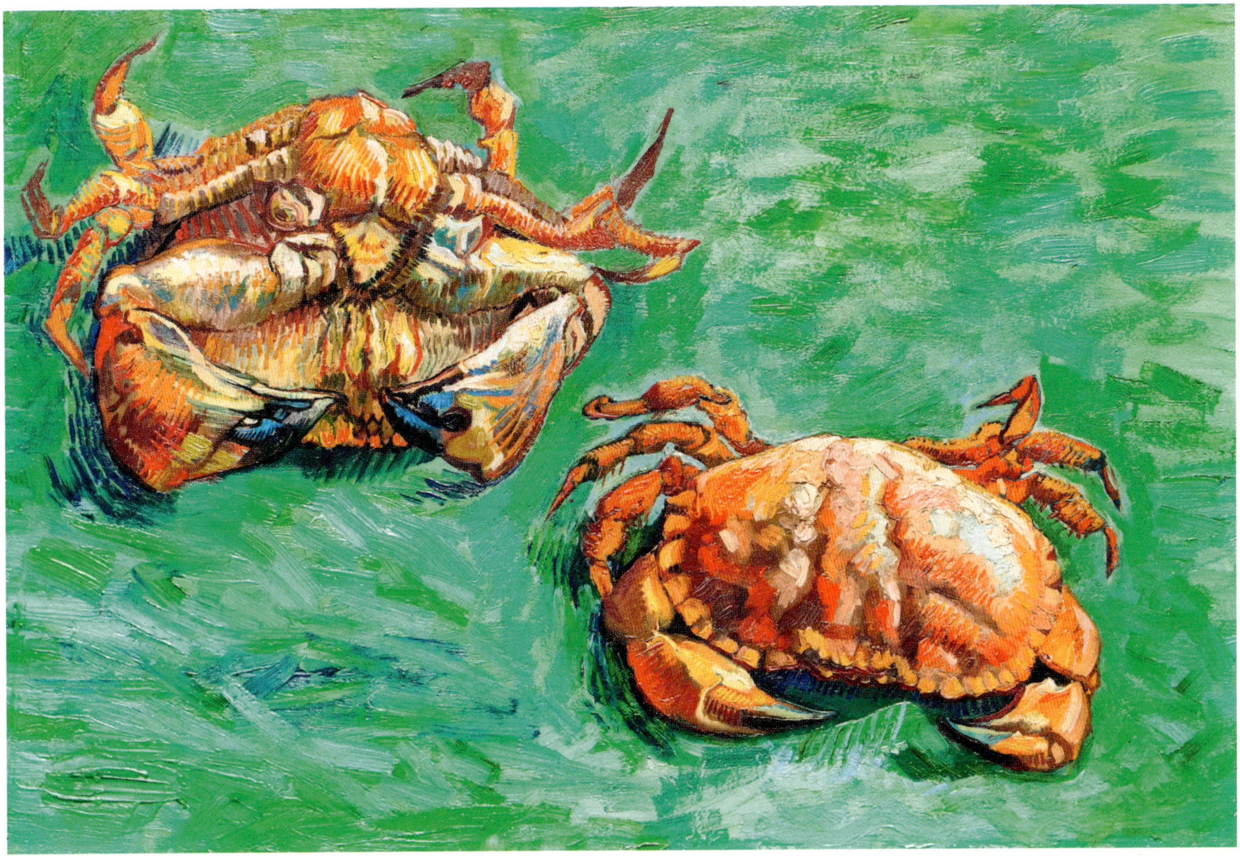

Palette

Red, orange, and yellow against pale and zingy greens.

Complementary works

- Paul Gauguin, *Self-Portrait*, 1889.
- Edvard Munch, *The Sin (Woman with Red Hair and Green Eyes)*, 1902.
- Henri Matisse, *The Dance*, 1909.

C0 M82 Y86 K0 R204 G71 B43

C0 M23 Y94 K0 R238 G194 B34

C60 M0 Y14 K0 R130 G193 B212

C90 M30 Y20 K65 R22 G65 B83

C40 M4 Y0 K100 R0 G0 B0

Let it all out

Edvard Munch

The Scream

1895

Pastel and crayon on cardboard, 36 × 28⅞ in (91 × 73.5 cm).

"I was walking along the road with two of my friends. The sun set —the sky became a bloody red. And I felt a touch of melancholy—I stood still, dead tired—over the blue-black fjord and city hung blood and tongues of fire. My friends walked on—I stayed behind —trembling with fright—I felt the great scream in nature." Munch wrote these words on a plaque attached to the gilt frame of this timeless pastel—one of a series of pastels, drawings, prints, and paintings that he made of the same motif. It has become one of the most iconic images in art history; it even has its own emoji.

A volcanic sky of red and yellow roils above a lone ghoulish figure, whose dark-purple dress threatens to slip through the gaps in the railings and into the torrent of purple water below. In this polychrome version of an earlier drawing, Munch used blunt pastel sticks and crayons to create linear bands of color that appear to ripple and sway. The medium itself gives the work a vivid and grainy rawness. The black shadow spreading out into the fjord follows the curve of the artist's contorted body, and the straight lines on the bridge are unrelenting. The stark contrast between what the Norwegian artist describes as the "bloody red" sky and the "blue-black fjord" adds to the intensity.

Munch uses bold and exaggerated color to recreate the overwhelming horror he experienced when he walked along this path to the east of his hometown of Oslo. Loneliness, fear, anguish, dread: these are just four of the emotions that swirl up and around the tormented figure, with his elongated palms pressed to his ears. The artist's friends linger near the board's edge—solid purple smudges looking out at the distant boats. Munch, on the other hand, is depicted with sinuous lines that conjure a sense of uprootedness. His eyes and nostrils are wide, his hair seemingly singed off by the flaming sky. You can almost hear the shriek escape from his open mouth.

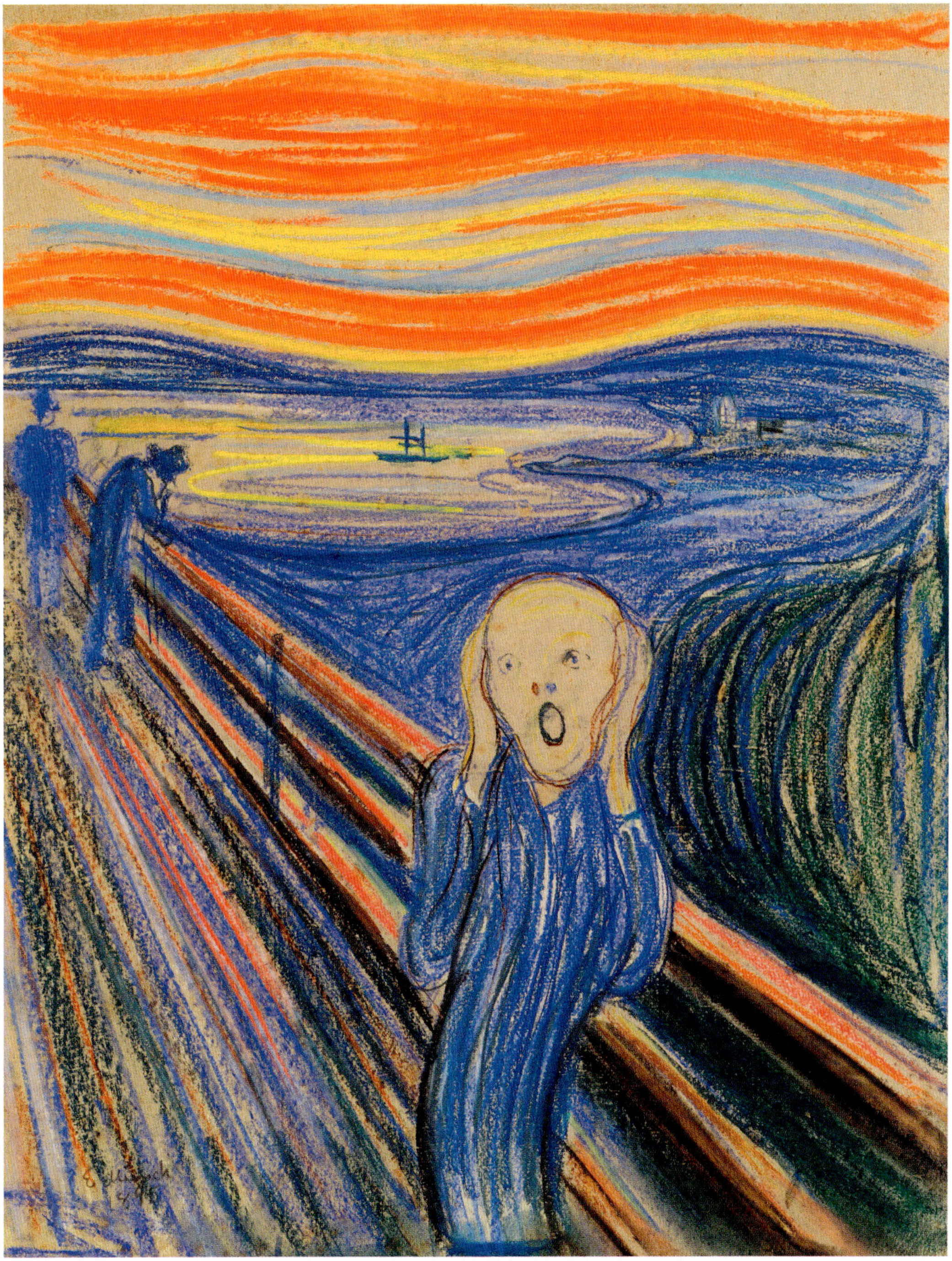

Palette

A volcanic sky of red and yellow; a lone figure dressed in dark purple; a black shadow and a blue-black fjord.

Complementary works

- Karl Schmidt-Rottluff, *Pharisees*, 1912.
- Erich Heckel, *Tired*, 1913.
- Marc Chagall, *The Blue Circus*, 1950.

C30 M16 Y45 K5
R180 G184 B145

C0 M20 Y26 K0
R241 G211 B184

C3 M0 Y0 K6
R237 G241 B243

C0 M46 Y70 K5
R214 G148 B83

C20 M63 Y65 K60
R96 G62 B43

Probing portrait

Paula Modersohn-Becker
Self-Portrait on Sixth Wedding Anniversary
1906

Tempera on canvas,
40⅛ × 27⅝ in (101.8 × 70.2 cm).

Modersohn-Becker imagines herself pregnant in this simple but powerfully emotive portrait. The artist is naked from the waist up, except for a long necklace strung with amber beads that falls between her breasts and glows warmly against her creamy pink skin. Her large eyes are the same shade of brown as her pinned-up hair, and her lips a rosy pink. She cradles her belly protectively with sturdy, workman-like hands—an artist's hands—and looks out at the viewer, head tilted to one side, pencil-thin eyebrows arched, cheeks flushed. Rather than a baby, when she painted this piece, the German artist was expecting to achieve her creative potential.

The life-sized portrait—which assumes a tragic undertone when you consider that Modersohn-Becker later did fall pregnant and died shortly after giving birth to a daughter—was painted with thick oil pigments in pale shades that seem suffused with light. The background has a softly mottled appearance, with green daubs emerging from a pale wash of greenish yellow. Some details are sharply delineated: from the sweeping outline of the artist's neck and shoulder to the shadowy dip of her belly button. Others are deliberately blurred: her left hand is a pale pink smudge, and the white cloth slung around her waist is tinged with blue and composed of loose brushstrokes, its right-hand edge on the brink of blurring with the background.

Self-portrait on Sixth Wedding Anniversary is the earliest known naked female self-portrait. Created at a time when women were more commonly painted rather than painters, it's a radical declaration of independence. The springlike green background is full of future promise; the earthy pink of Modersohn-Becker's skin is a nod to her capacity for work. In this image, she shuns conventional beauty and instead presents herself as a confident and capable young woman. Like the artist's gaze, the subdued palette is steady and self-assured. As she once said, "I will make something of myself."

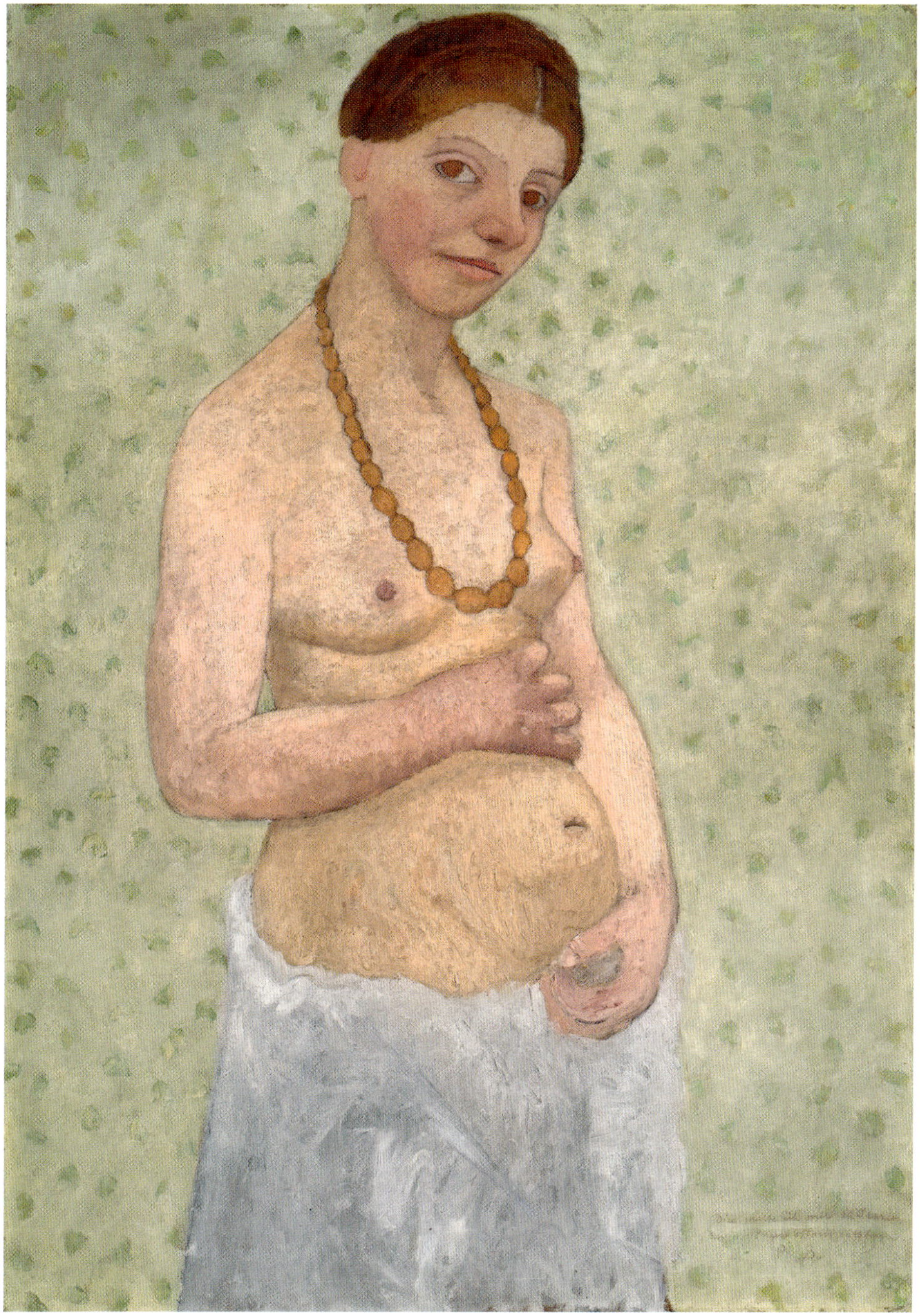

Palette

A springlike green background, a white cloth, creamy pink skin, and amber beads.

Complementary works

- Maria Lassnig, *Expressive Self-Portrait*, 1945.
- Winifred Nicholson, *First Prismatic*, 1976.
- Chantal Joffe, *Self-Portrait Pregnant II*, 2004.

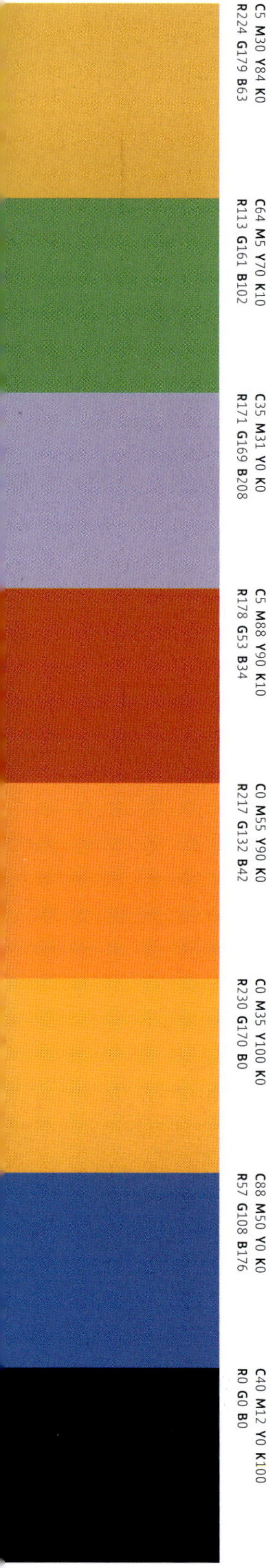

That's the spirit

Hilma af Klint
Group X, No. 1, Altarpiece
1907

Oil and gold leaf on canvas, 93½ x 70 11/16 in (237 x 179.5 cm).

In her will, af Klint requested that her work remain sealed for two decades after her death. The Swedish spiritualist believed that her contemporaries weren't ready for it, and that it would be better suited to a more mystically attuned future audience. Among her bold and colorful creations are 193 radically abstract paintings, created between 1906 and 1915, that she imagined installing in a three-story alabaster temple. The visionary image here is the first of three large canvases—she called them altarpieces—which she envisaged would preside at the top of a tower with a spiral staircase.

Painted with egg tempera and finished with gold leaf, the geometric work has a luminous quality. Set against a black background, a multicolored equilateral triangle points up toward the sun in the form of a golden circle, which is ringed with green and lilac and radiates yellow, blue, and pink beams. The triangle itself is a sort of color chart, with shades of red, orange, and yellow on the left, and blues and purples on the right. Each color is there for a reason: for af Klint, yellow and pink stood for masculinity, blue and lilac for femininity; green was harmony. In the center are different-shaped disks outlined in pink.

Af Klint found her voice as an artist when she formed an occult group called "The Five." Together with four female friends, she attempted to communicate with supernatural "High Masters" and painted at the service of her occult beliefs. *The Paintings for the Temple*, which culminated in the three altarpieces, were supposedly commissioned by an entity named Amaliel. In the second altarpiece, the beams are replaced with orbs, and the triangle has been inverted and painted black. In the third, there is no triangle—just a golden disk surrounded by a colorful star. As well as spiritual, af Klint was mathematical and scientific, and the advancements in the late 19th and early 20th centuries prompted her to question the universe. Above all, she sought to shed light on a new way of seeing—one that considered the upward and downward development between the spiritual and material worlds.

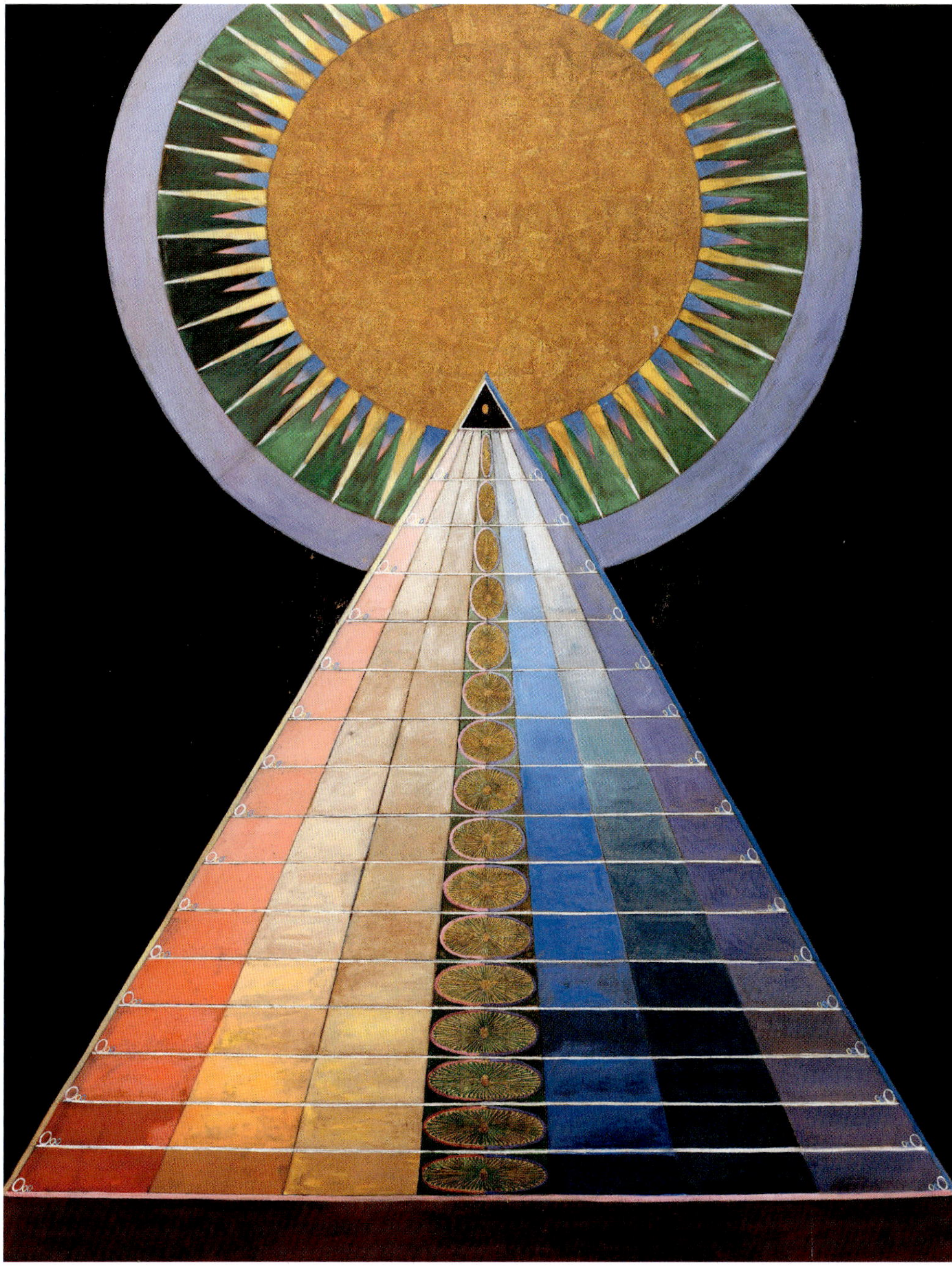

Palette

Set against a black background, a sort of color chart with shades of red, orange, yellow, blue, and purple; plus a golden circle ringed with green and lilac.

Complementary works

- Georgia O'Keeffe, *Grey Lines with Black, Blue, and Yellow*, 1923.
- Agnes Pelton, *Ahmi in Egypt*, 1931.
- Emma Kunz, *Work No. 003*, undated.

The psychology of color

Henri Matisse (*see page 166*) once said, "The chief aim of color should be to serve expression as well as possible." What he meant is that color is capable not only of giving form and shape, but also of recreating memories and arousing emotions. It ought to be based on interpretation rather than description, and what we feel rather than simply what we see. It's about expressing sensation and the nature of an experience.

Throughout art history, artists have used the relationship between mood and color to communicate and elicit emotion. An individual's psyche feeds into their work, and their work has the potential to feed into the psyche of the viewer. The palette of Pablo Picasso (*see page 140*), for example, was without doubt influenced by his state of mind: when he was poor, unsuccessful and in mourning, he painted with melancholy shades of blue; as he shrugged off his sorrow, he shifted his focus to blissful shades of pink. In his own words, "Colors, like features, follow the changes of the emotions."

Of course, there are no rules, and what a certain color represents differs from artist to artist. By late 1910, the German Expressionist Franz Marc—who, together with Wassily Kandinsky, founded a group of artists called Der Blaue Reiter (The Blue Rider)—had defined the characteristics of the three primary colors as such: "Blue is the male principle, stern and spiritual. Yellow the female principle, gentle, cheerful, and sensual. Red is matter, brutal and heavy, and always the color which must be fought and vanquished by the other two." The little-known Swedish spiritualist Hilma af Klint (*see page 160*), on the other hand, regarded yellow as masculine and blue as feminine.

Kandinsky and af Klint were among those heavily influenced by *Thought Forms*: a short but seminal book originally published in 1905 by the leaders of the Theosophical Society, Annie Besant and C. W. Leadbeater. The frontispiece features "Key to the Meanings of Colours," a chart that shows the spiritual and mental meanings of 25 colors. In the upper-left-hand corner is pale blue, which stands for high spirituality, and in the lower-right-hand corner is black, which denotes malice.

In between is everything from bright yellow ("highest intellect") and reddish orange ("pride") to pale pink ("unselfish affection") and purple ("depression"). The attributes of a particular color change according to tonal variations.

In their art, the Expressionists sought to make a mood. They engaged with the world around them, and conjured in color the way it made them think and feel. Van Gogh poured his energy into intense and violently contrasting colors. With charged shades of yellow, blue, purple, and black, Munch whipped up a crippling sense of anxiety and unease. And sometimes, the feeling for a color runs so deep, there's no explaining it. Take Matisse and his love affair with red.

Besant and Leadbeater's "Key to the Meanings of Colours" from *Thought-Forms*, 1901.

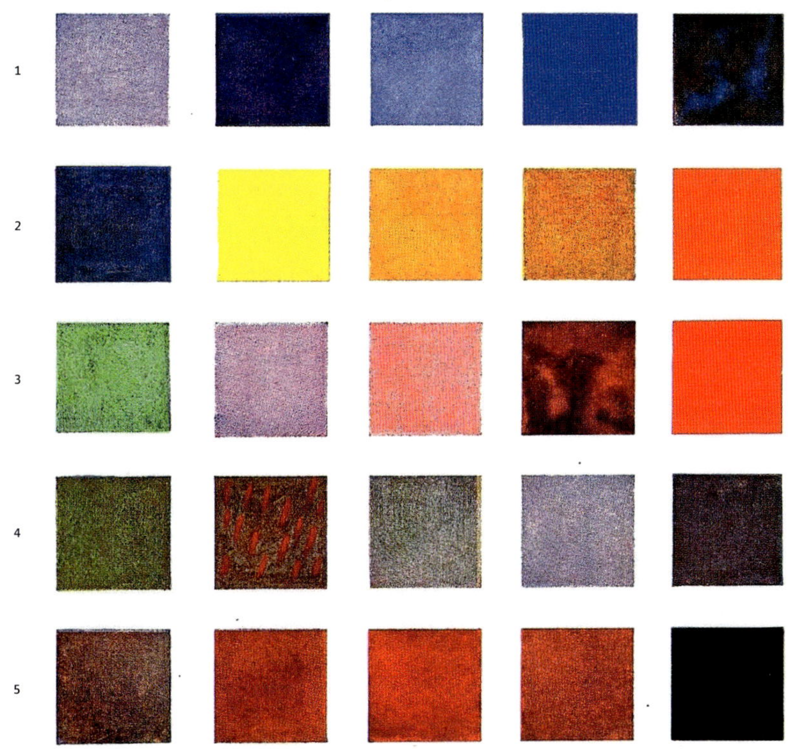

Key to the Meanings of Colours

1. High spirituality	1. Devotion mixed with affection	1. Devotion to a noble ideal	1. Pure religious feeling	1. Selfish religious feeling
2. Religious feeling, tinged with fear	2. Highest intellect	2. Strong intellect	2. Low type of intellect	2. Pride
3. Sympathy	3. Love for humanity	3. Unselfish affection	3. Selfish affection	3. Pure affection
4. Adaptability	4. Jealousy	4. Deceit	4. Fear	4. Depression
5. Selfishness	5. Avarice	5. Anger	5. Sensuality	5. Malice

C0 M0 Y60 K5
R245 G235 B127

C00 M24 Y100 K5
R228 G184 B0

C00 M44 Y100 K5
R215 G147 B0

Sun is shining

František Kupka
The Yellow Scale
*c.*1907

Oil on canvas,
31 × 29¼ in (78.7 × 74.3 cm).

Kupka is slumped in a wicker chair, his head propped up on a halo-like cushion with just the right amount of give. He's wearing what appears to be a rather plush bathrobe, bundled up to his lightly stubbled chin. A single finger of one hand has slipped between the pages of a book to mark his place; with the other hand, he pincers a half-smoked cigarette. The flashes of flesh and the wood frame of the chair are the only elements of this self-portrait that aren't coated with thick strokes of yellow. In fact, the color has leaked into the palm of the Czech modernist's open hand, and onto his unsmiling face.

Like af Klint (*see page 160*), Kupka was an abstract artist (though he didn't denounce realism entirely) with spiritualist inclinations. He, too, was drawn to spiritualist movements such as Theosophy and believed in the power of color. In his art, he sought to emancipate color from the shackles of description and enable it to reach its full potential as a profound means of expression. "Atmosphere in a painting is achieved through bathing the canvas in a single scale of colors," he once said. "Thus one achieves an *état d'âme* [state of being] exteriorized in luminous form."

Speaking of expression, what's Kupka thinking? He stares out at us with a self-possessed look on his face. The arch of his dark eyebrows, the same shade as his combed hair, and the turned-down corners of his mouth suggest a certain displeasure —a displeasure that sits in stark contrast with the sunny palette. The self-portrait may be depicted with various shades of a bright and cheery hue, but there's a dark and tingly undercurrent. Notice the sickly green streaks on the artist's cheeks—a nod, perhaps, to the envy he's experiencing as yellow takes over as the subject. Either that or yellow is a symbol of the artist's inner light, shining bright from within.

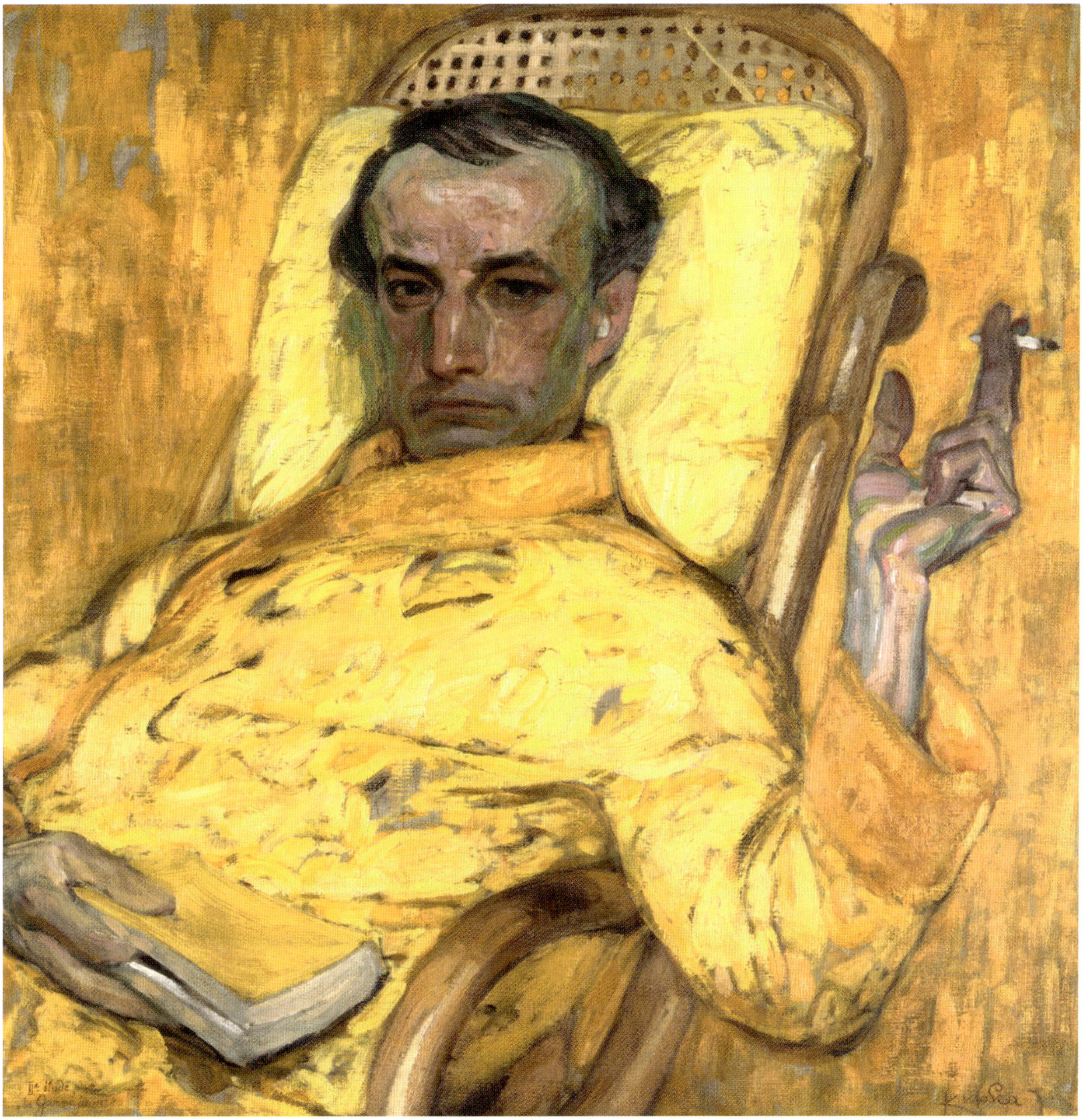

Palette

Thick strokes of yellow.

Complementary works

- Frederic Leighton, *Flaming June*, 1895.
- Loïs Mailou Jones, *Jennie*, 1943.
- Hedda Sterne, *Yellow Structure*, *c.*1952.

Fresh coat

Henri Matisse

The Dessert: Harmony in Red

1908

Oil on canvas,
71⅛ x 87 in (180.5 x 221 cm).

This painting was commissioned in 1908 by Sergei Shchukin, a Russian collector of modern art. He was a fan of pictures that gave him a shock and Matisse, the leader of Fauvism, was producing some of the peppiest art around. The work was to hang in the dining room of Shchukin's mansion, in Moscow, and to be called *Harmony in Blue*. But after the artist had handed over the canvas, which he painted in his studio in Paris, he decided he wasn't happy with the result. So, he demanded to have it back and painted over it in raspberry red.

The canvas shows a decorative room—Matisse himself called the work a "decorative panel." The floral wallpaper seeps into the cloth covering the table, which is topped with a couple of slender glass vases, and red, yellow, and green pieces of fruit. A single female figure in black and white tends to a fruit bowl; behind her is a chair, and a second sits opposite. Through the window is a childlike garden: blue sky, green grass, bushy trees; the small pink house on the hill picks up on the rosy interior. Or is it a landscape painting on the wall? The entire scene is devoid of perspective, which makes it hard to tell. The red itself appears to push at the surface of the canvas and resist the illusion of depth.

Matisse struggled to explain his love of this new hue. "Where I got the color red—to be sure, I just don't know," he once remarked. "I find that all these things ... only become what they are to me when I see them together with the color red." Regardless, this ornamental painting was the first of a number of red compositions. Here, bursts of blue remain in the twists of floral pattern, but there's no doubt the work is hot with color —a *Harmony in Red*.

C4 M100 Y60 K14
R170 G0 B62

C90 M70 Y3 K6
R55 G77 B145

C90 M10 Y55 K25
R43 G122 B109

C0 M45 Y100 K0
R223 G151 B0

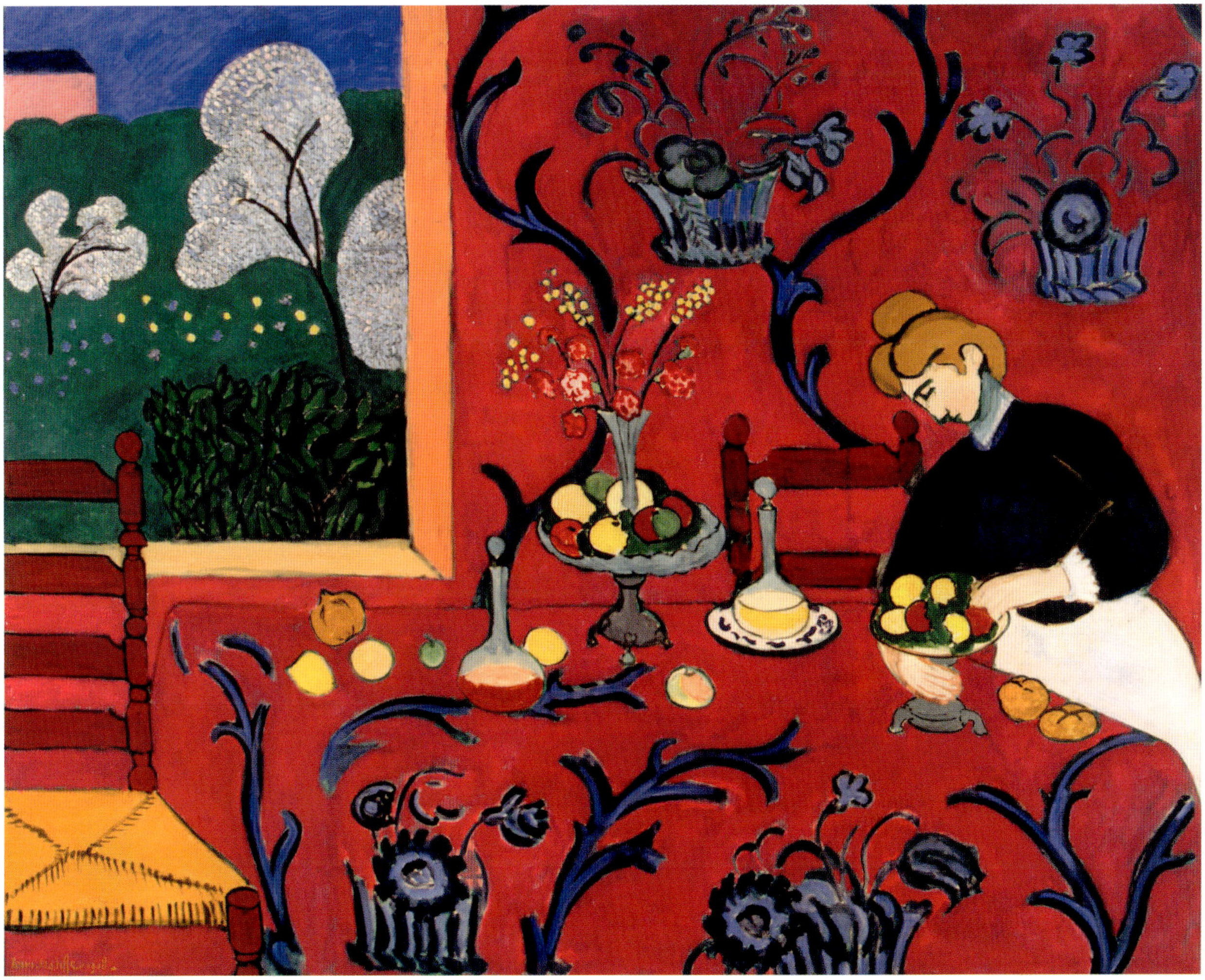

Palette

Raspberry red with twists of blue, plus red, yellow, and green pieces of fruit.

Complementary works

- André Derain, *Henri Matisse*, 1905.
- Georges Braque, *Still Life with Red Tablecloth*, 1934.
- Rene Magritte, *The Tomb of the Wrestlers*, 1960.

C82 M50 Y0 K5
R69 G107 B170

C75 M50 Y25 K65
R45 G57 B72

C0 M98 Y100 K0
R198 G21 B21

C0 M0 Y56 K0
R255 G245 B141

C0 M35 Y44 K0
R230 G179 B140

Walk this way

Ernst Ludwig Kirchner

Berlin Street Scene

1913

Oil on canvas,
47½ x 35⅞ in (120.6 x 91.1 cm).

There's something anxiety inducing about this painting. Something to do with the way it's been compressed and crammed full of figures. The scratchy brushstrokes are pent up with frustration, flickering like hot and angry flames. Against a wash of faded rose, the characters glow with intense colors: custard yellow, poppy red, dark and bright blue. Their facial expressions are harsh and angular, with long noses and pointed chins, and their posture strangely upright and stiff—apart from the man on the left, who's hunched over, leaning on the open door of a carriage being pulled along by a pair of bay horses.

Kirchner's juddering brushstrokes and caustic palette tallied with his character. He struggled with anxiety and addiction, suffered a nervous breakdown on the eve of the First World War, and killed himself in 1938 at the age of 58. He was a talented artist and a founding member of the Expressionist group Die Brücke (The Bridge), established in Dresden in 1905. In 1911 he moved to Berlin and became captivated by what he called "the symphony of the great city." There he met sisters Erna and Gerda Schilling, the models for the two women here.

The city's wild nightlife fueled Kirchner's artistic fantasies: to him, the busy streets crowded with unsavory men and gaudy prostitutes were creative kindling. A dark undercurrent runs through *Berlin Street Scene*, which captures the Schilling sisters parading in feathers and lace among a sea of glancing men. Bisecting them is a man in a bowler hat with his back to us, a menacing presence heading their way. To the right is another man, whose face we do see, with shadowy eyes and a cigarette dangling between his scarlet lips. Swirled up with it all are excitement, glamour, and danger, in which Kirchner reveled. As he once said, "I can't work rationally; I'm too much of a color man for that."

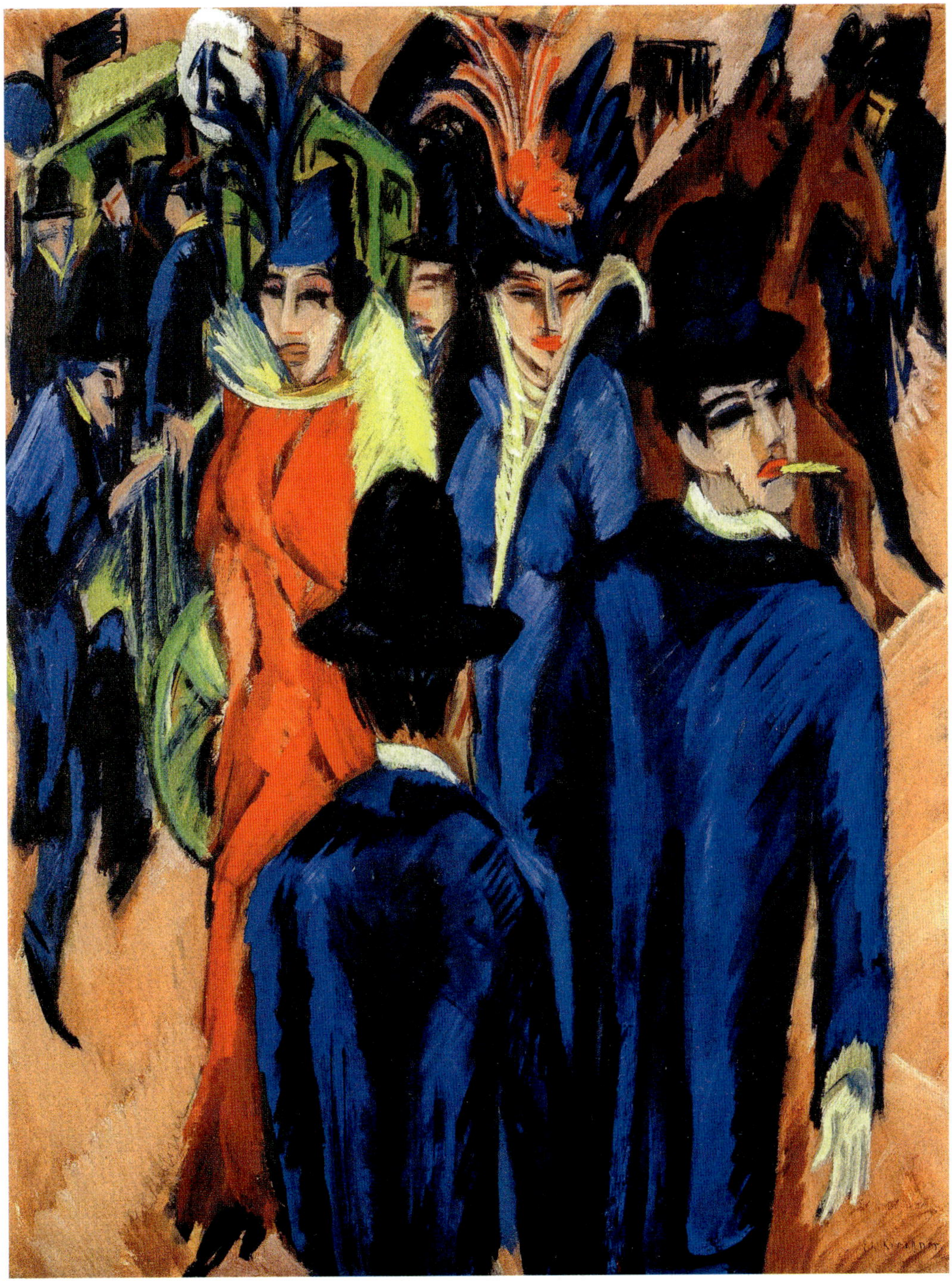

Palette

Against a wash of faded rose, characters glow custard yellow, poppy red, and dark and bright blue.

Complementary works

- Wassily Kandinsky, *Improvisation 19*, 1910.
- Franz Marc, *Blue Horse I*, 1911.
- Henri Gaudier-Brzeska, *Sophie Brzeska*, 1913.

Splash of color

Egon Schiele

Seated Woman with Legs Drawn Up

1917

Pencil and gouache,
18⅛ x 12 in (46 x 30.5 cm).

A pioneer of Expressionism in turn-of-the-century Vienna, Schiele used unprecedented color combinations and feverish lines to produce frank and erotic drawings, paintings, and watercolors. His preoccupation with sexuality and personal angst may have shocked his contemporary audience, but today it's regarded as groundbreaking for his time. Produced toward the end of his life, this beautifully balanced portrait is at once potent and tender. Schiele began his portrait as a drawing and later added color in patchy and rapidly applied brushstrokes.

The model—most likely the artist's sister-in-law, Adele Harms—wraps her arms around her left leg and rests her cheek wearily on her knee. She's hunched over, her hands loosely clasped at her shin. There's a vulnerability to the pose and the way she gazes up at us from her spot on the floor, and at the same time the look she gives us is intrepid. Over a pair of black stockings, she's wearing baggy off-white bloomers outlined in electric blue; a sleeveless sea-green blouse offsets her fiery orange hair. The crimson on her lips reappears in daubs on those bloomers, as well as her cheeks and arms, as though reminding us that there's blood pumping around her body. A particularly pronounced stroke on one of her fingers resembles broken skin.

The Austrian modernist's sexually explicit paintings were confiscated by the police on more than one occasion, and in 1912 he was charged with distributing obscene drawings. The 24-day imprisonment that followed might be why he decided to put some clothes on Adele, but the addition of garments does more than protect the model's modesty. The introduction of brightly colored clothes animates an otherwise static pose; surrounded by blank space, Schiele's sitter is brought to life with a palette of orange, blue, black, and green. The portrait might be of a single, lone figure, but it's brimming with emotion.

C86 M0 Y55 K5
R60 G156 B133

C0 M49 Y80 K0
R221 G146 B65

C70 M48 Y25 K65
R51 G60 B73

C0 M8 Y12 K5
R240 G228 B214

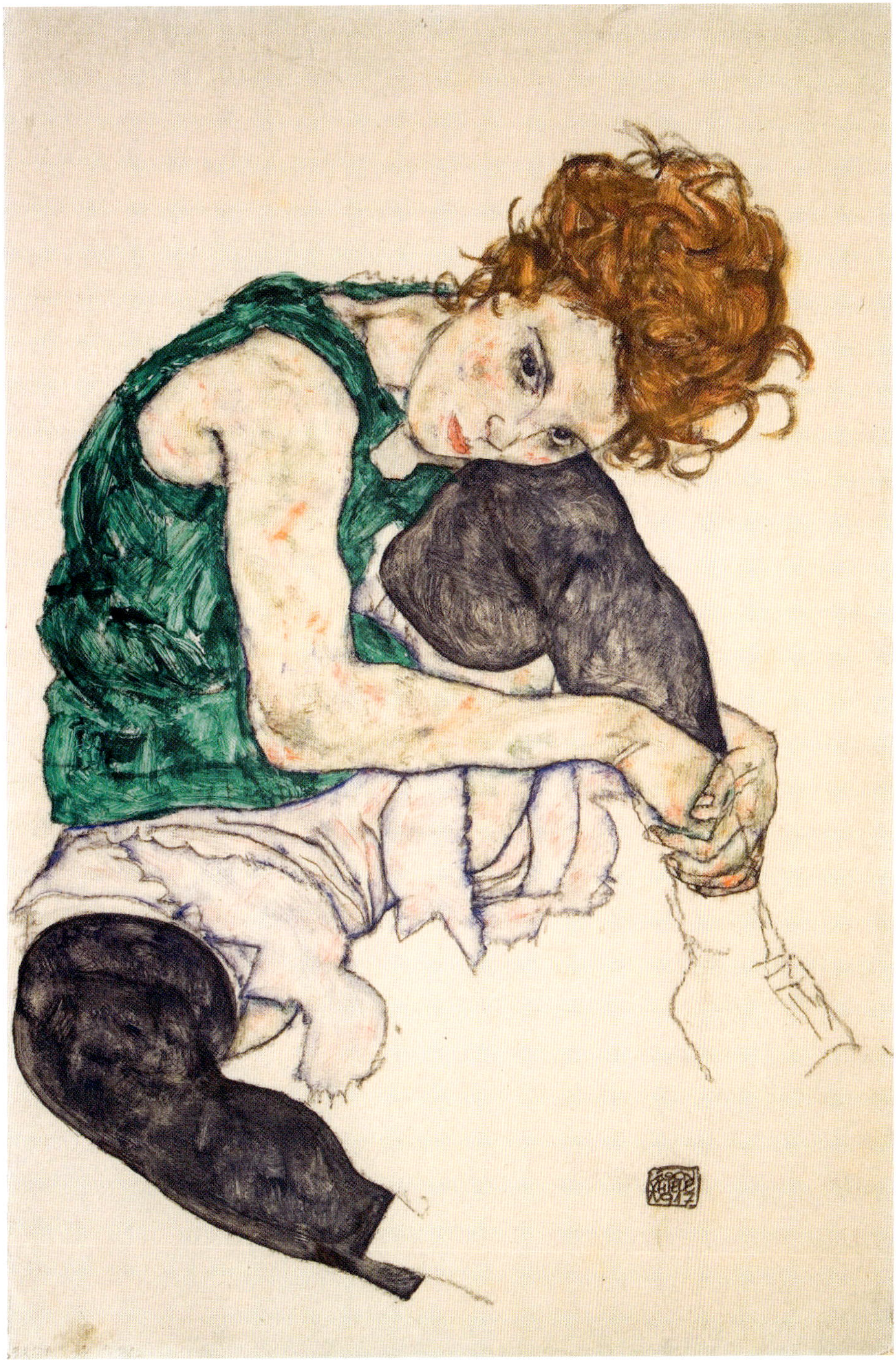

Palette

Baggy off-white bloomers over a pair of black stockings; a sleeveless sea-green blouse and fiery orange hair.

Complementary works

- Gustav Klimt, *Mäda Gertrude Primavesi*, 1912.
- Jules Pascin, *Nude*, *c.*1920.
- Paula Rego, *Lush*, 1994.

C63 M20 Y63 K30
R94 G123 B90

C34 M5 Y51 K0
R185 G204 B147

C29 M90 Y79 K20
R133 G48 B47

C66 M50 Y52 K80
R38 G42 B36

C40 M0 Y8 K100
R0 G0 B0

Death and decay

Helene Schjerfbeck

Still Life with Blackening Apples

1944

Oil on canvas,
$14\frac{3}{16}$ x $19\frac{11}{16}$ in (36 x 50 cm).

Toward the end of her life, Schjerfbeck created a series of unnerving still lifes that convey her physical and psychological deterioration. She moved from her native Finland to Sweden during the Second World War, and translated her sense of alienation and thoughts on mortality into haunting self-portraits and pictures of gradually decaying fruit. This and other works from those years, when she was in her 80s, have a ghostly quality—the muted tones and hazy finish suggest that the images before us are about to drift away; the lines blur, the pigments dissolve.

In *Still Life with Blackening Apples*, life literally appears to be leaking out of the fruit—the acid green of one apple has seeped onto the tabletop, where it forms a withered and wrinkled mirror image of the original. The corrosion appears to have started with the two black apples on the right, then spread to the moldy brown one behind. The background is a cloying green, a color that also crops up in Schjerfbeck's final self-portraits—radically abstract and ragged reflections of her weakening life. The brushstrokes don't quite hit the top of the canvas, as if they're low in energy. In the foreground, the tabletop is a rainbow of lilac, pink, green, and brown reflections.

The older she became, the more Schjerfbeck was interested in capturing a mood and a memory rather than a faithful likeness. Her forms and figures, which started out conventionally naturalistic, soon began to verge on abstract. When she died in 1946, Schjerfbeck drifted from the public eye—at least outside her native Finland, where she's a national icon. Gradually, and with the help of a solo show of her work at the Royal Academy in London in 2019, her contribution to modern art is being recognized for what it is. In this still life, and in the self-portraits she painted when she was dying from cancer, the artist detects a flicker of life within death. The fruit may be softening and blackening, but two perfectly rounded green and red apples remain.

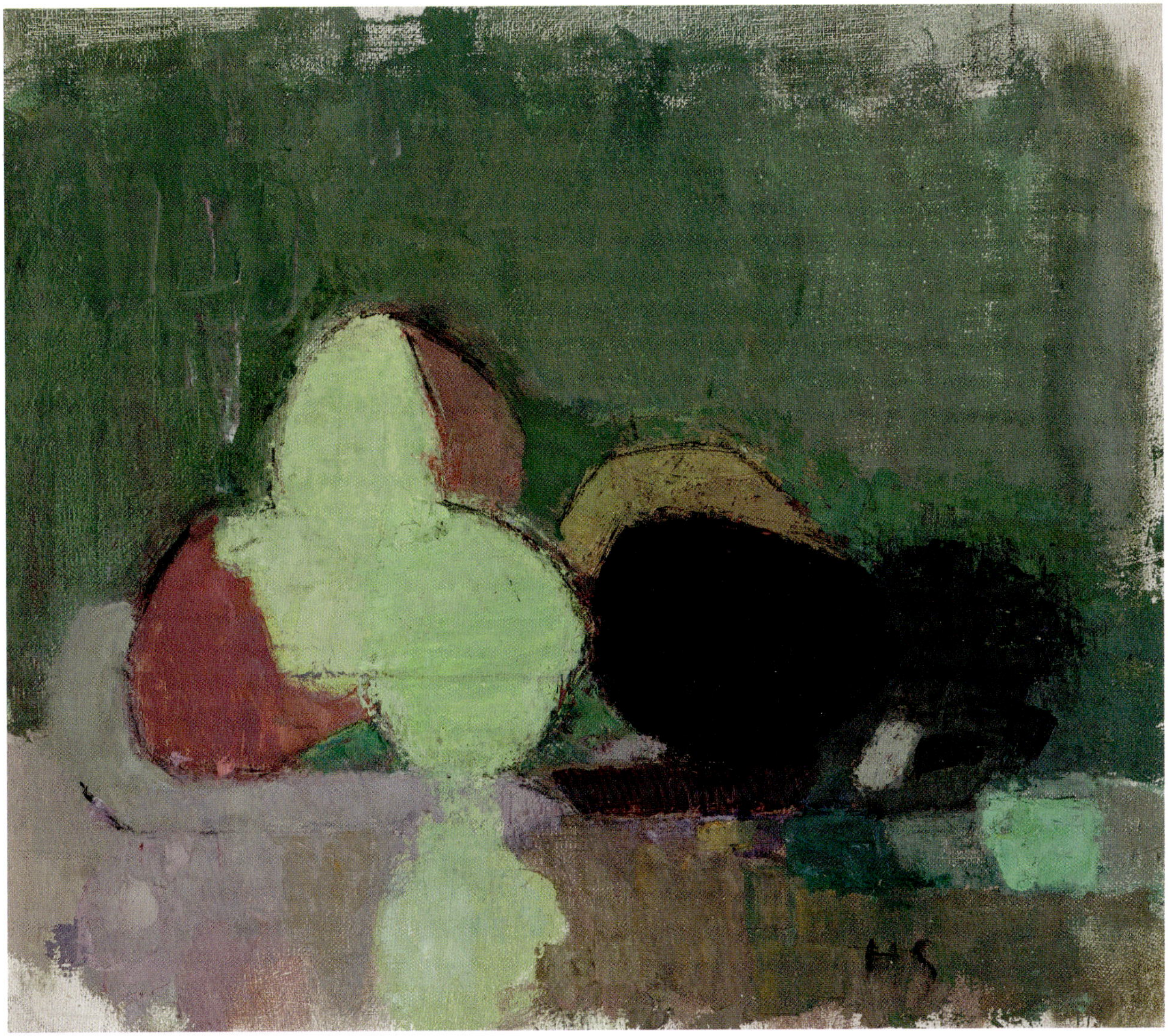

Palette

Apples in red, acid green, black, and moldy brown, and a cloying green background.

Complementary works

- Maria Wiik, *Out into the World*, 1889.
- Ellen Thesleff, *Echo*, 1891.
- Frank Auerbach, *Portrait of Catherine Lampert*, 1981–82.

Seeing it feelingly

Abstract Expressionism and color-field painting

C5 M95 Y50 K10
R176 G32 B76

Seeing it feelingly

Abstract Expressionism and color-field painting

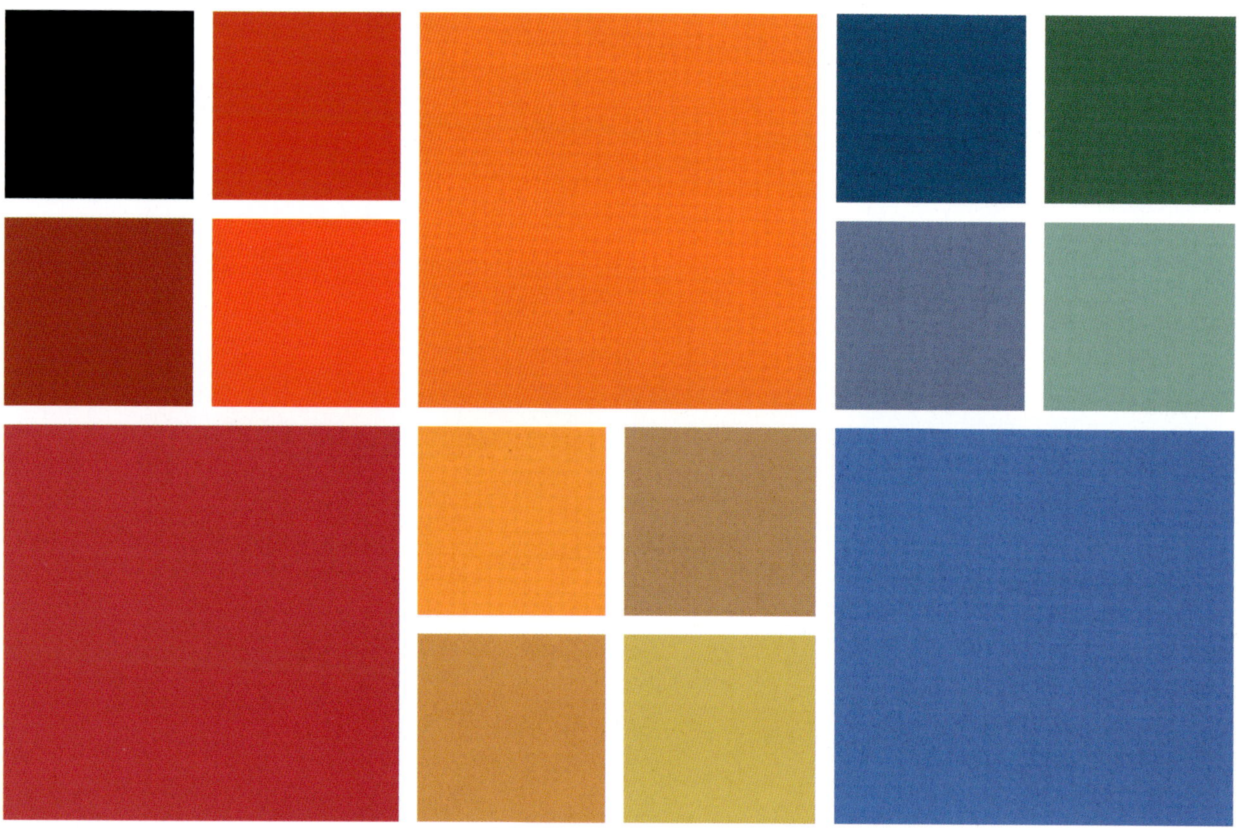

New York in the mid-20th century witnessed a watershed moment in art history. In the "age of anxiety" surrounding the Second World War, a group of loosely affiliated artists broke from tradition and unleashed a new kind of painting that required active engagement from the viewer rather than distant admiration. Troubled by dark times, the artists known as the Abstract Expressionists, or the New York School, considered it their responsibility to make art concerned with moral truths, freedom, humanity, and emotion.

War wasn't the only backdrop to what would become an unparalleled period in American art. Another influence was the arrival in the U.S. of avant-garde art from Europe: there were groundbreaking exhibitions of work by modernists across New York; the collection of the recently opened Museum of Modern Art was growing; and through his teachings, the German-born Hans Hofmann (*see page 186*) influenced both artists and critics. During the war, the Surrealists Salvador Dalí and Max Ernst sought refuge in the U.S., bringing with them their fascination with the unconscious. With the advent of Abstract Expressionism—a term that has its roots in Germany—New York took over from Paris as the center of the art world.

Though their often monumental canvases resist tidy categorization, the Abstract Expressionists can be roughly divided into two groups: the Action painters, who created direct and explosive images with energetic strokes and flicks; and the color-field painters, who filled their canvases with deeply contemplative swatches of flat color. Both placed great importance on process—and for both, imagery was mostly abstract and color key.

Abstract Expressionism as we know it is defined by Jackson Pollock's development of a radical new technique in 1947. Instead of using a brush to apply pigment to a stretched canvas on an easel, the artist dripped and poured industrial paint onto raw canvas laid out like a rug on the floor. At the same time, Pollock's wife, Lee Krasner (*see page 182*), was creating highly charged and dynamic abstract art, and Willem de Kooning was forging ahead with his own distinctive style. What each of these artists had in common was a love of immediacy, and a focus on painting as a physical and dynamic act of creation. It was this focus on process that prompted the American critic Harold Rosenberg to coin the term "action painting" in 1952: "At a certain moment the canvas began to appear to one American painter after another as an arena in which to act—rather than as a space in which to reproduce, redesign, analyze, or 'express' an object, actual or imagined. What was to go on the canvas was not a picture but an event."

From spontaneous mark-making to simplified swathes of color: if Pollock's drip paintings were about immediacy and placing his creative impulses onto the canvas, Mark Rothko's (*see page 184*) glowing veils were about enveloping the viewer in a field of color and eliciting an emotional response. Together with Barnett Newman and Clyfford Still, in a period of existential uncertainty, Rothko looked to religion and myth. Playing a pivotal role in the transition between Abstract Expressionism and color-field painting (a term coined by another American art critic, Clement Greenberg) was Helen Frankenthaler (*see page 180*), whose floating forms are at once gestural and fluid.

And so out of an extraordinary moment in time came an extraordinary movement in art. It redefined the nature and capabilities of painting—and of color—and it altered media from sculpture to photography too. In their own ways, the Abstract Expressionists celebrated art, unbound and free, and would go on to have a profound effect on what came later.

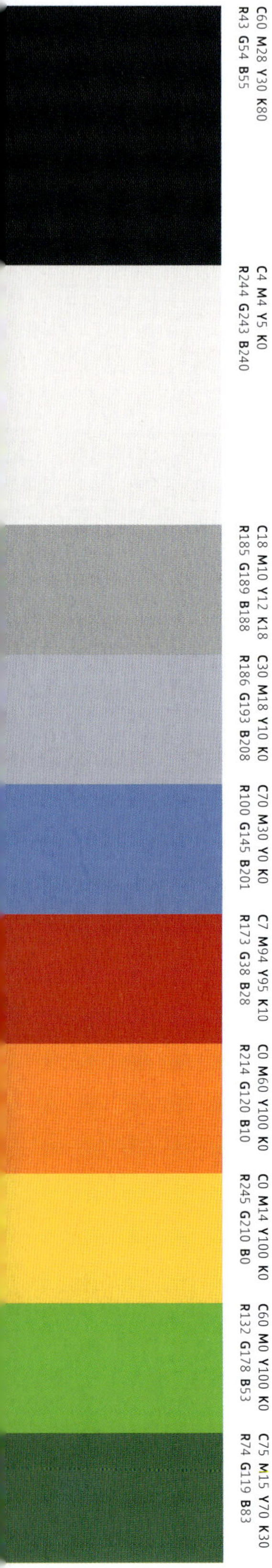

Twist and shout

Robert Delaunay
Endless Rhythm
1934

Oil on canvas,
63 11/16 x 51 3/16 in (161.9 x 130.2 cm).

Three large disks are strung out across a two-toned canvas in a diagonal line from lower left to upper right. The disks are composed of thick, interlinking white and black lines, each one leading to the next before looping back around at the ends. The two outer disks are outlined in lemon yellow and pastel blue, and a ribbon of red, greens, blue, and orange weaves through the center of all three; the round middle of each disk is divided into two halves of muted blue and gray. When Delaunay's wife and fellow artist, Sonia, saw the way the disks twist and turn in a limitless, looping chain, she came up with the title, *Endless Rhythm*.

A pioneer of abstraction, Delaunay's interest in the relationship between art, color, and music dominated his career. Together with Sonia, he explored new ideas about color theory; throughout their lives the pair practiced what Delaunay called Simultanism and his close friend, the poet Guillaume Apollinaire, renamed Orphism. They rejoiced in color—its contrasts, movement, and depth—and constructed paintings according to certain hues and shades. After dabbling in figurative work in the late 1920s, from 1930 he dedicated himself to complete abstraction, and made several compositions of wheels and arcs rendered in strong colors, harking back to *The First Disk* (1913).

Endless Rhythm is part of a series of color-based abstractions that uses the contrast between black and white to create a sense of rhythm and movement. Delaunay once said that "color is form and subject," and this painting is a continuation of that idea. Working during the first half of the 20th century, he observed the modern world of movement and technological innovation, and turned what he saw into abstract art. In Sonia's words: "Abstract art is only important if it is the endless rhythm where the very ancient and the distant future meet." Where color brings joy and the wheels just keep on turning.

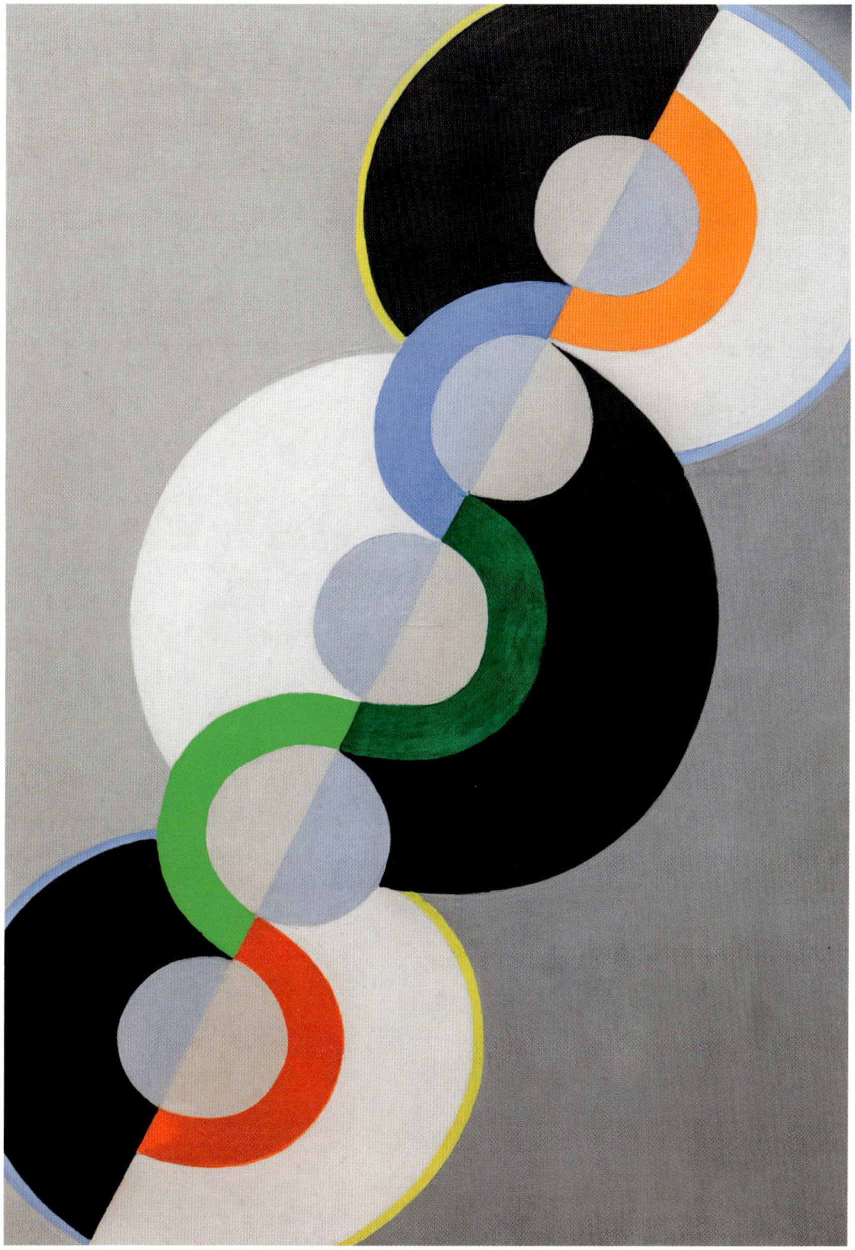

Palette

Interlinking white and black lines outlined in lemon yellow and pastel blue; a ribbon of red, greens, blue, and orange; halves of muted blue and gray.

Complementary works

- Wassily Kandinsky, *Color Study: Squares with Concentric Circles*, *c.*1913.
- Sonia Delaunay, *Electric Prisms*, 1914.
- Frank Stella, *Harran II*, 1967.

Soak and stain

Helen Frankenthaler
Mountains and Sea
1952

Oil and charcoal on unsized, unprimed canvas, 86⅜ x 117¼ in (219.4 x 297.8 cm).

C0 M39 Y74 K10 R209 G154 B76

C0 M35 Y35 K0 R230 G180 B155

C0 M91 Y85 K0 R200 G47 B42

C35 M12 Y30 K5 R173 G189 B173

C80 M36 Y0 K0 R70 G130 B192

C30 M16 Y8 K0 R187 G197 B214

Frankenthaler invented a new kind of painting with her pastoral abstraction *Mountains and Sea*. The 23-year-old had recently returned to New York from a trip to Nova Scotia, and the Canadian landscape remained fresh not only in her mind, but also in her arms and wrists. Like Jackson Pollock, she spread out a large canvas on the floor and poured liquid pigment onto it from above. Unlike Pollock, her canvas was unprimed and her oil paint was thinned with turpentine to the consistency of watercolor. Instead of sitting on top of the fabric, the paint soaked into its weave and stained it like dye. And there we have it—the invention of what would eventually become known as stain painting.

"One of the things that struck me," Frankenthaler later said of the Canadian landscape, "was the unique contrast between the great wooded peaks and the horizontal ocean—the mountains and the sea of its title." The abstract artist evoked that contrast not through line but through splashes of color, allowing soft pools of paint to define space and create a sense of depth. The impression of topography rises from the patches of sea-foam green, blue, gray, yellow, and red that fades into salmon pink. The pale-green wash that abuts the horizontal blue band recalls the rocky coastline, while the blue itself represents the Atlantic Ocean.

She painted quickly and freely, committing her memories of the landscape to canvas via soft and dissolving veils of translucent color. The fluidity of the paint injects movement into the work, as if the scene before us were living and breathing. In places, raw canvas is left exposed, and the atmospheric color washes rock against the light-filled space. Emerging around the watery stains is a kind of misty aura, evocative of weather and the seasons. Frankenthaler expanded the possibilities of abstract painting and of color itself, and this entrancing work secures her place as one of the greatest American artists of the 20th century.

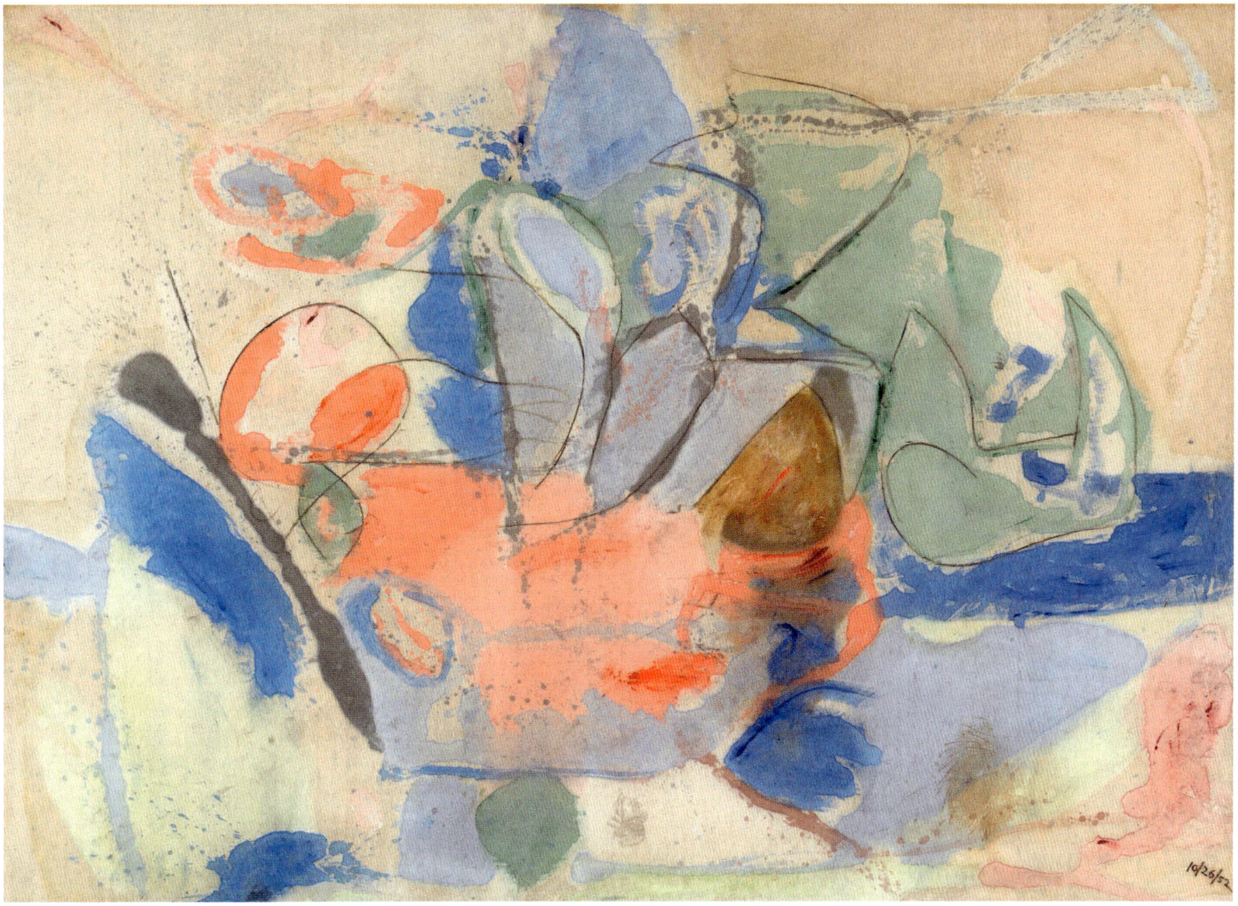

Palette

Patches of sea-foam green, blue, gray, yellow, and red that fades into salmon pink.

Complementary works

- Joan Mitchell, *City Landscape*, 1955.
- Morris Louis, *Tet*, 1958.
- Elaine de Kooning, *Desert Wall, Cave #96*, 1986.

Living in color

Lee Krasner

Bird Talk

1955

Oil, paper, photographs, and canvas collage on canvas, 58 x 56 in (147.3 x 142.2 cm).

C0 M95 Y95 K10
R183 G33 B25

C5 M96 Y50 K10
R176 G28 B75

C0 M69 Y95 K0
R210 G101 B29

C9 M39 Y60 K10
R195 G152 B102

C40 M12 Y0 K100
R0 G0 B0

From the prodigiously talented woman inspired by Pollock to the prodigiously talented woman married to him. Krasner's contribution to Abstract Expressionism was vast, and yet it was all but eclipsed by her husband, whom she met in 1941 and whose career she went on to support. She was on her way to achieving recognition herself, but doing so as a woman in the male-centered art world was no mean feat. It was only after Pollock died in an alcohol-fueled car accident that Krasner burst out with the enormous, energetic works that would define her as an artist.

A vibrant and offbeat collage of layered, colored paper, *Bird Talk* is packed full of swatches of raw canvas; scraps of paper drenched in crimson, fuchsia, and neon orange oil paint; and fragments of blurry black-and-white photographs taken by the New York artist herself. The bits and pieces come together to form a bird of prey, careening across a night sky. Roughly torn, the luminous prisms and jagged shards resemble feathers and beaks. Often, it was her own earlier work that she ripped up and rearranged in explosive compositions on canvas, the broken shapes fizzing as they clash and collide.

In Krasner's hands, destruction becomes an act of creation. Bringing together paintings, drawing, and photography, her work is at once wholly abstract and enticingly figurative. There's a sense of dynamism in the accumulation of disparate parts, even an air of menace—the carefully placed feather-like forms here could just as easily be razor-sharp shards of glass. The shredded pieces of paper pulse as they interact with each other and the negative space. "Color for me is a very mysterious thing," the artist once said. "I insist on letting it go the way it's going to go rather than forcing it." The result is an exuberantly playful and wild art moving through life to its own rhythm.

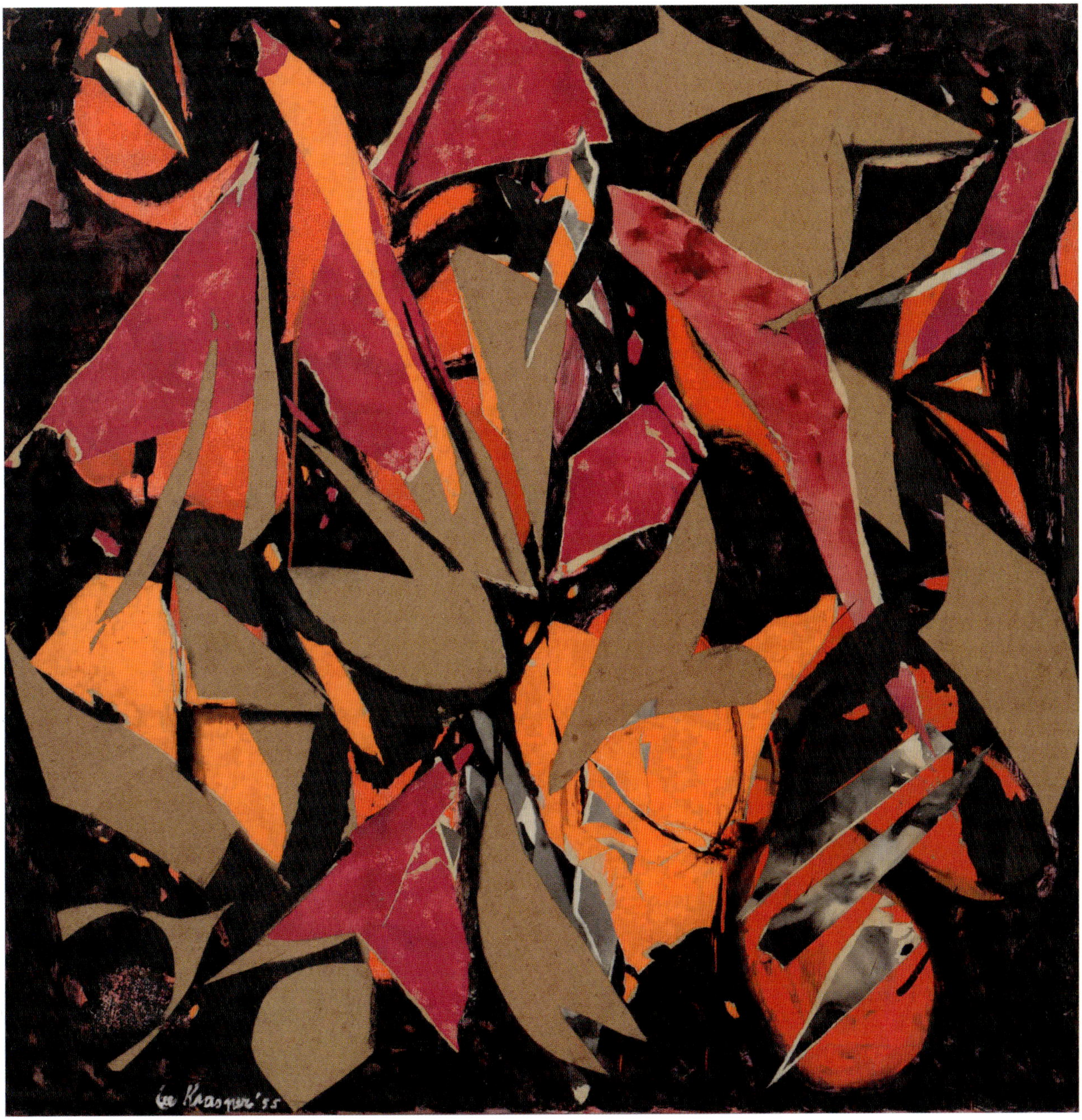

Palette

Raw canvas; paper drenched in crimson, fuchsia, and neon orange; blurry black.

Complementary works

- Robert Motherwell, *The Voyage*, 1949.
- Jackson Pollock, *Convergence*, 1952.
- Howard Hodgkin, *Leaf*, 2007–09.

C0 M69 Y100 K0
R210 G101 B13

C0 M48 Y100 K0
R221 G145 B0

C5 M9 Y9 K5
R230 G223 B218

Swallow you whole

Mark Rothko
No. 11 (Untitled)
1957

Oil on canvas,
79½ x 69$\frac{13}{16}$ in (201.9 x 177.2 cm).

Stare at Rothko's luminescent abstraction for long enough and the hazy swatches of gently contrasting colors will begin to vibrate and hum. Emerging from the rich orange backdrop are two rectangular bands of yellow-orange sandwiching a thin wash of white that teeters on transparent. The composition evokes a hot and dusty landscape at sunset—a desert, perhaps, with the white horizon a mirage. Despite its vast dimensions, this warm work is as intimate as it is magisterial; it's designed to be viewed up close, to surround and engulf the viewer. Rothko wanted his works to radiate such power that "when you turned your back to the painting, you would feel that presence the way you feel the sun on your back."

The Abstract Expressionist started out with a vibrant palette, before turning to more somber shades of purple, black, and maroon in his later years. *No. 11 (Untitled)* is the largest of a brightly colored series of paintings that glow orange and yellow. For Rothko, color was an "instrument" with which to create significant and meaningful content; he discouraged viewers from interpreting it as merely beautiful or decorative. "There is no such thing as good painting about nothing," he said early on in his career. "I'm interested only in expressing basic human emotions —tragedy, ecstasy, doom, and so on," he declared. "And the fact that a lot of people break down and cry when confronted with my pictures shows that I can communicate those basic human emotions."

Tragedy, ecstasy, doom. A combination of all three flicker beneath the surface of this seemingly sunny work. From afar, the luminescent billows of yellow-orange begin to fade into the fiery ground, but come closer and you'll appreciate the artist's subtle variations of tone and hue. The delicate layers are feathered at the edges, adding to the sense of ambiguity. It may be a sunset we're seeing, but it could also be a nuclear explosion. Rothko's art pulses with energy and emotion. Palpable and elemental, it's a form of communication hovering between beauty and violence.

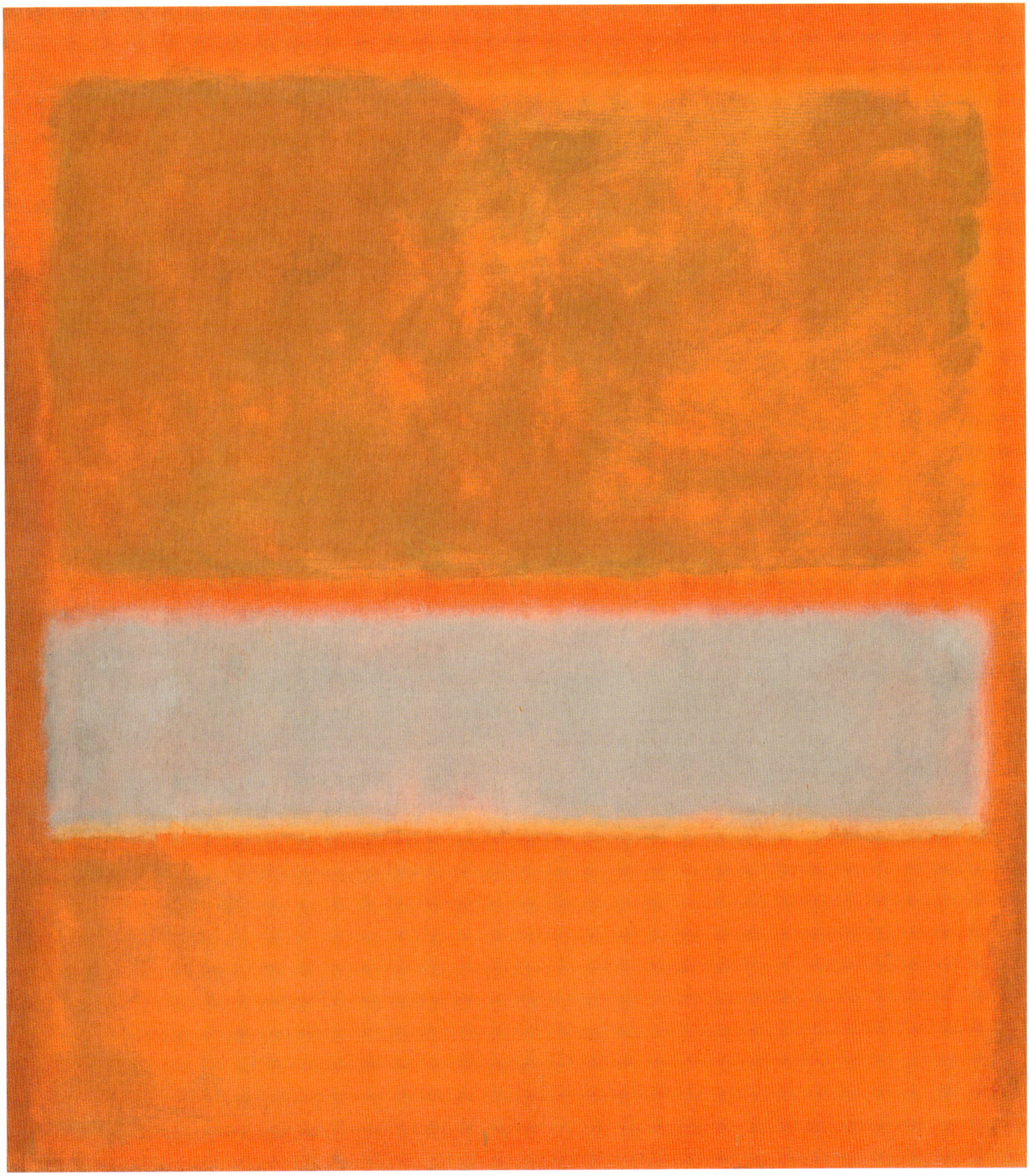

Palette

A rich orange backdrop, two rectangular bands of yellow-orange, and a thin wash of white that teeters on transparent.

Complementary works

- Barnett Newman, *Vir Heroicus Sublimis*, 1950–51.
- Robert Rauschenberg, *Banner (Stoned Moon)*, 1969.
- Susan Weil, *Musical Chairs*, 1995.

Properties of color

It will be clear by now—had it not been clear before —that color is more than hue. In fact, hue is just one of color's three attributes. The reason it's the one with which we're most familiar is because it refers directly to the color family or name, from yellow and red to blue and green. Beyond that, color is distinguished by intensity (or saturation), which denotes the amount of pure color present, and tone (or value), which is about how light or dark a color is.

Of course, the appearance of color depends on multiple factors, such as the texture of the pigment, the kind of surface to which it's applied (matte or gloss) and the environment (indoors or outdoors, viewing by candlelight or daylight). With scientific advancements have come longer-lasting pigments, which aren't as susceptible to change over time; remember that, like human beings, artworks can alter over the course of their existence. Above all, it's these three attributes—hue, intensity, and tone—that play the biggest part in color's expression.

While they're intrinsically linked, each attribute can be discussed separately, and throughout history there have been moments when one has taken precedence over the others because of context, taste, or simply an artist's or patron's personal preference. Caravaggio's (*see page 56*) drama-filled canvases are among the most theatrical when it comes to highlights and shadows, while the 20th-century Expressionists (*see page 151*) favored feverish, high-pitch saturation. During the 19th century, the Impressionists (*see page 103*) toyed with both tone and intensity, capturing with a vibrant palette the hazy effects of natural light and ever-shifting weather conditions.

For Hans Hofmann, color was a tool with which to shape space, and painting no more than "forming with color." He found the focus on linear perspective and tonal variations that occupied artists during the Renaissance (*see page 27*) limiting and preferred not to have viewers focus on any given area of a picture. In both his teaching and his practice, he acknowledged the fact that a painting is two-dimensional, and he devised a way to lend it a three-dimensional effect just by concentrating on hue. His late paintings are characterized by built-up, vivid rectangles floating on fields of color. Each hue is juxtaposed with the others, creating the impression of colored slabs advancing and receding, pulsing to a beat—an effect he called "push and pull."

With *Pompeii* (1959) and other works that featured such "color intervals," Hofmann sought to maintain an overall even intensity, and to evoke nature, living and breathing. In fact, in his mind, color was more powerful than nature itself: "In nature, light creates color; in painting, color creates light ... Color is the real building medium."

Hans Hofmann, *Pompeii*, 1959, oil on canvas, 84¼ x 52¼ in (214 × 132.7 cm).

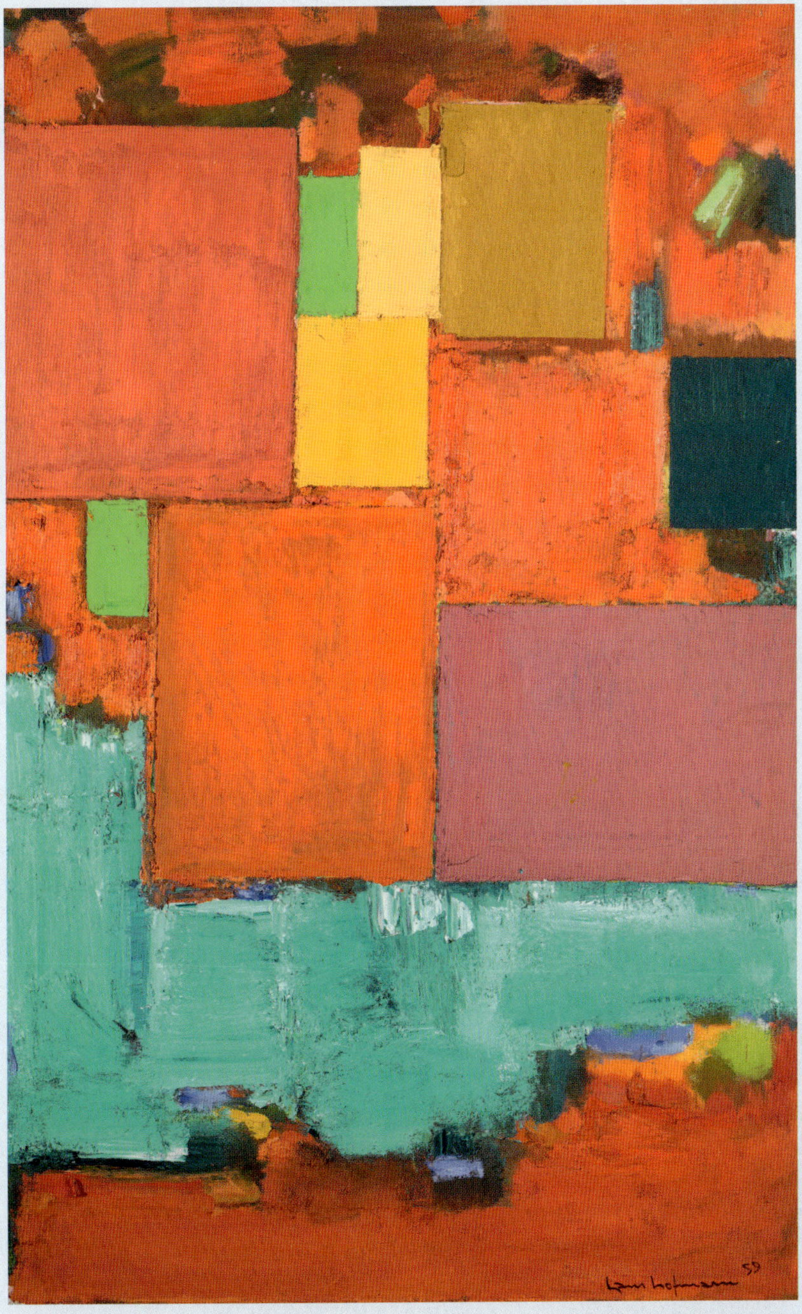

C65 M36 Y10 K5
R107 G134 B174

C55 M10 Y35 K0
R139 G180 B169

C35 M32 Y20 K5
R164 G159 B170

C5 M20 Y73 K5
R222 G192 B90

C3 M3 Y6 K6
R236 G234 B229

C80 M18 Y65 K20
R69 G125 B96

C10 M88 Y90 K20
R156 G50 B32

C90 M28 Y10 K30
R30 G105 B144

Sense of place

Richard Diebenkorn
Ocean Park #79
1975

Oil and charcoal on canvas,
93 × 81 in (236.2 × 205.7 cm).

This is one of a seminal series of 125 color-soaked geometric paintings made by Diebenkorn between 1967 and 1985, the third and final phase of his career. They all share the same name and evolve over time; they all evoke aerial views of Southern California, where he lived and worked, and at the same time windows and doors. Unlike the 20th-century American artist's early abstract works, which comprised dense and flowing forms, the Ocean Park series is decidedly flat and angular. The landscapes depicted in his previous patchwork compositions have become urban and architectural.

Like Frankenthaler (*see page 180*), Diebenkorn uses color to denote distance and space. This beautifully balanced canvas is divided into pronounced vertical columns and horizontal bands, with an empty wash of chalky Pacific blue giving way to turquoise, and then to pastel shades of sunset lavender and pink, desert yellow, and off-white. The artist applied his oil paint in thin, transparent washes, creating the impression that a dry, pale light is shining from within the canvas's weave. The colors evoke waves rocking against a sandy beach, and swimming pools glistening beneath the sun's rays.

Diebenkorn painted and repainted his contemplative abstractions, overlaying and blotting and boldening his veils of gently bleached colors. Look closer at *Ocean Park #79* and you'll notice flashes of green beneath violet, and white beneath green. He wanted to get the color and the light right, but he wasn't afraid of showing his workings: in the lower right-hand corner, a blue drip seeps to the edge of the canvas. There's a tranquility to the work, thanks to the breezy wash of blue, and yet small details add spark. Take the thin green and red lines running along the top, and the small solid rectangle of deep, burning blue. If Diebenkorn's artwork were a piece of music, these dashes of saturated color would be the high notes.

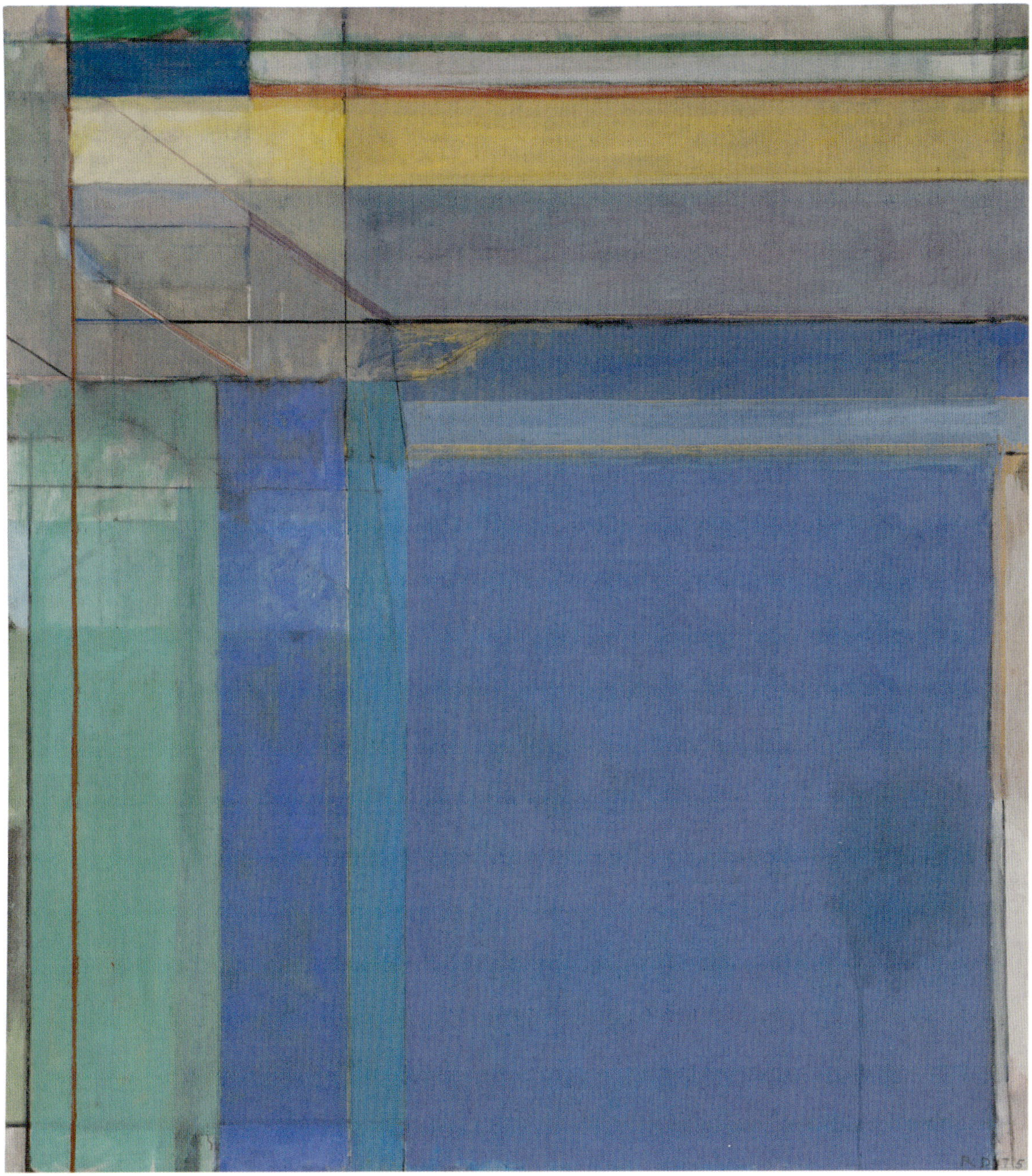

Palette

A wash of chalky blue gives way to turquoise, and then to pastel shades of lavender and pink, yellow, and off-white; thin green and red lines and a small rectangle of deep blue.

Complementary works

- David Park, *The Bus*, 1952.
- Clyfford Still, *1953*, 1953.
- Elmer Bischoff, *Orange Sweater*, 1955.

Show some restraint

Monochrome and Minimalism

C6 M6 Y10 K8
R224 G222 B214

Show some restraint

Monochrome and Minimalism

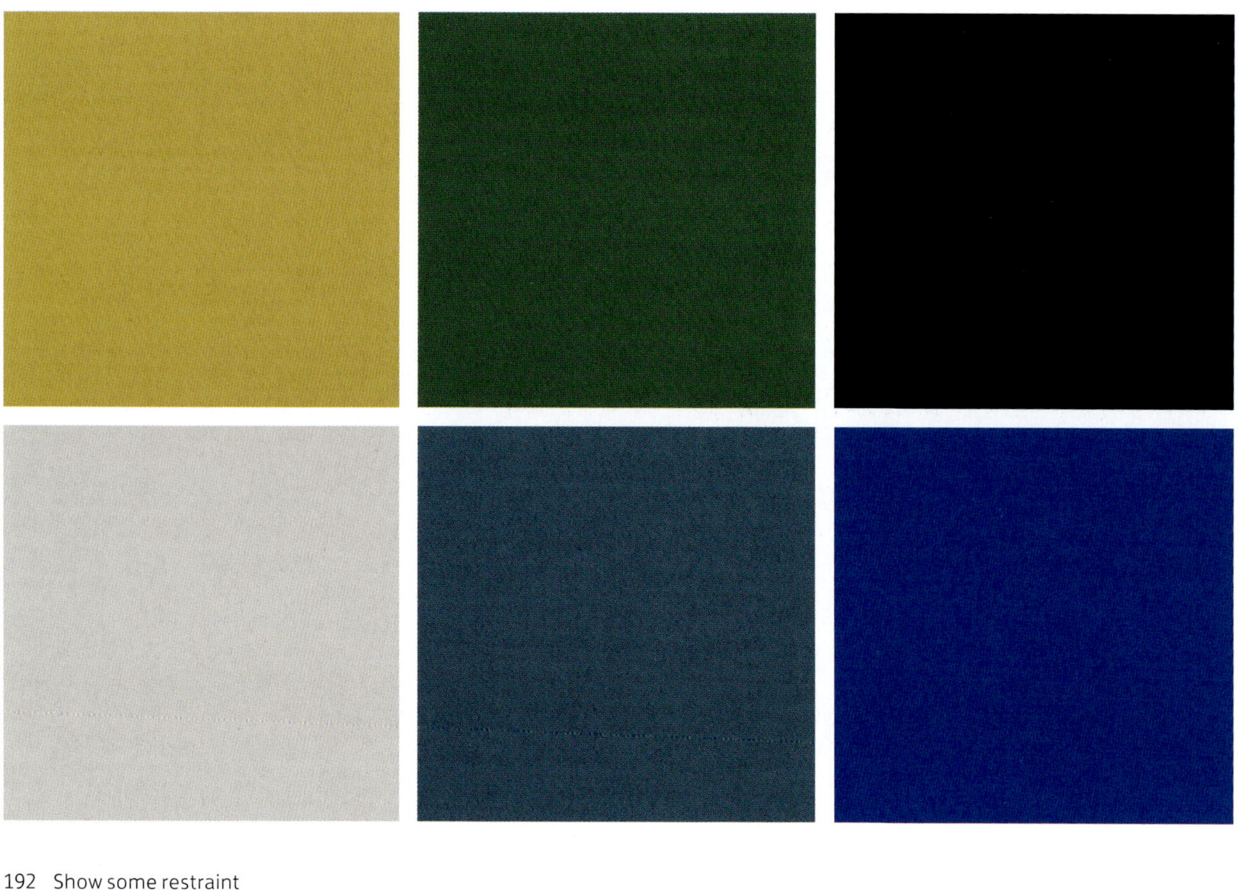

It was only natural that after the intense and emotional creations of the Abstract Expressionists, a group of artists would feel the need to give their work room to breathe. Minimalism emerged in the U.S. in the late 1950s and flourished in the two decades that followed. Among its pioneers were Donald Judd, Agnes Martin (*see page 202*), Sol LeWitt and Frank Stella (*see page 196*), whose *Black Series* (1958–60) was exhibited at the Museum of Modern Art in New York in 1959.

An extreme version of abstract art, Minimalism expands on the idea that art needs only to represent itself. It either seeks to communicate spiritual purity or focuses exclusively on the physical form that a work takes and the medium with which it's made. Where the Abstract Expressionists prized subjectivity and the act of creation, the Minimalists prized logic, order, and neutrality. Gestural brush marks and paint-splattered canvases were replaced with simple geometric shapes, straight lines, and repetitive grids.

Minimalism built on the concerns of abstract art movements that had come before. It was inspired in part by the pared-back elements and factory-manufactured materials of the Russian Constuctivist and Suprematist movements of the 1910s and 1920s. When Kazimir Malevich painted a white border on a medium-sized canvas and then applied black paint within it, he sought to liberate painting from representation and, in his words, reduce everything to the "zero of form." With his *Black Square* (1915), he achieved a painting of nothing, with no counterpart.

Minimalist art is often three-dimensional but, as the examples in this chapter show, there were plenty of Minimalist painters, too. No matter the medium, the aim was to create impersonal and non-referential art. In reducing their work to its essentials—color, form, and texture—Minimalists moved away from the idea that certain hues conjure a feeling or a mood. They also rejected the notion that hues only exist in relation to one another: enter monochrome. It should come as no surprise that, for some artists, creating totally abstract art entailed throwing out all but one color.

In fact, monochrome paintings had existed for centuries. The earliest surviving examples were made in the Middle Ages for devotional purposes and were painted in black, white, and gray—also known as grisaille. This was partly to focus the mind, free from distractions, and partly to signal a shift from the real, color-filled world to a spiritual realm. From the 15th century onward, artists occasionally turned to black and white to work through technical and compositional issues, such as the play of light and shadow. And with time, paintings in shades of gray were made as stand-alone works, from Jan van Eyck's sculpture-like *Saint Barbara* (1437) to Jean Auguste Dominique Ingres's *Odalisque in Grisaille* (1824–34).

By the mid-20th century, artists were able to pick and choose from a vast range of colors—which is exactly why some returned to black and white or another single hue. Faced with a limitless palette, there was something thought-provoking and radical about focusing only on a single color or its variations.

Admittedly, there's something a little cold about Minimalism—something a little too neat and systematic—and the same could be said of monochrome artworks. But in paring their images back, artists freed themselves up to test the limits of art and made room for viewers to appreciate elements they might have otherwise overlooked, from texture to subtle shifts in shade and tone. The result is a different kind of seeing, and an art that speaks for itself. It's a lesson in finding meaning in absence and, possibly, more in less.

Outside the box

Josef Albers
Homage to the Square: Apparition
1959

Oil on Masonite,
47½ x 47½ in (120.6 x 120.6 cm).

C10 M18 Y80 K10
R205 G183 B72

C24 M18 Y30 K14
R177 G176 B158

C75 M21 Y25 K25
R75 G124 B141

C68 M20 Y79 K35
R82 G113 B65

Albers described the square, which occupied him from 1950 until his death in 1976, as the "dish I serve my craziness about color in." He had been a student and a professor at the Bauhaus, a German school that combined fine art with arts and crafts. When the Nazis closed the campus in 1933, Albers emigrated to the U.S. to teach a generation of American artists (among them, Donald Judd and Robert Rauschenberg). *Homage to the Square* is a series in which he concentrated years of practice and that explores the instability of color, as well as the interplay of color and shape. Through his geometric abstractions, he showed how the same color can morph and shift, depending on its surroundings.

A deceptively simple work, *Apparition* features four superimposed flat squares of oil paint applied with a palette knife, straight from the tube, onto a panel primed with white ground. Nestled among planes of gray, blue, and green, the central yellow square appears to advance toward the viewer. The work demonstrates how subtle variations in hue, tone, intensity, and positioning can create an impression of contrast and depth. On the back of this, and every other panel in his signature series, Albers recorded the names and manufacturers of the paints.

"In order to use color effectively it is necessary to recognize that color deceives continuously," said Albers, who in this series and his influential book *Interaction of Color* (1963) sought to teach viewers how to observe the color spectrum, as well as to celebrate color's ability to transform itself and deceive the eye. *Homage to the Square* comprises more than a thousand variations of the same format of three or four squares nestled inside each other. "They all are of different palettes, and, therefore, so to speak, of different climates," wrote the artist in 1965. "Choice of the colors used, as well as their order, is aimed at an interaction—influencing and changing each other forth and back. Thus, character and feeling alter from painting to painting without any additional 'handwriting' or, so-called, texture."

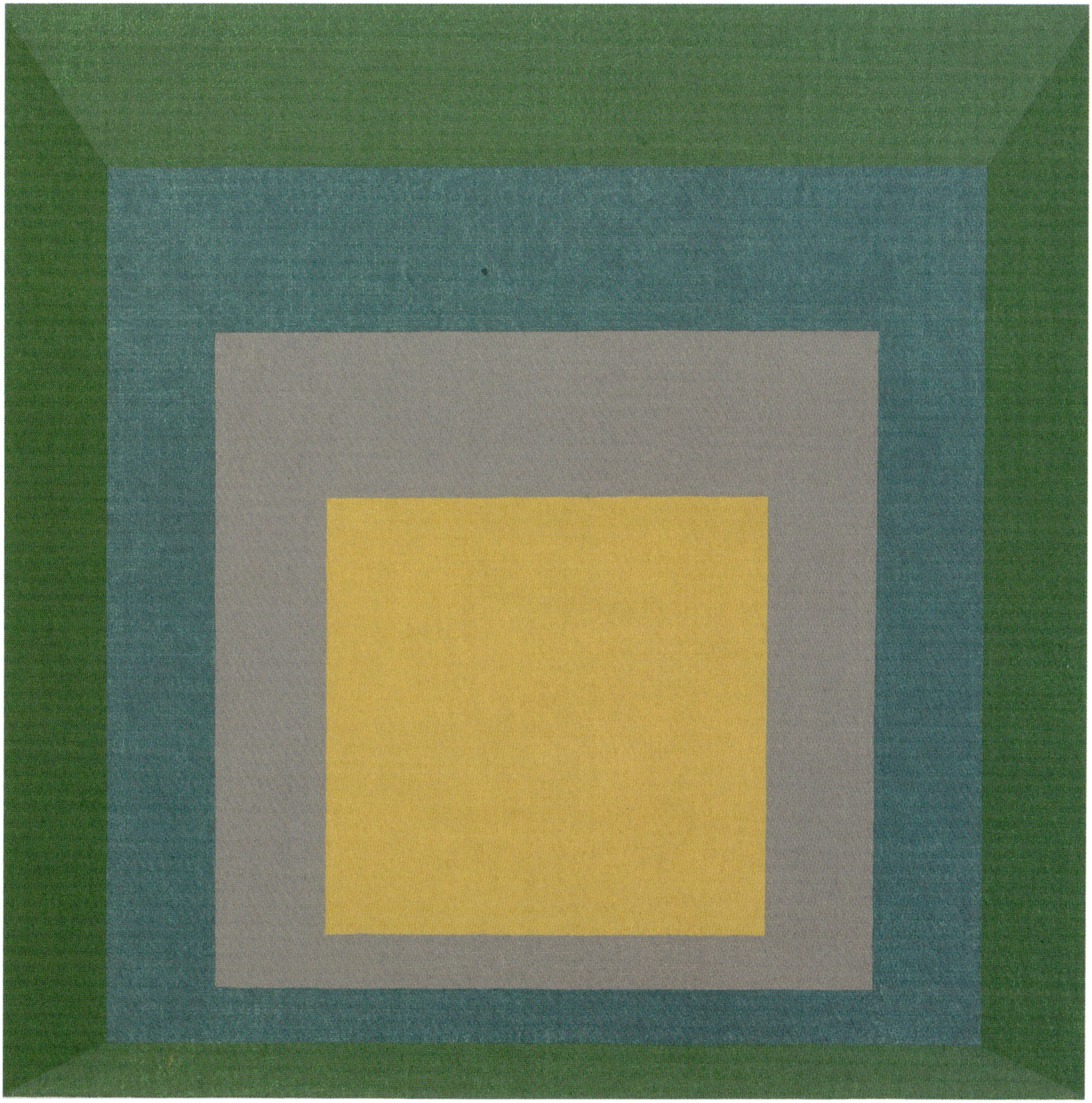

Palette

Yellow, gray, blue, and green.

Complementary works

- Anni Albers, *Black White Yellow*, 1926.
- Maria Lalić, *History Painting 17 Italian. Naples Yellow*, 1995.
- David Nash, *Oak Leaves Through May*, 2016.

C40 M4 Y6 K100
R0 G0 B0

Back to black

Frank Stella
The Marriage of Reason and Squalor, II
1959

Enamel on canvas,
90¾ x 132¾ in (230.5 x 337.2 cm).

Stella's monochromatic painting shows the tools of its making. The postwar American artist used commercial enamel paint that he applied with a house painter's brush, which was the same width as the thick black bands. Moving away from expressive brushstrokes, his stripes are the same size and run parallel to one another, to the edge of the canvas, leaving narrow gaps of unpainted, bare canvas in between. Stella drew attention to the structure of the artwork, and to the artwork as object. "My painting is based on the fact that only what can be seen there is there," he said in a radio interview in 1964. "What you see is what you see."

In other words, there is no hidden meaning in *The Marriage of Reason and Squalor, II* – or is there? Some say it nods to the bleak studio in which the artist first found himself working in New York. Primarily, though, the four simple and slightly varied dark works in Stella's famed *Black Series* (1958–60) of paintings, which gave way to maximalist canvases filled with color, prize form over content. Though there are slight inconsistencies in the black bands, which were painted freehand, there is nothing gestural about the abstract artist's stark and emotionless brush marks. The symmetrical composition of two sets of concentric lines adds to the sense of regularity. Stella set out to create "evenness, a kind of all-oneness, where intensity, saturation, and density remained regular over the entire surface."

He also tried to keep the paint "as good as it looked in the can," Stella sourced his paint from local hardware shops and was fond of an American brand called Benjamin Moore, which supposedly had the "nice dead kind of color" he was after. His paintings deny depth and any sense of spatial illusion; in paring them right back, he made them about the act of painting, its materials and the result. Stella wanted his minimalist paintings to have a strong and immediate visual impact, free from references to anything but the work itself.

Palette

Thick black bands with narrow gaps of unpainted, bare canvas in between.

Complementary works

- Bridget Riley, *Crest*, 1964.
- Cy Twombly, *Untitled*, 1970.
- Pierre Soulages, *Painting 181×244 25 February, 2009*, 2009.

The Pantone palette

It all began in New Jersey in 1963. Lawrence Herbert was a chemistry graduate who joined the American printing company Pantone in 1956 and bought it in 1962. He noticed how hard it was for designers and printers to communicate, and how often clients claimed that the colors used in their products were different to those they had agreed on. To reduce the number of variables, Herbert devised a universal color-matching system that enabled individuals and businesses around the world to faithfully articulate and reproduce consistent hues.

The world-renowned Pantone Matching System, which started off with 500 colors organized through a numbering system and chip format, today encompasses more than 10,000 color standards across materials, from pigments and plastics to textiles and coatings. By specifying the exact ink formula for each shade, this innovative tool ensures that—despite changes in light, medium, and weather—color is accurately standardized. Now available digitally as well as physically, it's used in industries such as printing, publishing, packaging, computer, fashion and film.

Herbert wasn't the first to attempt to create a universal color language. His predecessors include the German mineralogist Abraham Gottlob Werner, who in the late-18th century created a scheme that would allow him to describe subtle color variations with consistent terminology. That scheme was adapted by the Scottish flower painter Patrick Syme, who used the minerals described in Werner's handbook to create a series of color charts. *Werner's Nomenclature of Colours* (1814) is a precise and lyrical guide to the colors of the natural world that pre-photography enabled artists, naturalists, scientists, and anthropologists to accurately identify hues in animals, plants, and minerals. Charles Darwin famously used the guide during his seminal voyage to the Canary, Cape Verde, and Madeira islands on HMS *Beagle*.

The names of the colors used by Werner have a charm of their own, from Plum Purple and Asparagus Green to Wax Yellow and Hyacinth Red. Pantone also names its numerically identified hues: there's Sand Dollar, Chili Pepper, Mimosa, and Ultra Violet.

Color standardization is critical when it comes to global brand identities—think Coca-Cola and its signature red or Starbucks and its pine-green signage—and the Pantone of today has evolved into a global brand itself. In 1986 it established the Pantone Color Institute, which provides color consulting and trend forecasting to designers and brands, and since 2000 it has celebrated a Color of the Year (the first was Cerulean Blue, chosen to reflect the bright future promised by the new millennium). There are now color-keyed mugs, coffee pots, suitcases, and even hotels inspired by the iconic Pantone chart. And, of course, the color swatches themselves are considered design objects.

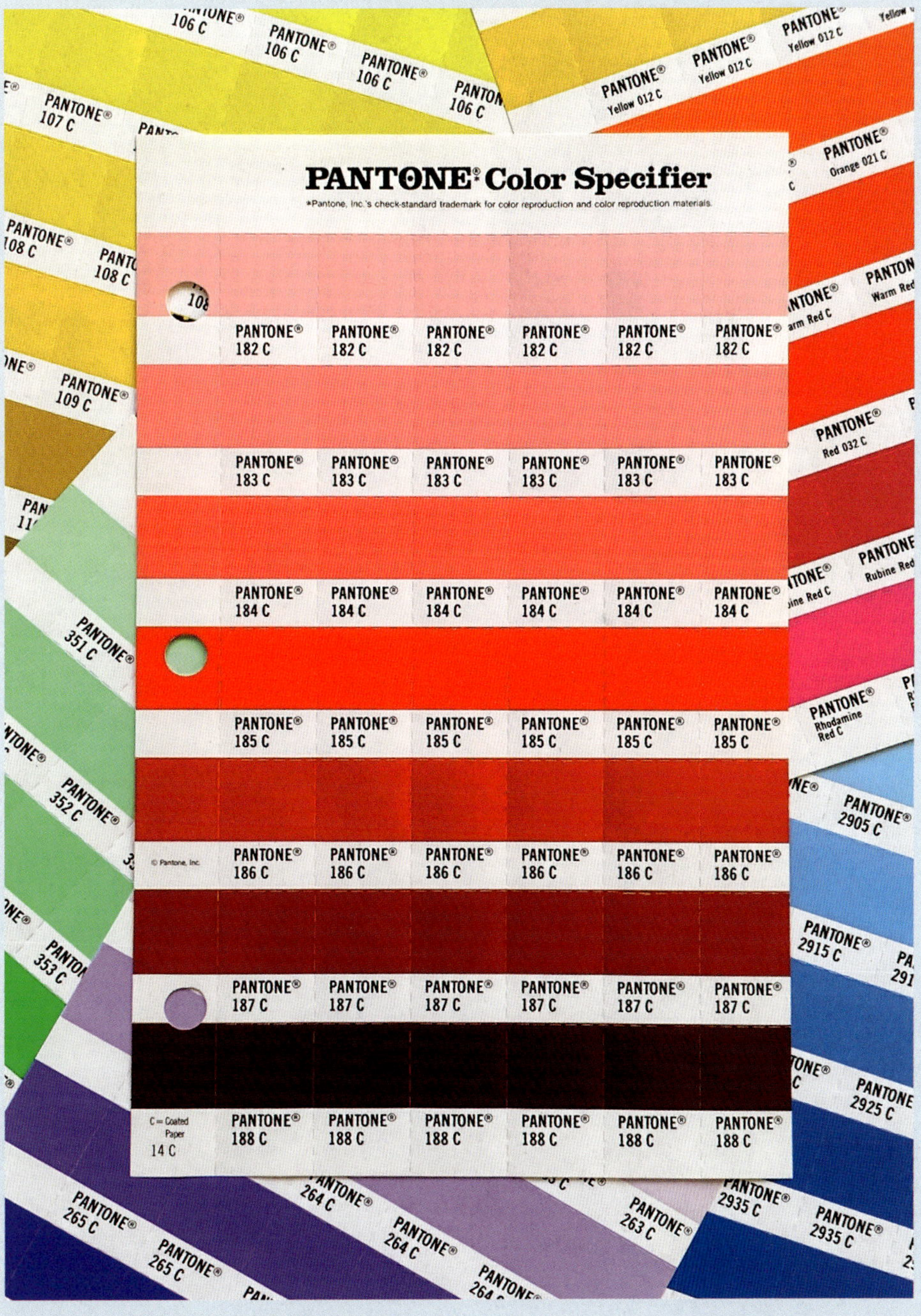

Pantone color charts.

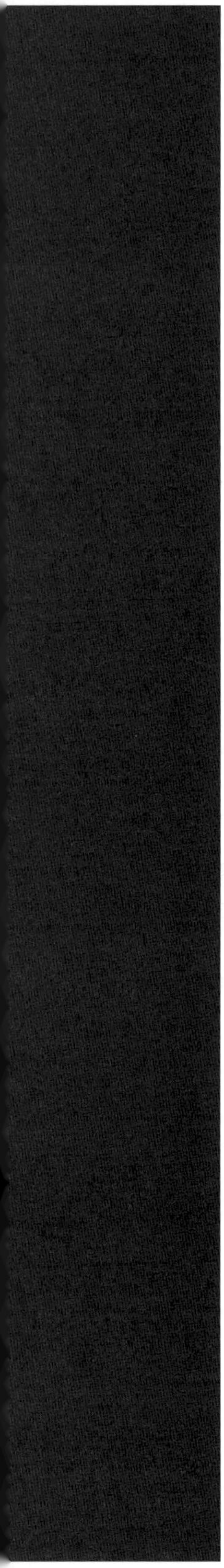

C100 M92 Y0 K0
R44 G50 B133

One-stop shop

Yves Klein
IKB 79
1959

Paint on canvas on plywood,
55 x 47⅛ in (139.7 × 119.7 cm).

When it comes to artists who have focused on one specific color, the first name that springs to mind is Yves Klein. The French artist began making monochrome paintings in 1947, and a decade later collaborated with a Parisian paint supplier to create a particular shade of ultramarine blue, which he called International Klein Blue and registered as a trademarked, patented color in 1957. Klein described it as "a Blue in itself, disengaged from all functional justification," and he used it to create saturated fields of pure powdery color.

IKB 79 is one of almost 200 entirely blue paintings that Klein made during his career, and by the time he'd reached number 79, he'd discovered how to maximize the hue's luminosity and achieve a fine and even surface. While medieval and Renaissance artists mixed the raw pigment with oils, which had a dulling effect, Klein worked with chemists and a color vendor called Edouard Adam to create a synthetic binder that preserved the pigment's radiance. He would treat his canvas with a milk protein that encouraged the paint to stick, mix his paint with a fixative, and apply it with a roller, which left no marks. Once dry, the pigment appeared to hover over the surface, giving the work an unmodulated velvety finish, with no center, hierarchy, or form.

For Klein, making monochrome art was a way of rejecting representation and achieving creative freedom—and what better shade to paint with than one associated with infinite space? He took inspiration from the French philosopher Gaston Bachelard, who said, "First there is nothing, then a depth of nothingness, then a profundity of blue." Klein once mused: "What is blue? Blue is the invisible becoming visible. Blue has no dimensions, it is beyond the dimensions of which other colors partake." He dedicated himself to his signature shade and dubbed himself the painter of dreams.

Palette

A saturated field of pure powdery International Klein Blue.

Complementary works

- Lucio Fontana, *Spatial Concept, Expectations*, 1966.
- Ellsworth Kelly, *Lake II*, 2002.
- Callum Innes, *Exposed Painting Delft Blue*, 2018.

C6 M8 Y12 K8
R223 G218 B208

Read between the lines

Agnes Martin
White Stone
1964

Oil and graphite on linen, 71⅞ x 71⅞ in (182.6 x 182.6 cm).

It would be easy to pass by Martin's solitary plain field without pausing, and what a shame that would be. From afar, it may look like a hazy blank canvas or an untouched enamel surface, but up close you'll discover that *White Stone* is composed of a delicate veil of subtly nuanced color—ivory from some angles, pink and silvery gray from others—laid over a hand-drawn grid. Although regularly spaced, the faint, graphite lines are far from mechanical, shifting as they crisscross the support, like mesh. They're skinny and delicate, on the brink of dissolving beneath the paint. Martin once said of her paintings: "They are light, lightness, about merging, about formlessness, breaking down form."

It took time for Martin to develop her signature grid, but by 1960 she had it down, and she continued to produce large, square canvases of close-knit horizontal and vertical lines for the rest of her life. She was inspired by spirituality and the natural world—notably the New Mexico desert. Let your eyes relax and you can almost glimpse daylight in the muted color. Martin's monochromatic abstractions are mellow, meditative. They're also painstaking in their obsessive repetition and desire for order—a trait that can perhaps be traced to the artist's schizophrenia, with which she was first diagnosed as a young woman.

Although this is abstract art (Martin is often associated with both Minimalism and Abstract Expressionism), the artist's hand is never far away—in *White Stone* it's there in the quietly controlled lines and the rhythmic field of color that looks soft to touch. You can almost sense her taking care as she works, straining to make her marks precise and exact, to achieve clarity. There's an absence and at the same time a presence, which is what makes her work so memorable and gently soothing—a balm in past and present times of unrest. To appreciate it in all its subtleties, in Martin's words, "You go there and sit and look."

Palette

Ivory from some angles, pink and silvery gray from others.

Complementary works

- Kazimir Malevich, *Suprematist Composition: White on White*, 1918.
- Ad Reinhardt, *Number 107*, 1950.
- Jasper Johns, *White Flag*, 1955.

By popular demand

Pop Art and the Pictures generation

C60 **M**0 **Y**5 **K**0
R129 **G**194 **B**228

By popular demand

Pop Art and the Pictures generation

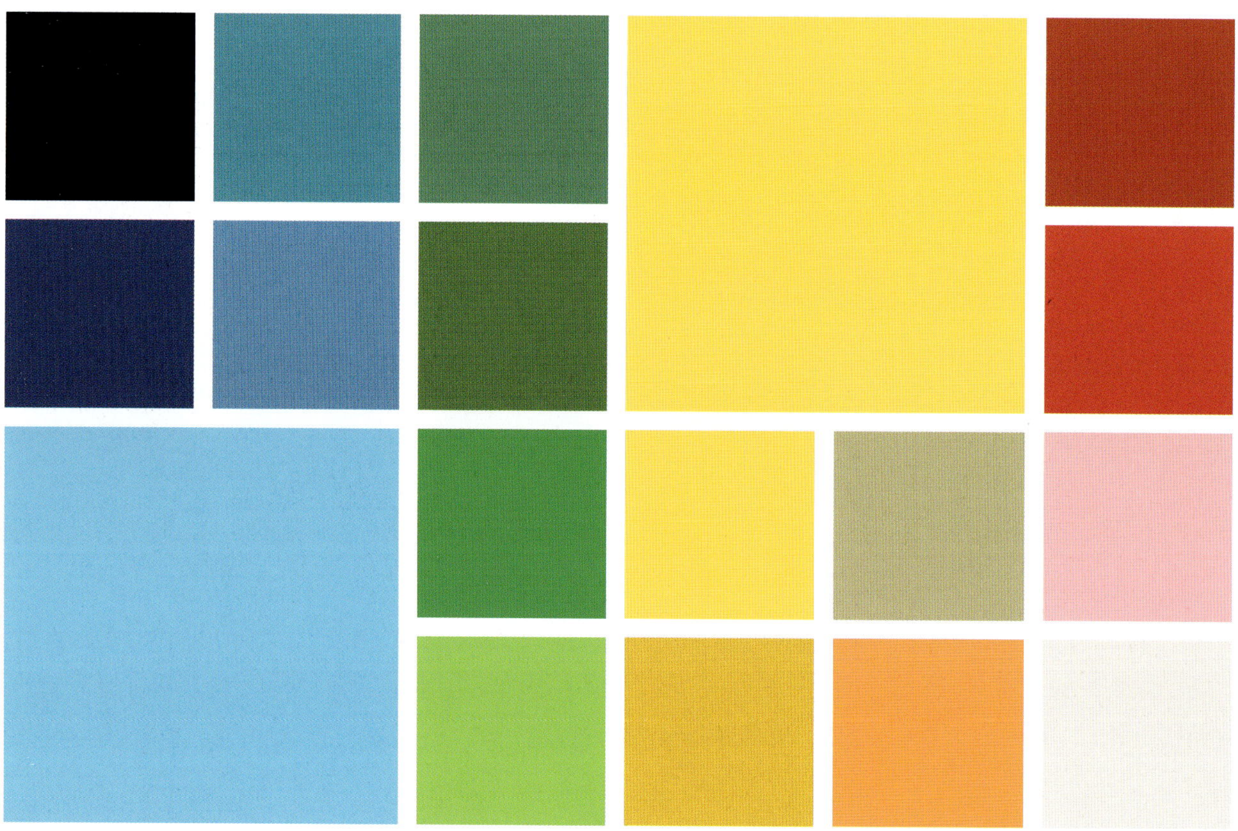

"Pop Art is: Popular (designed for a mass audience), Transient (short-term solution), Expendable (easily forgotten), Low cost, Mass produced, Young (aimed at youth), Witty, Sexy, Gimmicky, Glamorous, Big business." These are the "characteristics of Pop Art" that the British artist Richard Hamilton listed in a letter to his friends, the architects Peter and Alison Smithson, in 1957.

Emerging in both the U.S. and the U.K. in the late 1950s and the early 1960s, during a period of economic and political growth that followed the Second World War, the Pop Art movement was no less than a cultural revolution. It began as a revolt against increased consumerism and the conformity of mass production, as well as the mainstream art world and conventional views of what art should (and shouldn't) be. And it wasn't the only uprising taking place at the time: the Vietnam War was sparking protests, the Civil Rights Movement gaining momentum, and the women's liberation movement finding its voice.

Against this backdrop of unrest and experimentation, a generation of bright young artists got to work. They wanted to free themselves from the elitism and ideals they had encountered in the classroom and museums, and instead make art from subjects and materials that mirrored and critiqued their immediate surroundings. They turned to everyday items, advertising, product packaging, car design, magazines, comic books, and cigarette packets. Hollywood and pop music, too: Marilyn Monroe was an icon; TV had replaced radio as the leading media outlet, and popular culture played out to a soundtrack of rock and roll. They took the existing subjects of the day and transfigured them into art that engaged with popular culture and had popular appeal.

How did they do it? With a bright palette of primary colors, often applied directly from the can or tube in bold strokes and planes. With the arrival of fast-drying acrylic paint—more on this later—artists were able to apply vast swathes of color and, without waiting, swiftly add extra layers and details. Moving away from the highly gestural canvases of the Abstract Expressionists (*see page 177*), Pop artists produced work that bore little to no sign of their hand. Inspired by commercial advertising techniques, they began to work with silkscreens and multiples—anything that tied in with the idea of mass production and, in turn, subverted the notion of originality. They rejected the boundaries between high and low art, and disparate mediums and methods, bringing together painting, printmaking, and photography—the handmade and the readymade.

Pop Art was a male-dominated movement, and in the U.S. Andy Warhol (*see page 216*) was its brightest star. From The Factory (even the name of his studio was a reference to mass production), he replicated brands from Campbell's Soup to Coca-Cola and made multiples of celebrities such as Elvis Presley and Elizabeth Taylor. Other notable names include Jasper Johns and Robert Rauschenberg. In the U.K. there was the previously mentioned Hamilton and Eduardo Paolozzi. In fact, Pop Art spread beyond the U.S. and the U.K., and was interpreted differently according to the context; also, though their contribution was for some time sidelined, women played a key part. In their art, Pauline Boty (*see page 208*) and others used the language of Pop Art to critique the depiction of women in popular culture.

Pop Art is familiar and accessible and optimistic. But it's also subversive—a site of criticism and protest. The birth of Pop Art was a liberating moment in art history, one that celebrated the everyday and the throwaway, too. The artists on the following pages took the eye-popping colors and images of commercial design and media culture, and turned them into entertainment for the masses.

C5 M96 Y100 K15
R168 G31 B19

C33 M30 Y35 K30
R136 G132 B122

C0 M48 Y25 K0
R222 G155 B157

C49 M10 Y79 K25
R124 G146 B73

Nostalgia for now

Pauline Boty
Colour Her Gone
1962

Oil on canvas,
48 x 48 in (121.9 x 121.9 cm).

The word that springs to mind when looking at Boty's collage-like image of Marilyn Monroe is "lush." The ill-fated film star, who died shortly before the portrait was painted, appears in front of a swatch of rosy, red wallpaper, with swirling abstractions in gray, pink, and green either side. The impression is that she's peering out of a window, her platinum-blonde hair bobbed, her eyes and mouth stretched into a smile. Boty, whose highly regarded work disappeared from public view after her death and who has only recently been recognized for her startling contribution to British Pop Art, was fascinated by Monroe—by her fame, her beauty, and her status as a sex symbol.

Trained as a stained-glass artist, Boty had a feel for color and composition. Her relaxed depiction of Monroe in a casual baby-blue top is in stark contrast with the overtly sexualized images produced by the artist's male contemporaries, such as Andy Warhol (*see page 216*). The wallpaper of blooming red roses appears to have peeled off at the bottom of the board and is inching up toward Monroe's neck. Still, she smiles for her audience—or does she? There's something tense about the way her teeth are clamped together, her chin raised. Any moment, she could be eclipsed.

"It's almost like painting mythology," Boty said of Pop Art, "a present-day mythology—film stars, etc ... the 20th-century gods and goddesses. People need them, and the myths that surround them, because their own lives are enriched by them. Pop Art colors those myths." Like Monroe, Boty was beautiful and vivacious, and died tragically young—in her case, from cancer, aged 28 (doctors discovered the tumor when she was pregnant, and she turned down the offer of abortion and treatment in favor of having the baby). She was the first and only female British Pop artist, and in her fresh and vibrant art she asserted her own sex and femininity.

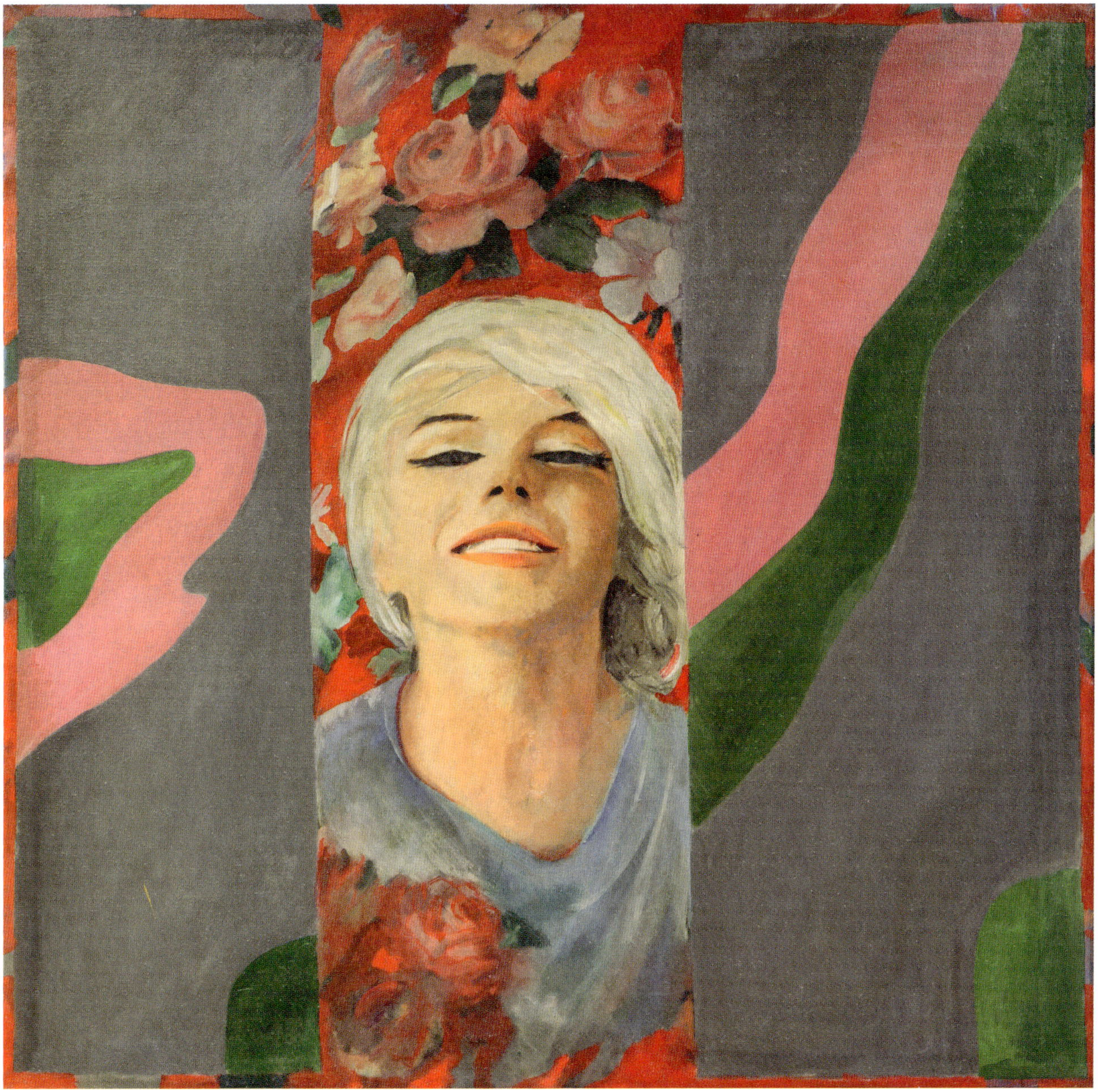

Palette

Rosy, red wallpaper, with swirling abstract patterns in gray, pink, and green.

Complementary works

- Richard Hamilton, *My Marilyn*, 1965.
- Andy Warhol, *Marilyn Monroe*, 1967.
- Peter Blake, *Diamond Dust Marilyn*, 2010.

C0 M90 Y100 K0
R201 G50 B20

C0 M10 Y80 K0
R248 G221 B78

C88 M70 Y10 K30
R49 G65 B113

C78 M5 Y85 K5
R85 G153 B80

C39 M0 Y80 K0
R177 G202 B88

C0 M28 Y10 K0
R235 G198 B202

C40 M4 Y6 K100
R0 G0 B0

C0 M0 Y0 K6
R243 G243 B243

Melt in your mouth

Evelyne Axell

Ice Cream 1

1964

Oil on canvas,
31½ x 27⅝ in (80 x 70 cm).

When the Philadelphia Museum of Art uploaded an image of this provocative oil painting to its Facebook page in 2016, the social media site censored it on account of it "containing excessive amounts of skin or suggestive content." In response, the museum reuploaded the image, along with a message. It said that Axell's work can be understood as a critique of mainstream Pop Art, in which women are regularly depicted as "passive, decorative objects," and that in contrast she portrayed "active, confident women who pursue satisfaction on their own terms—such as the protagonist of *Ice Cream 1*, who unabashedly enjoys her dessert."

Like Boty, Axell uses color to evoke a sense of female freedom and the sexual revolution of the 1960s. The monochrome face of a beautiful woman is juxtaposed with cherry-red hair and appears to float free in an undulating abstract sea of yellow, blue, and green spirals. There's no sign of the woman's body—just her hand, wrapped around a pale beige cone. As she pushes out her tongue to lick her melting ice cream—a neon blob of strawberry pink and mint green—she rapturously closes her eyes, her long lashes lying flat on her skin. Yes, she's taking pleasure in her dessert, which is leaking onto her fingers, but she's not here for male viewing pleasure. Instead, she's losing herself in the technicolor sweetness.

Amid the male-dominated Pop movement, the Belgian actress turned artist, who trained under the Belgian Surrealist René Magritte, created highly saturated images of self-sufficient, pleasure-seeking women. Rejecting the passive portrayals produced by her male counterparts, she sought to liberate women while drawing on the vocabulary of Pop Art. The result is art that's bold and bright, and above all joyful and unapologetically erotic. In Axell's paintings, women can be whatever and whoever they want to be—including aroused to the point of abstraction.

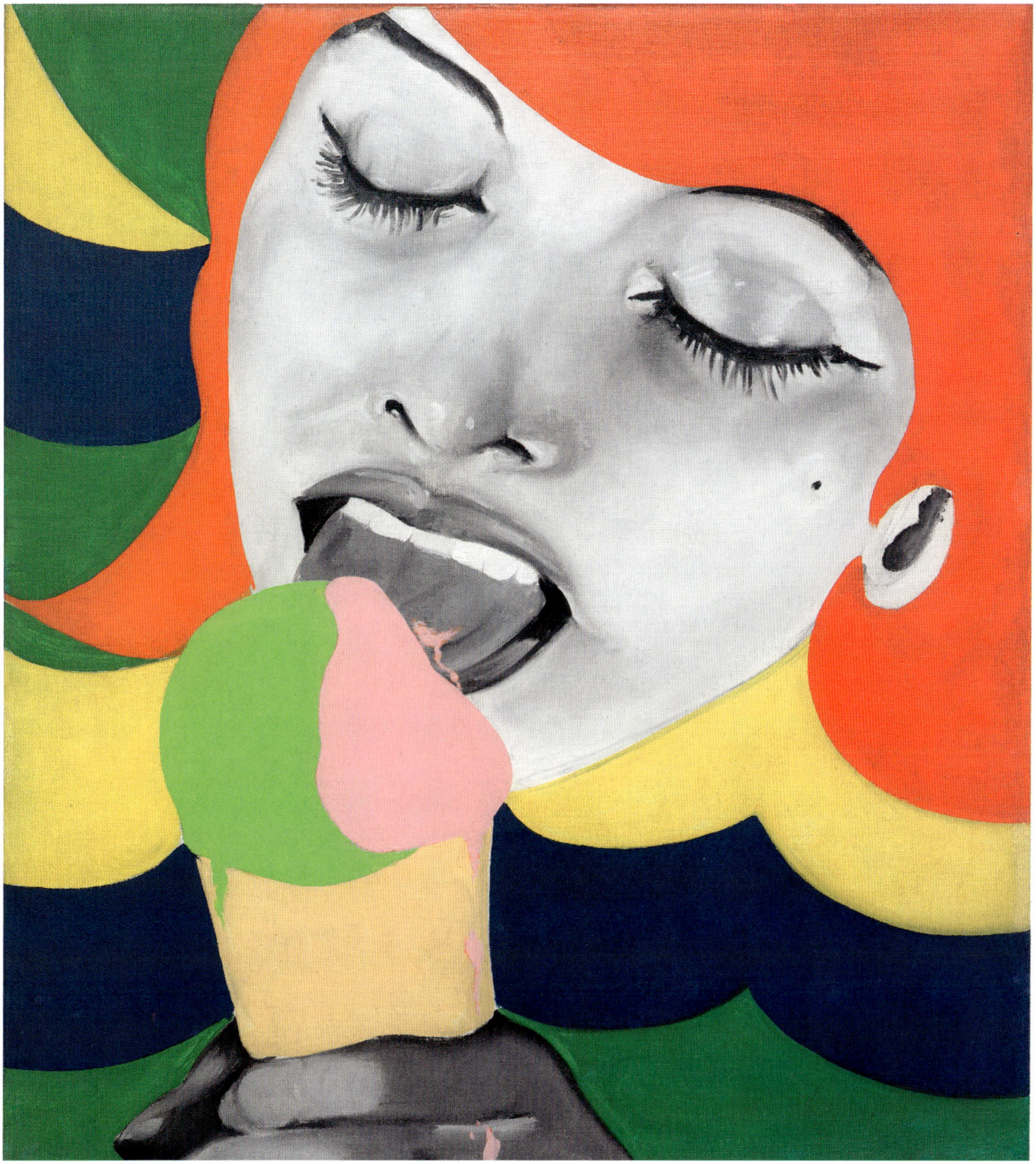

Palette

A black-and-white face with cherry-red hair in an abstract sea of yellow, blue, and green spirals.

Complementary works

- James Rosenquist, *Smoked Glass*, 1962.
- Marjorie Strider, *Come Hither*, 1963.
- Alex Katz, *Ariel 3*, 2020.

Anything is possible

After Jan van Eyck's (*see page 38*) masterful manipulation of oil paint in the 15th century, and the technological innovations in paint storage in the 19th century, the most significant advancement in artists' materials was the development of acrylic paints in the late 1940s and early 1950s. During the Second World War, synthetic resins had become cheaper and more readily available than natural materials.

Initially used to bind the pigments of household paints, acrylic resin solutions were soon being designed specifically for artists. Created by the pioneering New York-based Bocour Artists Colors and marketed under the brand name Magna, these paints could be diluted with solvents, such as turpentine, and mixed with oils. Roy Lichtenstein was a dedicated follower, favoring their smooth, matte finish, and it was with this medium that Mark Rothko (*see page 184*) was able to achieve his shimmery saturated surfaces.

In the mid-1950s, acrylic emulsion paints arrived on the scene. Unlike the Magna colors, which resolubilized when topped with fresh paint, these were waterproof once dry, making it quick and easy to build up layers. Andy Warhol (*see page 216*) was an early champion, as was Helen Frankenthaler (*see page 180*). When they arrived in the U.K. in the 1960s, David Hockney (*see page 214*) used them to create some of his most celebrated works.

As well as giving artists the freedom to paint over their work without disturbing what lies beneath, acrylic paints—which don't affect paper and textiles to the same degree as oil paints—enable them to make work on more diverse supports. Depending on how much water is added, they can be thinned to watercolor-like glazes, used as they are to build up thick amounts of impasto or applied on top of a synthetic gesso (or primer) to create texture. They're versatile in terms of both thickness and gloss, and neither crack nor fade with time.

But what about color beyond the medium of painting? From the 20th century onward, the possibilities have been endless when it comes to color experiments and new materials. Artists freed color from the two-dimensionality of painting and presented it as sculpture, installation, performance. In 1968, Gilberto Zorio presented an asbestos bowl filled with yellow sulfur and iron filings, and two years later Bruce Nauman created a narrow corridor of acid-green light. Anish Kapoor made a mountain out of wood, gesso, and red pigment in 1985. And in 2014, Kara Walker carved a giant white sphinx from sugar and polystyrene.

The avant-garde feminist artist Judy Chicago took things one step further. It was in the late 1960s that she turned to pyrotechnics, and began making art out of pastel-colored smoke and painted female bodies. Using fireworks and flares, she sought to "feminize" and soften her surrounding environment, setting these technicolor figures and plumes against the stark backdrop of the California desert. As she once said, "This was a very different time: artists could just go out into the environment and do things without a permit."

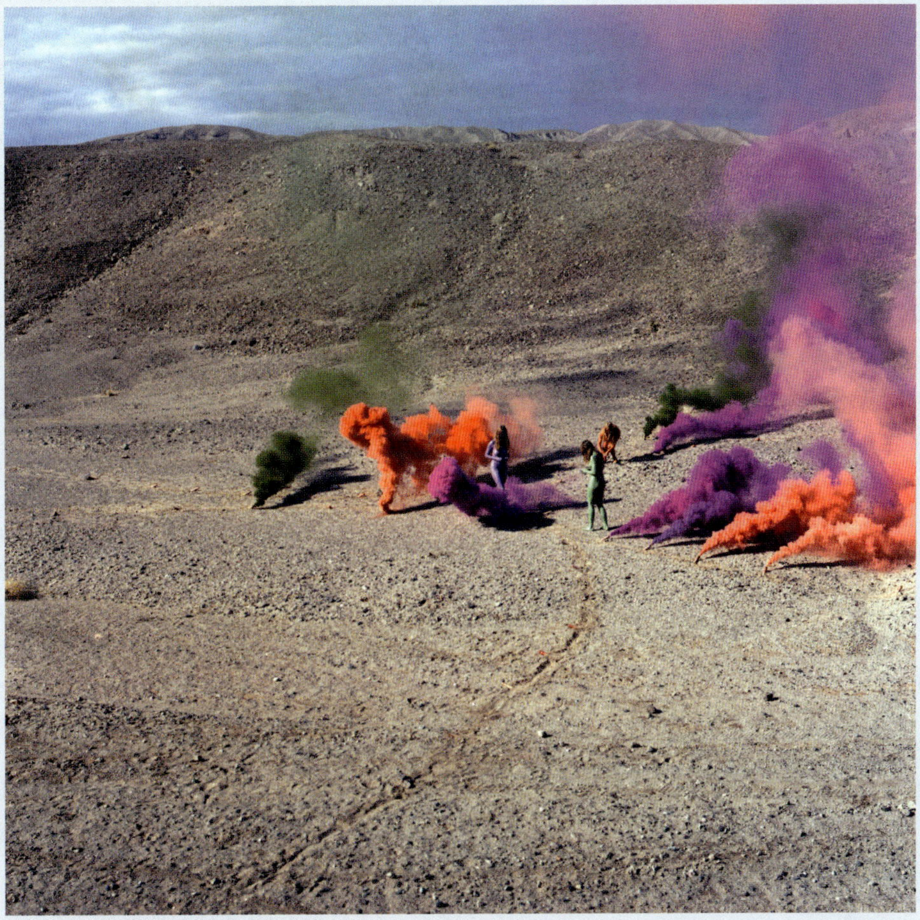

Judy Chicago, *Smoke Bodies III* from the *Women and Smoke Series*, 1972, Flares. Performed in the California desert.

C62 M0 Y0 K0
R124 G193 B236

C78 M8 Y10 K9
R76 G155 B193

C13 M26 Y26 K3
R208 G186 B173

C15 M13 Y54 K5
R208 G200 B133

C0 M0 Y0 K6
R243 G243 B243

C70 M10 Y60 K15
R95 G146 B112

Dive right in

David Hockney
A Bigger Splash
1967

Acrylic on canvas,
96 x 96 in (243.8 x 243.8 cm).

If it weren't for the smooth strip of pale-pink concrete cutting across the middle of Hockney's masterpiece, the canvas before us would be almost entirely blue. The sky is the kind that contains a full-beam sun and it's a shade lighter than the crystalline swimming pool. Apart from the splash—a tip of the hat to Jackson Pollock—that appears fluid and wet, the composition has been divided into sharply delineated planes of still color. After visiting Los Angeles, the U.K.'s best-known living artist created a series of three "splash" paintings, of which this is the largest—and in all of them he uses color to create a sense of place.

Hockney first visited LA in 1963, and he found there a light-filled Californian fantasy land of openness and freedom. As a gay man, he felt more comfortable with its laid-back lifestyle, and after returning to London, in 1966 he decided to make California his home. It was between the summers of 1966 and 1967 that he painted his "splash" paintings—canvases that combine realistic imagery with saturated colors and razor-sharp lines. With its modernist buildings, palm trees, neatly manicured grass, and sun-kissed pools, LA was Hockney's aquamarine paradise.

In *A Bigger Splash*, Hockney commits to an almost minimalist canvas the split-second act of an unseen diver slipping beneath the surface of the cerulean water. Look closely and within the foaming wake—a mix of fine white lines, specks and veillike washes of acrylic diluted with detergent—you can almost see a blur of pink. There's an air of intrigue in that suggestion of flesh, not to mention the empty chair opposite and the faded yellow diving board that extends toward the viewer, tempting you to follow. Without the splash, we'd be left with an image that was too cool and geometric, too refined. The stillness of the composition enhances the spontaneity associated with the riot of water. This is Californian living, frivolous and iconic.

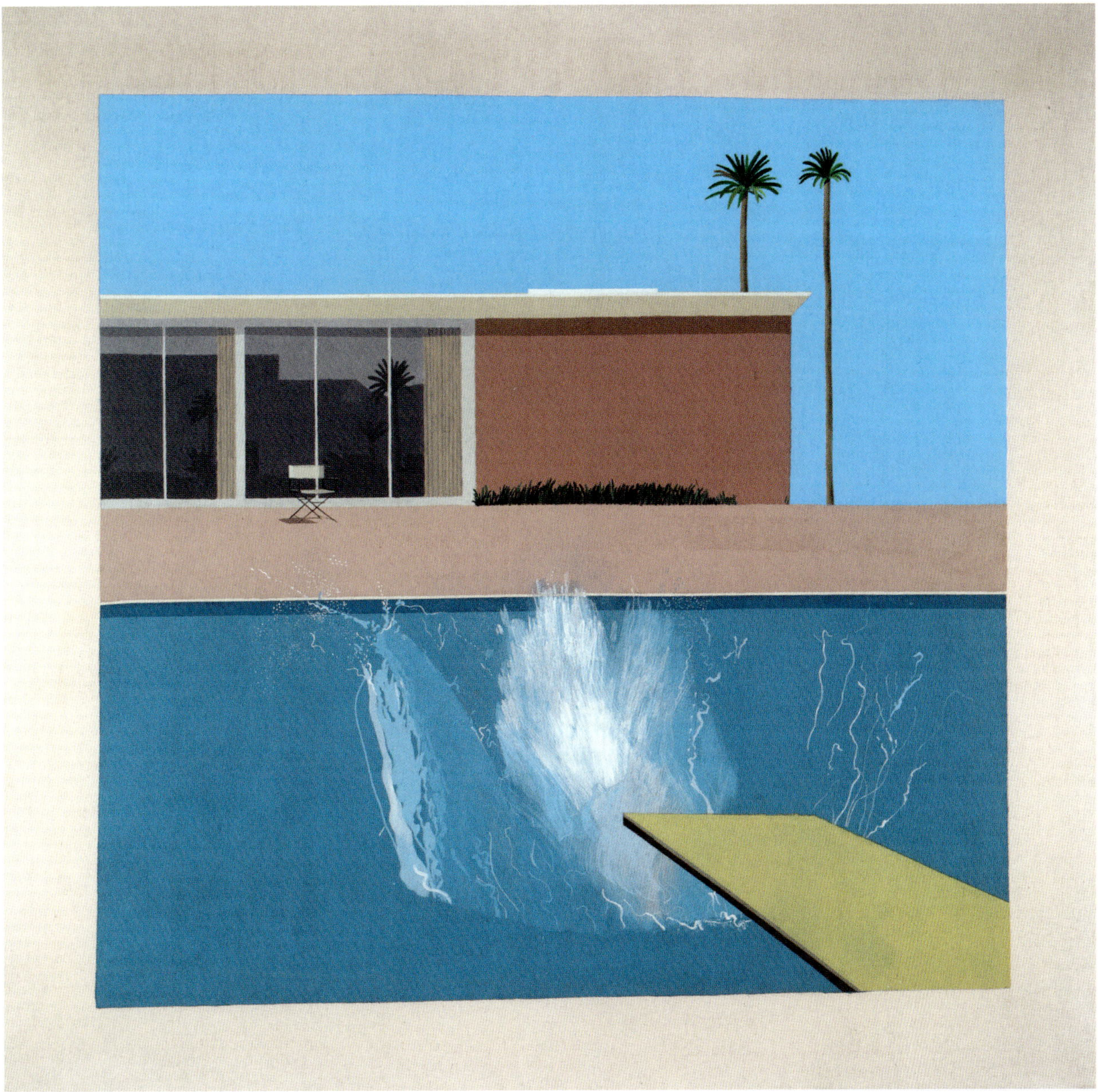

Palette

A blue sky and a crystalline pool, pink concrete, a faded yellow diving board, foaming white wake, and neatly manicured green grass.

Complementary works

- Henri Matisse, *The Swimming Pool*, 1952.
- Edward Hopper, *Office in a Small City*, 1953.
- Ramiro Gomez, *No Splash* (after David Hockney's *A Bigger Splash*, 1967), 2014.

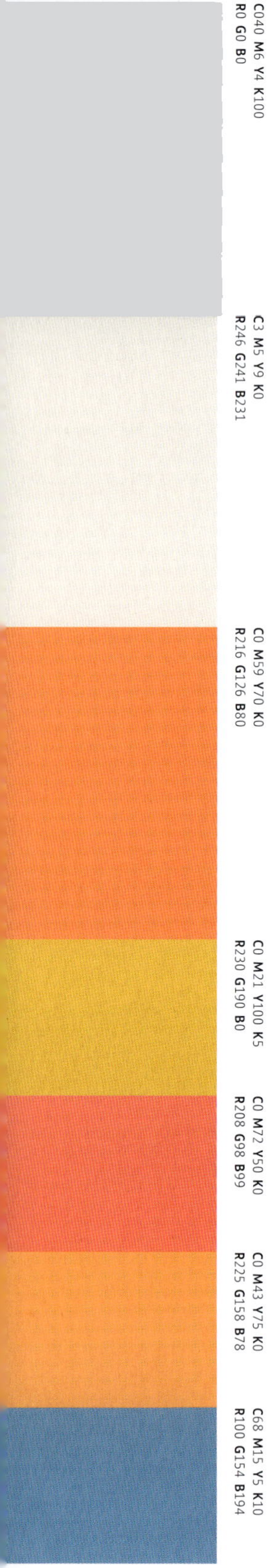

Life's a drag

Andy Warhol
Ladies and Gentlemen (Iris)
1975

Screenprint on Arches paper (F&S.II.135),
43⅓ x 28½ in (110 x 72.4 cm).

In 1974 the Italian art dealer Luciano Anselmino commissioned Andy Warhol to make a series of portraits of New York's Black and Latinx drag queens. Too recognizable to go himself, the Pop artist sent friends to a Manhattan club called the Gilded Grape to recruit those willing to model in exchange for $50. Back in the Factory (his studio and social hangout), Warhol took several Polaroids of each sitter and then enlarged a selection onto vibrantly colored silkscreens. In total, he snapped more than 500 photographs of fourteen models. And so, the man who was fascinated by the rich and famous turned his attention to an altogether different community.

It wasn't until 2014 that researchers discovered the models' names and identities. Among them was Iris (*pictured*), a petite trans performer who posed for Warhol with and without her wig. Here she drapes her right arm up and over her head. The faded black-and-white photographic portrait is enlivened with lush splashes of acrylic. Her face and neck are a warm brown, her eyelids yellow, and her lips smeared pink. There's a hint of glamour in the makeup-like daubs, and an air of exhibitionism. Matching blue, pink, orange, and yellow marks swirl energetically around her, confetti-like, their edges jagged and torn.

In total, Warhol created 268 silkscreens, and 26 feature Iris. Some see the theatrically named series as exploitative, while others regard it as an opportunity for these beautiful individuals to shine; in his art, Warhol reinstated Iris's missing tooth. There's a confidence to her pose but, at the same time, the way the color leaks from her eyelid into her eye, and smudges from her lips to her chin, suggests a certain vulnerability. One thing is for certain, though: in this series, a bold and spirited community of ladies and gentlemen is immortalized, iconic, their story pressingly relevant.

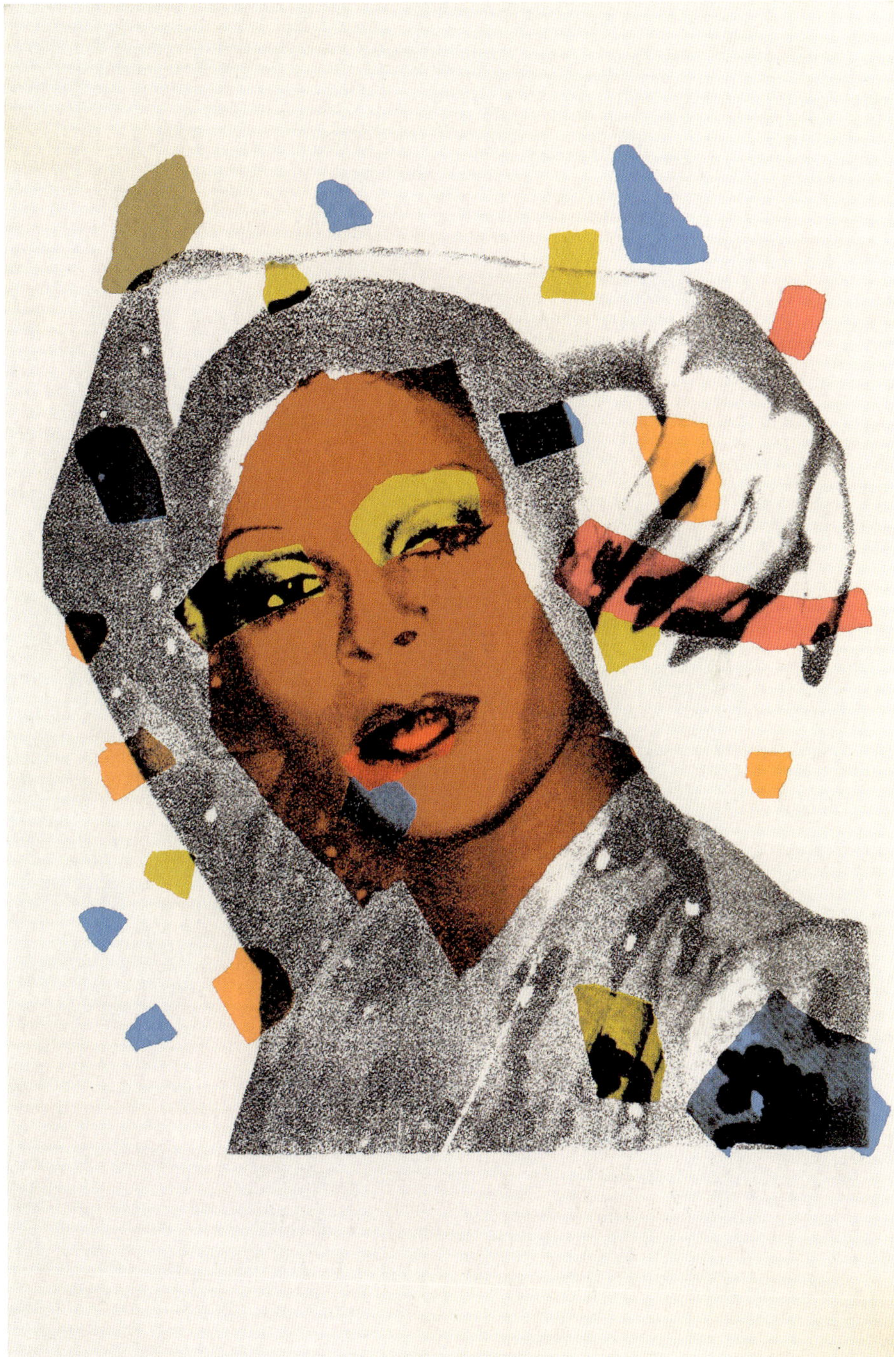

Palette

A faded black-and-white portrait with lush splashes of warm brown, yellow, pink, orange, and blue.

Complementary works

- Byron Kim, *Synecdoche*, 1991–present.
- Marlene Dumas, *Chlorosis (Love sick)*, 1994.
- Jenny Saville, *Meridian,* 2019–20.

Sending a message

Barbara Kruger
Untitled (Your body is a battleground)
1989

Photographic silkscreen on vinyl, 112 x 112 in (284.5 x 284.5 cm).

C40 M8 Y4 K100
R0 G0 B0

C0 M0 Y0 K6
R243 G243 B243

C00 M100 Y82 K10
R181 G0 B39

Kruger's art is nothing if not assertive. It's likely you're familiar with it even if you've never set foot in one of her shows, or stumbled upon it on a billboard or the side of a building. There are variations, of course, but her best-known format is a monochrome photograph overlaid with a colored box stamped with monolithic letters in her trademark Futura Bold Oblique typeface. It's brash, it's brilliant—the phrase pity and terse spring to mind—and it's wrought with a limited palette of black, white, and red.

Untitled (Your body is a battleground) shows a close-up of a woman staring out at the viewer, lips pursed, eyes unwavering, brows arched. Her steadfast expression is emphasized by the overall symmetry of the image, which in turn is highlighted by the sharp line bisecting her face. To the left, the glossy photograph exists in its original state; to the right we have its negative, the model's lipsticked mouth and scraped-back hair now a ghostly white. Originally created as a flier for a pro-choice rally in Washington, D.C., in the 1980s, this is one of several works that the American conceptual artist created to draw attention to the fight over women's reproductive rights. The halved face represents the stark divide in reactions to the new string of anti-abortion laws that were sweeping the country at the time.

Kruger, whose background was in graphic design, appropriated the propagandistic techniques and images of mass media to comment on gender and identity politics. In this seminal work she combines a monochrome photograph with bold, bright-white letters on a scarlet strip. The colors hark back to those of Russian Constructivism, as seen in El Lissitzky's *Beat the Whites with the Red Wedge* (1919), an agitational lithograph in black, white, and bloody, revolutionary red. The main role of the minimal palette, though, is to draw attention to the message—striking in its simplicity—and spur us into action.

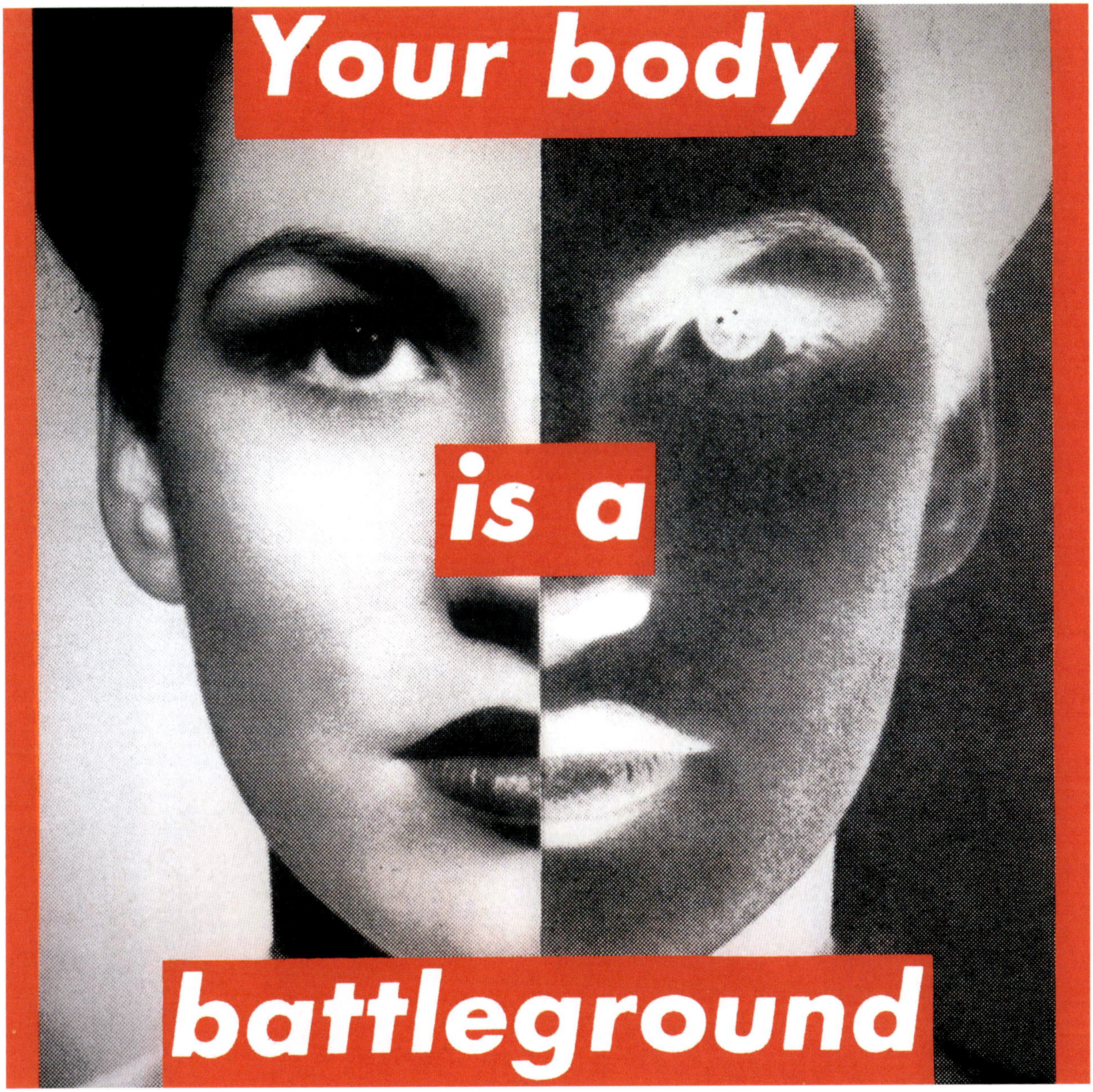

Palette

A monochrome photograph and bold, bright-white letters on a scarlet strip.

Complementary works

- El Lissitzky, *Beat the Whites with the Red Wedge*, 1919.
- Piet Mondrian, *Composition with Red, Blue and Yellow*, 1930.
- Linder, *She's too much for my mirror*, 1979, 2008.

Here and now

1970s to the present

C40 **M**0 **Y**90 **K**5
R168 **G**192 **B**63

Here and now

1970s to the present

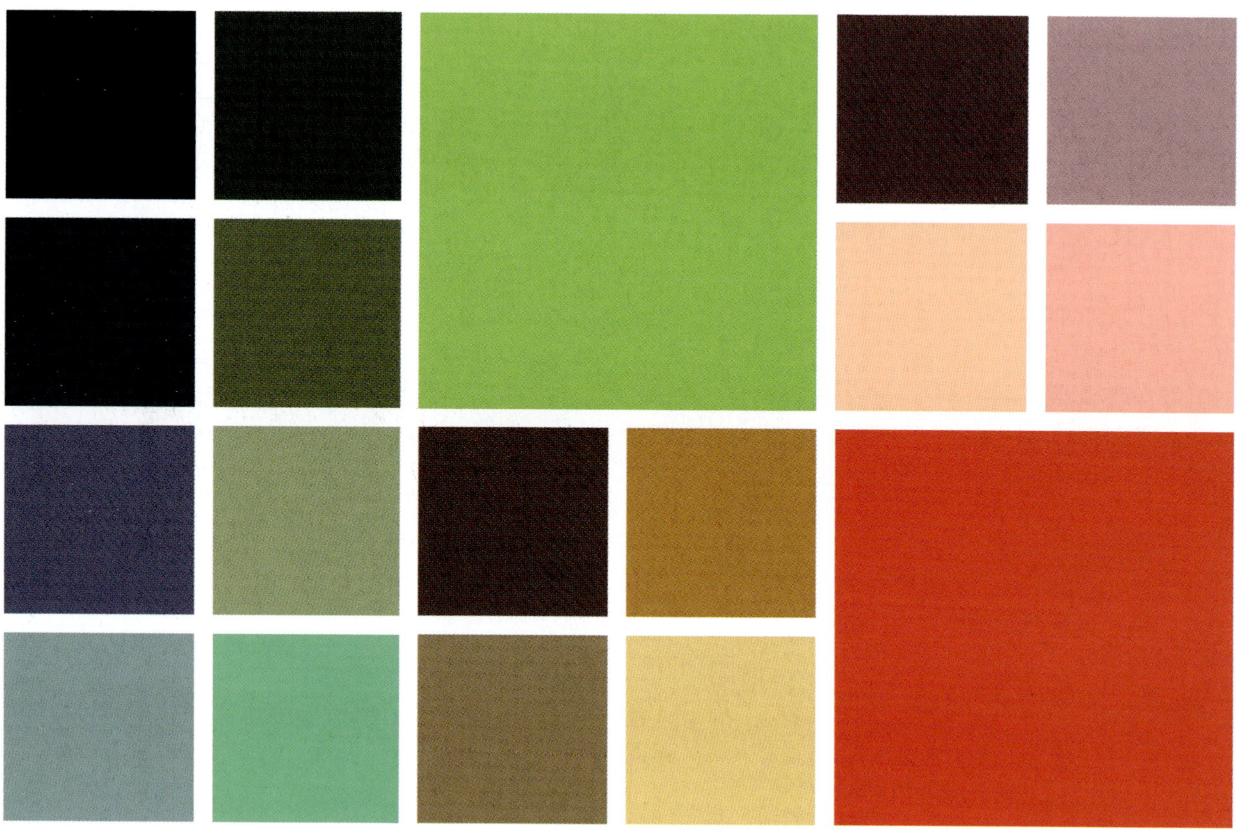

The history of color has developed hand in hand with advancements in materials, science, technology, psychology, and human development itself. So, what happens now, in the 21st century, when artists have infinite options, as well as a vast pool of knowledge and reference points at their fingertips? The opportunities are endless.

When it comes to contemporary art, or art that has been made between the 1970s and the present, color remains one of the most expressive elements that an artist has to hand. It continues to create a look, an energy, a mood; it can be used to elicit at times thoughtful and at times emotional responses. It's capable of sparking an immediate reaction in the viewer, as well as a quiet contemplation. Like line, it will always be there, one way or another.

Gone, however, are the color rules that governed previous generations, and the abidance to theories and hierarchies that evolved over centuries. Today, color retains a vital role in art, but that role is more fluid and open to interpretation. Each individual artist is free to pick and choose how they use color and the form that it takes.

Naturally, an artist's choice of color depends on their choice of materials: from traditional media—such as wood and stone, and oil- and water-based paints—to more modern ones, such as synthetic emulsions, resins, electrical and mechanical components, and vegetable and animal matter (think Damien Hirst's pickled cow and calf). As has been the case throughout this book, the focus here is primarily on artists working with a paint-based palette, but beyond these pages you'll find a free-for-all. The British painter Christopher Ofili is best known for decorating his paintings with elephant dung, while the German painter and sculptor Anselm Kiefer has incorporated earth into his investigations of destruction and regeneration. Annie Morris's *Stack* series (2014–ongoing) comprises jaunty columns of irregular spheres made from plaster and sand, coated with raw powdered pigments in ultramarine, viridian, and ocher. Yayoi Kusama's legendary mirror rooms transport viewers into worlds of bright hues and endless reflections.

The purpose of making art isn't always to look ahead, and just because artists today have access to the latest techniques, materials, and palettes, it doesn't mean that old and established models are cast aside. Several artists in this chapter recognize the value in revisiting the past—among them is Kiki Smith (*see page 236*), whose vast tapestries are decked with gold to highlight their otherworldliness, much like Renaissance altarpieces. Flora Yukhnovich's (*see page 242*) contemporary abstractions are inspired by the flamboyant canvases of the Rococo, while Kara Walker's (*see page 240*) incendiary art takes its cues from 19th-century silhouette portraits.

Color in the 21st century is as much about politics and culture as it is about description. As Walker's powerful murals show, it can be a corrective and a tool for change. Lisa Brice (*see page 238*) paints intimate portraits of women in blue to blur any easy reading of her subjects along ethnic lines, while Lynette Yiadom-Boakye (*see page 234*) evokes Blackness through her low lighting and sober tones. More on this to come (*see page 230*).

And so, without further ado, here is a sprinkling of artists working today who are doing smart and stimulating things with color. You might assume that the more choices an artist has, the easier their job is. But with options come decisions—let's see which ones they've made.

C80 M54 Y0 K10
R70 G99 B160

C8 M6 Y6 K0
R235 G235 B235

C10 M38 Y90 K18
R181 G140 B42

C60 M8 Y60 K15
R116 G156 B113

See change

Alice Neel

Self-Portrait

1980

Oil on canvas,
53¼ x 39¾ in (135.3 x 101 cm).

The artist sits in the blue-striped armchair that appears in so many of her portraits. She's naked except for a pair of glasses that nod to a lifetime of looking; their frames, a golden ocher, match the left side of the floor. The right side is a forest green, and the upper half of the canvas is left largely blank. The artist's body is outlined in the same electric blue that features on the chair, and a halo-like cloud wafts above her. Neel painted this candid and unconventional self-portrait at the age of 80. Turning her unflinching yet compassionate gaze on herself, she eschews traditional notions of idealized femininity and youth, and instead captures her aging body in all its glory, with slumped shoulders, swollen ankles, and sagging breasts and belly.

In the midst of Abstract Expressionism, as other artists turned their backs on figuration, Neel continued to paint portraits. As such, she was overlooked until her rich contribution to the art world was recognized by two retrospectives in the early 1970s. "Life begins at seventy!" she exclaimed, and in 1975 she began this work, her first proper self-portrait, which took her five years. She later said, "The reason my cheeks got so pink was that it was so hard for me to paint that I almost killed myself painting it."

Working without preparatory sketches, Neel painted directly onto the canvas with both somber and vibrant colors. Note the green on her neck, arm, and face—a hint of deterioration, perhaps. Her application of paint is sometimes harsh, sometimes soft. The self-portrait has an unfinished look about it, with the ocher patch of floor not quite reaching the edge, and the washy swathe of blue. In one hand she clasps a paintbrush, in the other a white rag—a shade brighter than her fluffy hair. Some believe that the white rag is a sign of the artist surrendering to age and decline, but with her swift brushstrokes and fresh palette, Neel shows that she was still very much alive and kicking.

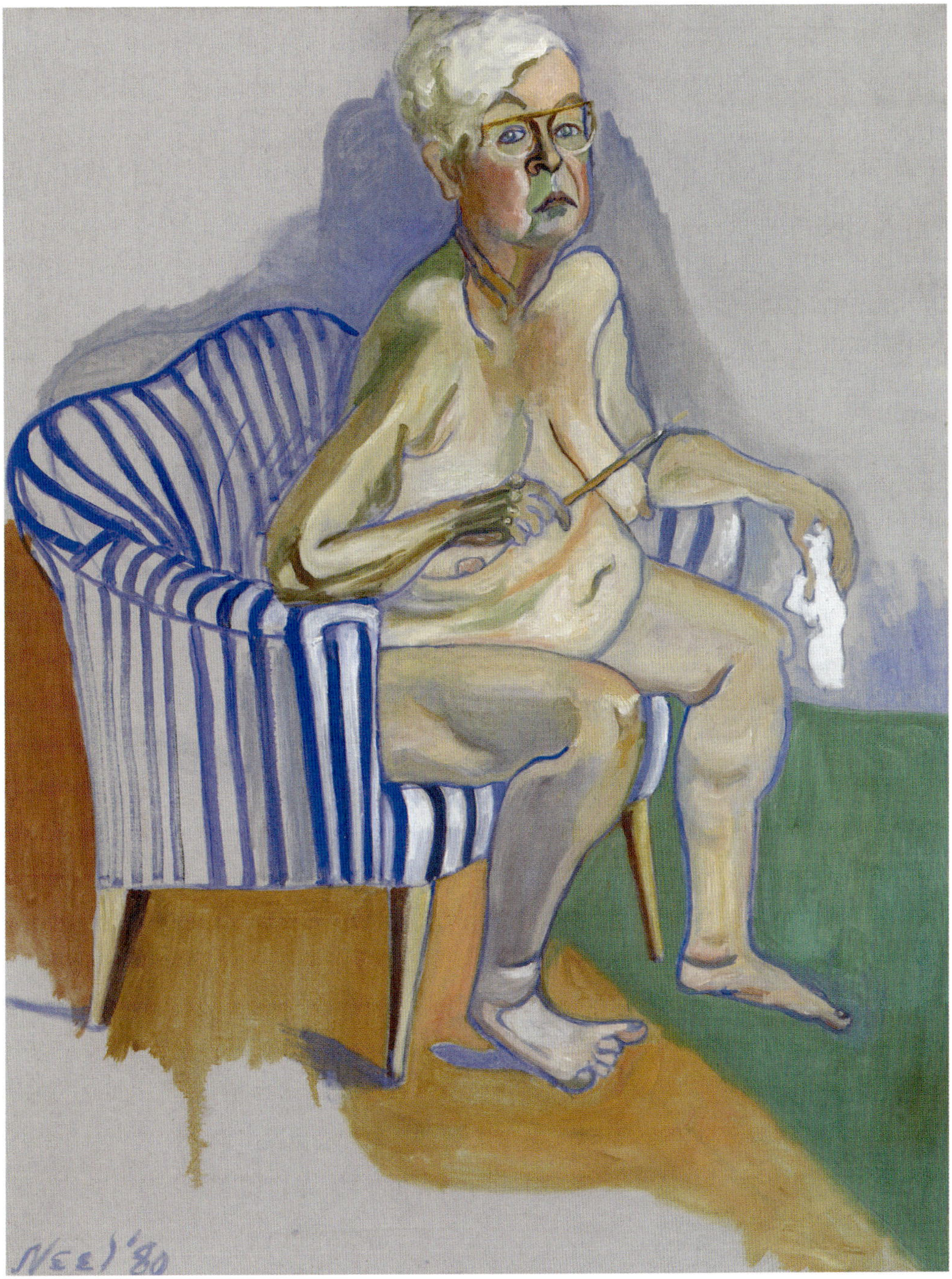

Palette

Blue and white, golden ocher, and forest green.

Complementary works

- Sylvia Sleigh, *Imperial Nude: Paul Rosano*, 1977.
- Anna Ancher, *Sunlight in the Blue Room,* 1891.
- Celia Paul, *Painter and Model*, 2012.

C0 M100 Y100 K10
R181 G0 B18

C0 M39 Y25 K0
R228 G174 B166

C42 M0 Y90 K5
R164 G190 B64

C65 M0 Y55 K0
R120 G181 B139

C100 M82 Y0 K0
R42 G63 B142

C00 M31 Y75 K5
R223 G175 B80

Straight from the tube

Etel Adnan
Untitled 17
*c.*1980

Oil on canvas,
13 3/16 x 17 7/8 in (35 x 45.5 cm).

The late Lebanese-born American artist, essayist, and poet Etel Adnan began to paint in the 1950s, while teaching philosophy of art and aesthetics at the University of California. From the start, she was drawn to the immediacy of pure color, and her geometric compositions comprise thick swatches of oil paint squeezed directly from the tube and laid on firmly with a palette knife. Within her geometric designs are flashes of Lebanon, as well as her adopted home in northern California and its landmarks, such as Mount Tamalpais. Adnan explored the tension between abstraction and recognizable landscapes, and she did so by paying attention to colors, which she said "exist for me as entities in themselves, as metaphysical beings, like the attributes of God exist as metaphysical entities."

A small, intense work created late in her career, *Untitled 17* is, like many of her paintings, composed around a cherry-red square. If it weren't for the majestic mountain peak in a mix of verdant greens rising above it, it could pass for a burning sun or low-hanging moon. The canvas comprises horizontal blocks of luscious color that, when viewed in conjunction, become familiar elements of a landscape—sand, sea, and sky. The band of rich blue offsets the strip of creamy ocher, while the slope of candyfloss pink is a paler version of the painting's elemental red heart.

Adnan's art is shot through with optimism. Within the bright colors and bold forms is a playful energy and an appreciation of life. In her art, she responded to the environment —conjuring in paint the enormity and intricacy of nature and open air. Horizon lines and geological masses emerge in and among huddles of color. "My painting is very much a reflection of my immense love for the world, the happiness to just be, for nature, and the forces that shape a landscape," the artist said. It's a means of slowing down and appreciating the world around us, or our memories of it.

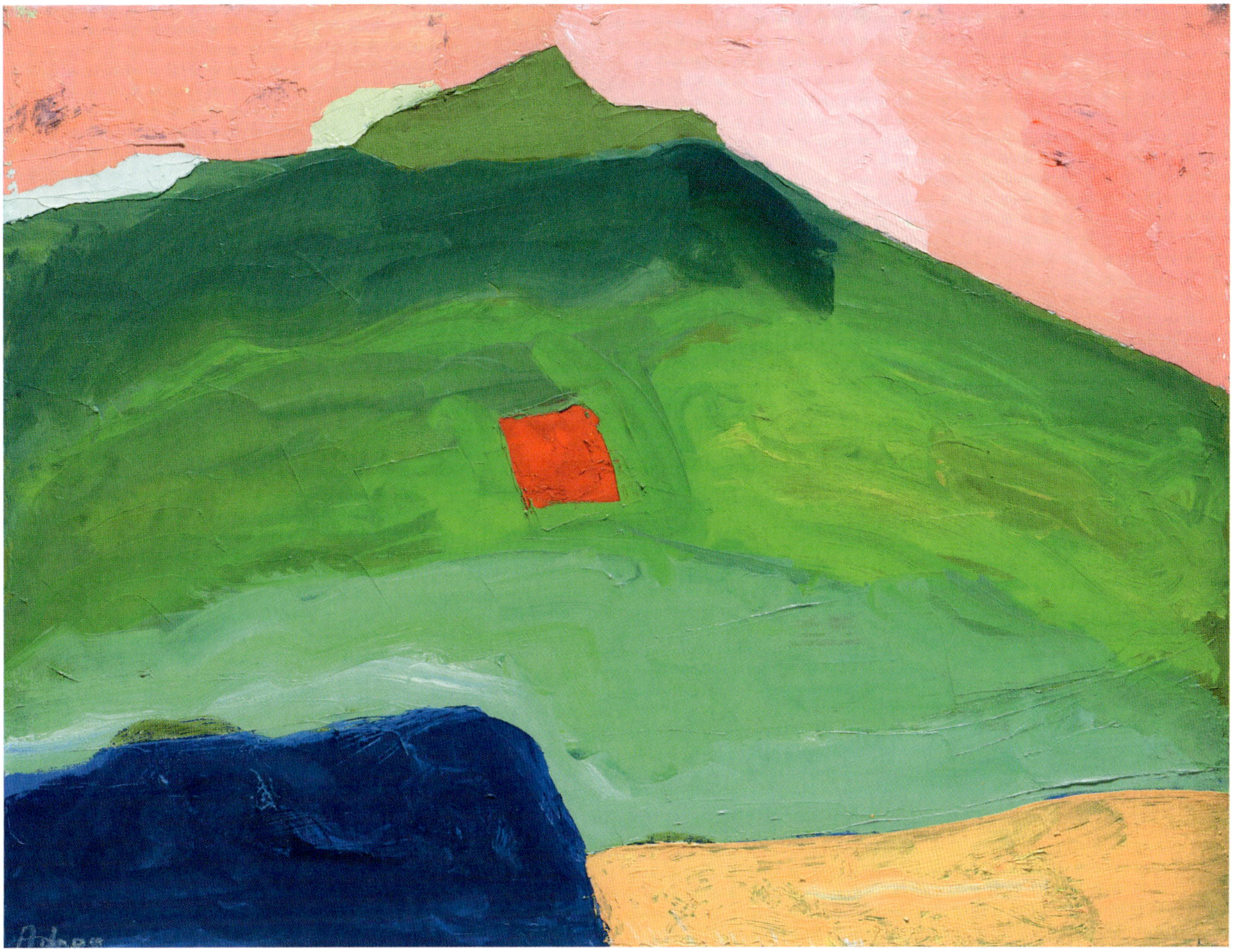

Palette

Bands of rich blue, creamy ocher, candyfloss pink, verdant greens, and a cherry-red square.

Complementary works

- Saloua Raouda Choucair, *Composition in Blue Module*, 1947–51.
- Simone Fattal, *La Baie de Beyrouth*, 1973.
- Lois Dodd, *Red Curtains and Lace Plant*, 1978.

C10 M96 Y90 K0
R183 G36 B38

C034 M70 Y48 K55
R91 G58 B59

C40 M8 Y4 K100
R0 G0 B0

C0 M0 Y0 K6
R243 G243 B243

C94 M40 Y0 K4
R37 G115 B180

Stick it to the man

Basquiat
Self-Portrait
1984

Acrylic and oil stick on paper mounted on canvas, 39⅜ x 27⅝ in (100 x 70 cm).

Basquiat's career was remarkable and also remarkably brief—born in 1960 to a Haitian father and a Puerto-Rican mother, he died at the age of 27 from an accidental drug overdose. When he was seventeen, he left home and started to scrawl enigmatic messages in Magic Marker around New York as part of the duo SAMO (a contraction of "same old shit"). In 1981 he traded the city's doors and walls for canvases, and began to paint and draw, and by the following year, the underground graffiti artist had emerged onto the international art scene as a fêted neo-Expressionist whose work was in great demand.

Rendered in Basquiat's trademark faux-naïf style with acrylic and oil sticks—a medium that he and other artists made popular in the 1980s—the figure before us is depicted from the chest up, arms out of sight. He stands in front of a sky-blue backdrop that has been hastily whitewashed and scratched at, with clawlike markings dangerously close to the artist's cheeks. The blood red of his top is echoed in his bloodshot eyes, one of which appears to be leaking, and his burning ears, unevenly placed and different in size. The artist's skin is blotted with black—the same shade as his sticking-up hair—and X-ray-like dashes of white evoke bones and gnashing teeth, as well as African masks. The overall impression is of an alienated and haunted man unable to defend himself.

In each of his anguished figures, Basquiat weaves together autobiography, Black history, popular culture, and moral truths. His art holds a mirror up to the traumas of everyday racism and the psychological effects of a rocket-like rise to fame. In this vibrant self-portrait, he explores his identity as a Black American man, and as a successful Black artist within a mostly white history of art. It's surely no coincidence that the wall is white, and his torso is the color of blood.

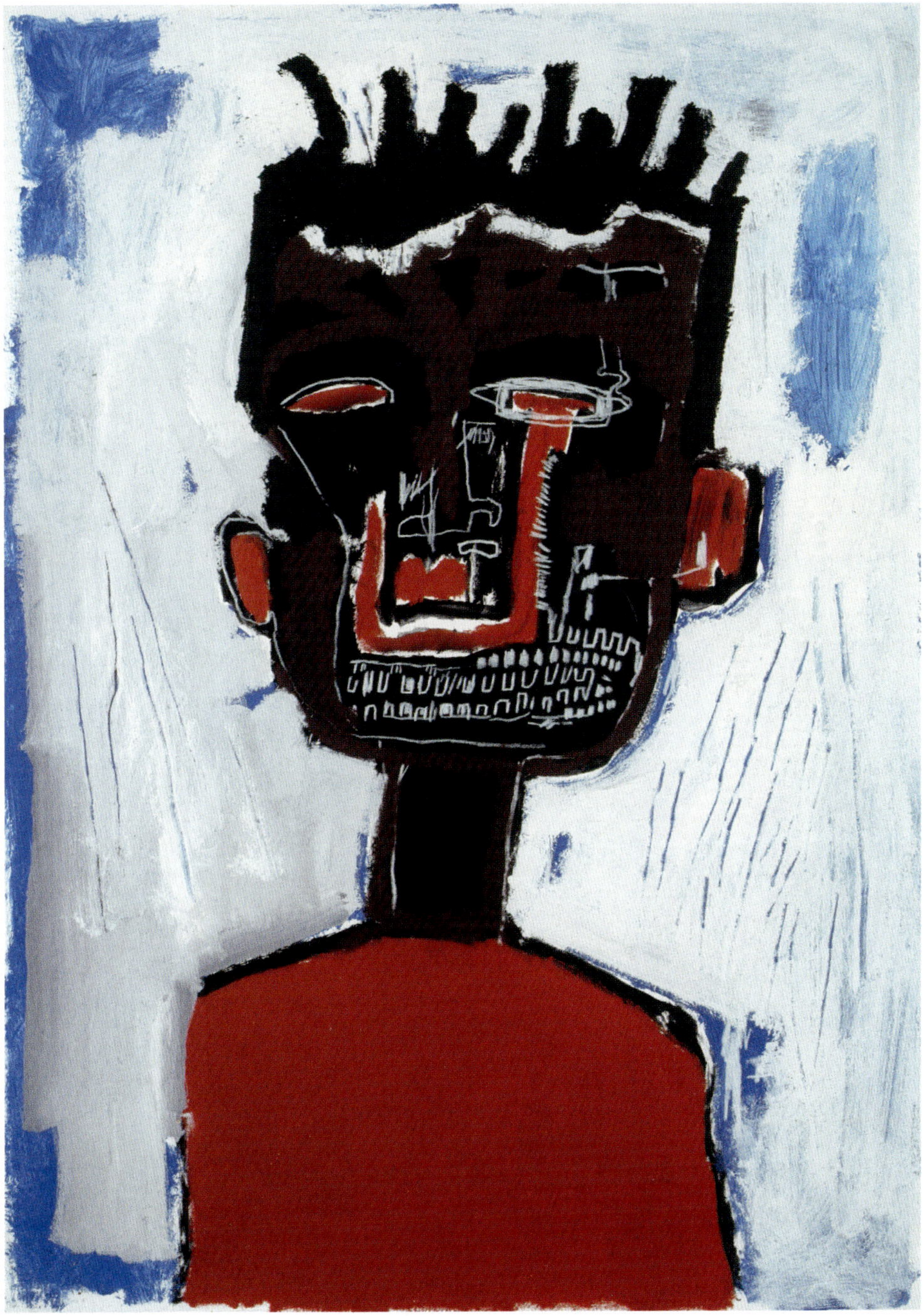

Palette

Sky blue, blood red, brown blotted with black, and dashes of white.

Complementary works

- Jean Dubuffet, *Skedaddle (L'Escampette),* 1964.
- Frank Auerbach, *Seated Figure*, 1966.
- Willem de Kooning, *Untitled XIII*, 1982.

The color of art history

It would be overly simplistic to say that a new generation of figurative painters are inserting Black figures into the white canon. But for several Black artists at work today, redressing the imbalance in art history is part of their mission. Portraiture has for centuries been the predominant art form of white male artists, who traditionally dominated it; then in the 20th century it was all but eclipsed by abstraction. Now it's back and more vital than ever before—what was once idealistic and isolating is now humanizing and essential.

The resurgence is in part down to Kerry James Marshall, who in his paintings responds to the absence of Blackness in the history of art. The Chicago-based artist and professor depicts African American subjects in the studio, at the hairdresser's, in parks. He uses three kinds of black —carbon black, mars black, and ivory black—and adds to them dashes of raw umber, yellow ocher, and a couple of shades of blue. The result: seven blacks without a hint of white in them. "The idea of those paintings is that Blackness is nonnegotiable in those pictures," Marshall has said. "It's also unequivocal—they are Black—that's the thing that I mean for people to identify immediately. They are black to demonstrate that blackness can have complexity. Depth. Richness."

In *Past Times* (1997), Marshall takes the kind of pastoral scene that would ordinarily be populated with European aristocrats and instead presents us with a Black family. There they are, in their starched white clothing and trainers, playing croquet and golf on a grassy knoll, steering a speedboat around a lake, water-skiing under the sun. The figures in the foreground meet and question the viewers' gaze.

Among those following in Marshall's footsteps in the U.S. are Amy Sherald, who in her own words seeks "versions of myself in art history and in the world," and Kehinde Wiley, best known for his portraits of contemporary Black and Brown men in poses and settings associated with Baroque paintings. In 2018, Wiley became the first African American to paint a presidential portrait—that of Barack Obama. Housed in the Smithsonian's

National Portrait Gallery in Washington, D.C., together with Michelle Obama's portrait, painted by Sherald, the pair are already iconic.

Others reimagining the possibilities of portraiture include the young British-Nigerian painter Joy Labinjo, who started out making big, colorful portraits inspired by archival family photos, and London-based Kudzanai-Violet Hwami, who in her art captures Southern African life. Toyin Ojih Odutola is another example: born in Nigeria, she moved to the U.S. as a young child, and her beautiful monochrome portraits—made from charcoal, chalk, and pastel—rework traditional figurative compositions with a society that's Black, mostly female, and queer.

The work of these artists is about more than the exploration of Black selfhood, and just as they share certain characteristics, they're also unquestionably unique. What they do have in common, though, is the ability to remake figuration with color. Theirs are affirming images that don't shy away from Blackness, and that explore Black identity and visibility. Portrait by portrait, they are reinscribing the Black community into the history of art—and its future.

Kerry James Marshall, *Past Times*, 1997, acrylic and collage on canvas, 114 x 156 in (289.6 × 396.2 cm).

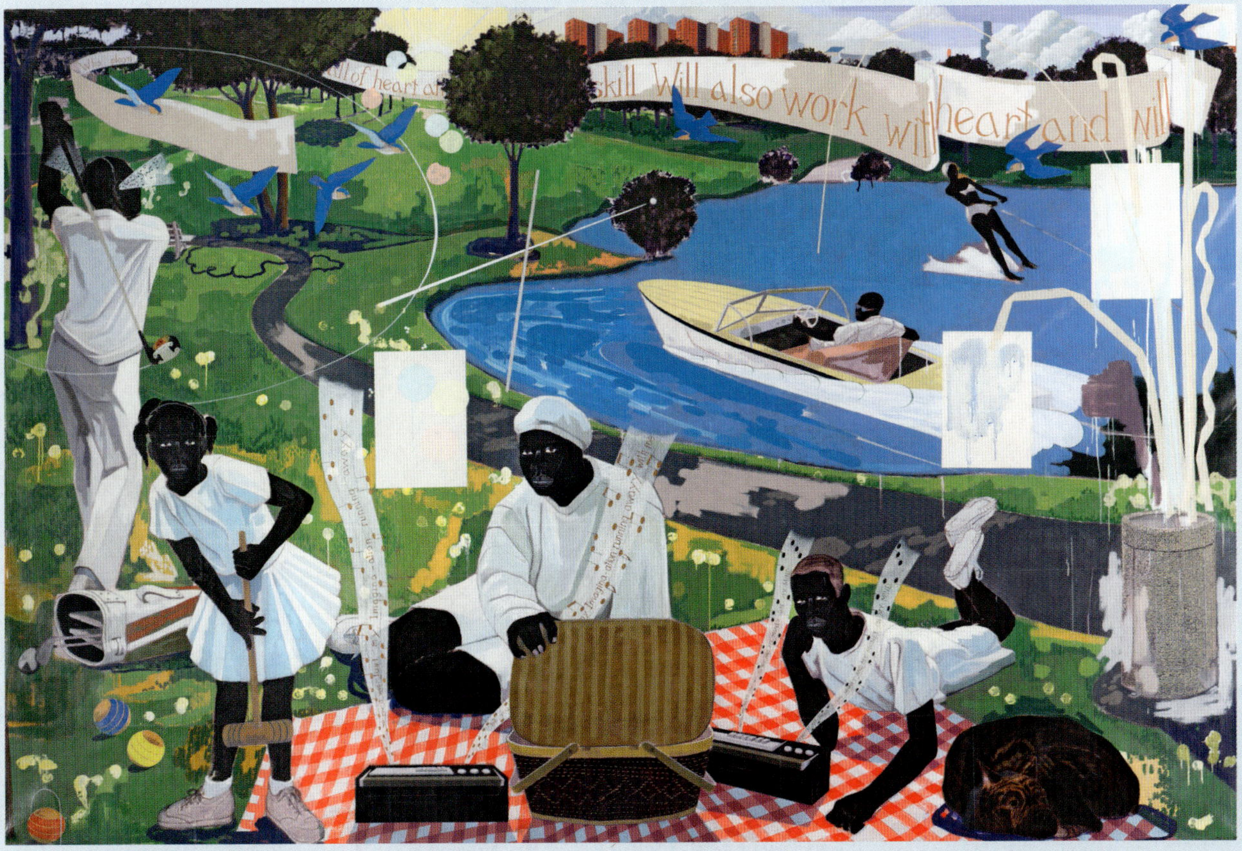

C3 M3 Y11 K0
R247 G245 B229

C8 M8 Y20 K0
R234 G229 B206

C20 M24 Y31 K8
R189 G177 B159

Into the fold

Alison Watt
Sabine
2000

Oil on canvas,
84 x 84 in (213.5 x 213.5 cm).

You can almost feel the weight of the painted fabric, which falls across the canvas in smooth swoops and folds. On the left-hand side the plain painted material lies mostly flat, while on the right the sheet has been gathered and bunched. Watt achieves an effect akin to trompe l'oeil thanks, in large part, to her expert handling of the color white, which she subtly blends with gray, ocher, sienna, vermilion, and black. The highlights and shadows have been so convincingly depicted that the painting has a sculptural quality, inviting the viewer to reach out and touch it.

Watt, who lives and works in Edinburgh, made her name as a figurative painter in the 1980s. She started out painting intimate portraits and female nudes, often alongside bleached backdrops and furnishings. In the 1990s she began to take inspiration from Jean-Auguste-Dominique Ingres (*see page 100*), who depicted his undressed figures against sensuous fields of drapery. Then she bypassed the figure altogether, focusing solely on swathes of suspended and creased fabrics, which in her poetic paintings are both intricate and loosely rendered.

Stripped of pattern and decoration, *Sabine* is part of a seemingly simple series inspired by the rich and sensuous textiles found in Ingres's suggestive paintings of women. The combination of color palette and composition evokes empty bed sheets and discarded clothes, as well as the folds and creases of skin that such fabrics usually conceal. The vast, chalky canvas contains within it a human presence—or perhaps a human absence. It's there in the bodily curves and openings, and the way the creamy cloth has been carefully nipped and tucked. The result is a tantalizing almost-portrait and a sense of absence that's at once soothing, seductive, and haunting. Lean in and you might just smell a lingering note of perfume hanging in the air, or the memory of cigarette smoke.

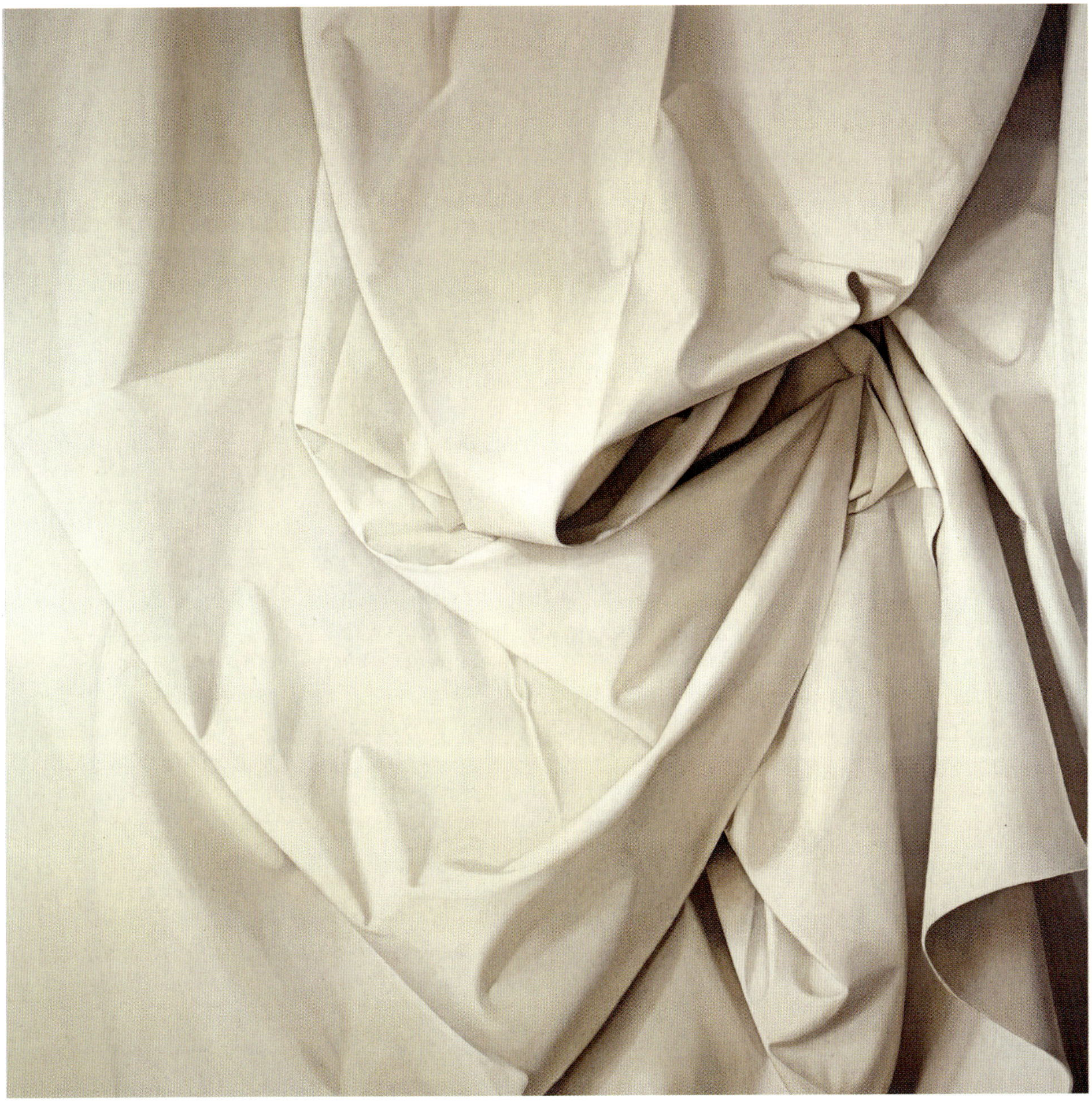

Palette

Cream, or a subtle blend of white, gray, ocher, sienna, vermilion, and black.

Complementary works

- Francisco de Zurbarán, *Saint Francis in Meditation*, 1635–39.
- Jean-Auguste-Dominique Ingres, *Madame Moitessier*, 1856.
- Rachel Kneebone, *Rise*, 2017.

C69 M34 Y75 K65
R52 G67 B42

C88 M30 Y28 K75
R19 G53 B62

C30 M60 Y60 K60
R89 G63 B48

C19 M35 Y45 K15
R175 G150 B123

C14 M30 Y66 K30
R160 G138 B81

Fact or fiction

Lynette Yiadom-Boakye

To Tell Them Where It's Got To

2013

Oil on canvas,
23⅝ x 21⅝ in (60 x 53.3 cm).

Yiadom-Boakye learned to paint from life before realizing that she was less interested in capturing a particular person and more interested in the act of painting itself. Working with oil paint and canvas, the British-Ghanaian artist says she begins each piece with "a color, a composition, a gesture, a particular direction of the light." Her source materials vary from her own memories and thoughts to found images and literature, all of which come together in her striking composites of fictional individuals and groups.

To Tell Them Where It's Got To shows a young woman in profile, her shadow cast on the golden-green wall behind. She's wearing a deep-green rollneck jumper, and her hair is pulled back into a bun at the nape of her neck. She's relaxed, her chin lowered, her eyes open but downcast. Like all of Yiadom-Boakye's fictitious figures, the woman is in her own world; she doesn't look at us and her expression is unclear, though within the gentle uptick of her lips and lashes is a hint of a sad smile. Apart from her rollneck, there are no temporal or cultural signifiers, giving the portrait a universality and a timeless feel. There's an air of mystery about her, and an absence into which we, the viewer, project our own interpretations. Yiadom-Boakye is a writer as well as an artist, and she refers to the teasing titles of her paintings as "an extra brush mark"—a prompt for our imagination.

Yiadom-Boakye's muted palette seems restricted at first, but the closer you look, the more colors you see. Within the jumper are different gradations of green, while the woman's skin varies from dark to light brown—note the contrast between cream and almost black on her ear. There are rough strokes of green in her hair, while the ocher background is patchy in places, tempered by unpainted canvas. The artist never uses pure black pigment—always a dark shade of brown or blue—and yet her low lighting and sober tones evoke Blackness, as well as a sense of freedom and introspection that suits her imagined characters.

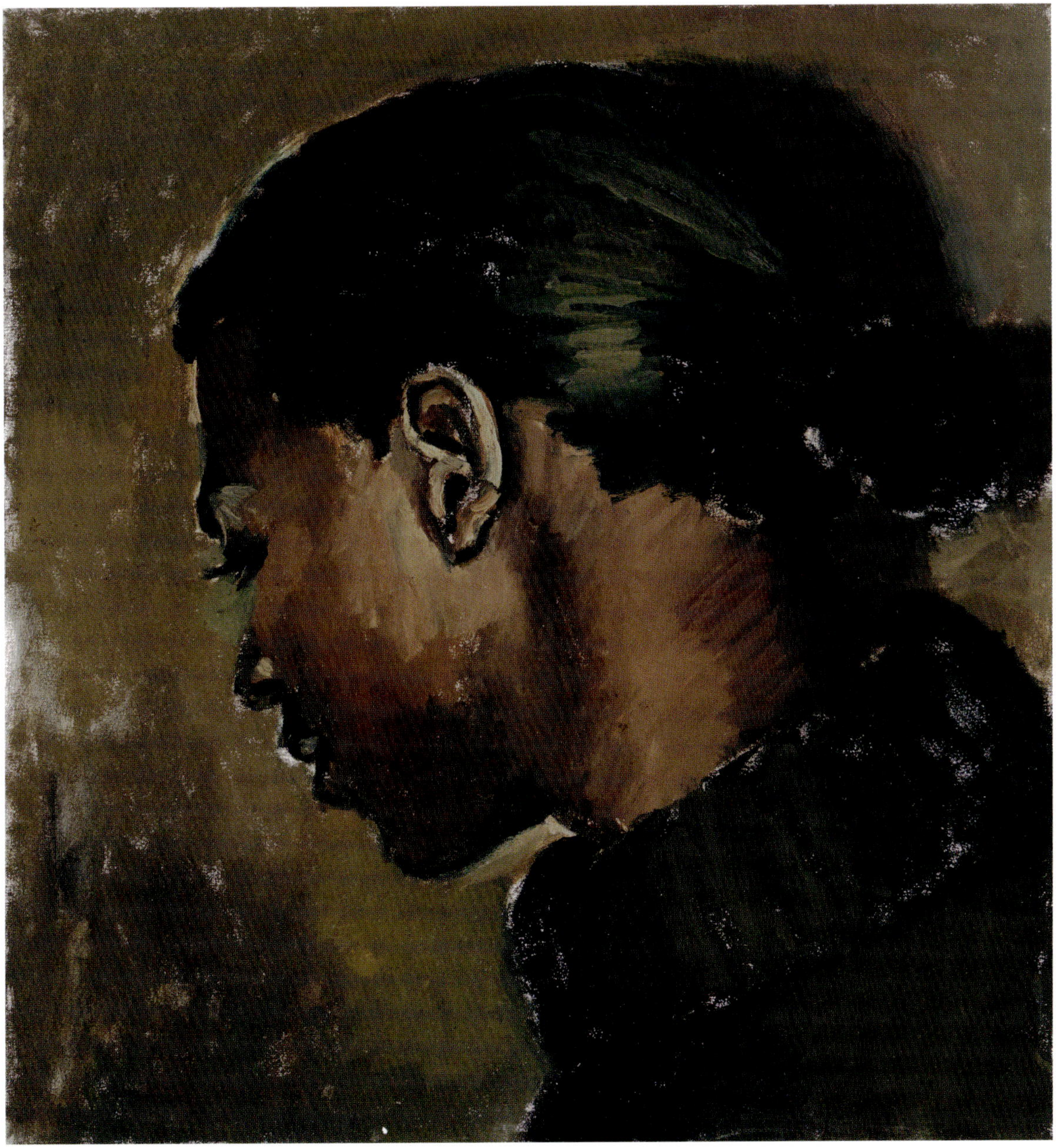

Palette

A deep-green rollneck jumper, skin that varies from dark to light brown, dark brown and blue shadows, and an ocher background.

Complementary works

- Walter Richard Sickert, *Ellen Heath*, 1896.
- Kehinde Wiley, *Portrait of Lynette Yiadom-Boakye, Jacob Morland of Capplethwaite*, 2017.
- Amy Sherald, *What's different about Alice is that she has the most incisive way of telling the truth*, 2017.

Golden touch

Kiki Smith

Spinners

2014

Cotton Jacquard tapestry, hand-painting, and gold leaf, 117⅗ x 76⅘ in (298.7 x 195.1 cm).

From afar, Smith's ethereal, new-age tapestry evokes camera flashes, a constellation of stars, or the blink of headlights on full beam in the dark. Look closer, though, and you'll start to notice the intricate details mapping out each pocket of light. They are, of course, spiderwebs, their threads silky and ultrafine. Each iteration whirls out from its center in concentric circles, while straight lines cut across the cotton fabric, creating a collective web that's fragile yet beautifully dense.

In her art, the New York-based multidisciplinary artist creates restless worlds that exist outside time and space, and reflect on the human condition. After rising to prominence in the early 1990s, she moved away from the physical—namely her figurative sculptures that challenge bodily taboos—and toward the celestial. Ever since she visited the medieval Apocalypse Tapestry in Angers in France, Smith had dreamed of doing her own embroidery. Works such as *Spinners*—transformed from Smith's large-scale collages into towering tapestries using a computerized Jacquard loom in collaboration with the Californian art studio Magnolia Editions—comment on life, spirituality, and nature. The silk moths radiate beauty but also instability, with some of their finely woven wings not yet spread. Among the shadow and light, otherworldly pussy willow drifts toward the sky, a clump of stalks covered with furred flowers.

Like the artists of the Renaissance, Smith adds flickers of gold leaf to her colossal tapestries to highlight their enchanted qualities. Set against a marbled dark-blue backdrop, *Spinners* is composed of silver and gold, with hints of hand-painted pinks, purples, and greens. These bright jolts of color appear to radiate from the central spiderweb and pick up on the flecks of color at the tapestry's base. The intricate dreamscape that Smith has woven is both familiar and full of wonder: a serene realm hanging delicately in the balance.

- C5 M40 Y95 K20 R183 G136 B27
- C10 M0 Y6 K45 R153 G161 B158
- C75 M60 Y40 K80 R32 G35 B39
- C10 M38 Y20 K15 R187 G153 B155
- C70 M58 Y20 K30 R78 G83 B114
- C40 M22 Y80 K45 R109 G113 B53

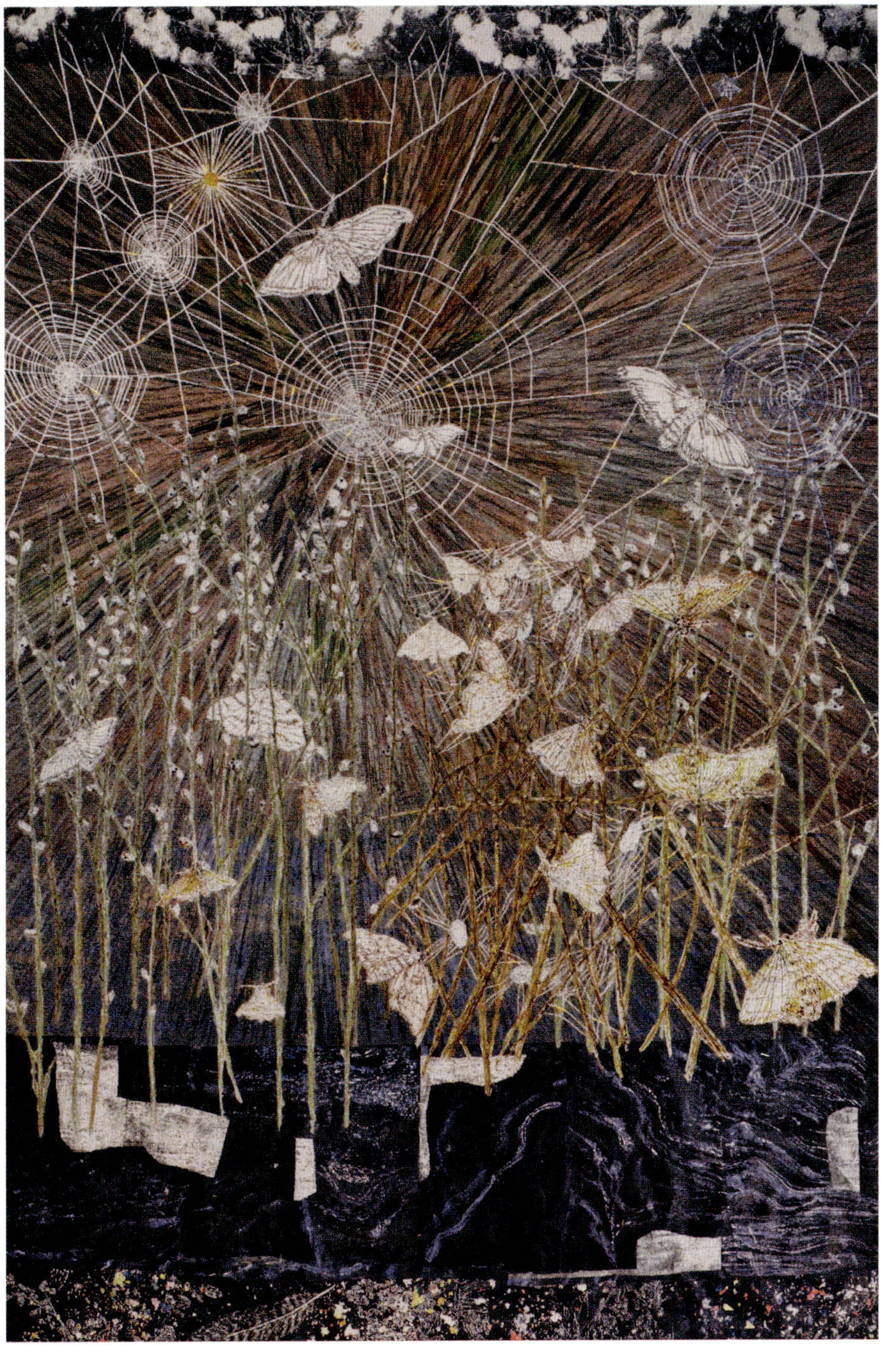

Palette

Silver and gold, together with hints of hand-painted pinks, purples and greens, against a marbled dark-blue backdrop.

Complementary works

- Jean Dubuffet, *Landscape with Argus*, 1955.
- Louise Bourgeois, *Lady in Waiting*, 2003.
- Anselm Kiefer, *Ramanujan Summation – 1/12*, 2019.

C100 M70 Y0 K0
R37 G79 B154

Ladies in blue

Lisa Brice

Untitled

2016

Gouache on paper,
16½ x 11¾ in (41.9 x 29.6 cm).

Brice's portraits are immediately recognizable, thanks to their dimly lit shade of blue. A combination of cobalt and ultramarine, it evokes the fluidity of twilight, with its hazy not-yet-light and not-yet-dark hues. The South Africa-born artist associates it with the Trinidadian carnival character of the blue devil, and the revelers who coat themselves in cobalt blue paint (a tradition that has its roots in colonial times) to mask their identities. "In my work this color can suggest skin veiled in paint or tinted mud, obscuring naturalistic skin tones and interrupting an easy or preconditioned reading of the subject along ethnic lines," she has said. "This all reinforces the idea of transformation and adds to the ambiguity of the narrative."

Untitled shows two women taking a cigarette break. One stands tall in a striped tube dress; her skin is painted a solid blue, save for brief dashes that mark her features. Her companion, on the other hand, is suggested by a sketchily rendered blue line—without it, her spotty dress would disappear into the backdrop. She reaches around a doorway, her hands clasping at the door's edge, with her head tilted in question. Her traits are barely visible; color is contained mostly within her hair. She's out of reach of the viewer, in another realm.

The anonymous women in Brice's paintings are pieced together from photographs, magazine clippings, and art history. The artist interrogates the male gaze by taking women from the paintings of Félix Vallotton (*see page 132*), Édouard Manet (*see page 112*), and others, and transforming them into self-assured characters who are drinking, chatting, smoking, undressing. She gives these women a new lease of life, a chance to exist as part of a group, to riff off one another in a different time and place, often with props such as cigarettes and beer bottles. Color keeps their identities at bay and discourages us from making assumptions about their relationships or ethnicity. As in the liminal moments of dusk and dawn, sunrise and sunset, in Brice's art, everything is fluid.

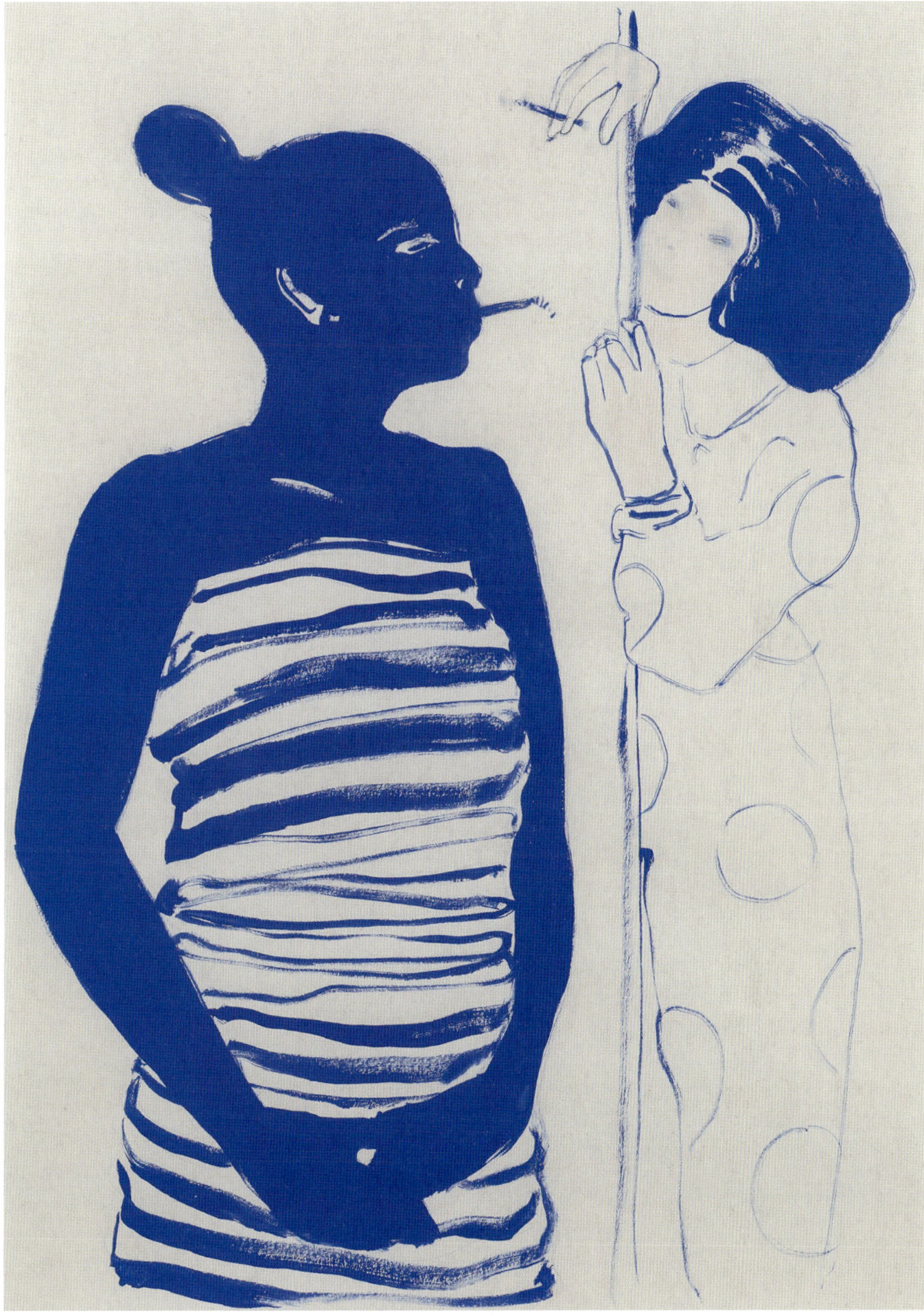

Palette

A combination of cobalt and ultramarine.

Complementary works

- Edgar Degas, *The Absinthe Drinker*, 1875–76.
- Félix Vallotton, *The White and the Black*, 1913.
- Roger Fry, *Nina Hamnett*, 1917.

C40 M8 Y4 K100
R0 G0 B0

C3 M3 Y3 K6
R236 G235 B234

Out of the shadows

Kara Walker
Slaughter of the Innocents (They Might be Guilty of Something)
2016

Cut paper and acrylic on linen, 79 x 220 in (200.7 x 558.8 cm).

Walker's art is beautiful and challenging. Reimagining the sentimental 19th-century genre of silhouette portraits, she uses cut paper, acrylic, and graphite on canvas to explore the history of slavery and the way it permeates society today, as well as other issues of gender and violence. Confronting viewers with disturbing large-scale murals of stereotypes of the antebellum American South, she brings to life this bitter legacy and dares us to confront its continued forceful presence.

In *Slaughter of the Innocents (They Might be Guilty of Something)*, Walker reworks the biblical narrative into a composition crammed with mourning, eroticism, violation, and abuse. The realities of racism are highlighted by the medium—placing Black characters against a seemingly whitewashed backdrop—and in the depictions of vicious masters and their slaves. On one side of the mural-like scene, a large, hunched man wearing a wide-brimmed hat carries a limp body on a long-handled sickle, and a child flees from grappling hands. On the other side, a young girl holds an open-mouthed skull, and above her a devilish figure with a sharp goatee and a twisted tail smiles a wicked smile. One woman, kneeling, holds a lifeless baby in her arms, while another clasps a small child by the ankle and prepares to strike a blow. Along the top, inverted characters share moments of intimacy. Throughout, exaggerated Black features expose white male fantasies.

Walker's racially charged monochrome images, which have caused controversy in the U.S., visualize the relationship between power and oppression, and the original sin of owning and selling bodies. As well as being critiques of slavery, they shine a light on the casual racism that permeates the world today. Her work is hard to look at, which, in a way, is the point. With their vast scales and stark contrasts of black and white, Walker's parables are provocative and honest, strange and unforgettable—a haunting bridge between past and present, oppressor and oppressed.

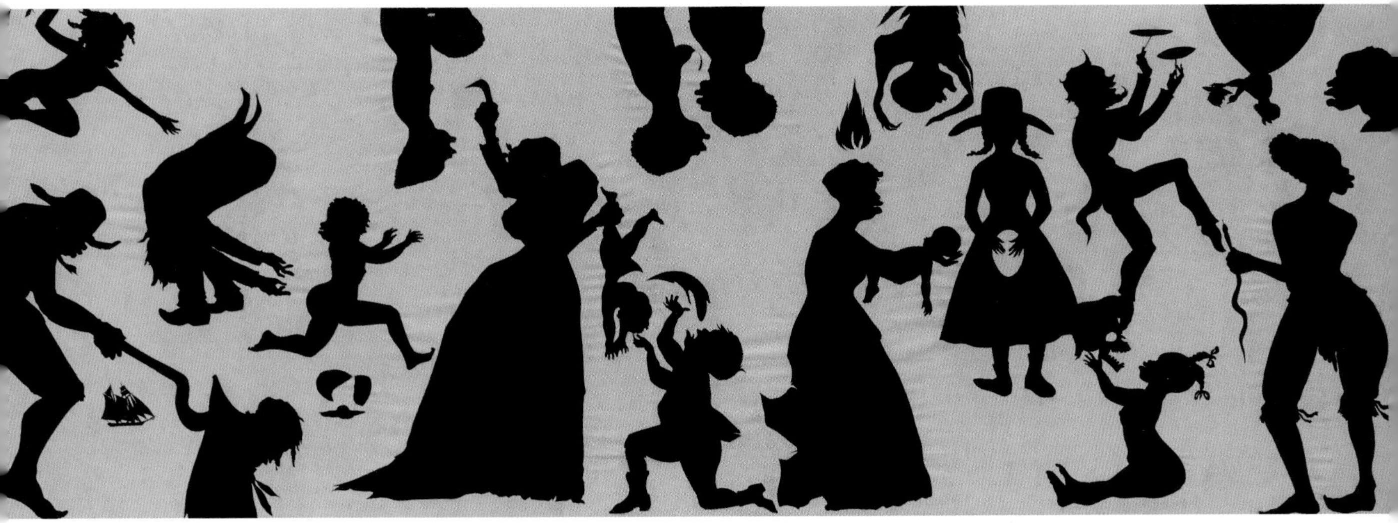

Palette

Stark contrasts of black and white.

Complementary works

- Adrian Piper, *Safe #1*, 1990.
- Lorna Simpson, *Then and Now*, 2016.
- Toyin Ojih Odutola, *The Ruling Class (Eshu)*, 2019.

The politics of pink

Flora Yukhnovich

In the Pink

2018

Oil on linen,
86⅝ x 74¾ in (220 x 190 cm).

Leaf back a few pages and you might notice a resemblance between the paintings of Yukhnovich and François Boucher (*see page 64*). The London-based artist uses the Rococo—that 18th-century movement associated with indulgence and ornamentation—to explore feminine aesthetics throughout art history. She finds connections between the flamboyant paintings of Boucher, Jean-Honoré Fragonard, and Giovanni Battista Tiepolo, and contemporary popular culture. “It feels like Disney, like Hallmark cards,” she has said. “In many ways, it’s revved-up silliness—but I think there’s a seriousness there.” A seriousness to do with the gendering of the color pink, and the items, imagery and packaging targeted at young girls.

In the Pink is at once entirely abstract and tantalizingly figurative. The backdrop—step back and you’ll see it—comprises pale washes of green and blue, as suggestions of a natural landscape, and a sky blotted with vague lemon-yellow clouds. Luminous colors create the impression of otherworldliness, and yet, emerging from the ether are true-to-life sprigs and branches. Bare-bottomed cherubs prance in the sky. Hazy impressions of half-submerged nudes lounge lazily or prop themselves up on an elbow, faces obscured and limbs dissolving into paint—these women are both in plain view and hidden, refusing to be seen. Abstraction allows the artist to free her figures from form, and invites the viewer to focus instead on color and the sensation of the medium.

Yukhnovich’s paintings have an energy all of their own, with boldly applied textural brush marks giving way to patches of pastel-colored calm. She prefers to work with oil paint because it stays wet for longer than acrylic, meaning that she can add and remove layers over a period of eight or so days; it also makes sense because this was the chosen medium of the artists of the Rococo. There’s a fluidity to her works, which is in part down to the loose application of her fleshy colors, and in part down to the way her components slip in and out of focus.

C0 M25 Y35 K0
R237 G200 B164

C0 M10 Y30 K5
R238 G221 B180

C0 M15 Y58 K5
R235 G207 B124

C0 M38 Y80 K10
R210 G155 B63

C49 M15 Y30 K5
R145 G173 B168

C36 M15 Y61 K10
R163 G172 B113

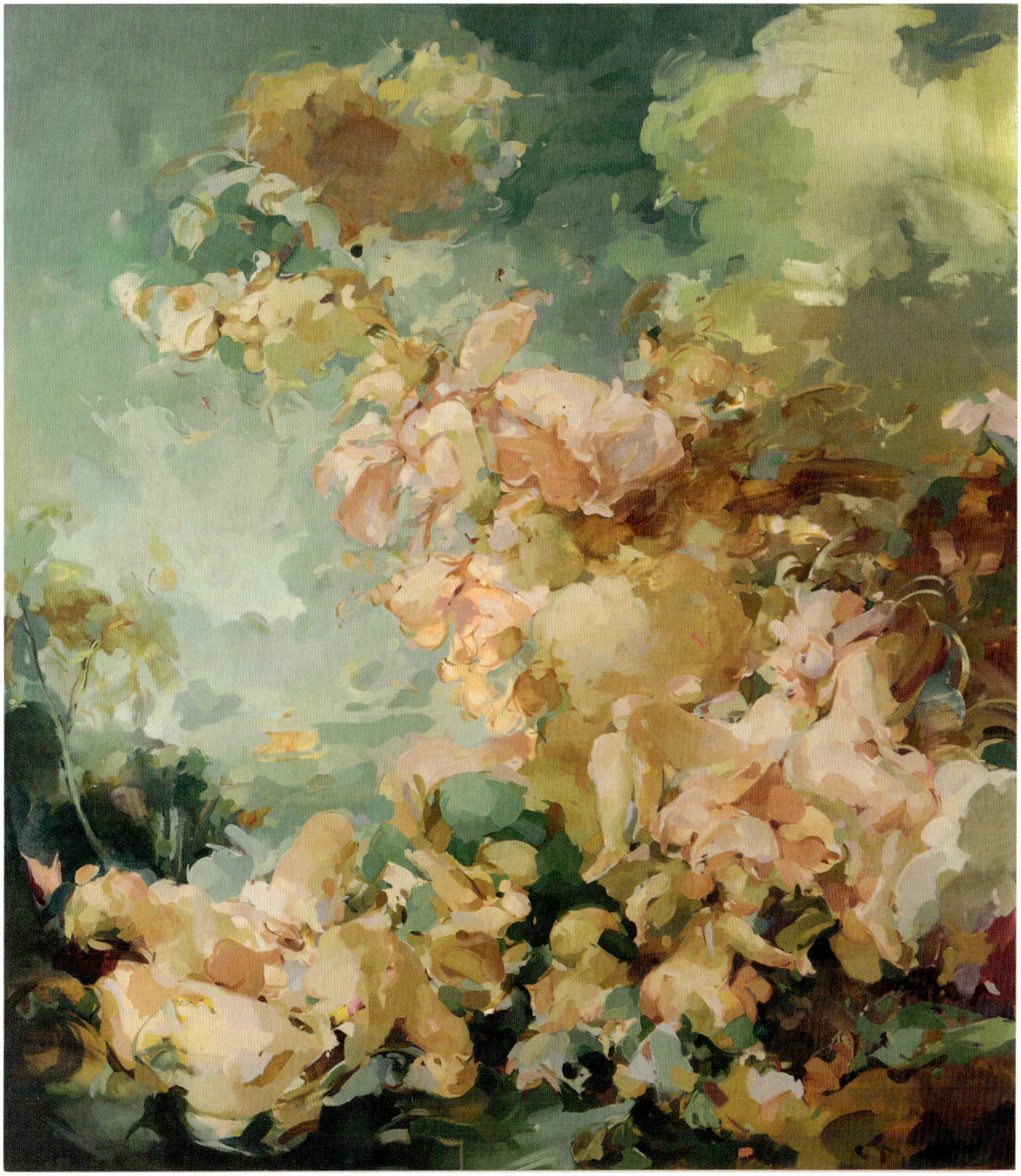

Palette

Pale washes of green and blue, vague lemon-yellow clouds, and smudgy impressions of half-submerged nudes in rose, ocher, and cream.

Complementary works

- Jean-Honoré Fragonard, *The Musical Contest,* *c.*1749–52.
- François Boucher, *The Setting of the Sun*, 1752.
- Giovanni Battista Tiepolo, *Olympus or The Triumph of Venus*, 1761–64.

Further reading

Albers, Josef, *Interaction of Color* (Yale University Press, 2013).

Anfam, David and Susan Davidson et al., *Abstract Expressionism* (Royal Academy of Arts, 2016).

Ashby, Chloë, *Look At This If You Love Great Art: A critical curation of 100 essential artworks* (Ivy Press, 2021).

Ball, Philip, *Bright Earth: The Invention of Colour* (Viking, 2001).

Barnes, Julian, *The Man in the Red Coat* (Jonathan Cape, 2019).

Baty, Patrick et al., *Nature's Palette: A colour reference system from the natural world* (Thames & Hudson, 2021).

Bomford, David and Ashok Roy, *A Closer Look: Colour* (National Gallery, 2009).

Chambers, Eddie, *Black Artists in British Art: A History since the 1950s* (Bloomsbury, 2014).

De Kerangal, Maylis, tr. Jessica Moore, *Painting Time* (MacLehose Press, 2021).

Fox, James, *The World According to Colour: A Cultural History* (Allen Lane, 2021).

Fox Weber, Nicholas, *Anni & Josef Albers: Equal and Unequal* (Phaidon, 2020).

Fuga, Antonella, *Artists' Techniques and Materials* (Getty, 2007).

Gabriel, Mary, *Ninth Street Women: Lee Krasner, Elaine de Kooning, Grace Hartigan, Joan Mitchell, and Helen Frankenthaler: Five Painters and the Movement That Changed Modern Art* (Little, Brown & Company, 2019).

Gale, Matthew, ed., *The CC Land Exhibition: Pierre Bonnard: The Colour of Memory* (Tate Publishing, 2019).

Gayford, Martin, *Man with a Blue Scarf: On Sitting for a Portrait by Lucian Freud* (Thames & Hudson, 2012).

Gayford, Martin, *The Yellow House: van Gogh, Gauguin, and Nine Turbulent Weeks in Arles* (Fig Tree, 2006).

Mason, Wyatt, "Kerry James Marshall Is Shifting the Color of Art History," *T Magazine* (2016).

Nairne, Eleanor, *Lee Krasner: Living Colour* (Thames & Hudson, 2019).

Nelson, Maggie, *Bluets* (Jonathan Cape, 2017).

Pamuk, Orhan, *My Name Is Red* (Faber & Faber, 2001).

Proctor, Alice, *The Whole Picture: The colonial story of the art in our museums & why we need to talk about it* (Octopus Publishing Group, 2020).

St Clair, Kassia, *The Secret Lives of Colour* (John Murray, 2016).

Steele, Valerie, *Pink: The History of a Punk, Pretty, Powerful Colour* (Thames & Hudson, 2018).

Stubbs, Phoebe, *Colour in the Making: From Old Wisdom to New Brilliance* (Black Dog Press, 2014).

Pastoureau, Michel, tr. Jody Gladding, *Black: The History of a Color* (Princeton University Press, 2008).

Pastoureau, Michel, tr. Jody Gladding, *Blue: The History of a Color* (Princeton University Press, 2018).

Pastoureau, Michel, tr. Jody Gladding, *Green: The History of a Color* (Princeton University Press, 2014).

Pastoureau, Michel, tr. Jody Gladding, *Red: The History of a Color* (Princeton University Press, 2017).

Pastoureau, Michel, tr. Jody Gladding, *Yellow: The History of a Color* (Princeton University Press, 2019).

Paul, Stella, *Chromaphilia: The Story of Colour in Art* (Phaidon, 2017).

Von Goethe, Johann Wolfgang, *Theory of Colours* (MIT Press, 1970).

Picture credits

pp.9, 10, 39, 45, 47, 49, 51, 61, 67, 91, 111, 113, 123, 159, 163, 171 Courtesy of Wikimedia; p.11 Courtesy of Nmuim/Alamy; p.17 Courtesy of Centre National de Préhistoire; p.19 © Fine Art Images/Heritage Images/Alamy; p.21 Courtesy of Art Collection/Alamy; p.23 Courtesy of Heritage Images/Alamy; p.25 Courtesy of Prisma Archivo/Alamy; p.31 Courtesy of Niday Picture Library/Alamy; p.33 Courtesy of Peter Horree/Alamy; pp.35, 135, 139 Courtesy of The Picture Art Collection/Alamy; pp.37, 99, 145 Courtesy of Album/Alamy; p.41 Courtesy of Peter Barritt/Alamy; p.43 Courtesy of World History Archive/Alamy; pp.57, 75, 95 Courtesy of Heritage Images/Getty; p.59 © Detroit Institute of Arts/Gift of Mr Leslie H. Green/Bridgeman Images; p.63 L: Courtesy of CPA Media Pte Ltd/Alamy, R: © ADAGP, Paris and DACS, London 2022. © Philadelphia Museum of Art/The Louise and Walter Arensberg Collection, 1950/Bridgeman Images; p.65 © Wallace Collection, London, UK/Bridgeman Images; p.69 Courtesy of Akademie/Alamy; pp.77, 107, 169 Courtesy of incamerastock/Alamy; p.79 Courtesy of Peter Horree/Alamy; p.81 Courtesy of Classicpaintings/Alamy; p.83 Courtesy of FineArt/Alamy; p.85 Courtesy of The National Gallery. Bequeathed by Alan Evans, 1974; p.93 Courtesy of Christophe Fine Art/Getty; p.96 Agefotostock/Alamy; p.97 Asar Studios/Alamy; pp.101, 133, 137 Courtesy of Art Heritage/Alamy; p.109 Courtesy of Art Reserve/Alamy; p.115 Courtesy of World History Archive/Alamy; p.117 Photo © Christie's Images/Bridgeman Images; p.119 Courtesy of Picturenow/Getty; p.121 Courtesy of Niday Picture Library/Alamy; p.129 Courtesy of Art Collection 2/Alamy; p.131 Purchased with the Drayton Hillyer Fund, Smith College Museum of Art, Northampton, Massachusetts. Courtesy of Smith College Museum of Art; p.141 © Succession Picasso/DACS, London 2022. Courtesy of Art Library/Alamy; p.143 Image © The Metropolitan Museum of Art/Art Resource/Scala, Florence; p.147 © Banco de México Diego Rivera Frida Kahlo Museums Trust, Mexico, D.F./DACS 2022. Courtesy of Archivart/Alamy; p.149 © Estate of Leonora Carrington/ARS, NY and DACS, London 2022. Photo © Sainsbury Centre for Visual Arts/Robert and Lisa Sainsbury Collection/Bridgeman Images; p.155 Andrea Dhanani/Alamy; p.157 Courtesy of Artepics/Alamy; p.161 Courtesy of IanDagnall Computing/Alamy; p.165 © ADAGP, Paris and DACS, London 2022. Photo © Museum of Fine Arts, Houston/Museum purchase funded by Audrey Jones Beck/Bridgeman Images; p.167 © Succession H. Matisse/ DACS 2022. Photo: Courtesy of The State Hermitage Museum, St Petersbourg.; p.173 Courtesy of Didrichsen Art Museum, Helsinki; p.179 Courtesy of Steve Vidler/Alamy; p.181 © Helen Frankenthaler Foundation, Inc./ARS, NY and DACS, London 2022. Courtesy of The Artchives/Alamy; p.183 © The Pollock-Krasner Foundation ARS, NY and DACS, London 2022. Courtesy of Bridgeman Images; p.185 © 1998 Kate Rothko Prizel & Christopher Rothko ARS, NY and DACS, London 2022. Photo © Christie's Images/Bridgeman Images; p.187 © ARS, NY and DACS, London 2022. Photo: Tate; p.189 © Richard Diebenkorn Foundation. Courtesy of Richard Diebenkorn Foundation; p.195 © The Josef and Anni Albers Foundation/DACS 2022. Courtesy of The Solomon R. Guggenheim Foundation/Art Resource, NY/ Scala, Florence; p.197 © Frank Stella. ARS, NY and DACS, London 2022. Digital image: The Museum of Modern Art, New York/Scala, Florence; p.199 Courtesy of Glenn Howard; p.201 © Succession Yves Klein c/o ADAGP, Paris and DACS, London 2022. Photo: Tate; p.203 © Agnes Martin Foundation, New York/DACS 2022. The Solomon R. Guggenheim Foundation/Art Resource, NY/ Scala, Florence; p.209 Image © Wolverhampton Art Gallery/Bridgeman Images; p.211 © ADAGP, Paris and DACS, London 2022; p.213 © Judy Chicago. ARS, NY and DACS, London 2022. Photo courtesy of Judy Chicago/Art Resource, NY; p.215 © David Hockney. Collection Tate UK. Photo: Tate; p.217 © 2022 The Andy Warhol Foundation for the Visual Arts, Inc./Licensed by DACS, London. Photo © Christie's Images/Bridgeman Images; p.219 Courtesy the artist, The Broad Art Foundation and Sprüth Magers; p.225 National Portrait Gallery, Smithsonian Institution © The Estate of Alice Neel. Courtesy the Estate of Alice Neel and Victoria Miro; p.227 Courtesy of the artist and Sfeir-Semler Gallery Beirut/Hamburg. Private Collection; p.229 © The Estate of Jean-Michel Basquiat/ADAGP, Paris and DACS, London 2022. Courtesy of Adagp Images, Paris,/SCALA, Florence; p.231 © Kerry JamesMarshall. Courtesy the artist and Jack Shainman Gallery, New York; p.233 © Alison Watt. All Rights Reserved. DACS, London 2022. Image courtesy of National Galleries of Scotland; p.235 © Lynette Yiadom-Boakye. Courtesy of the artist, Jack Shainman Gallery, New York and Corvi-Mora, London; p.237 © Kiki Smith. Published by Magnolia Editions, Oakland. Photograph by Tom Barratt, courtesy Pace Gallery; p.239 Copyright Lisa Brice. Courtesy the artist; Stephen Friedman Gallery, London and Salon 94, New York. Photo by Mark Blower. Private collection; p.241 Artwork Kara Walker, courtesy of Sikkema Jenkins & Co. and Sprüth Magers; p.243 © Flora Yukhnovich. Courtesy the artist and Victoria Miro; p.255 © Sophie Davidson.

Index

S

Acknowledgements

First, thanks to Alice Graham, for thinking of me when you needed a writer, and for your insight and edits. Also, to Charlotte Frost, Daniela Nava, and the rest of the team at Frances Lincoln for taking my manuscript and turning it into this beautiful book. As always, thanks to Adam, my stepfather and in-house editor, for reading these pages as you do everything I write. Thanks to my mother, Anne, for your tireless support, and to my father, Charlie, and my brother, Tristan, for your enthusiasm. Thanks to Ollie, for everything. And finally, to the artists for creating these works, and to the galleries and museums for sharing them – thanks to you all for teaching me about the colors of art, rich and vital, infinitely varied.

About the author

Chloë Ashby is an author and arts critic who writes and reviews for publications such as *The Times*, the *Guardian*, *Harper's Bazaar,* and the *TLS*. She is the author of two non-fiction books on art history, and the novels *Wet Paint*, *Second Self,* and *Family Friends*.

www.chloeashby.com

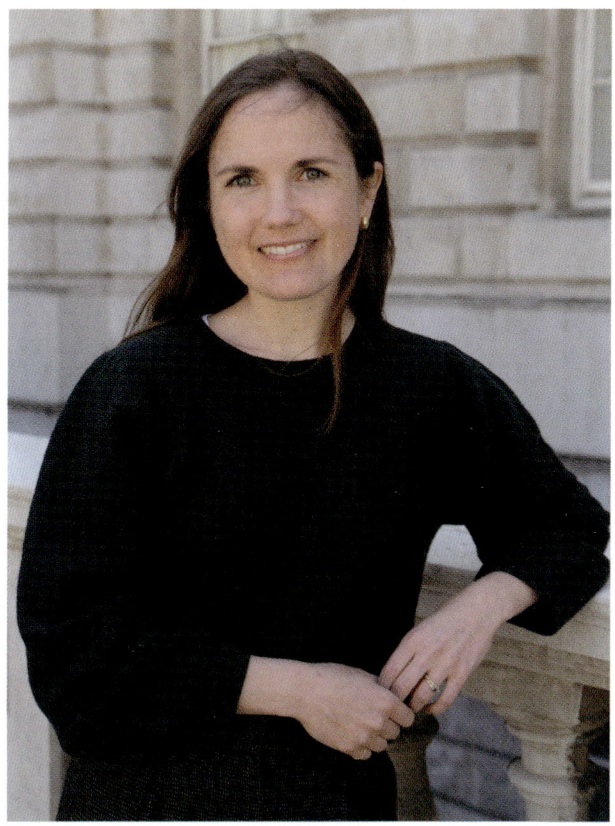

Quarto

First published in 2022 by Frances Lincoln Publishing
an imprint of The Quarto Group.
One Triptych Place, London, SE1 9SH,
United Kingdom
T (0)20 7700 9000
www.Quarto.com

This edition published in 2026 by Frances Lincoln.

EEA Representation, WTS Tax d.o.o., Žanova ulica 3,
4000 Kranj, Slovenia
www.wts-tax.si

A catalogue record for this book is available from the British Library.

ISBN 978-1-80570-149-1
Ebook ISBN 978-0-71127-941-4

10 9 8 7 6 5 4 3 2 1

Design by Glenn Howard

Printed in Guangdong, China TT062026

FSC www.fsc.org MIX Paper | Supporting responsible forestry FSC® C016973

Front cover image:
The Ten Largest, No. 2, Childhood, by Hilma af Klint (1907). Photo via ArtVee.

Back cover image:
Newton's colour wheel from Book I, Part II, Proposition VI, Problem 2 of *Opticks*, 1704. Courtesy of CPA Media Pte Ltd/Alamy.

Front flap image:
The Rising of the Sun, by Francois Boucher (1753). © Wallace Collection, London, UK / Bridgeman Images.

Back flap image:
Seated Woman with Legs Drawn Up, by Egon Schiele (1917). Photo via Wikimedia Commons.